Philosophy of Social Science

A New Introduction

Edited by

Nancy Cartwright and Eleonora Montuschi

OXFORD

UNIVERSITY PRESS

OXFORD

UNIVERSITY PRESS

Great Clarendon Street, Oxford, OX2 6DP,
United Kingdom

Oxford University Press is a department of the University of Oxford.
It furthers the University's objective of excellence in research, scholarship,
and education by publishing worldwide. Oxford is a registered trade mark of
Oxford University Press in the UK and in certain other countries

Published in the United States of America by Oxford University Press
198 Madison Avenue, New York, NY 10016, United States of America

British Library Cataloguing in Publication Data
Data available

Library of Congress Control Number: 2014938929

ISBN 978-0-19-964509-1 (hbk.)

ISBN 978-0-19-964510-7 (pbk.)

Printed and bound by
CPI Group (UK) Ltd, Croydon, CR0 4YY

Links to third party websites are provided by Oxford in good faith and
for information only. Oxford disclaims any responsibility for the materials
contained in any third party website referenced in this work.

Acknowledgements

Chapter 4: iPinCH (the Intellectual Property Issues in Cultural Heritage project), especially Sheila Greer for helpful advice and the Champagne and Aishihik First Nations for their generosity.

Chapters 7, 14, 16: The Order project, Templeton Foundation (London School of Economics and University of California, San Diego); AHRC-funded research project on 'Choices of Evidence' (London School of Economics); in Chapter 7, material on suicide originally appeared in E. Montuschi, *The Objects of Social Science* (Continuum Press, 2003), chapter 2; and on AIDS/HIV spread in Africa in E. Montuschi, 'Evidence, Objectivity, Social Policy', in E. Viola (ed.), *Epistemologies and the Knowledge Society: New and Old Challenges for 21st-Century Europe* (Nemesis Publisher, Roma-Acireale, 2010). A version of the case study on Dutch RCT on heroin users appeared in E. Montuschi, 'Questions of Evidence in Evidence-Based Policy', *Axiomathes*, 19(14) (2009): 429–31.

Chapter 13: National Science Foundation-funded research on the controversy over screening mammography (Award number SES-1152050). Some of the material in this chapter appeared in an early version in Miriam Solomon, ' "A Troubled Area": Understanding the Controversy Over Screening Mammography for Women Aged 40–49', in Christoph Jager and Winfried Loffler (eds), *Epistemology: Contexts, Values, Disagreement. Proceedings of the 34th International Ludwig Wittgenstein Symposium* (Heusenstamm, Germany: Ontos Verlag, 2012), 271–84.

Chapter 15: The British Academy and Wolfson Foundation-funded research project: 'Re-Thinking Case Studies Across the Social Sciences'; parts of the chapter appeared in M. S. Morgan, 'Case Studies: One Observation or Many? Justification or Discovery?', *Philosophy of Science*, 79(5), (2012), 667–677.

We are grateful to Alex Marcellesi, Rebecca Robinson, and Rosa Runhardt for editing and assisting with the completion of the volume.

Contents

Contents

Notes on Contributors

Anna Alexandrova is a University Lecturer in Philosophy of Science at the Department of History and Philosophy of Science in Cambridge and a Fellow of King's College. She has written on the nature of rational choice explanation in the social sciences, the use of abstract and idealized models in science and policy, and on the science of well-being.

Cristina Bicchieri is the S. J. P. Harvie Professor of Philosophy and Psychology at the University of Pennsylvania and the founding director of BeLab, the behavioural ethics lab at Penn. Her research interests include social norms and their dynamics, behavioural ethics, and social epistemology.

Nancy Cartwright is Professor of Philosophy at the Department of Philosophy, University of Durham, and at the University of California, San Diego (UCSD). Her research interests include philosophy and history of science (especially physics and economics), causal inference, objectivity, and evidence, especially in evidence-based policy.

Sharon Crasnow is Professor of Philosophy at Norco College in Southern California. Her current research interests include feminist philosophy of science and epistemological questions raised by methodologies in the social sciences.

Heather Douglas is Waterloo Chair of Science and Society in the Department of Philosophy at the University of Waterloo and a Fellow of the Institute for Science, Society and Policy at the University of Ottawa. Her research focuses on the science–policy interface and the role of values in scientific reasoning.

Sophia Efstathiou is a Researcher in Philosophy at the Norwegian University of Science and Technology (NTNU). She is interested in the conditions of scientific innovation within interdisciplinary biomedical cultures, and especially in how scientific ideas are invented from common ones.

Helen Longino is C. I. Lewis Professor in Philosophy at Stanford University. Her teaching and research interests are in philosophy of science, especially the interface between biology and social science, social epistemology, and feminist philosophy. Her latest work is on the relationship between logical, epistemological, and social aspects of behavioural research.

Zara Mirmalek is a Postdoctoral Fellow with the Program on Science, Technology and Society at the Harvard Kennedy School of Government, Harvard University. Her research focuses on cultural, historical, and structural arrangements of science and technology, innovation and identity in post-industrial organizations, and politics of representation.

Eleonora Montuschi is an Associate Professor in Philosophy of Science at the Department of Philosophy and Cultural Heritage at the Ca' Foscari University of Venice and Senior Research Fellow at the London School of Economics and Political Science. She works on scientific objectivity, on the theory and practice of evidence, and on methodological issues in the social sciences.

Mary S. Morgan is Professor of History and Philosophy of Economics at the London School of Economics and Political Science. Her work ranges over the history and philosophy of statistics and the social sciences (especially economics). She is currently researching the ways in which cases and case studies are used in the generation of scientific knowledge.

Eileen Munro is Professor of Social Policy at the London School of Economics and Political Science. Her current research interests include how best to combine intuitive and analytic reasoning in risk assessment and decision-making in child protection, and on the role of the wider organizational system in promoting or hindering good critical thinking.

Wendy Parker is a Reader in Philosophy at Durham University. Her research interests include the epistemology of computer simulation (especially climate modelling), concepts of scientific evidence, and the roles of science in public policy.

Rosa Runhardt is a Ph.D. candidate in the Department of Philosophy, Logic and Scientific Method at the London School of Economics and Political Science. Her research interests include measurement and concept formation for causal analysis in social science, especially international relations.

Miriam Solomon is Professor of Philosophy and Affiliated Professor of Women's Studies at Temple University. Her research interests are in philosophy of science, philosophy of medicine, gender and science, bioethics, and social epistemology.

Katie Steele is Senior Lecturer in the Department of Philosophy, Logic and Scientific Method at the London School of Economics and Political Science. Her research lies at the intersection of rational choice and scientific inference/evidence. She is interested in applications in both the social and natural sciences (particularly climate science and climate change economics) and in the relations between science and policy.

Deborah Tollefsen is Associate Professor of Philosophy at the University of Memphis. Her research and teaching interests include collective intentionality, philosophy of mind, and epistemology.

Alison Wylie is Professor of Philosophy and Anthropology at the University of Washington. She works on philosophical issues raised by archaeological practice and by feminist research in the social sciences: ideals of objectivity, the role of contextual values in research practice, models of evidential reasoning, and issues of accountability to research subjects and others affected by research.

Introduction

Nancy Cartwright and Eleonora Montuschi

When it comes to studying science, the philosophy of the social sciences has long been a poor sister to philosophy of the natural sciences. This is no surprise. It is far easier to study, and critique, what goes on in fields that—rightly or wrongly—are taken to include well-articulated, widely accepted theories, concepts, and methodologies than to study fields where concepts appear vague, methods are in dispute, and there either is no theory on offer or far too many. Probably that is why for a long time among topics in the social sciences it was work on the logic of statistical inference that seemed to command the most respect in the philosophy of science community and then later, work on the philosophy of economics, which developed as a separate field of philosophical inquiry in a discipline considered to be closer to the natural than to the social sciences.

The last decade has seen a big turnaround. The philosophy of the social sciences has become a vibrant field with exciting research on a host of topics, and not just in the more exact areas, like economics, social statistics, and experimental psychology, but widely across the social science disciplines. Philosophers seem to have figured out how to dig in and do detailed work on more elusive material, like studies of happiness, the role of standpoint in explanation, what a society is, the measurement of inexact concepts like 'civil war' or the description of 'rape' (just to mention a couple discussed in chapters to come in this volume).

Undergraduate teaching has followed this new trend. A typical undergraduate syllabus for philosophy of social science used to focus on the differences between natural and social science, *verstehen* versus *erklären*, covering-law explanation, and holism versus individualism. Nowadays in a philosophy of the social sciences course you can find yourself discussing the prisoner's dilemma, intervention theories of causality, we-intentions, and qualitative versus quantitative methods, as well as topics of heated contemporary debate, such as climate change, evidence-based policy, and social well-being, where it seems that philosophical understanding may make a difference to the formulation of practical solutions.

We have aimed here to provide an introductory-level textbook that reflects the topics and concerns of much of the exciting new research in the philosophy of the social sciences. It is intended both for students with central interests in philosophy and those planning to concentrate on the social sciences, so we have tried to presuppose no particular background in either domain. From the wide range of topics at the forefront of contemporary debate in philosophy of social science, we have chosen ones that we think are representative of the work now being done and that we take to be accessible to introductory-level students. Because the topics are so diverse, we have a whole team of distinguished authors at the top of the field, both junior and senior, each writing on a subject we both teach and research on. This hopefully will make for a lively and engaging presentation.

The new directions in the philosophy of the social sciences go hand-in-hand with several other changes in the intellectual landscape, which are reflected in the topics taken up in this textbook. One is the spread of game theory from economics outward across the social sciences. It is in game theory and the theory of rational choice that you hear of the prisoner's dilemma, Nash equilibria, and the dictator game. It is a natural home for philosophers, where formal methods intersect with issues of rationality, cooperation, social conventions and social norms, and the social good versus that of the individual. One section of our text is devoted to teaching the basic ideas of rational choice models and how they can be of help in thinking about social issues. We suggest that students who are unfamiliar with game theory and rational choice theory study Chapter 10 first, which will explain what these are. Chapter 11 shows how they are deployed in the social sciences to understand norms and conventions better.

A second change, in intellectual attitudes more generally, has been in the understanding of the role of values in the sciences. Concerns that values may play a special role in the study of society have been around at least since the rise of positivism, the movement that emerged in France in the first half of the nineteenth century and then spread in the second half to other European countries, Britain included. Positivism preached that the only source of knowledge is empirical facts, which can be logically or mathematically treated, measured, and, if we are careful and rigorous enough, predicted by science. In the social sciences disputes about the positivist view of science surfaced in the battle of methods (the *Methodenstreit*) at the end of the 1800s, which saw at opposite sides the supporters of a lawlike, causal model of social science and the proponents of a historical, value-informed social science. The battle culminated in the compromise position of the father of sociology, Max Weber, in the early decades of the twentieth century, which you will read about in Chapters 7 and 9: values should affect the choice of topics studied in social enquiry but not the choice of which results to accept. This is how, Weber argued, social science can retain the objectivity of science. During the second half of the twentieth century the ideal that scientific results can and should be entirely value-free dominated.

Matters began to change in the 1970s, and on two fronts. First, the recognition that factual evidence is always insufficient to determine the choice among scientific theories and hypotheses raised concerns, driven home by the work of Thomas Kuhn and Paul Feyerabend, about what can fill in after the evidence has been considered. Perhaps there are special virtues that all and only true theories can be expected to have, such as simplicity, coherence, and explanatory power. Or perhaps one theory is chosen over another because it has special advantages, maybe it solves problems that are particularly pressing at the moment. Maybe a worldview dictates. Maybe scientists get excited by the new ideas of the most recent theory or by the newest methods and concepts from other disciplines. Or perhaps adopting a particular theory serves some special interest groups over others or fits better with our views or prejudices.

These last are related to the second front of attack on the value-free ideal during the 1970s, led by feminists and disadvantaged minorities, who argued that science never has been value-free. It has always been done by privileged white men, or privileged classes, using ideas and methods natural to them and their worldviews and that, it was argued, ultimately serve their own interests. Over the years the debates on both these fronts became more sophisticated and views on both sides mellowed. Encounters and battles diminished but not so much because differences were resolved; rather, people on both sides focused on developing work along their own lines rather than on arguing against those with opposed positions.

In the last decade matters have changed again, both in philosophy and in many of the sciences. As you will see, we have come to recognize a great variety of roles that values can play, especially in the social sciences, from the choice of what gets funded to decisions about what modelling techniques to use or how to measure our social concepts. Values are then inextricably related to the evaluation of the objectivity of scientific results. This made the relationship between facts and values far more complicated to assess and describe than a first naïve distinction would have it. This is the central topic of Chapter 9 (which appears in the section on objectivity for this reason) and a running theme through several others (Chapters 4, 7, and 14).

A third change has been a shift within the philosophy of science along a number of interconnected dimensions: from a focus on general issues across the sciences to separate philosophies of the separate sciences, from a predilection for theory to more emphasis on scientific practices and problems, and from single method studies to multidisciplinary ones, engaging with other ways of looking at the sciences, especially in what is now called 'Science Studies'. In this volume we do not focus on the separate sciences individually since those kinds of studies require background knowledge in the specific subject under investigation.[1]

We do though look at both practices and problems and how to deal with them in an interdisciplinary fashion. Our text begins with a sample of four problems of current social concern where philosophy of social science has been at work: what counts as well-being (Chapter 1), what is evidence-based policy and how much is it to be encouraged (Chapter 3), what is the social impact of climate change (Chapter 2), and, for archaeological findings, how to negotiate between the interests of indigenous peoples in their ancestors and the interests of people in general in human history (Chapter 4). We focus on practices in the social sciences in Parts V and VI. You will read about interdisciplinarity and science studies in Chapter 12, about the role of knowledge in social practice in Chapter 13, and about the practical concerns of using appropriate methods in social research in Chapters 14, 15, and 16.

A fourth change is the obsession with objectivity over the last two decades, both in society and among the sciences and those who study them. We live in an audit society that counts everything to make sure that we have got it right. Students are continuously examined and re-examined to ensure that both they and their schools are performing properly, hospital waiting times are recorded and monitored, league tables are constructed for everything from dishwashers to universities, even happiness is measured, on a scale of 1 to 10—and in the UK currently getting improvements in this measure is supposed to be one of the central goals of government policy. On the scholarly side, historians write books with provocative titles like *Trust in Numbers* (Ted Porter) and *The History of Objectivity* (Lorraine Daston and Peter Galison), which show how trust is socially constructed and how objectivity, far from being a simple reflection of undisputed facts, has changed its nature over the centuries. Social and biomedical scientists argue about whether there are any objective methods for establishing causal claims other than the randomized controlled trial, and social scientists quarrel about how to measure everything from the consumer price index to the number of civil wars in the last decade.

---

[1] Happily subject-specific texts have begun to appear in many of the separate social sciences, for instance, Julian Reiss's *Philosophy of Economics: A Contemporary Introduction*, Routledge 2013, or the various volumes in the Elsevier *Handbook of the Philosophy of Science* series edited by M. Gabbay, P. Thagard, and J. Woods, e.g. on philosophy of anthropology and sociology (2006) and the philosophy of economics (2012). Or also see Eleonora Montuschi's *The Objects of Social Science*, Continuum Press 2003, which examines how different social sciences—economics, sociology, anthropology, history, human geography—design their different objects of inquiry.

Current philosophy of social science is deep into this issue. Chapter 7 is dedicated to objectivity—what it is, how much of it we want, and how we can get it in social science—but you will see this critical concern about objectivity reflected across several chapters (e.g. Chapters 4 and 8). The objectivity of the sciences was notoriously challenged by the social constructivists of the late 1900s. Science, they argued, is a social enterprise, like others, embedded in specific social, economic, and historical contexts. The decisions that scientific communities arrive at will thus be subject to the same kinds of causal influences as those in other domains. A good many scientists were appalled at this thought and rose up in arms. The 'science wars' ensued in the 1990s (well described e.g. in A. Ross (ed.), *Science Wars*). As with the debates of the late 1900s on values in science, after a while views on both sides mellowed, and at least some people from both camps settled for acceptable compromises. Conciliatory positions emerged, more credible than many of the radical caricatures from the first season of the wars. Rather than arguing that facts are either discovered by science or totally invented by theories, it has proved more fruitful to suppose that facts can be both discovered and invented: theories can creatively represent the world without creating fictional worlds.

More recent work on objectivity in the philosophy of both the natural and the social sciences has had different, though related, concerns that reflect a more general erosion of trust in the scientific method. Philosophers used to think they could teach you what this is and why there should be only one truly scientific method. Karl Popper, for instance, demanded that scientific claims be falsifiable: They are properly 'scientific' only if they run the risk of being empirically proven false. For him this is what sorts the sciences from the non-sciences. Philosophers also taught the importance of experiment, measurement, and theory testing to the development of Western science; and movements from positivism to Bayesianism (a doctrine that supposes that probabilities represent rational degrees of belief) tried to construct rigorous methods for using the facts to choose among theories.

But much of the recent thinking about what knowledge is and how we acquire it, both in philosophy in general and in philosophy of the social sciences, is less sanguine about scientific method, which has been notoriously slippery to pin down. Perhaps it is not after all reliance on specific regimented methods that makes for objectivity, since these come and go, getting refined, developed, and replaced as we learn new facts, acquire new technologies, get new ideas, and adopt new theories. Rather, it is now widely argued, what makes scientific knowledge trustworthy is the intense critical debate, analysis, and review that scientific claims are subject to in the best of circumstances and the institutions that secure this, such as peer review, university-funded not-for-profit research, and for some results like pharmaceutical claims for safety and effectiveness, government regulation and oversight. This approach generally goes under the title 'social epistemology' and you will learn about it in Chapter 13.

To follow the text it will help those new to the field to recognize a three-way distinction that philosophers make all the time, between *ontology, epistemology,* and *methodology*. 'Ontology' is the study of what there is and of what 'what there is' is like. It is the explicit focus of Part II. The two chapters there reflect the recent renewed concern in the philosophy of the social sciences about how social reality is constructed and about the ontological status of social groups and social causes. Chapter 5 investigates whether we can attribute attitudes like belief and intention to groups, or do only individuals have intentions? Chapter 6 contrasts 'methodological individualism'—the view that social behaviour is entirely the effect of the behaviours of individuals which in turn are entirely the effect of biological and psychological factors within them—with a *multi-scale* approach that also looks for the determinants of individual and social behaviour within the social environment as well.

'Epistemology' is the study of what knowledge is and how we come to have it. Clearly the social epistemology discussed in Chapter 13 is part of this enterprise but so too is all the work on objectivity. The interesting question about objectivity concerns how we represent the world in science, and what and how much of it, rather than worrying fruitlessly about whether the world corresponds exactly to the ways we represent it.

'Methodology' is the study of methods. Much of the current work in this area reflects a recent sensitivity to the need for methods and subject matter to match: what is a good method to use in a study depends on the features of the particular subject matter the study deals with. Students will learn in this text about three areas of methodology that are of current concern in the philosophy of social science. Chapter 14 studies what makes for a good measurement of a social concept, Chapter 15 treats the use of case studies, and Chapter 16 describes methods for causal inference.

We have tried to keep the number of references in the text down so as not to inundate beginning students with too much new material, though this has proven easier in some chapters than in others. A handful of works for further reading are suggested at the end of each chapter. These should give students a good start for topics they want to explore in more detail and the references found in these further readings will take them even further.

There are sixteen chapters in this text, surely too many for a one-term course, perhaps even for a year-long course, especially since instructors may want to supplement with other materials already readily available, such as some introduction to probability and social statistics. What we hope is that we here provide a solid and engaging introduction for undergraduates to many of the exciting new topics in the philosophy of social science not found in earlier texts.

Part I
Current Debates

1

Well-Being*

Anna Alexandrova

1. Introduction

Why discuss well-being in a textbook on philosophy of social science? A better question is how could one *not*. Concern with human well-being is at the very root of modern social science. The phrase '*science sociale*' was coined by the French constitutional theorist Emmanuel-Joseph Sieyès in 1789 in his pamphlet on the third estate. For Sieyès, social science was to provide the justification for democratic decision-making based on majority rule, for this is the best way to marry the selfish interests of all. But the political ideals of justice and democracy were only part of the picture. Soon after, in 1798, Jean-Jacques Régis de Cambacérès, a statesman and the author of the Napoleonic Code, in his *Discours sur la science sociale* explicitly identified social science with the means of securing happiness (*bonheur*) for all (Sonenscher 2009). Binding the individual wills into a common will was the best way to secure it. Social science began its life as a form of knowledge devoted to the advancement of well-being.

Though the precise definitions of social science continued to change, its founders in the Enlightenment and nineteenth-century France, Scotland, and England—Jeremy Bentham, Adam Smith, Nicolas de Condorcet, James and John Stuart Mill, Auguste Comte—all conceived of social science as central in the project of bringing about happiness, relieving suffering, furthering progress, or whatever else they took to be the main value in human life and the guiding principle of government. And so they shaped the subject matter and the methodologies of the new sciences to serve this goal. Psychology would help us measure and predict changes in happiness, sociology to advance society to the next more perfect stage of development, economics to predict the macro-consequences of

---

* Some of the material in this chapter has previously appeared in Alexandrova, A. (2012). 'Well-being as an Object of Science', *Philosophy of Science*, 79(5): 678–689.

individual pursuit of happiness, etc. Even when the language of happiness was purged from social science because of the early twentieth-century behaviourist concerns with unobservable mental states, the economists' preoccupation with 'efficiency' still betrayed their focus on these old values.

Social sciences have changed much since then, but well-being still figures in their motivation and subject matter. It does so less as some abstract final goal, but more as a direct object of study. Economists, psychologists, sociologists, gerontologists, anthropologists, especially in the English-speaking world, now study causes, correlates, and consequences of well-being in large populations, individuals, and communities. The search for 'well-being' and 'happiness' turns up about 7,000 papers in the relatively small but important Social Science Research Network database and almost 2 million on PubMed, the giant database of all medical literature. Well-being is the second most popular keyword in all psychology articles cited in the Social Science Citation Index and the Science Citation Index between 1998 and 2005. Journals focusing specifically on well-being multiply across disciplines, so do books for mass audience by eminent academics. Even the traditional hard science journals such as *Science* and *Nature* now publish articles on well-being.

These changes do not go unnoticed by policy-makers, who eagerly enlist the experts from the social sciences into projects to measure and improve well-being of various groups from local schoolchildren to entire nations. At the national level, the Center for Disease Control, among other governmental agencies in the USA, is now measuring well-being of the nation, as does the UK's Office of National Statistics, and governmental agencies in France, Australia, and Canada. At the international and NGO level, agencies such as UNICEF and the UN, and many major charities and foundations are putting together measures and surveys on well-being of one group or another. Exactly what to do on the basis of such knowledge is subject to debate. It is not widely accepted that governments, for example, should be in the business of promoting well-being. However, small-scale projects using scientific findings to make, say, schoolchildren or older people happier are not seen as controversial and are well under way.

Perhaps the most remarkable fact about all this research is how many different definitions and measures of well-being coexist at once. Some researchers take well-being to be life satisfaction or happiness or another subjective indicator. Others adopt objective person-independent constructs such as health, consumption, and legal protection. Still others combine the two. Moreover different subjective and objective indicators are chosen for different subjects of study: toddlers, the chronically ill, refugees, teenaged boys, etc., each get to have their own unique questionnaires, which often differ substantially in what they take well-being to consist in.

What justifies all these conceptions of well-being? How do we know if these scientists really study well-being, as it matters to us, and not something else? These are philosophical questions and it is natural to expect philosophy to provide resources for answering them. In search for these I survey, first, the current landscape in the philosophical theories of well-being and, second, the many uses of well-being in the sciences. But securing the connection between the two turns out to be far from straightforward: philosophical theorizing proceeds at too high a level of abstraction, while the scientists make tacit philosophical assumptions and only use philosophy when they need a gloss on their already existing views. I conclude with a proposal for how to make the connection work and how the two areas of inquiry should feed into each other. In my view it requires a change in the status quo of philosophy of well-being—a move away from traditional high-level theorizing and towards a more mid-level theorizing—and a change in the status quo of social science—an explicit admission of philosophical arguments into the way scientists justify their choices of measures of well-being.

Before we start an important emphasis is in order. This chapter will not aim to cover the empirical findings of the well-being research but concentrate instead on how we conceptualize and measure well-being. But one empirical finding is crucial to note even for my more methodological focus. Early studies of subjective well-being emphasized the idea of *adaptation*—that major events in our lives might push our sense of happiness up or down, but ultimately we return to a certain *set-point* (or a set-point range) given to us by our ultimate personality determined by genes and early environment. We are perpetually running on a 'hedonic treadmill', in which our feelings quickly catch up with changes in our material circumstances, so that we can never stay too happy or unhappy for a long time. If this is true, not much can be done to improve our subjective well-being, and it isn't clear whether it is worth monitoring all that much.

After much research, it is now relatively clear that this simple version of set-point theory is false. There are many circumstances we indeed adapt to—promotions, weather, minor health changes, good looks, among a few—and the links between happiness and personality are indeed strong and heritable. But that is not the whole story. There are events that have a lasting effect on happiness—they include unemployment, divorce, loss of a spouse, and disability. People who lose jobs recover a bit after the initial shock, but never quite to the levels they were at before, even once a new job comes along. This shows that subjective well-being can be intervened upon and thus is worth measuring. Reports to the contrary are much overstated, so let us get on with our business.

2. The Problem of Science–Value Coordination

Science and philosophy always go together: an empirical study of, say, light must start with a view on what light is. Such a view is part of fundamental theory, or philosophy. Same for any other object of science. But sometimes science and philosophy are entangled in a further way. Such as when the object of science also happens to be the object of normative, not just metaphysical, theorizing. Such objects include rationality, poverty, health, crime, and well-being. One just cannot classify an action as rational or criminal, and a community healthy or poor, by merely stating facts or reporting opinions, as you will also see discussed in Chapters 9 and 14. For any standard of rationality, criminality, health, or poverty is already a claim about the appropriateness of an action or a state in the light of some assumed value. A definition of well-being is similarly sensitive not just to facts, philosophical or empirical, but also to values. Well-being simply would be something else if it was not *good for one*, and if it did not create reasons to promote it. When we deal with such objects we face a special problem. A scientific study of this object can only be successful if it also gets the values right. When a headline proclaims that a happy marriage requires a wife slimmer than the husband, as the *Daily Telegraph* recently did,[1] I need to know that what these researchers mean by 'happy marriage' is indeed good for me, before I put away my chocolate bar. Let us call this the problem of *science–value coordination*. Accepting a piece of scientific research, let alone basing action on it, sometimes requires that we coordinate science and values. It is not a problem we can solve once and for all and forget about, but rather we face it every time we contemplate using science.

Science–value coordination—how to do it and how not to—is, in my view, one of the central problems facing philosophers of social science, as other chapters—especially 9 and 14—also stress. It is our professional responsibility to show how to connect scientific findings about 'well-being' with well-being proper, that is, with the sort of value that should help to regulate our lives just because it is good for us. And, clearly, no scientific study on its own can tell us what is good for us. Philosophy, especially its normative branches, must be called to testify.

3. The Philosophy–Science Disconnect

So what value are we talking about when contemplating well-being? Philosophers call this value 'prudential', and distinguish it from moral,

---

[1] <http://www.telegraph.co.uk/news/8646930/Happiness-is-based-on-wife-being-slimmer-than-husband-according-to-study.html>. Accessed Sept. 2013.

aesthetic, epistemic, and other values. They theorize about it as part of ethical theory and moral philosophy, and have been doing so for over two millennia. Prudential value is supposed to bear a special relationship to us: well-being is not merely good, it is also *good for us.*

Back to our problem then. When a scientist says she has identified a major contributor to well-being—a standard pronouncement in press releases nowadays—should we take her to be talking about prudential value? 'Why not?', you might reply, 'Presumably the scientist picked her characterization of well-being for a good reason, because it corresponds to prudential value.' But this assumes that we have an uncontroversial and readily usable theory of prudential value that a philosopher can pick off the shelf and hand over to a scientist or a policy-maker. It also assumes that this theory comes with well-articulated 'bridge principles' to take us from the theory to constructs and measures that can be used by the sciences. We do not have such a theory, despite the abundance of philosophical work on well-being.

What I call the philosophy–science disconnect is just that—the theories of prudential value developed by philosophers have a very tenuous connection to what is called 'well-being' in the sciences. The applicability of these theories remains a mystery and, what is more, a mystery that seems to be of little concern to philosophers. This does not bode well for addressing the problem of science–value coordination.

But before we say any more we need a crucial three-way distinction between *theories, constructs,* and *measures* of well-being. Very roughly, theories are the preoccupation of philosophers, while constructs and measures preoccupy scientists. A theory of well-being is a study of well-being's *essential* properties, those that make it well-being rather than something else. Philosophers often provide such theories by attempting to specify necessary and sufficient conditions for classifying a person as 'doing well'. A brief survey of these theories follows shortly. The term 'construct' is just another name for an attribute or a phenomenon, in our case the state of well-being in the subjects of a scientific study. Constructs are usually unobservable, but have various observable manifestations. For example, those who do well are less likely to commit suicide. Measures are the observable indicators of constructs. For example, a score on a questionnaire might be such an indicator. If this questionnaire is really good at detecting well-being it is said to be a valid measure of this construct. Defining or characterizing what the construct is, either by use of a general philosophical theory or some other way, corresponds to what in Chapter 14 is called 'characterization'; the observable indicators will be specified in what are there called 'procedures'.

To tackle science–value coordination, theories, constructs and measures must be put in the right relation to each other. As Chapter 14 stresses, measures must reliably track constructs and our choice of constructs must be properly informed by theories. What are the sources of the disconnect between theories of well-being, on the one hand, and constructs and measures on the other? I identify two sources. The first one is a disagreement between philosophers, the second one a discrepancy between what philosophers do with the notion of well-being and what everybody else does with it.

The first disagreement concerns the nature of well-being. Some philosophers are *subjectivists* about well-being and others are *objectivists*. Subjectivists insist that nothing can be good for you unless you desire or prefer or endorse this good. The objectivists disagree: a loving relationship, among other things, is good for you even if you don't want it. There are other divides among philosophers of well-being—each of which has its own technical name—the importance of virtue (*perfectionism*), of living in accordance with one's nature (*eudaimonism*), the value of having one's aims or desires realized (*desire fulfilment* views), or of having an overall pleasant life (*hedonism*). Still each of these views has counterexamples, i.e. made-up scenarios which fit the theory but intuitively do not count as well-being (or the other way around). At this time the literature on philosophy of well-being is extensive and each of the major options has grown elaborate and intricate under the weight of counterexamples. More on that in section 5.

Still, this disagreement should not in itself discourage us. Debates in philosophy are not about *which* goods are prudentially valuable, but rather about the *reasons* why they are so valuable. So philosophers might all easily agree that pleasant experience matters, success in personal projects matters, living within one's limits matters, and possibly more. This level of agreement might be enough for addressing the problem of science–value coordination. The second feature is more problematic however. It concerns not the theory of well-being but the very concept.

Take the question: 'How is Mo doing?' This question might be asked in two ways: a general and a contextual one. A general context considers Mo's life as a whole, all things considered. Say, Mo's close friend asks him 'how are you?' in that significant tone of voice in a heart-to-heart conversation. This is a context in which Mo is invited to take account of all the important things in his life, evaluate how he is doing on each account, and then aggregate all the important elements to produce an overall judgement. This is what I mean by general evaluation. If, on the other hand, Mo hears 'how are you?' from his family doctor on an annual check-up, the same question invokes a context-specific evaluation—are you feeling healthy? This would be a contextual evaluation—only a particular kind of well-being is in question here.

Philosophers theorize only about the first kind of well-being—the agent's overall all-things-considered well-being—not the second kind. If you are a hedonist philosopher, you take well-being to consist in all the pleasures, in all aspects of one's life, over the course of life as a whole. If you are a desire theorist, you identify well-being with the fulfilment of all the desires in their order of overall importance, etc.

I call this a discrepancy between philosophers and everybody else, because philosophers sometimes act as if the general kind is the only well-being concept there is. But in life, science, and policy, such a general focus is actually quite rare. For the most part we make context-specific judgements of well-being, using a narrower concept. How is a toddler with Down's syndrome just adopted from an orphanage some place in Eastern Europe doing? Is he still extremely malnourished and weak? Does he still spend the day staring at the ceiling? Does he still hit his head against the wall? Is he learning to trust people? Learning to smile and to play? The very fact that we ask these questions about this child and not others reveals that we are engaged in a contextual, rather than general, evaluation. Only some aspects of his well-being count and others, for instance, whether he is trying to communicate as many 3 year olds (even with Down's syndrome) do, are irrelevant for this context. Compare this to the general context: a funeral of a woman with normal abilities at which the friends and family of the deceased reflect on her life as a whole. Dominant philosophical theories equip us to think only about the latter, which, though important, is hardly the only, or even the most important concept of well-being. We might be tempted to think of the distinction between overall and contextual well-being as just a distinction between the general and the particular, with the particular contextual well-beings making up the general overall well-being. But this is not helpful; the philosopher's notion of well-being is concerned only with one kind of evaluation—the general kind. Contextual evaluation has different rules and they are not detectible just by looking at the philosophical theories.

4. Variantism and Invariantism about Well-Being

You might think it is just the measures of well-being that will differ from context to context, not the definition of well-being. Let us explore this option. In this case we have an agreed-on concept of well-being that applies to all—adopted toddlers with disabilities, elderly widows with fragile bones, depressed middle-class fathers, etc. What might this construct be? Taking the major proposals in philosophy for our guidance, we might say it is their pleasure/pain balance, or satisfaction of their desires, or some such. (More on these options in the next section.) We then can measure this phenomenon directly, by providing a measurement operation that we suppose gives the right result, or indirectly by measuring factors that cause, or correlate with, whatever the agreed-on phenomenon of well-being is. Call this picture *invariantism* about well-being because on this view the construct of well-being does not vary with circumstances, only the measures do.

Invariantism has a lot to recommend itself. For starters it is the natural default picture: when there is a single term such as 'well-being', it probably refers to a single unified concept that serves its purpose in all contexts in which we apply the term. And a single theory is supposed to tell us what this concept refers to, i.e. what well-being really is. It is plausible to assume invariantism at least at the start of one's inquiry. But it is an assumption we should be ready to abandon if it does not earn its keep. Just as we have learnt from psychology that memory is not a unified phenomenon, but rather many different phenomena, we may question that a single concept and a single theory of that concept is sufficient for well-being.

I believe we should consider the possibility that it is the actual stuff that gets called 'well-being', not just the measures, that differ. Perhaps well-being as the concept is generally used is what Chapter 14 calls a *ballung* concept, a loose concept embracing a variety of different aspects, where the use of the concept in different contexts can focus on different aspects. A version of this view might be called *variantism* about well-being. According to this picture, we do and should adjust the notion of well-being to the circumstances in which it is used. We adjust it in two ways. First, a different threshold of well-being applies in different situations. Doing well in an emergency refugee camp might have a lower threshold than doing well in a middle-class Western community. Secondly and perhaps more controversially, the very stuff, or in philosophical parlance, the *constituents* of well-being, depend on circumstances. Realization of personal values might constitute the well-being of an adult, but not of a child; it's the other way around with play. Variantists maintain that there may not be a single correct theory of well-being to do all the jobs. At least, as far as the social sciences are concerned.

Naturally, in philosophical theories of well-being there is no place for contexts and for variation. It's not that they are not allowed. (No theorist of prudential value would claim that well-being has only one measuring stick.) But they are invisible precisely because philosophical theories of well-being are after a theory of prudential value in the most abstract and general sense. That theories are abstract is obviously no criticism so long as we know how to apply them. So, the all-things-considered focus would not be a problem if we had a practical way of connecting the two projects, the general philosophical and the contextual scientific. I do not deny that this connection exists but it is very tenuous and certainly not suitable for addressing the problem of science–value coordination.

I summarize the problem in Table 1.1. Each row represents an area of social science that uses a notion of well-being. The columns aim to give,

Table 1.1 Different notions of well-being in different areas of the social sciences

	(1) Philosophical theory of well-being	(2) Scientific construct of well-being	(3) Measures of well-being
Psychological sciences	Hedonism	Average affect	Experience sampling methods, happiness questionnaires
Psychological sciences	Subjectivism (or desire fulfilment)	Life satisfaction	Satisfaction With Life Scale, World Values Survey, Gallup World Poll
Psychological sciences	Eudaimonism or perfectionism	Flourishing	Seligman's PERMA, Ryff's Psychological Well-being Index, Huppert's Flourishing
Development economics	Objective list theory	Quality of life	Dasgupta's aggregate quality of life, Human Development Index, various capabilities measures
Gerontology and medicine	?	Quality of life under various social and medical conditions	Nottingham Health Profile, Sickness Impact Profile, World Health Organization Quality of Life, Health-Related Quality of Life, QUALEFFO, etc.
Child well-being	?	Adequate satisfaction of children's physical and mental needs	US Department of Health and Human Services, Children's Bureau Child Well-Being Measure (3 domains of assessment: family, education, mental health and physical needs), among many other measures
National well-being	?	A consensus on the many values of a nation	UK's Office of National Statistics Measure of National Well-Being, Legatum Prosperity Index

respectively, a philosophical theory commonly assumed by this area of research (1), the constructs built on the basis of this theory (2), and the measures that are supposed to capture the construct (3). Notice how in some rows I put a question mark in the theory column. Why? Because in these areas researchers use a context-specific, not a general, notion of well-being, and because of this it is not clear what philosophical theory is supposed to justify the choice of construct. So long as these question marks remain in column (1) we will not be able to evaluate the adequacy of the contextual constructs in column (2). In my view, it is these missing contextual theories for the column (1) that philosophers should be busy developing, instead of chiselling out yet another fool-proof version of the standard theories of overall well-being.

But the problem is bigger than it looks. How come four different theories of well-being are used in the first four rows? What justifies a different choice in each case? If invariantism is correct, this should not be the case.

Before we proceed any further, we need a brief field guide to the views in the column (1).

5. Theories of Prudential Good

Derek Parfit, an Oxford philosopher, in a short but famous Appendix I to his *Reasons and Persons*, distinguished between mental state, desire fulfilment, and 'objective list' theories of well-being and this way of carving up the options, with a few tweaks here and there, has become standard (Parfit 1984).

Let us be clear at the outset what sort of debate philosophers are engaged in. The debate is not about what sort of life to pursue and what choices to make in order to be well. It is not a 'how to' debate. So a person in crisis wishing to reform their life for better would be ill advised to look for help here. (For this purpose there exists a growing semi-popular literature on positive psychology.) Indeed, in the vast majority of cases philosophers will all agree on whether a given life or a choice is good or bad for you. Rather their differences are in *why* they are good for you. Very roughly, for desire theorists (a kind of subjectivism) it is because you want them, for hedonists (a kind of mental state theory) it is the way they make you feel, for objectivists it is the way they suit your nature.

Mental state theorists, as the name suggest, take our mental states, and only them, to constitute our well-being. Not just any mental states, of course, but only experiences with a positive valence. What states exactly? Hedonists take the relevant state to be pleasure, or satisfaction, or enjoyment, which for present purposes are synonymous. Here is, for example, a recent statement of a hedonist theory of well-being from another Oxford philosopher Roger Crisp (2006: 622): 'What is good for any individual is the enjoyable experience in her life, what is bad is the suffering in that life, and the life best for an individual is that with the greatest balance of enjoyment over suffering.' Hedonists can accept that things other than enjoyment can be good for us, but only instrumentally. Great art, friendship, virtue can all benefit us, but only via their causal effect on our experiences.

However, much rides on how we define enjoyment. What makes an experience pleasurable? Is it pleasurable in virtue of how it feels or in virtue of our liking it? Very roughly these positions are respectively *internalist* and *externalist*. They are called so because in the first case pleasures are identified by their internal quality, whereas in the second by something external to the pleasure—our liking it. The outcome of this debate is not trivial, for externalists about pleasure have more affinities with desire fulfilment theories than with hedonism. If pleasure is that which you desire, then the hedonist view that pleasure is good for us becomes a version of a desire satisfaction view. That is, the view that it is good for us to satisfy our desires, of which pleasure is one. But in that case why focus only on pleasures? We might as well conceive of well-being as having access to *any* desired object. This would bring us squarely into the territory of desire fulfilment views of well-being.

This view prides itself on not falling victim to the experience machine argument now popular in philosophy. Take two people with identical experiences. One lives them 'for real', the other by being connected to a machine that simulates his brain in precise ways. Hedonists have no option but to bite the bullet and admit that neither life is any more prudentially valuable. The desire fulfilment theorist can claim that the denizen of the experience machine has not *really* got his desires fulfilled, he only thinks he has.

This view has another advantage. For something to be good for me, this good has to have a special relationship to me, it has to engage me, or resonate with me, or be responsive to my priorities, or some such. Classical hedonism takes pleasure to be good for me without consulting me. But we can all imagine monks or tortured artists with no desire for pleasure and yet a great satisfaction with their lives. Are they not doing well?

The main version of subjectivism is the desire satisfaction view. According to it, it is good for you to get what you want, and that is the only thing that's good for you. But of course, sometimes people want things for themselves that seemingly do them no good whatsoever. Perhaps they are uninformed, or indoctrinated, or perhaps their desires are only for things that have nothing to do with themselves, like survival of polar bears, or their desires are for trivial things like another piece of chewing gum. For those cases, there are many bells and whistles we can attach to the basic desire satisfaction view. First we can say that it is not *desire* fulfilment, but *goals* or *value* fulfilment that matters. Second, we can restrict which desires or goals or beliefs count, any actual one or perhaps only idealized ones, for instance only those that one would have after good reflection or with full information. These are known as *idealized* versions of subjectivism.

We can even try to tweak the theory to exclude the famous counterexample of the grass-counter. A grass-counter is a person who with full information and sincerity announces that his goal in life is to count blades of grass on all the lawns he encounters. He does so and claims to be doing perfectly well, thank you very much! But if you want your theory of well-being to exclude the grass-counter you might as well admit to being objectivist (the view that well-being can encompass goods that benefit a person no matter what her attitudes, life plans, or tastes are). Perhaps the most famous such theory is Aristotle's *perfectionism*—the best life for a person is to function at the highest level a normal human could, which involves exercising distinctly human virtues of justice, friendship, contemplation, etc. Because Aristotle, along with other Classical Greek philosophers, thought that the exercise of virtues is *eudaimonia* (often translated as happiness), this approach is also known as *eudaimonism*. Modern versions of this view all preserve the main idea—some things are good for us because of our nature as human beings, not because of our tastes and attitudes.

The dialectic of this debate should start becoming clear. There are standard counterexamples and objections to each of the major theories and many attempts to respond by introducing various fixes. The unending back and forth and the appeals to intuition have left many a philosopher frustrated. The scientists interested in well-being do not engage in these debates, but they freely help themselves to whatever concepts seem convenient to them in their projects.

6. Major Constructs of Well-Being in the Social Sciences

Now we move on to the columns (2) and (3), i.e. the major constructs and measures of well-being in the social sciences. There are so many of them, especially in fields of research concerned directly with policy and therapy, that I concentrate only on the most central ones.

6.1 Psychological Sciences

I start with psychology because the definition of well-being here is the closest to the all-things-considered focus in philosophy. Perhaps, because of this affinity, psychology sports three traditions in measurement of well-being, each inspired by one of the Big Three theories in philosophy.

The first tradition takes well-being to be 'hedonic balance', i.e. the ratio of positive to negative emotions in a person over time. Nobel prize-winner Daniel Kahneman is famous for, among other things, reviving classical hedonism and adapting tools of modern psychology for measuring the day-to-day experience of life (Kahneman et al. 2004). This can be done by 'experience sampling', a methodology for obtaining immediate reports on the subject's experience while she is engaged in it. Nowadays in happiness studies it is done with hand-held devices that prompt subjects, regularly or randomly, to rate the level of a given positive or negative emotion. Then these ratings are combined to form the subject's 'hedonic profile'. If the horizontal axis represents duration and the vertical axis represents the level of positive emotion at a given time, then the area under the curve formed with individual ratings refers to what Kahneman once called 'objective happiness'. It is objective in the sense that the subject herself does not judge her overall happiness, but only her happiness at a given moment. This sense of 'objective' is not to be confused with objective theories of well-being, where objectivity has to do with goods that are good for an individual irrespective of her desires or attitudes.

It can also be done by having subjects keep a diary that records the duration and intensity of their experiences. But most importantly it should not be done by asking subjects to summarize their experience with an overall judgement about their lives of the kind, 'How happy are you overall?' People, modern hedonists maintain, inevitably distort their experience, introducing all sort of biases rooted in their immediate surroundings.

The second tradition embraces these biases as a feature not a bug. For them well-being is life satisfaction, i.e. an endorsement of the balance of the many values and priorities in life. We care about lots of things and life satisfaction reflects how we are doing taking them all into account. If experience is only one of our priorities, it is no wonder life satisfaction judgements diverge from hedonic balance. The Satisfaction With Life Scale (SWLS) developed by the psychologist Ed Diener consists of five questions that all invite people to make such a summary judgement. Note that, though I put life satisfaction in the same row as desire fulfilment, the two are not identical. Desire fulfilment theorists define fulfilment as *actual*, not just felt, realization of the person's wishes. You may think your desire to win an Olympic medal was realized, but if you are a resident of an experience machine or are otherwise radically deceived, the desire theorist will not count you as doing well. The SWLS, on the other hand, can, of course, only pick out the person's own sense of how they are faring.

The union of hedonic balance and life satisfaction is often referred to as 'subjective well-being' and it is this combination construct that has been gaining much prominence in academia and policy circles.

Finally, the third tradition identifies well-being with flourishing, taking inspiration from perfectionism and/or eudaimonism. Again it is not quite the flourishing that Aristotle talked about, but rather *a sense* of flourishing, a subjective version of the theory. But notably, unlike the other two traditions, eudaimonists in psychology understand flourishing not as a unified phenomenon but as encompassing several components: a sense of autonomy, mastery, purpose, connectedness to people, etc. Unlike in philosophical eudaimonism, these distinct components of well-being are derived not from a theory of human nature, but rather from *psychometric* tests. Very roughly, psychometric tests identify how much different items of a questionnaire correlate with each other and these tests are widely used throughout psychological and medical sciences to 'validate' measures. I use scare quotes because this is a very different sense of validation than that used in philosophy. To validate a measure in psychology is to show that it has favourable psychometric properties, which, in my view, is very different from showing that a measure actually measures what it is supposed to. I will return to these points in section 7.

As we can see, all of these constructs are subjective, but all in different senses. Hedonic balance requires favourable emotional balance, life satisfaction a favourable judgement of one's life, and flourishing a sense of meaning and accomplishment.

All three of these constructs are used widely, but none as widely as life satisfaction because of its brevity and ease of use. This is despite the many critiques directed at life satisfaction. Is there really one correct judgement as to how satisfied one is with his or her life? Unlikely, when we see just how sensitive this judgement is to the perspective one adopts, norms that one endorses, and, research shows, arbitrary changes in the context of the speaker. To some extent these critiques have succeeded and life satisfaction is no longer the dominant construct. It is notable that the new questionnaire for measuring UK's national well-being, recently unveiled by the UK Office of National Statistics, incorporates questions from each of the three traditions: one question on life satisfaction, one on flourishing, one on positive emotions and one on negative. More on this in section 6.5.

In psychology then it is common to use philosophical theories as resources for developing constructs of well-being, but selectively and opportunistically.

6.2 Economics

Traditionally economics operated with a preference satisfaction view of well-being, which is closest to the desire fulfilment view, but does not restrict preferences in any way. What we want is what's good for us. Welfare economics is a theoretical system based on this simple (to many philosophers, dangerously simple) view of well-being. Moreover, this view is standardly supplemented with a definition of preferences as *revealed* choices. What you want is, roughly, what you choose when given an opportunity. Whether the choices are horrible, or whether you yourself are deceived, weak-willed, or irrational does not matter on this view. This is the actual, rather than idealized, preference satisfaction view of well-being.

Writing for the *New York Times*, Harvard economist Edward Glaeser couples this view with the idea that freedom consists in having lots of options; together they make up what he calls 'the moral heart of economics'. He elaborates (2011):

> Improvements in welfare occur when there are improvements in utility, and those occur only when an individual gets an option that wasn't previously available. We typically prove that someone's welfare has increased when the person has an increased set of choices. When we make that assumption (which is hotly contested by some people, especially psychologists), we essentially assume that the fundamental objective of public policy is to increase freedom of choice.

As Glaeser acknowledges, this project is under pressure from many sources, especially its assumption that people have stable and consistent preferences and act rationally so as to get the most of what they prefer. The main source is the empirical research into various biases and irrationalities that afflict choices of actual human beings. Psychologists and behavioural economists have been studying these biases since the 1970s. It turns out we do not have stable preferences, but make them up as we go along in response to arbitrary changes in environment; we make systematic and predictable mistakes in our judgements and choices and in general do not look like the rational agents economic theory assumes. As a result of these studies, even mainstream economists now recognize that actual choices do not reveal 'real' preferences, or at least not under a broad range of conditions. A different conception of well-being is slowly making its way into economics, a conception that recognizes the importance of psychological states, such as happiness.

But even without these changes, not all economists are wedded to a preference satisfaction view of welfare. Development economics, for instance, has its own robust tradition of theorizing about well-being along entirely different lines.

Development economists need tools to evaluate large-scale public policy in poor countries. Such evaluation starts with a question, 'How well is this country doing?' Though up until recently this question was answered with purely income-based measures, such as the Gross National Product, the tide is changing. A new approach was first pioneered by economist-philosopher Amartya Sen and philosopher Martha Nussbaum as a framework for measuring justice, development, and progress. The idea is that humans need the freedom to pursue distinct capabilities, their 'beings and doings', which may include health, education, political rights, social relationships, emotional life, creativity, etc. A person's *capability set* is the set of all the combinations of doings and beings possible for that person given their constraints—constraints like their physical abilities and the resources available to them—all the different lives that person could live. The core of the capability approach is that having a lot of options about the lives you can live is a good thing, at least if these are 'lives worth living'.

Human well-being is here understood using the notion of capabilities, rather than the traditional economic utility. Capabilities are different from utility in that their value cannot be measured on a single scale and as a result they do not admit simple trade-offs. Sacrificing political rights for access to health care, for example, could be utility maximizing. But in the capabilities approach both are essential and neither can be purchased at the expense of the other. Capabilities also make room for the fact different people might need different amounts of goods or services to have the same doings and beings available or to have the same combinations available. In practice capabilities are usually defined using a theory of objective human needs (e.g. an Aristotelian theory) rather than by consulting people's preferences, let alone the ones revealed by choices. The capabilities approach inspired the United Nations Development Project's Human Development

Index described in Chapter 14, now over twenty years old and still serving as the measure of progress of development.

Even economists who do not subscribe to the capabilities approach claim that development contexts need an objective understanding of well-being. Partha Dasgupta, a Cambridge economist, proposes the notion of *aggregate quality of life*. It is aggregate in two senses: first, it represents the state of many people and, secondly, their quality of life is constituted by several elements. Dasgupta writes (2001: 54): 'A minimal set of indices for spanning a reasonable conception of current well-being in a poor country includes private consumption per head, life expectancy at birth, literacy, and civil and political liberties.' Private consumption is food, shelter, clothing, and basic legal aid. Life expectancy at birth is the best indicator of health, while literacy is the best indicator of basic primary education. Civil and political rights allow people to function independently of the state and their communities. Each of these is necessary. They cannot be reduced to some one item or replaced by a monetary value, for they may be undervalued by people themselves and hence by the market.

However, current quality of life is not the only thing we mean when we ask 'How well is a country doing?' Sometimes we also mean to inquire about what Dasgupta calls a country's *social well-being*. This concept encompasses, along with the current quality of life, the *sustainability* of this current lifestyle—how well does a country balance the needs of its current population with the needs of its future generations? The concept of social well-being is necessary for evaluating policy because planning is a forward-looking exercise and the future generations are sometimes included in the calculation of the nation's well-being. A high quality of life at a time may conceal the fact that a community is consuming its resources without an adequate provision for the future, so Dasgupta defines social well-being as a pattern of consumption that strikes the best balance between current and future quality of life. Measuring social well-being, Dasgupta claims, requires a concept of a country's *wealth*. He defines wealth in broad terms, which include the nation's capital: human, intellectual, natural, and manufactured. Importantly the value of this capital needs to be judged not by market prices but by its social value. Clearly this is a departure from both the preferentist approach of classical economics and from the overwhelmingly subjective approach of psychology.

6.3 *Gerontology and the Medical Sciences*

When the focus is on an individual person, especially one with a disability or a chronic condition, the construct of well-being is yet again different. What gets called 'quality of life' and 'well-being' in gerontology and specialized medical contexts has little in common with the eponymous constructs in economics or even psychology. Rather, well-being here is a combination of subjective satisfaction and objective functioning, where the latter is understood as the ability to go through one's day reasonably autonomously and the standard of functioning is adjusted specifically by age and the specific illness.

Some studies of the elderly identify quality of life as general healthy functioning. Measurement instruments such as the World Health Organization Quality of Life questionnaire, Nottingham Health Profile, and the Sickness Impact Profile provide a general picture of the subject's health, both subjective and objective, including pain and environmental stressors.

Because these instruments gauge health as a whole they are known as generic. Non-generic measures are developed for people with a specific illness. For example, QUALEFFO is a questionnaire developed by the European Foundation for Osteoporosis especially for people with vertebral fractures and osteoporosis. This questionnaire consists of forty-eight questions falling in five areas: pain, physical function (activities of daily living, i.e. sleep, bath and toilet, dressing, jobs around the house, mobility), social function, general health perception, and mental function.

Non-generic measures abound. Many ageing people care for their spouses with heavy chronic illnesses. This is frequently a time of great hardship in the life of the caregiver, as they are at an increased risk of depression and complications with their own health. Researchers invented the notion of Caregiver Strain to mark this hardship: sleep disturbance due to the illness of the care recipient, loneliness, lack of control over personal and social plans, family adjustments and arguments, upsetting behaviour of the care recipient, his or her loss of the former self, worry, fatigue, and financial strain. Freedom from this strain is then combined with life satisfaction to make a special measure of well-being for caregivers.

6.4 *Child Well-Being*

Children are yet another special category whose well-being is not captured by the constructs and measures used for adults. It is hard to find anyone who thinks that a child low on life satisfaction is therefore necessarily unwell or a child high on life satisfaction is therefore necessarily well. Children are just not capable of judging their own well-being appropriately, or at least are less capable than adults are. Children, more than adults, can be manipulated, abused, and maltreated without realizing that they are. And as any parent knows, children can be very dissatisfied indeed even when they have everything they need. It is no surprise then that all serious measures of well-being for children incorporate objective indicators such as medical care, family dynamics, access to education, play, adequate food, and hygiene. Subjective indicators are increasingly added to objective measures, but always as a secondary ingredient.

Naturally children are a diverse group: infants are very different from teenagers, malnourished children from Darfur are very different from obese children in suburban USA. Actual measures of child well-being reflect these differences; some are specialized to schoolyard bullying victims, others to former child soldiers, others to schoolchildren with anxiety or specific disabilities.

Still, what justifies these various collections of indicators as unified wholes? What makes them all good indicators of child well-being? Worryingly, a theory of child well-being simply does not exist. The three major theories of prudential value have not been extended to the case of children, nor is it easy to see how they could be. For the most part science proceeds without the necessary philosophy to back it up, a concern that drives much of this chapter and motivates my formulation of the problem of science–value coordination.

6.5 National Well-Being

Our final example is the construct of national well-being. It is hard to draw up a summary here because the debates about what exactly such a construct should encompass are ongoing. As this chapter was being written the UK Office for National Statistics (ONS) was conducting a country-wide inquiry called 'What matters to you?', soliciting views and recommendations from the public, the experts, and communities all across the UK. The outcome of this exercise will be a measure of UK's well-being, which would provide an alternative way of evaluating how the country is doing than the traditional economic measures. That these traditional measures are inadequate for capturing national well-being was eloquently argued by Bobby Kennedy in his 1968 address at the University of Kansas, Lawrence:

> Our gross national product...counts air pollution and cigarette advertising, and ambulances to clear our highways of carnage. It counts special locks for our doors and the jails for those who break them. It counts the destruction of our redwoods and the loss of our natural wonder in chaotic sprawl. Yet the gross national product does not allow for the health of our children, the quality of their education, or the joy of their play. It does not include the beauty of our poetry or the strength of our marriages; the intelligence of our public debate or the integrity of our public officials. It measures neither our wit nor our courage; neither our wisdom nor our learning; neither our compassion nor our devotion to our country; it measures everything, in short, except that which makes life worthwhile.

What measure would capture that which makes life worthwhile at the level of a nation? That it should include more than the traditional economic indicators is slowly becoming the mainstream view. In 2009 three major economists. Joseph Stiglitz, Amartya Sen, and Jean-Paul Fitoussi produced a report commissioned by the then French President Nicolas Sarkozy outlining a multi-dimensional measure of national well-being that includes even subjective well-being indicators (Stiglitz et al. 2009). But which ones? It is true that sometimes answering this question does not matter for policy. On any conception of subjective well-being (SWB) people suffer acutely the effects of unemployment and social isolation, which explains why these areas are often proposed as crucial for policy interventions. Still a great deal rides on which elements of SWB we choose to focus on. One fascinating recent study offers evidence that income and economic indicators correlate much better with life satisfaction than with hedonic balance (Kahneman and Deaton 2010). So depending on which measure of well-being we pick, pursuit of economic growth, rather than job protection, may or may not be a national priority.

Two requirements seem to be crucial to a notion of national well-being. First of all, such a measure needs to capture the values and priorities of the people whose well-being it is supposed to represent. Philosophers Dan Haybron and Valerie Tiberius coin the term *pragmatic subjectivism* precisely for this purpose (Haybron and Tiberius 2012). They argue that, even if one adopts an objectivist theory of well-being, when it comes to well-being policy at a governmental level one should adopt a kind of subjectivism. Not an actual preference satisfaction view, but a more sophisticated subjectivism: one that differentiates between stated or revealed preference and deeply held values and prioritizes the latter. Because policy contexts present special dangers of paternalism and oppression, governments defer on the nature of well-being to the individuals they represent. (None of this implies that governments should stay out of promoting the well-being of its citizens.) Second, a measure of national well-being needs to represent a certain level of consensus, not a mere sum of individual well-beings. Together these two requirements explain why, in this context, more than in any others, it is particularly important to consult people on their prudential values and to use these views as the most important basis for a measure. (This is presumably what the UK's ONS tried to do in their consultation.)

But these requirements still leave much room for variation. Should measures of national well-being be linked specifically to happiness and positive emotions? The new hedonists believe so, urging that national well-being be measured by the population average of the ratio of positive to negative emotions (Kahneman et al. 2004). Others think that the Satisfaction With Life Scale, which asks respondents to evaluate how their lives are going all-things-considered, is a better measure (Diener et al. 2008). The UK's ONS has already announced that the UK measure will contain both subjective well-being and objective indicators, such as life expectancy and educational achievements. There are also well-worked-out proposals such as the Prosperity Index of the Legatum Institute—a multi-index indicator encompassing eight sub-indices from economy to safety and social capital.

Social capital, a measure of cohesiveness of a community, is particularly notable as a plausible candidate for inclusion in a measure of national well-being. As argued famously by Harvard sociologist Robert Putnam in his book *Bowling Alone*, social capital has been decreasingly steadily in the West since the Second World War: we spend less time around each other, volunteer less, join organizations and societies less, trust strangers less, and so on (Putnam 2001). Social capital is most probably tightly connected to subjective well-being, but even independently of this link we might want to ask, 'What sort of community are we if we don't trust or remotely like each other?', and on this ground alone include social capital into our understanding of national well-being.

7. Conclusion

As we can see, constructs of well-being in the sciences do not present a unified front and, more worryingly, they do not connect well to the philosophical theories of well-being. In this chapter we have seen the great distance between philosophical theorizing about well-being and the sort of value judgements that underlie constructs of well-being in the social sciences. This is what I have called the philosophy–science disconnect. It exists because philosophers talk about well-being in an all-things-considered sense, whereas scientists and policy-makers tend to make contextual evaluations. And we simply do not have the principles that connect the general philosophical theories of prudential value to the context-specific constructs needed in science and policy. Not yet anyway. I hope this will change soon because it matters greatly which construct we choose for which purpose, as these constructs are used to assess the progress of policies, therapies, and personal decisions. Since different constructs often result in different answers to these vital questions, a choice of a construct needs to have a thorough justification by appeal to what matters in a given context. How well we can use current philosophical theories for these purposes remains to be seen. I do not believe they are sufficient by themselves. My bet is that the current theories need to be supplemented with other more grounded theories if they are to connect with scientific constructs in a genuine way.

We also need to change the status quo in the social sciences. In disciplines that rely on questionnaires the matter of validity of constructs and measures is usually settled by *psychometrics*. When great numbers of people fill in a questionnaire about well-being, psychometricians run various statistical tests on these answers. They are able to detect how much answers to different questions of a test correlate with each other, how much they 'bunch together', how well they correlate when the test is administered again after a time interval or under different circumstances. When these correlations are strong enough, a test is described to be a 'valid' measure of the underlying construct.

Whatever 'valid' means in psychometrics, it cannot be a genuine justification of a measure. The fact that replies to a questionnaire have certain correlations, even very strong ones, can show that people understand these questionnaires to refer to some unified stable phenomenon. But whether this phenomenon deserves the name of well-being is a philosophical question that cannot be settled by statistics. So psychometrics does not give us a licence to ignore fundamental normative questions about well-being. (And besides, many disciplines, most notably economics, do not rely on psychometrics.) Philosophical arguments about well-being need to become part and parcel of the practice of the science of well-being.

Take for instance the Genuine Progress Indicator (or GPI), which inspired the Canadian Index of Well-Being. It calculates costs of economic growth and subtracts them from GDP. When social scientists speak of its 'theoretical foundation', they cite models and theories about the diminishing returns of economic growth for ecology, resource depletion, social costs, etc. GPI reflects these costs and is thus thought to gauge well-being better than GDP alone. Implicit in these arguments are value judgements about what matters. Money matters presumably because it helps people satisfy their basic needs, but at a certain point more money no longer serves human needs and might indeed take away from them. So satisfying human needs matters—these needs include material comforts, belonging, connection with nature, etc.

These sorts of judgements have very little connection to any of the prevailing philosophical theories of well-being. Sure, they can be recast in terms of hedonism, eudaimonism, or desire fulfilment, but do they come from these theories? And are they made right by these theories? As a matter of methodology, should social scientists rely on these theories in order to develop measures of well-being? These questions should be on the agendas of philosophers of social sciences and ethicists. We need to develop theoretical foundations for the various projects on well-being in different branches of science and medicine. Whether this work will assume variantism and propose different theories of well-being for different purposes with only thin unity among them, or invariantism, whereby different contextual theories of well-being follow from a single general theory, remains to be seen.

References

Crisp, R. (2006). 'Hedonism Reconsidered', *Philosophy and Phenomenological Research*, 73(3): 619–45.

Dasgupta, P. (2001). *Human Well-Being and the Natural Environment.* Oxford: Oxford University Press.

Diener, E., Lucas, R., Schimmack, U., and Helliwell, J. (2008). *Well-Being for Public Policy.* New York: Oxford University Press.

Glaeser, E. (2011). 'The Moral Heart of Economics', *New York Times*, 25 Jan. <http://economix.blogs.nytimes.com/2011/01/25/the-moral-heart-of-economics/?smid=pl-share>. Accessed Sept. 2013.

Haybron, D., and Tiberius, V. (2012). *The Normative Foundations of Well-being Policy.* Papers on Economics and Evolution, 1202, Evolutionary Economics Group. Jena: Max Plank Institute, Jena.

Kahneman, D., and Deaton, A. (2010). 'High Income Improves Evaluation of Life But Not Emotional Well-Being', *Proceedings of the National Academy of Sciences*, 107(38): 16489–93.

Kahneman, D., Krueger, A., Schkade, D., Schwarz, N., and Stone, A. (2004). 'Toward National Well Being Accounts', *American Economic Review*, 94(2): 429–34.

Kennedy, R.F. (1968). 'Remarks at the University of Kansas', speech delivered at the University of Kansas, Lawrence, 18 Mar.

Parfit, D. (1984). *Reasons and Persons.* Oxford: Oxford University Press.

Putnam, R. (2001). *Bowling Alone: The Collapse and Revival of American Community.* New York: Simon & Schuster.

Sonenscher, M. (2009). ' "The Moment of Social Science": The Decade Philosophique and Late Eighteenth Century French Thought', *Modern Intellectual History*, 6(1): 121–46.

Stiglitz, J., Sen, A., and, Fitoussi, JP. (2009). *Report of the Commission on the Measurement of Economic Performance and Social Progress.* Paris: Commission on the Measurement of Economic Performance and Social Progress.

Further Readings

Crisp, R. (2008). 'Well-Being', in E. Zalta (ed.), *The Stanford Encyclopedia of Philosophy* (Winter 2008 edition), <http://plato.stanford.edu/archives/win2008/entries/wellbeing>.

Hausman, D., and McPherson, M. (2006). *Economic Analysis, Moral Philosophy and Public Policy.* Cambridge: Cambridge University Press.

Haybron, D. (2008). *The Pursuit of Unhappiness: The Elusive Psychology of Well-Being.* New York: Oxford University Press.

Layard, R. (2011). *Happiness: Lessons from a New Science.* New York: Penguin.

Nussbaum, M., and Sen, A. (1993). *The Quality of Life* (Wider Studies in Development Economics). Oxford: Clarendon Press.

2

Climate Change

Wendy Parker

Climate change is often framed as an issue for the physical sciences, concerned with the extent to which greenhouse gas emissions are causing—and will in the future cause—Earth's climate to warm. Indeed, much of the public controversy surrounding climate change has focused on precisely these matters. In its 2007 assessment report, the Intergovernmental Panel on Climate Change (IPCC) reaches some clear conclusions: warming of Earth's climate is now unequivocal, and it is very likely that much of the warming that occurred since the mid-twentieth century was caused by increased emission of greenhouse gases from human activities, especially the burning of fossil fuels and the clearing of forests (IPCC 2007). Moreover, the IPCC concludes that, if greenhouse gas emissions continue at or above current rates, there is good reason to expect that significant additional warming will occur and will be accompanied by other changes in climate, such as more frequent heat waves and heavy precipitation events.

Yet climate change is not just an issue for the physical sciences. It is a remarkably interdisciplinary problem, requiring expertise from a host of disciplines, including the social sciences. In fact, the human dimensions of the issue are particularly salient: recent warming is attributed to *anthropogenic* emissions of greenhouse gases; concern that future climate change will have very negative impacts on *human societies* drives much of the investment in climate change research; and decision-makers grapple with how *individuals, communities, and governments* can respond to the threat of climate change. The social sciences will be integral to understanding the consequences of climate change for human societies as well as the feasible responses.

So far, however, the social sciences have been somewhat slow to engage with the issue of climate change. Part of the explanation for this may lie in the issue's physical science framing, but other factors, such as ordinary disciplinary inertia, also probably have contributed. This is not to imply that social scientists have had nothing to say on the issue of climate change. Far from it. Perhaps the best-known work has come from economists, who have analysed the costs and benefits of limiting greenhouse gas emissions and who have offered a distinctly economic characterization of climate change as 'the greatest and widest-ranging market failure ever seen' (Stern 2006: p. i). Nevertheless, there is now broad recognition of the need for much greater involvement on the part of the social sciences in understanding and responding to climate change.

This chapter aims both to give a sense of the range of climate-related topics in need of attention from social scientists and to highlight related questions that are of interest to philosophers. I begin with a basic introduction to the topic of anthropogenic climate change from a physical science perspective, providing background and context. I then discuss some of the important ways in which the social sciences have already contributed to the study of climate change, focusing in particular on the areas of: scenario development; impacts, adaptation, and vulnerability; economic analysis of mitigation options; and science and politics. Next, I call attention to a few priority areas for future research: social change; equity and justice; and assessment, judgement, and justification. In the closing section, I review some of the philosophical questions that have emerged along the way. The discussion reveals significant opportunities for social scientists and philosophers alike to engage further with the issue of anthropogenic climate change.

1. A Climate Science Perspective

'Climate' refers to the totality of a region's or planet's weather conditions over several decades or longer.[1] A change in climate, then, can be seen only over a relatively long period of time. For instance, suppose we examine weather conditions recorded for a region over five consecutive thirty-year periods, and we find that in each successive period the region experiences warmer night-time temperatures, more extremely hot days, and more frequent heavy precipitation events; we might conclude that the region is undergoing climate change. By contrast, the occurrence of a few cooler-than-average years in a row or one especially hot and dry summer would not qualify as climate change, as the timescale considered is too short.

---

[1] When describing the climate of a region, scientists typically make use of statistics, indicating averages and extremes, but climate should not be defined as the average weather in a region.

By the late 1980s, climate scientists were expressing serious concern about anthropogenic climate change. Earth's climate appeared to be warming, they said, and increased human emissions of greenhouse gases might well be causing it. The idea that emission of gases like carbon dioxide and methane would heat the planet was not new; it had long been known that these gases help to keep Earth's atmosphere warmer than it would otherwise be, and increasing their concentrations was expected to warm the atmosphere further still. In fact, rough theoretical calculations of the warming that would result from doubling atmospheric concentrations of carbon dioxide had been performed already in the nineteenth century. Nor was there much doubt that atmospheric concentrations of these gases had increased significantly since pre-industrial times, nor that these increases were due in large measure to human activities—especially the burning of fossil fuels to power our cars, heat our homes, etc. Nevertheless, it remained plausible that other factors, such as increased energy output from the sun, might be responsible for the warming that seemed to be occurring. Indeed, it was not yet clear that the warming was not just a manifestation of 'internal variability'—the year-to-year, decade-to-decade, and century-to-century fluctuations in weather conditions that occur even in the absence of any forcing of the climate system. Further investigation was called for.

That investigation has occupied climate scientists for well over two decades now. To a significant extent, it has focused on three overarching questions. Is Earth's climate changing in ways that are unlikely to be just a manifestation of internal variability? If so, can observed changes in climate be attributed to human activities? What will climate be like in the future on global and regional scales? The first question concerns the *detection* of climate change, the second concerns its causal *attribution*, and the third is a matter of *prediction*. On the questions of detection and attribution, a broad scientific consensus—underwritten by a substantial body of evidence—has emerged: the IPCC and other expert bodies have concluded that Earth's climate is warming significantly on a global scale and that anthropogenic greenhouse gas emissions are very likely to be a major cause of that warming. Progress also has been made in projecting future changes in climate under different assumptions about future greenhouse gas emission levels, though significant uncertainties about the timing and magnitude of changes remain.

Scientific arguments for detection and attribution of climate change are complex, appealing to observational data, basic physical reasoning, and computer simulations. A first step is to estimate how much warming actually occurred over the last century or so. For this, climate scientists must develop global temperature datasets; there is no thermometer from which they can simply read off the average near-surface temperature of Earth's atmosphere, so temperature records from around the world have to be collected, subjected to quality control, and carefully combined. These temperature reconstructions have been the source of much controversy, but the IPCC-reported finding that Earth's mean surface temperature has increased by about 0.76 [±0.19] degrees Celsius since 1850 continues to survive scrutiny. The question of detection, however, is not whether Earth's climate is warming, but whether the warming is unlikely to be just a manifestation of the climate system's natural internal variability. Since available observational data are mainly from the twentieth century, when significant forcing factors (e.g. changes in solar output, greenhouse gas concentrations, aerosols, etc.) are believed to have been operating, they are of limited help in estimating internal variability. So climate scientists also base their estimates on the variability seen in computer simulations of the climate system when these forcing factors are held constant. Given current estimates, they find that recent warming is extremely unlikely to be merely a manifestation of natural internal variability.

Attribution arguments consider not only changes in global mean surface temperature, but also geographical patterns of change. Results from computer simulations are important here too. Simulations that take into account only natural forcing factors, such as changes in solar output and volcanic eruptions, fail to display the global warming seen in twentieth-century observations. It is only when historical greenhouse gas emissions and aerosols from human activities are also represented in climate models that their simulations show changes in global temperature similar to those observed. Spatial patterns of temperature change in observational data also more closely resemble the patterns that increased greenhouse gas emissions produce in simulations than the patterns that increased solar output produce in simulations. In fact, climate scientists argue that these greenhouse gas 'fingerprints' are clearly detectable in observational data. Moreover, by adding together the fingerprints/patterns that climate models indicate would be contributed by the different known forcing factors individually, climate scientists can account roughly for the spatial patterns of temperature change seen in recent observational data. For these reasons and others, the IPCC has concluded that it is very likely that most of the global warming that occurred in the late twentieth century was due to anthropogenic greenhouse gas emissions.

Predicting the quantitative details of future climate change presents greater challenges. Here, scientists must rely more heavily on climate simulations, and the simulations usually target possible futures in which greenhouse gas concentrations are much higher than in the past, outside the range for which the models have been directly tested and tuned. Because estimates of future climate change are made conditional on these assumptions about future emissions (known as 'emission scenarios'), climate scientists refer to them as *projections* rather than predictions. Exactly how to quantify and communicate the uncertainty associated with these projections continues to be a contentious topic. In the 2007 assessment, IPCC scientists assigned a 'likely' range of global warming for each of several emission scenarios. This is the range into which these IPCC experts, after reflecting on the available modelling results and other background information, judged there to be a probability of at least 0.66 that actual twenty-first-century warming would fall, if emissions were to unfold as specified in the scenario. For the A1B 'medium' emission scenario, for example, this likely range was 1.7–4.4 degrees Celsius, while for the A2 'high' emission scenario it was 2.0–5.4 degrees Celsius.

Nevertheless, some conclusions about future climate change are not very uncertain. There is good reason to expect global warming to continue as the twenty-first century unfolds, since even the effects of past emissions have not been felt fully yet, due to ocean-related lags in the climate system. Likewise, the greater the accumulation of greenhouse gases in the atmosphere, the warmer Earth's climate is expected to become. According to the IPCC, if emissions continue at or above current rates, it is very likely that the twenty-first century will bring many changes in climate that are larger than those seen in the twentieth century. They further conclude that it is very likely that hot extremes, heat waves, and heavy precipitation events will continue to become more frequent, and likely that hurricanes and typhoons will become more intense. Such expressions of likelihood are explicitly acknowledged to reflect expert judgement and, in many cases, are based both on modelling results and on basic physical reasoning about the consequences of adding energy to the climate system.

These key conclusions related to detection, attribution, and prediction are the culmination of more than two decades of intensive research by climate scientists. They were not established by any single study, but rather gained support as evidence accumulated and anomalies were resolved, over a long period of time. Of course, none of these findings (nor any other in science) has been established with certainty. Future research might overturn any or all of them, and it is important for climate scientists to remain open to that possibility. But at the present time the available evidence—in the form of observational data, theoretical analysis, and computer simulations—clearly favours these conclusions over alternatives that have been proposed (e.g. that changes in solar output are the primary cause of recent global warming). There is good reason to believe that anthropogenic climate change is occurring and will accelerate if greenhouse gas emissions are not curbed considerably.

2. Important Contributions from the Social Sciences

Climate scientists study the causal links between greenhouse gas emissions and changes in weather and climate. But these links are just a portion of the larger causal chain that is of interest in the study of anthropogenic climate change (see Figure 2.1). The latter encompasses not only the physical

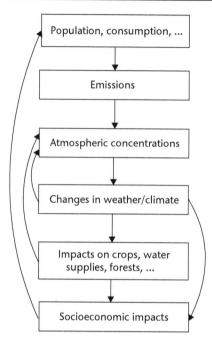

Figure 2.1. A schematic depiction of the causal chain leading from anthropogenic drivers of climate change to its impacts on humans and the environment. Numerous feedbacks between elements in the chain also occur, although only a few are depicted here. Inspired in part by Parson and Fisher-Vanden (1997: fig. 1).

dimensions of the issue, but also the human and environmental dimensions, which motivate much of the recent investment in climate change research in the first place: there is concern that climate change, by bringing more frequent extreme weather events and by affecting crop yields, water supplies, animal migrations, ecosystems, etc., will have very negative impacts on human societies, and there is debate over what governments and individuals should do to try to avoid or prepare for these impacts. Once this larger causal chain is considered, it becomes clear that understanding and responding to anthropogenic climate change will require the expertise of researchers in a host of disciplines, including the social sciences.

The social sciences have already made important contributions to the study of climate change. In fact, when the IPCC performs its periodic scientific assessments, two of the three IPCC working groups focus to a significant extent on research in the social sciences: Working Group I assesses the physical science basis, but Working Group II assesses research on how climate change might impact humans and the environment and how humans might adapt in the face of anticipated climate change ('adaptation'), and Working Group III assesses options for reducing greenhouse gas concentrations ('mitigation'), including economic costs and benefits of these options. Mapping this to Figure 2.1, Working Group II is especially concerned with the impacts represented by the bottom two boxes, while Working Group III investigates how humans might reduce greenhouse gas emissions via changes in the drivers represented by the top box.[2]

It is far beyond the scope of this chapter to review even a modest fraction of the social scientific research that informs these recent IPCC reports, much less the broader body of related work on anthropogenic climate change that is currently available. This is the case even though research conducted so far has only scratched the surface of the many climate-related questions that social scientists might investigate. The aims of this section are more modest, namely, to briefly introduce a few important topics that have received attention from social scientists so far and to highlight related themes and questions that may interest philosophers.

2.1 Scenario Development

The emission scenarios mentioned in the last section are an important ingredient in the investigation of future climate change. They specify hypothetical future trajectories for greenhouse gas emission/concentration levels, aerosol levels, and (in some cases) land use. Climate models require this information in order to make projections of the extent of future climate change. But what range of future emission levels is worth investigating? How high—or low—might greenhouse gas concentrations plausibly go over the course of the next century? Since the emissions of interest are those due to human activities, such as the burning of fossil fuels to power cars and industry, the answers to these questions depend on which socio-economic futures are plausible.

Thus, a standard approach to the development of an emission scenario is to first envision a more or less plausible *socio-economic scenario*, which initially may be described in a narrative storyline. The storyline characterizes qualitatively how important socio-economic drivers of emission levels—such as population, consumption, energy technologies, policy commitments— might unfold over the course of the future period of interest. For example, a very abbreviated storyline might look like this:

> The A1 storyline and scenario family describes a future world of very rapid economic growth, global population that peaks in mid-century and declines

---

[2] Figure 2.1 is itself a somewhat physics-centric depiction, as it gives more detail on the path from emissions to climate change than, say, from climate change to socio-economic impacts. An alternative depiction might expand or collapse the causal chain in various ways; see Figure 2.2 for an example.

thereafter, and the rapid introduction of new and more efficient technologies. Major underlying themes are convergence among regions, capacity building, and increased cultural and social interactions, with a substantial reduction in regional differences in per capita income. The A1 scenario family develops into three groups that describe alternative directions of technological change in the energy system. The three A1 groups are distinguished by their technological emphasis: fossil-intensive (A1FI), non-fossil energy sources (A1T), or a balance across all sources (A1B) (where balanced is defined as not relying too heavily on one particular energy source, on the assumption that similar improvement rates apply to all energy supply and end use technologies). (IPCC 2007: 18)

The storyline is typically given a quantitative interpretation in order to provide input for one or more 'integrated assessment models'—computer models that combine economic-energy models with simplified climate models and sometimes other models as well. These integrated assessment models are used to produce quantitative estimates of the emissions associated with a given socio-economic storyline.[3] Since there are a number of different integrated assessment models available at research centres around the world, as well as various legitimate ways of quantifying a given storyline, numerous emission scenarios may be produced for (and consistent with) a single socio-economic storyline.

Recently, the IPCC has adopted a somewhat different approach to scenario development. Rather than starting from detailed socio-economic storylines, the new approach identifies four 'representative concentration pathways' that depict very different future trajectories for greenhouse gas and aerosol concentrations and for land use. These pathways were selected from the published literature and are intended to span most of the range that is considered plausible in light of past work on emission scenarios. They are being used as input to the latest generation of climate models, in order to produce new projections of future climate change. At the same time, social scientists are being called upon to develop a range of socio-economic scenarios consistent with these representative concentration pathways, taking into account new research on future population growth, technological development, policy options, etc. that has become available since the last major IPCC scenario development effort more than a decade ago. Among other advantages, this parallel approach to scenario development encourages greater exploration of the range of socio-economic and policy futures consistent with a given concentration pathway, since it does not fix the storyline from the beginning; such exploration may be quite useful both in policy discussions and for assessments of climate change impacts.

---

[3] As noted below, integrated assessment models are also commonly used to investigate the economic costs of stabilizing greenhouse gas concentrations.

The development of socio-economic scenarios for climate research and assessment is an ongoing activity. A current priority is the development of scenarios on regional and local scales, where many studies of climate change impacts are now focused. Because the extent to which a community is harmed by climate change can depend significantly on socio-economic factors, socio-economic scenarios are an important input to these impact studies. Among the many challenges faced when developing socio-economic scenarios on regional and local scales is learning how to involve stakeholders in the process in such a way that the resulting scenarios (and subsequent impact assessments) are credible and useful to them as they consider how to respond to the threat of climate change. This is just one instance of the more general challenge of making climate change research responsive to the needs of communities and decision-makers.

2.2 Impacts, Adaptation, and Vulnerability

Climate models are used to make projections of future climate change under different emission scenarios. But what would these changes in climate mean for human societies? How might individuals and communities be impacted? If negative impacts are anticipated, what could be done to limit the damage? These questions are of obvious importance and are plausibly answered only with the help of the social sciences, since social, economic, and cultural factors can influence significantly the extent to which changes in climate lead to harm.

Many studies investigating climate change impacts and adaptation strategies have already been performed, and many more are currently under way. These studies examine various locales and sectors (e.g. fresh water resources, ecosystems, crops and food supply, human health, industry, etc.), and they employ a wide range of approaches and methods, from formal cost–benefit analysis to qualitative anthropological and sociological methods. Collectively, they demonstrate the serious risks posed by future climate change, even under moderate emission scenarios.

Over time, the concept of 'vulnerability' has become important in this area of work. The IPCC defines vulnerability as 'the degree to which a system is susceptible to, and unable to cope with, adverse effects of climate change, including climate variability and extremes' (Parry et al. 2007: 27). As depicted in Figure 2.2, vulnerability is understood to be a function not just of the anticipated *exposure* of a population to variations in climate and the *sensitivity* of the population to those changes—which together determine *potential impacts*—but also the 'adaptive capacity' of the population, i.e. its capacity to alter its characteristics or behaviour to cope with changes in external conditions, such as changes in climate. The core concepts employed here,

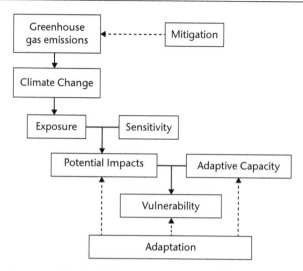

Figure 2.2. A simple model of relations among concepts that are commonly employed in assessments of vulnerability to climate change. After Giupponi et al. (2012: fig. 1).

including those of *adaptation, vulnerability,* and *adaptive capacity,* have them-selves been the subject of significant discussion (see Smit and Wandel 2006), and there is room for further analysis and clarification.

Vulnerability assessments have many uses. For instance, studies that evalu-ate the relative vulnerability of different populations under plausible emission scenarios can be useful for prioritizing efforts to increase adaptive capacity or to provide resources for adaptation measures. Different adaptation policies can also be evaluated in terms of their effectiveness in reducing vulnerabil-ity, facilitating choice among those policies. Indeed, as concern about future climate change has grown, research is increasingly being conducted with the aim of identifying feasible adaptation measures for specific communities. This work sometimes takes a 'bottom up' or participatory approach in which stakeholders contribute directly to the analysis, e.g. by helping to identify the exposure variables, conditions, and possible adaptive strategies that are most relevant for the community, rather than leaving this up to the researcher.

Some adaptation measures are already being implemented in light of recent and/or anticipated climate change. A commonly cited example is that of Confederation Bridge in Canada, which was built with a higher vertical clearance to help ensure that future sea level rise due to climate change would not prevent ships from passing underneath it. However, adaptation studies often face large uncertainties when they look beyond the near term, since long-term climate change projections and socio-economic futures them-selves remain significantly uncertain. Consequently, there is growing interest in identifying response strategies that are robust across a range of plausible futures and flexible going forward in time, encouraging periodic adjustments as new information becomes available.

Despite the considerable research investment already made in studies of impacts, adaptation, and vulnerability, further work is needed. Important practical goals include: advancing understanding of the non-climatic factors that can increase vulnerability or strengthen adaptive capacity in various populations; expanding the range of socio-economic futures considered when conducting assessments; and learning more about synergies between adaptation and sustainable development (Parry et al. 2007). Other perceived needs are more theoretical. According to a recent report from the US National Academies, 'although much is known about specific elements or facets of the processes of adaptation, no general integrative theory or framework now exists to guide a coherent research agenda or to suggest a set of best practices' (NRC 2010: p. viii). It remains to be seen whether a useful general theory can be found and, if so, what it will look like.

2.3 Economic Analysis of Mitigation Options

Adaptation is one type of response to the threat of future climate change. But it is also possible to aim 'earlier' in the causal chain depicted in Figure 2.1, trying to limit the extent to which future climate change occurs by preventing atmospheric concentrations of greenhouse gases from climbing too high in the first place.[4] Such *mitigation* of climate change would involve limiting emissions and/or increasing the rate at which greenhouse gases are removed from the atmosphere, e.g. by planting more trees. International policy discussions have largely focused on mitigation, but agreement on concrete emission targets remains difficult to achieve, in part because of concerns about the economic costs of meeting such targets.

Economic analyses of mitigation options have been performed both within particular sectors and economy-wide, in some cases for the global economy. Often, these global analyses rely on integrated assessment models, assuming particular stabilization goals. For instance, the aim might be to estimate the costs of stabilizing atmospheric concentrations of greenhouse gases at 550 parts per million CO_2-equivalent over some time period.[5]

---

[4] Geoengineering approaches that do not focus on limiting greenhouse gas concentrations are also possible. One proposal, for instance, calls for injecting aerosols into the stratosphere to reflect more sunlight back to space.

[5] Typically, the goal is to keep the total radiative forcing produced by a set of greenhouse gases—not just carbon dioxide—under some limit, but the goal is expressed as an equivalent carbon dioxide concentration; this is the concentration of carbon dioxide that (on its own) would be expected to produce that level of radiative forcing.

These studies typically require assumptions about, among many other things, the policy mechanisms available, the rate at which technological innovation occurs, and the baseline emission rates that would otherwise occur in the absence of any stabilization requirement. As with other modelling results in the study of climate change, there is significant uncertainty surrounding estimates of mitigation costs; for stabilizing concentrations at 550 ppm CO_2-equivalent, for example, some modelling studies show a cost of around 3 per cent of world GDP in 2050, while others give results closer to 1 per cent.

A major source of contention surrounding economic analyses of mitigation options is the so-called 'discount rate'—a parameter (or group of parameters) that represents the extent to which goods obtained in the future are considered less valuable than similar goods obtained today. The discount rate can significantly influence the conclusions of cost–benefit analyses of mitigation policies, because while the costs of reducing emissions in the near term will be felt in the near term, most of the benefits of mitigation—in the form of avoided damages—will not occur for many decades; to the extent that future benefits are discounted, economic analyses are more likely to conclude that mitigation policies that require strong emission reductions in the near term are not worth it. As discussed in more detail in Chapter 7, reliance on different discount rates led two prominent economists to reach very different conclusions regarding mitigation policies. *The Economics of Climate Change* (2006), commissioned by the UK government and led by economist Nicholas Stern, used a low discount rate and concluded that even mitigation policies requiring significant near-term emission reductions would have benefits that far exceed their costs, while an analysis by US economist William Nordhaus (2008) used a higher discount rate and reached the opposite conclusion about such aggressive mitigation policies

Differing approaches to the choice of discount rate may reflect a deeper divide in the philosophy of economics, concerning the appropriate role of ethical considerations in economic analysis. For instance, Stern justifies his choice of a low discount rate on explicitly ethical grounds, assuming that future generations have 'the same claim on our ethical attention as the current one' (Stern 2006: 31). Nordhaus, on the other hand, seems to view the discount rate as something constrained by observational data, such as data on interest rates and rates of return on capital; advocates of such a 'descriptive approach' take the view that discount rates should conform to these empirical data. The debate over discounting is far from resolved and has sparked broader discussion of the practice of economics and its ideals, especially its conceptualization of the ideal of objectivity (see Chapter 7).

2.4 Science and Politics

Beyond research related to climate change impacts, adaptation, and mitigation, a wide-ranging body of work addresses questions where the science and politics of climate change intersect. Much of this work can be placed under the broad umbrella of science and technology studies (STS), which you can learn more about in Chapter 12. Only a few areas of focus will be mentioned here.

The IPCC assessment process itself is of considerable interest. One reason is its sheer ambition: it aims to assess not just research on the physics of climate change but also work on impacts, adaptation, and mitigation, in order to provide decision-makers with a clear picture of the current state of knowledge about climate change. The size and diversity of the 'panel' involved is also remarkable: hundreds of natural and social scientists from around the world contribute to the drafting process, and many more are involved as reviewers. A second reason is that IPCC assessments are explicitly acknowledged to be hybrid scientific-political exercises. The IPCC is an *intergovernmental* organization; scientists volunteer to participate in the assessment process and are responsible for drafting and reviewing the detailed chapters, but the precise language of key conclusions in the report's 'Summary for Policymakers' must be approved by representatives from governments around the world who (along with lead scientists) attend plenary meetings for this purpose. Negotiation of language at such meetings can be extensive and heated. A third reason is the unrivalled prominence of the reports that the IPCC assessment process produces; they have become the standard reference for information about climate change. For these reasons and others, the IPCC process receives considerable attention and scrutiny.

The notion of *consensus* in science has also been explored and problematized in connection with the issue of anthropogenic climate change. The IPCC aims to produce consensus reports, and the existence of a broader scientific consensus regarding key conclusions (e.g. that climate change is occurring and that human activities are contributing significantly) is often emphasized. On the flip side, there have been repeated efforts to deny this consensus, often by pointing to petitions signed by scientists who purportedly reject various conclusions about climate change. This has sparked discussion over the nature of legitimate consensus, how it can be measured or demonstrated, and how it relates to opinion, proof, and evidence. You will see similar discussion of how consensus is measured and demonstrated in the case of a medical example in Chapter 13.

A third, related area of research investigates the motivations and strategies of individuals and groups variously described as 'contrarians' or 'deniers' or 'sceptics'—those whose views on the science of climate change are significantly different from the views expressed in IPCC reports and other 'mainstream' scientific publications. Often, the focus is on political commitments of these contrarian actors and how those commitments might be shaping their views or depictions of climate science. Recently, Oreskes and Conway (2010) have argued that a small group of prominent scientists, in conjunction with think tanks and private corporations, has worked to prevent policy action on a variety of health and environmental issues, including anthropogenic climate change, by sowing doubt about the scientific basis for claims of risk or harm. They refer to this obstructive strategy as the 'Tobacco Strategy'—due to its early use in debates about smoking and lung cancer—and argue that it has been motivated in part by an ideological commitment to free market fundamentalism.

3. Some Priority Topics for Future Research

Many important questions related to anthropogenic climate change stand in need of further attention from social scientists. Three research areas that also raise interesting philosophical questions are very briefly discussed here: social change; equity and justice; and assessment, judgement, and justification.

3.1 Social Change

Climate scientists have made clear that continued high rates of greenhouse gas emission may well bring futures with very significant climatic change—enough to mean seriously negative impacts on humans and the environment. Yet many people seem unconcerned about climate change, uninterested in doing much to respond to the threat, and perhaps even unconvinced that climate change is actually occurring. Social scientists have already identified some of the factors likely to be contributing to this state of affairs. The question is how to move beyond it, especially if adequately responding to climate change will require significant changes in lifestyle or even broader social transformation. This is a critical matter that social scientists can help to address. While understanding how to effect change in behaviours and choices that lead to high emission rates will no doubt be important, Shove (2010) argues for the need to look beyond what she calls the 'attitude-behaviour-choice' models of social change that are inspired by paradigms in psychology and economics and often deeply embedded in policy discussions; she calls for exploring approaches that make use of other resources in the social sciences, such as social theories of practice and transition.

3.2 Equity and Justice

The issue of anthropogenic climate change cannot be divorced from questions of equity and justice. It is well known that, while most historical emissions of greenhouse gases have come from relatively wealthy nations, the most severe impacts of climate change are likely to be felt by those who are impoverished. Likewise, while people living today benefit from high levels of emissions, it is people of the future who will bear most of the burden of climate change. Thus, the first principle of the United Nations Framework Convention on Climate Change (UNFCCC) begins: 'The Parties should protect the climate system for the benefit of present and future generations of humankind, on the basis of equity and in accordance with their common but differentiated responsibilities and respective capabilities' (UNFCCC 1992: 3.1). Yet considerations of equity and justice are often downplayed in discussions of climate change. Moreover, questions remain about what such equity and justice would call for in practice, in terms of policy agreements and actions on the ground as well as in climate-related research contexts.

3.3 Assessment, Judgement, and Justification

IPCC authors are tasked with providing a clear account of the current state of knowledge in their chapter domains. This involves reviewing, evaluating, and synthesizing dozens if not hundreds of published papers and offering conclusions that are suitably qualified to reflect remaining uncertainties. For instance, in light of the available evidence, it might be reported as 'likely' or 'very likely' or 'unlikely' etc. that such-and-such would occur. These qualifiers have agreed-upon meanings, e.g. a 'likely' outcome is one that is judged to have a probability of at least 0.66 of occurring, while a 'very likely' outcome has a probability of occurrence of at least 0.90 (see IPCC 2007: box TS.1). As noted earlier, these expressions of likelihood are explicitly acknowledged to reflect expert judgement. Sociologist Steven Yearley suggests that, unless more is said about how expert judgement comes into play, this acknowledgement 'opens [the IPCC] to the charge that judgements have been made in tendentious ways or that the reports are not compelling since a different set of authors might have reached a different set of judgements' (2009: 398). This is just one reason why it would be valuable to examine in more detail how diverse evidence is evaluated and synthesized by IPCC experts and how judgements are justified during the assessment process. Such research might also contribute to broader discussions of the role of judgement in science and the place of values in policy-relevant science, a topic you can learn more about in Chapters 7 and 9. Both sociologists and philosophers of science could play an important role here.

4. Concluding Remarks

Understanding and responding to anthropogenic climate change requires expertise from both the natural and social sciences—and beyond. The foregoing discussion highlighted some of the areas in which the social sciences have made significant contributions already and identified a few priority areas for future research. The presentation was necessarily selective; other important areas, such as climate change and decision theory, communication of uncertain climate risks, business perspectives on climate change, and climate change and governance might also have been included.

From the areas that were discussed, a number of philosophically interesting questions emerged.

- Can there be an integrative general theory that usefully guides adaptation research?
- How does the involvement of stakeholders facilitate decision-relevant science?
- How should a discount rate be selected in economic analyses of climate change mitigation options?
- Would alternatives to attitude-behaviour-choice models of social change facilitate the development of more effective climate change policies?
- How can considerations of equity and justice be better incorporated in policy discussions and in climate change research?
- How is diverse evidence evaluated and synthesized by expert panels like the IPCC?
- What constitutes a scientific consensus and what is its import?

These are questions that both social scientists and philosophers could help to address, with the potential for payoffs far beyond the issue of anthropogenic climate change.

References

Giupponi, C., Giove, S., and Giannini, V. (2012). 'A Dynamic Assessment Tool for Exploring and Communicating Vulnerability to Floods and Climate Change', *Environmental Modelling and Software*, <http://dx.doi.org/10.1016/j.envsoft.2012.05.004>.

IPCC (2007). 'Summary for Policymakers,' in S. Solomon et al. (eds), *Climate Change 2007: The Physical Science Basis. Contribution of Working Group I to the Fourth*

Assessment Report of the Intergovernmental Panel on Climate Change. New York: Cambridge University Press, 1–18.

Nordhaus, W. D. (2008). *A Question of Balance: Weighing the Options on Global Warming Policies*. New Haven: Yale University Press.

Oreskes, N., and Conway, E. (2010). *Merchants of Doubt*. New York: Bloomsbury Press.

Parry, M. L., et al. (2007). 'Technical Summary', in M. L. Parry et al. (eds), *Climate Change 2007: Impacts, Adaptation and Vulnerability. Contribution of Working Group II to the Fourth Assessment Report of the Intergovernmental Panel on Climate Change*. Cambridge: Cambridge University Press, 23–78.

Parson, E. A., and Fisher-Vanden, K. (1997). 'Integrated Assessment Models of Global Climate Change', *Annual Review of Energy and the Environment*, 22: 589–628.

Shove, E. (2010). 'Beyond the ABC: Climate Change Policy and Theories of Social Change', *Environment and Planning A*, 42: 1273–85.

Smit, B., and Wandel, J. (2006). 'Adaptation, Adaptive Capacity and Vulnerability', *Global Environmental Change*, 16: 282–92.

Stern, N. (2006). *The Economics of Climate Change: The Stern Review*. Cambridge: Cambridge University Press. <http://webarchive.nationalarchives.gov.uk/+/http://www.hm-treasury.gov.uk/independent_reviews/stern_review_economics_climate_change/stern_review_report.cfm>. Accessed Dec. 2011.

Stern, P. C., and Kasperson, R. E., eds (2010). *Facilitating Climate Change Responses: A Report of Two Workshops on Knowledge from the Social and Behavioral Sciences*. NRC (National Research Council). Washington, DC: National Academies Press.

UNFCCC (1992). *United Nations Framework Convention on Climate Change*. <http://unfccc.int/resource/docs/convkp/conveng.pdf>. Accessed Dec. 2011.

Yearley, S. (2009). 'Sociology and Climate Change after Kyoto: What Roles for Social Science in Understanding Climate Change?' *Current Sociology*, 57(3): 389–405.

Further Readings

Gardiner, S. et al. (2010). *Climate Ethics: The Essential Readings*. Oxford: Oxford University Press.

Hulme, M. (2009). *Why we Disagree about Climate Change: Understanding Controversy, Inaction and Opportunity*. Cambridge: Cambridge University Press.

Lever-Tracy, C., ed. (2010). *Routledge Handbook of Climate Change and Society*. London: Routledge.

Miller, C. A., and Edwards, P. N., eds. (2001). *Changing the Atmosphere: Expert Knowledge and Environmental Governance*. Cambridge, MA: MIT Press.

Oreskes, N. (2007). 'The Scientific Consensus on Climate Change: How do we Know we're Not Wrong?' in J. F. C. DiMento and P. Doughman (eds), *Climate Change: What it Means for us, our Children, and our Grandchildren*. Cambridge, MA: MIT Press. 65–99.

3

Evidence-Based Policy

Eileen Munro

1. Introduction

Evidence-based policy (EBP) is a relatively new approach that it is becoming widely recommended as the way to improve decisions about what policies to implement, from deciding how to reduce youth crime in a rich economy to reducing child malnutrition in a developing economy. On first hearing this, many might feel puzzled about what is 'new' about this. Of course policy-makers have always drawn on evidence when deciding what to do, including using evidence from scientific research. What is new about EBP is that it is not just the simple exhortation to draw on scientific evidence when making policies; it seeks to replace ideologically driven politics with more rational decision-making. While claiming that it does not tell politicians what goals to have, it sees its role as encouraging a more rational, rigorous, and systematic appraisal of options on how to achieve those goals.

Some have queried the phrase 'evidence-based policy', suggesting that it gives the impression of determinism—that research can determine what policy is adopted. This of course is not correct since there are several other influences on policymaking (discussed later). Alternative phrases such as 'evidence-informed' or 'evidence-influenced' have been suggested as having less potential to mislead, but 'evidence-based policy' remains the dominant phrase and is used here.

Its primary focus is on testing the strength of causal claims: if we do X then we shall achieve our goal Y. It has led to numerous books, articles, and reports with titles such as 'What works in crime prevention', 'What works in child protection', etc. Focusing on 'what works' is a simple and appealingly practical option but this short phrase covers many contested issues so the topic of EBP has generated a lot of debate and study.

This chapter explains what claims are made for EBP, and examines some of the most controversial aspects.

2. What is EBP?

Policy-makers have always called on evidence to some degree in deciding what to do, and in persuading others that their policy is well-founded. As long ago as 1086 in England, King William the Conqueror sent men all over the country to collect systematic data on who owned what land and livestock, all the reports being compiled into the Domesday Book that was then used as a source of reliable information to inform tax policy. The late nineteenth century saw a further spurt in political interest in research. The London School of Economics and Political Science was founded in 1895 by Sidney and Beatrice Webb, among others, with the motto: 'to know the causes of things', meaning to undertake rigorous social science research to inform policy-makers so that they made better decisions on how to improve society.

However, EBP encompasses more than simple encouragement to draw on scientific evidence when making policies. Although it has many variations, in most of them it embodies a positivist epistemology that assumes that it is possible to develop objective, universal knowledge about the social world that can inform politicians and other policy-makers on how to solve problems. It seeks to reduce the role of ideology, prejudice, and speculative hunches in policy-making, and encourages policy-makers to aspire to a model of rational decision-making where they make every effort to minimize the risk of bias and inaccuracy in their reasoning, and use research evidence wherever possible. Testing claims about causality is the central concern, whether it is at the earlier stage of deciding what policy to choose by looking at the evidence that it is likely to work, or the later stage, after implementation, of judging whether a policy is working well or not.

For example, UK policy-makers in the 1990s wanted to know what services would help children from poor families to achieve better at school. Head Start, a US programme, has some evidence of effectiveness so the UK government decided to copy this programme, under the name Sure Start. A major evaluation was then conducted to see whether, when implemented, it was producing the desired results.

Pawson (2002: 160) offers the following definition of EBP:

> Like all the best ideas, the big idea here is a simple one—that research should attempt to pass on collective wisdom about the successes and failure of previous initiatives in particular policy domains. The prize is also a big one in that such an endeavour could provide the antidote to policy making's frequent lapses into crowd pleasing, political pandering, window dressing, and god-acting.

The term 'evidence-based policy' has come into common usage relatively recently, with most of the political interest starting in the 1990s. In the UK, the Labour Government made it a key aspect of their 'Modernising Government' agenda: 'This Government expects more of policy makers. More new ideas, more willingness to question inherited ways of doing things, better use of evidence and research in policy making, and better focus on policies that will deliver the long term goals' (Cabinet Office 1999: 16). A similar message is expressed in the slogan of the US 'Coalition for EBP': 'Increasing Government Effectiveness Through Rigorous Evidence About What Works'.

EBP is now widely adopted in developed countries and is being advocated for use when helping developing economies. In discussing its Millennium Development Goals, the United Nations recommend EBP because: 'evidence-based policymaking refers to a policy process that helps planners make better informed decisions by putting the best available evidence at the centre of the policy process' (UNICEF 2008).

EBP has been influenced by evidence-based medicine (EBM), which has gained prominence since the 1980s. Because of this link, sources in both EBP and EBM will be cited in this chapter. Sackett, who has been the leading proponent, defines EBM as 'the conscientious, explicit, and judicious use of current best evidence in making decisions about the care of individual patients. The practice of evidence-based medicine means integrating individual clinical experience with the best available clinical evidence from systematic research' (Sackett 1996).

What has driven the increased interest? One factor has been a growing scepticism about the expertise of professionals. Doctors, police officers, and teachers, for example, had been trusted to make good judgements, and had therefore been left relatively unchallenged to do their work. A more educated population started to challenge their judgements, and ask for more reassurance that their money was being well spent. For advocates of EBP, professional judgement is viewed as very susceptible to error so its high status in many societies needs to be challenged. At the same time as this growing scepticism, more data were becoming available. Developments in information technology led to an explosion in the amount of data that could be studied relating to policy implementation.

A third and biggest factor is the attraction of EBP. Tony Blair, when UK Prime Minister, argued that government 'must produce policies that really deal with problems, that are forward-looking and shaped by evidence rather than a response to short-term pressures; that tackle causes not symptoms' (Cabinet Office 1999: 15). Blair talks of 'really' dealing with problems, getting to the root causes, and of getting away from short-term pressures, with the implication that these take you away from really tackling problems. This illustrates the two key claims made for EBP: it offers solid evidence and evidence is objective, free from personal bias and self-interest. Consequently, policies based on evidence will 'really' work. The claim of the US Coalition for EBP illustrates this, saying it offers: 'a validated resource to distinguish research-proven social programs from everything else'.[1]

3. What is 'Best' Evidence?

The idea that doctors and policy-makers have only recently been encouraged to use evidence is worrying, and of course they have always drawn on evidence in some form or another. For EBM and EBP, however, it is 'current best evidence' that is important. Consequently a big element of EBP involves developing explicit criteria for judging evidence, and appraising existing research, in order to offer guidance to policy-makers in determining what is the best evidence for their purposes. A number of organizations have been established that review, critique, and form a judgement on the quality of research findings. These judgements are then made available on their websites for use by policy-makers. For example, the Campbell Collaboration has the mission to help 'people make well-informed decisions by preparing, maintaining, and disseminating systematic reviews in education, crime and justice, and social welfare'.[2]

Before discussing what counts as 'best', it is necessary to define 'evidence'. It is often mistakenly spoken of as if it were a fixed property of a statement. It is more correctly seen as in a three-place relationship. It is *of* something, and it is useful *to* someone to use as good grounds *for* accepting some assertion or claim. Research results become evidence only when someone decides that they will support the case they are trying to make. But what is noticed and considered relevant depends on the thought processes of the individual who decides to use it as evidence. For example, data about the exam results of 16 year olds will become evidence if someone wants to draw on them to back up claims that parental income has a big influence on children's performance at school. This brings out how being an item of evidence is not a neutral, objective fact but the result of someone, in some context, deciding that it is evidence for their purposes.

In general usage, 'evidence' can refer to many types of information. It can refer to the facts in a legal case. It may be expert opinion. It can mean the evidence of our senses, what we see, hear, etc. In EBP, the type of evidence

---

[1] See <http://coalition4evidence.org>. Accessed Jan. 2013.
[2] <http://www.campbellcollaboration.org>. Accessed Dec. 2012.

that matters most is evidence that supports claims about causal connections. Typically, it is often used in a very narrow way, referring only to the findings of empirical research, other types of information being considered too unreliable. So the conclusions of a well-conducted randomized controlled trial (RCT) count as evidence but, for example, the observations of a teacher derived from extensive teaching experience are not considered robust enough to count as evidence to support a theory about how children learn. This is because the latter is seen as unreliable due to being based on one person's limited experience, and potentially biased by the teacher's personal beliefs and preferences.

The need for methodological rigour derives from the many sources of error that can creep into evaluations of policies. Davies provides a useful summary:

Ethical concerns: Randomly allocating individuals to different interventions raises serious ethical and sometimes legal issues to do with informed consent.

Learning curves: Many interventions may take time to be perfected. The question then arises as to when evaluations of these should be undertaken. Too soon and even those with potential are likely to be rejected; too late and ethical considerations may preclude randomization.

Variable delivery: The delivery of many interventions may rely on the skills of the deliverer. Ensuring consistent and replicable delivery may be difficult leading to concerns about what, exactly, is being evaluated.

Interactions: There may be interactions between the intervention deliverer and the intervention recipient, which affect the likelihood of achieving beneficial outcomes.

Individual preferences: Individuals may have strong prior preferences that make their random allocation to groups problematic or even unethical.

Customised interventions: Some interventions may need considerable customizing to individuals to achieve best effect. Concerns again rise as to what is being evaluated.

Lack of group concealment: Knowledge of group allocation may lead to changes in behaviour or attitudes, which undermine the unbiased nature of any evaluation.

Contamination: Understanding by participants of the nature of the evaluation may lead to convergence between the groups diminishing any effect sizes.

Lack of blinding: Blinding is difficult or impossible for many interventions, with the attendant irks of bias being introduced by study subjects' behaviour, compensatory activities by external agents, or differential outcomes assessment.

Poor compliance: Individuals allocated to one intervention or another may fail to comply with stipulations thus undermining the assessment. (Davies et al. 2000: 256)

The concern with gauging the robustness of evidence as support for causal claims has led to the formulation of hierarchies of evidence based on the research methods by which it was obtained. This stems from assumptions that some study designs are better than others at providing strong evidence

I: Properly powered and conducted randomised controlled trial (RCT); well
conducted systematic review or meta-analysis of homogeneous RCTs

II-1: Well-designed controlled trial without randomization

II-2: Well-designed cohort or case-control analytic study

II-3: Multiple time series with or without the intervention; dramatic results from
uncontrolled experiments

III: Opinions of respected authorities, based on clinical experience; descriptive studies
or case reports; reports of expert committees

Figure 3.1. The US government's evidence hierarchy for medical research (US Preventive Service Task Force 2008: section 4).

1a: evidence from meta-analysis of randomised controlled trials

1b: evidence from at least one randomised controlled trial

2a: evidence from at least one controlled study without randomisation

2b: evidence from at least one other type of quasi-experimental study

3: evidence from non-experimental descriptive studies, such as comparative studies,
correlation studies and case-control studies

4: evidence from expert committee reports or opinions and/or clinical experience of
respected authorities.

Figure 3.2. Categories of evidence accepted by NICE.

for causal claims. They are better in the sense that they are more likely to have reduced bias and eliminated alternative plausible explanations of the findings. A number of hierarchies have been developed with some minor variations among them.

A typical example is the US government's evidence hierarchy for medical research (see Figure 3.1). An example from the UK is provided by National Institute of Clinical Excellence (NICE) (see Figure 3.2).

The results of a randomized controlled trial (RCT) and of systematic reviews of RCTs are generally seen as the gold standard evidence for causal claims so they come at the top in most hierarchies. Therefore the methods of RCTs and of systematic reviews deserve closer examination. I shall outline the case for them before looking at the criticisms that are raised. You will find a related discussion in Chapter 16.

4. Randomized Controlled Trials

RCTs are seen as having a special, high status as the source of evidence for causal claims. For example, the Coalition for EBP says:

> The Coalition advocates many types of research to identify the most promising social interventions. However, a central theme of our advocacy, consistent with

the recommendation of a recent National Academy of Sciences report, is that evidence of effectiveness generally cannot be considered definitive without ultimate confirmation in well-conducted randomized controlled trials.[3]

Why are RCTs said to be so important? Policy-makers want to know if their policies work so it might seem that they just need to implement them, and see if they are successful or not. However, there may be what are called 'confounding factors'—factors that are causally significant in producing the observed improvement but are not part of the new policy.

Historically, society has given weight to the views of experienced practitioners. Doctors who treat patients, and see them recover or deteriorate, form views about what works or not. Teachers, too, develop ideas about how best to teach their classes on the basis of what has gone well or badly in previous years. Philosophers call this line of reasoning 'post hoc ergo propter hoc'— after this, therefore on account of this. These kinds of judgements are vulnerable to inaccuracy for a number of reasons.

Any practitioner sees only a small number of service users and their sample may not be representative of the general population, so any lessons they draw cannot be reliably generalized to other groups.

Human beings are dynamic and changing, so it may be that any improvements the practitioner observes would have happened anyway—many illnesses have a natural history that includes recovery without medical intervention.

Linked to this, the service users might have made *more* progress if the practitioner had not intervened, i.e. the service had a negative effect.

Practitioners may be biased in what they observe, tending perhaps to be very aware of their successes and overlooking their failures.

Even if we increase the scale of appraisal from the individual to a broader check on progress, the possibility of confounding factors is still present. Say, for instance, that a government has introduced a substantial rise in university fees in the belief that this will improve university finances, allow a reduction in public funding and *not* deter potential students. If you then find that there is a drop in the number of people applying for university places, is this evidence that the policy has failed? You need to consider what else is going on besides the change in fee policy. There are a number of rival hypotheses that could account for the drop in applications. Birth rates fluctuate: does this year coincide with a smaller group of people in the appropriate age group? People are influenced in deciding to apply to university by their belief about whether it will help them get a well-paid job and, since the economy is struggling, the current circumstances make many people decide it will not be financially worthwhile. In

---

[3] <http://coalition4evidence.org>. Accessed Jan. 2013.

summary, the point is that you cannot assume that the group of people applying to university prior to the policy change is the same in all causally important respects as those considering applying after the policy change.

RCTs are designed in a way that seeks to control for confounders, and so avoid or minimize the risk of bias and inaccuracy in making causal claims. The central idea is that two groups are created that are alike in all respects *except* that one group, the experimental group, receives the intervention and the other group, the control group, does not. Any differences in outcomes are then attributed to the presence or absence of the intervention. The control group may receive no intervention but typically, in policy research, they will receive the normal service.

The key features of RCTs are, first, a study in which participants are assigned to an experimental or control group. In a randomized controlled trial, participants are assigned to a group at random (i.e. they have an equal probability of being assigned to any group). This increases the probability that any confounding factors that could affect the outcomes you are studying will be equally distributed between the groups.

Procedures are controlled, seeking to ensure that all participants in all study groups are treated the same except for the factor that is unique to their group. The unique factor is the type of intervention they receive. When the study involves interactions between a service provider and a service user, as most medical and social interventions do, knowledge of whether the user is in the experimental or control group can influence the way the service is administered and how progress is measured, both consciously and unconsciously. Therefore, ideally, both the person providing the service and the person evaluating it are 'blind', i.e. ignorant of which group the individual belongs to.

Random assignment and the use of a control condition seek to ensure that any extraneous variation not due to the intervention is either controlled experimentally or randomized. That allows the study's results to be causally attributed to differences between the intervention and control conditions.

In sum, the use of an RCT design gives the investigator confidence that differences in outcome between treatment and control were actually caused by the treatment, since random assignment (theoretically) equalizes the groups on all other variables. Although, as noted in Chapter 16, one cannot claim that randomization can guarantee that there are no differences between the two groups, the RCT design is still a robust if not perfect way of supporting causal claims.

4.1 *Example of an RCT*

4.1.1 THE RESEARCH DESIGN

A Randomized Control Trial (RCT) was used to explore the effect of class size on pupil test scores (taken from Krueger 1999). 11,600 students and their teachers were randomly assigned to different size classes in the summer before students entered kindergarten. The study followed them through to the third grade. The research began in the 1985–6 school year and took place in the state of Tennessee, USA.

The design included two treatment groups: small classes (13–17 students per teacher) and regular/aide classes, which included a full-time teacher's aide (22–5 students). The control group consisted of regular-size classes (22-25 students). Once students had been assigned to classes, the research design called for them to stay in the same class type for four years. Eighty schools were involved. Each was required to have at least one of each class-size type and random assignment took place within schools. The students completed standardized tests at the end of each school year. No baseline data were collected.

At the time of the study kindergarten attendance was not mandatory in Tennessee and so new students entered the programme in first grade. Students were also added to the sample over time because they repeated a grade or because they moved to a school participating in the research. In all, 2,200 new students entered the project in first grade and were randomly assigned to three classes. A further 1,600 and 1,200 new students entered the experiment in the second and third grades, respectively. In total 11,600 students were involved.

4.1.2 THE RESEARCH IN PRACTICE

In practice there were some deviations from the research design. First, regular classes often had a teacher aide. This was because ethically students in the control group could not be prevented from receiving resources that they ordinarily would receive. Secondly, at the beginning of the first grade students in regular-size classes were randomly reassigned between classes with and without a full-time aide. This was done to placate the parents of students who had initially been assigned to regular-sized classes without a full-time aide. Thirdly, approximately 10 per cent of students switched between small and regular classes between grades, primarily because of behavioural problems or parental complaints. Fourthly, because some families relocated during the school year, actual class size varied more than intended in small classes (11–20) and in regular classes (15–30). Finally, there was a high rate of attrition (dropout) from the project. Only half the students who entered the project in kindergarten were present for four years.

4.1.3 RESULTS

The study concluded that 'on average performance on standardized tests increases by four percentile points the first year students attend small classes'

(Krueger 1999: 497). In subsequent years, the test score advantage of students in small classes 'increases by about one percentile point' (Krueger 1999: 520) per year. The study also sought to control for a number of variables. It found that teacher education, measured as teachers having/not having a master's degree, 'does not have a systematic effect'. Teacher experience had a small positive effect. The effect of having a full-time teacher aide was significantly positive only at one grade level. Finally, the results indicated that students on free lunch and black students tended to have a larger initial effect and a larger cumulative effect than those not on free lunch and white students.

5. Systematic Reviews

At the top of the evidence hierarchy comes the systematic review. Meta-analysis is a widely used strategy for integrating the findings from multiple studies using statistical methods aimed at increasing the population size and thereby strengthening the reliability of the results. The basic idea is that, if policy P has been shown to be effective in achieving the desired goals in several RCTs conducted in different places, then there is more confidence that policy P really achieves those results.

Systematic reviews are contrasted with narrative reviews. Narrative reviews of healthcare research have existed for many decades, but are often not systematic in the sense that they have not been conducted according to an explicit set of rules about how they search for literature and how they decide what to include and what to leave out. They may have been written by a recognized expert, but usually no one individual has explicitly tried to identify and bring together all relevant studies. Of more concern, an individual or company might actively seek to discuss and combine only the research which supports their opinions, prejudices, or commercial interests. This may not indicate deliberate distortion but arise from the biases in what studies the author knows about or the common bias of looking more critically at the methodology of a study whose results you do not like (and so finding reasons for excluding them in your review). In contrast, a systematic review aims to circumvent this by using a predefined, rigorous, and explicit methodology. The Cochrane Collaboration, which undertakes and disseminates systematic reviews for the health professions, make this claim for their methods:

> A Cochrane Review is a scientific investigation in itself, with a pre-planned methods section and an assembly of original studies (predominantly randomised controlled trials and clinical controlled trials, but also sometimes non-randomised observational studies) as their 'subjects'. The results of these multiple primary

investigations are synthesized by using strategies that limit bias and random error. These strategies include a comprehensive search of all potentially relevant studies and the use of explicit, reproducible criteria in the selection of studies for review. Primary research designs and study characteristics are appraised, data synthesized, and results interpreted.[4]

Some argue that, despite having an explicit methodology in searching for and appraising studies, the process still involves numerous judgements. For instance, decisions have to be made about which studies are included. Quality factors are listed to assist in this decision but how are they to be combined? How do you reach a judgement that requires you to combine the contribution of the study having a large sample (a good feature) plus measurements of progress being made by people who were not 'blind' to whether the person belonged to the control or experimental group (a bad feature)? Detailed guidance is provided but, in practice, there is still scope for judgement and therefore it cannot be guaranteed to be reliable in the sense that any two people conducting the review would have reached the same conclusions.

6. Criticisms of EBP 1: The Claim to Be Objective

In Chapter 7, Montuschi gives a general account of the philosophical issues relating to objectivity. EBP takes the approach that she reports has been so dominant in the social sciences generally; it assumes that the natural sciences are the role model to aspire to, so the issue of objectivity is framed as 'can EBP be as objective as the natural sciences?' The three main demands that Montuschi discusses are all apparent in the EBP discussions: are social facts and objects 'really there' to be studied like mountains or stars? Can we/should we eliminate values? Are quantitative methods the only way to secure true outcomes?

To deal with these in turn, social facts and objects that are the focus of EBP do look to be of a different type than natural phenomena. 'Money', 'family', and 'education' clearly take their meaning because of human agreement and would not exist without humanity (the variation in meaning from one social group to another or over time is discussed later when considering the universality of research findings).

A challenge to EBP comes from those who claim that the concepts that are used in empirical social research are framed and chosen by particular groups in society. There is a fear, which we see echoed in Chapter 8's discussion of feminist philosophy of social science, that those in power have a

---

[4] <http://www.cochrane.org/cochrane-reviews>. Accessed Jan. 2013.

dominant influence, and this may distort or omit the way the issues might be understood by less powerful groups. This challenge is of particular significance in social policy because it so often involves powerful policy-makers making decisions that affect the most vulnerable in society who often have weak political representation—children, those suffering mental illness, or the disabled, for example. The implication is that the apparent 'objectivity' of research hides the extent to which it is influenced by the values and preferences of the more powerful in a society. Increasingly, policy-makers and politicians seek to reduce any such distortion by including those who will be the subject of the policy in discussions. For instance, health services have patient representatives on major committees. In studies on policy provision, representatives from those who will receive the service are increasingly being involved at the design stage.

Eliminating values is the ambition of some who argue for EBP. They acknowledge that values influence the choice of questions to be studied (e.g. education is good for the individual and for society, so it is desirable to find ways of improving it) and the types of solutions that are acceptable (e.g. you cannot solve the problem of increasing numbers of frail elderly people by introducing a compulsory death date, however effective this might be). But they argue that the way the research is conducted can be value-free, and so its findings are not biased by the values of the researchers.

However, as we see in Chapters 7, 8, and 14, critics argue that values have a pervasive influence, and this needs to be acknowledged. The main thrust of the political science literature serves as a warning against idealized visions of pure data being applied in depoliticized arenas. Although generalizations about an entire discipline inevitably are oversimplifications, the centre of gravity within the field encourages scepticism about proposals for a rational, comprehensive science of public policy-making and regards data and information as sources of power first and foremost (Henig 2012).

Partly, the influence comes in the language used—as discussed, we are dealing with concepts that are socially constructed and so reflect the values of the social group that constructs them to some degree. For example, in the UK there is a current policy of tackling 'troubled families', but the description of being 'troubled' is imposed on the families concerned and is one that many of them would vehemently reject. Values also influence what questions are seen as important enough to receive funding for evaluative research. This can mean that the available RCTs are very skewed towards some types of policy interventions. The vast majority of existing RCTs have been conducted in the US and so reflect the priorities and preferences of that country.

The preference for quantitative data that has traditionally been a part of the search for objectivity in the social sciences is now disputed even within the EBP movement, with many arguing for the importance of research collecting both quantitative and qualitative data in order to form a rounded view of the impact of a policy. Quantitative data can be too crude to capture the individual nuances of human understanding and experience, so research restricted to the quantitative can overlook important dimensions of any policy implementation.

For example, a study of unemployment policy can measure the number of people claiming welfare support because they are unemployed, but within this group there may be many varied experiences. Some may be desperate to find work; others pleased to have the time free. The benefit may be adequate for one person's needs but grossly inadequate for someone with additional health problems. To judge whether a policy is meeting its objectives it may be necessary to gather this type of personalized data. The preference for quantitative data can lead researchers to overgeneralize about the population and underestimate the variety of human experience.

7. Criticisms of EBP 2: The Claim to Produce Universal Knowledge

How universal are the results of social research? A key tenet of EBP is that the findings about causal connections that are established by a well-conducted RCT can be used by others to inform their decision-making. As a limit to universalizability, there is some proviso of the form that the new population has to be 'sufficiently similar' to that in the RCT. The problem is in determining what is 'sufficiently similar'. Some argue that this issue of generalizability is a major problem to which advocates of EBP pay insufficient attention, and that social knowledge is inevitably tied to its context in ways that make it less straightforwardly portable from one social context to another than the results of research in the natural sciences.

7.1 *External Validity*

The concepts of internal and external validity are central to this issue. A study has internal validity when the study provides strong warrant for the study results, and well-conducted RCTs can provide strong warrant for causal conclusions about the study population. A study is said to have external validity when the 'same intervention' has the 'same result' as the RCT when used with a new population. However, there is little guidance on how to judge whether the new population is sufficiently similar.

First, there is a problem in deciding what counts as the 'same' intervention. An accurate and complete description of the tested intervention is needed. This is extremely important since if people look to the RCT to provide reliable evidence that 'it' works, they need to know enough about 'it' to reproduce it in their policy area. This is called 'fidelity to model'. This requires some theoretical assumptions about what aspects of the intervention are of causal significance. Does it matter whether the intervention is provided by someone of the same gender as the recipient? In some interventions dealing, for example, with sexual abuse, gender might be a very important factor. In others, it might not matter. There are countless aspects of the intervention in the RCT and decisions about which of them need to be included in a description of the intervention. Which factors are chance and irrelevant associated factors is not a factual matter that can be decided by just observing practice, but derives from theoretical assumptions about how the intervention has its observed effects.

Also, even with a precise description of the intervention, it will, in practice, have drawn on myriad support factors in being implemented, and those considering using the findings of an RCT need to know those support factors so that they can decide whether they are likely to exist in the context in which they plan to use the RCT findings. For instance, a policy to improve children's nutrition by educating the mothers was found to be effective in an RCT in one country but failed when tried in a different country because, in the second society, mothers did not have the social role of being responsible for buying food or deciding what food their children would eat. The assumptions about the maternal role were taken for granted in the RCT because they were such familiar aspects of family life there.

> Causes work in teams. What gets highlighted as the cause—where for you that means your policy—is rarely enough to produce a contribution to the effect on its own. It needs team support. If any of the essential team members is absent, the policy won't make any contribution at all. It is like trying to make pancakes with no baking powder. (Cartwright and Hardie 2012: 52)

This point is well illustrated by the subsequent history of the Tennessee RCT on class size that was discussed earlier. Some other states in the US used the positive results of this RCT to inform their policy and hence to reduce class sizes in their state. However, they failed to reproduce the positive results for children's achievements. The different problems they found have revealed that reducing class size is not sufficient to produce improved educational achievements. Also needed are:

- sufficient high quality teachers (one state sought to get the extra teachers needed to teach smaller classes by taking on many newly qualified staff);
- adequate facilities; many more classrooms are needed (one state found the extra rooms by closing many support services that had been helping children);

- sufficient money so that the smaller class sizes are not funded by cutting other services that contribute to good achievement.

While not rejecting EBP, Nancy Cartwright and Jeremy Hardie argue that the task of making a prediction about whether the results of an RCT will work in your context is far more complicated than most proponents of EBP acknowledge. It requires a line of argument that leads to the prediction that the policy will work for you, involving an exposition of the causal principles that explain the demonstrated effectiveness. As they explain: 'Causes do not produce their effects willy-nilly but for a reason. They produce effects in some systematic way, in accord with some causal principles. A causal principle for a situation lays out all the factors that operate to bring about the outcome in question in that situation and shows how these combine to produce it' (Cartwright and Hardie 2012: 51)

Their point is that one must have reason to think that the same causal principles hold in the target population as in the study population. Otherwise results from the study are simply not relevant to predictions about the target population. When it is social causes that are at stake, one cannot assume that causal principles are the same across different societies or different social groups. You will find a related discussion in Chapter 15 on case studies.

7.2 The Social Construction of Key Concepts

As mentioned earlier, another argument that points to the problems in generalizing from research findings is that key concepts in the social world are socially constructed. Concepts such as 'family', 'money', or 'crime' are given meaning by a social group. An American dollar bill does not have intrinsic monetary value but becomes money because people have the appropriate beliefs about what it is. These beliefs are not just that it is money but also about its practical implications: it will be accepted as money by another American.

Societies and cultures differ radically so the meanings of key concepts in social research may vary from one social group to another and, in the same social group, may vary over time. Family structures, for example, and the distribution of duties and responsibilities are very varied. Homosexual acts were illegal in the UK until 1967 and are still seen as criminal in some countries.

This means that one cannot simply treat any research finding as having universal relevance. More thought has to be given to considering whether the social context in which it was generated is sufficiently similar to the context in which you wish to use it. This has major consequences for conducting systematic reviews in which findings from many different RCTs are brought together.

7.3 *The Wrong View of Causality in the Social World*

A criticism is that standard EBP takes too simplistic a view of causal processes in the social world, assuming a degree of regularity that allows for generalizing from observed causal connections. The complexity of the social world is presented as an obstacle to this assumption. Instead of conceiving of causality as simple and linear, independent of context with controllable outcomes, it is argued that the social world is an open system in which causal processes are non-linear. A system that is open, as all social systems are, receives input from outside and this creates a problem for evaluating change within an organization as we cannot control for all the possible factors that can influence the organization that are additional to, or even emerge from, the intervention we are interested in. This has major implications for our ability to predict and control processes. 'When social science tries to focus on what seems a uniform pattern of behaviour it soon discovers that it is shaped by historical forces, with the result that it may occur in one culture but not the next' (Pawson 2006: 18).

Institutional forces are also influential so that the same 'policy' may take on different forms as it is implemented in different contexts. People's individual volitions and choices add another layer of influences, rendering simple prediction impossible. Finally, social research itself has a tendency to disturb what it is trying to describe or measure.

A new policy on examining achievement in schools, for example, will be modified as it is implemented in each school, producing varying effects. Introduction of targets for exam results may lead some teachers to strive harder to teach a good understanding of the topic, while others prefer to focus on helping children with the exam (teaching to the test) and avoiding a deeper study of the topic. Even if both achieved improved exam results, it might be due to very different causal pathways.

While viewing causality as complex makes EBP a harder option, the critics tend to still agree that it is valuable to undertake empirical research to adjudicate between alternative explanations, but the results are more limited than some would claim. Progress will depend not just on more research but also on theory development: the more we understand of the variables that contribute to an outcome and how they bring it about, the more we shall be able to judge whether findings are of relevance to us.

The standard methods of undertaking systematic reviews are criticized for glossing over the possible, important variations between the RCTs, but cumulative learning is still seen as possible, though this will be at least as much from building theories as from building collections of research results.

8. Criticisms of EBP 3: The Preference for RCTs Limits the Questions that are Studied

Some areas of knowledge are not well served by quantitative research or raise questions that are not answered by the methodology of RCTs. The prominence given to RCTs as a source of evidence is feared by some to lead to prominence being unreasonably given to questions about whether an intervention has achieved its intended goals, its effectiveness, and the questions that RCTs can answer, thereby undervaluing other questions. One critic challenges the view expressed by some politicians that 'what matters is what works':

> But what works is not all that matters. To interpret the call for evidence-based policy and practice in these terms alone is to disregard a whole set of other important questions in policy development, like what is going on? What's the problem? Is it better or worse than…? What causes it? What might be done about it? At what cost? By whose agency?…There needs to be research that is descriptive, analytical, diagnostic, theoretical, and prescriptive. That is, an evidence base to policy in all stages of the policy cycle—in shaping agendas, in defining issues, in identifying options, in making choices of action, in delivering them, and in monitoring their impact and outcomes. (Solesbury 2001: 8)

Another critic, referring to evidence-based medicine, complains that treating RCTs as 'gold standard' evidence has implied that qualitative research methods are inferior, yet they are superior if you are trying to answer certain research questions, for example, if you wish to gain insights into the patient's experience of illness and of treatment (Davies et al. 2000: 192).

Petticrew and Roberts argue that the 'evidence hierarchy' in EBP should be replaced because of the impression it conveys that questions about effectiveness are the key issues (Petticrew and Roberts 2003). They suggest that instead EBP needs to have typologies of research methods for the many different questions that can be asked with relevance to policy-making. Questions about *how* the intervention works or how satisfied users are, for instance, can be best studied by qualitative research and surveys rather than RCTs but are equally important questions within the whole context of policy-making.

9. The Limited Role of Research Evidence in Policy-Making

The final area to be covered is not so much a criticism of EBP itself but a caution that its contribution to policy-making is modest, and research evidence cannot determine what policy to follow. Many other factors have to be taken into consideration.

Politics is the art of the possible and acceptable. Policies tend to affect many different groups in society, and they often have different values and views on the merits of the various options available to policy-makers. In practice, making policies involves adjudicating between and seeking to reconcile the preferences of many different people.

Many have sought to list the numerous factors that influence policy-making. Weiss (1977) offers the four *I*s:

- *I*nformation: the range of knowledge and ideas that help people make sense of the current state of affairs, why things happen as they do, and which new initiatives will help or hinder;

- *I*nterests: i.e. self-interests;

- *I*deologies: philosophies, values, political views;

- *I*nstitutions: shaping how individuals interpret their own interests and views and affecting the decision process itself—who gets to speak, who makes the decisions.

10. Conclusion

Evidence-based policy is gaining a strong following in policy circles in many countries. While policy-makers have always drawn on science for some guidance in formulating policies, EBP is a more systematic approach which follows evidence-based medicine in emphasizing the importance of policy-makers considering the 'best evidence'. The key interest is in evidence that supports causal claims and so informs predictions about the impact a policy is likely to have. Consequently, the second-best form of 'best evidence' is seen as the results of randomized controlled trials in which confounding factors have been controlled for, so that one can confidently claim that any observed differences in outcome are due to the policy. The best evidence of all is a systematic review of the results of several RCTs.

Criticisms of EBP challenge the positivist assumptions that the social world can be studied in the same way as the natural world and that regular causal pathways can be identified, allowing prediction and control.

One set of criticisms is directed at claims to produce findings that are neutral, not influenced by values or biases. Some argue that, on the contrary, the way that problems are framed and studied reflects values and beliefs, and the most powerful in society can have undue influence on EBP.

Criticism is also levelled at the claim that the findings of one study can be generalized to other contexts. While those who advocate EBP acknowledge the need for the reader of research to decide whether the context in which he or she wishes to use the findings is sufficiently similar, critics argue that this demand is much more difficult than existing EBP literature recognizes.

The nature of social reality—the social construction of key concepts—is one obstacle to generating universally valid findings about causal pathways. The complexity of causality in an open system is another. The causal impact of any policy will be shaped by its interactions with other parts of the social system as it is implemented and this, in turn, will produce varied outcomes in different locations.

Some reject outright the possibility of generalizations from social research, arguing for a relativist view of knowledge that means that findings are only of local significance. The majority of critics, however, still consider that empirical research can be a useful resource for policy makers but argue that it is much more complex and limited than EBP assumes.

References

Cabinet Office. (1999). *Modernising Government*. London: Stationery Office.

Cartwright, N., and Hardie, J. (2012). *Evidence-Based Policy: A Practical Guide to Doing it Better*. Oxford: Oxford University Press.

Davies, H., Nutley, S., and Smith, P. (2000). *What Works? Evidence-Based Policy and Practice in Public Services*. Bristol: Policy Press.

Henig, J. R. (2012). 'The Politics of Data Use', *Teachers College Record*, 114(11): 1–32.

Krueger, A. B. (1999). 'Experimental Estimates of Education Production Functions', *Quarterly Journal of Economics*, 114(2): 497–532.

Pawson, R. (2002). 'Evidence-Based Policy: In Search of a Method', *Evaluation*, 8(2): 157–81.

Pawson, R. (2006). *Evidence-Based Policy: A Realist Perspective*. London: Sage.

Petticrew, M., and Roberts, H. (2003). 'Evidence, Hierarchies, and Typologies: Horses for Courses', *Journal of Epidemiology and Community Health*, 57(7): 527–9.

Sackett, D. L. (1996). 'Evidence-Based Medicine: What it is and What it isn't', *British Medical Journal*, 312(7023): 71–2.

Solesbury, W. (2001). *Evidence-Based Policy: Whence it Came and Where it's Going*. London: ESRC Centre for Evidence Based Policy and Practice.

UNICEF (2008). 'Bridging the Gap: The Role of Monitoring and Evaluation in Evidence-Based Policy Making' <http://www.unicef.org/ceecis/evidence_based_policy_making.pdf>.

US Preventive Services Task Force (2008). *Procedure Manual*. Rockville, MD: Agency for Healthcare Research and Quality.

Weiss, C. (1977). 'Research for Policy's Sake: The Enlightenment Function of Social Research', *Policy Analysis*, 3(4): 531–45.

Further Readings

Haynes, L., Service, O., Goldacre, B., and Torgerson, D. (2012). *Test, Learn, Adapt: Developing Public Policy with Randomised Controlled Trials*. London: the Cabinet Office. <http://www.cabinetoffice.gov.uk/resource-library/test-learn-adapt-developing-public-policy-randomised-controlled-trials>. Accessed January 16, 2013.

4

Community-Based Collaborative Archaeology

Alison Wylie

Although many still hanker for universally true, value-free knowledge of the social world—the proverbial 'view from nowhere'—some of the best, most compelling research in the social sciences is credible not because it somehow transcends all interests and contexts of practice, but because it is self-consciously situated and brings diverse angles of vision to bear on its central claims. Traditions of inquiry that actively engage non-scientific local knowledge in various ways have taken shape in a great many fields, most visibly under the banner of 'participatory action research' and 'community-based participatory research'. In these research programmes practitioners recognize that the subjects of inquiry, and any number of other stakeholders, have their own distinctive forms of expertise from which researchers stand to learn a great deal.

Archaeology might seem to be a field where this kind of community engagement is impossible, inasmuch as the subjects of inquiry are often long dead, or especially risky given worries that archaeological interpretation is notoriously vulnerable to speculation. But in fact, a growing number of archaeologists now work closely with community groups of all kinds and, despite sharp opposition from critics who fear that this cannot but undermine scientific integrity, they argue that their research is significantly enriched by these collaborations.

I focus here on archaeologists who work with Indigenous descendant communities in North America and address two key questions raised by their practice about the advantages of situated inquiry. First, what exactly are the benefits of collaborative practice—what does it contribute, in this case to archaeology? And, second, what is the philosophical rationale for collaborative practice? Why is it that, counter-intuitively for many, collaborative practice has the capacity to improve archaeology in its own terms and to provoke critical scrutiny of its goals and methodological norms? The broader import, I argue, is a rethinking of traditional views of objectivity that takes social, contextual values to be a resource for improving what we know, rather than inevitably a source of compromising error and distortion (as discussed in detail in Chapters 7 and 9).

I begin with an account of the context in which collaborative practice has taken shape in archaeology. I consider a pivotal example of this practice and then address the two questions I pose here. I conclude with a brief comparison between lessons drawn from long-standing PAR and CBPR research traditions and those recently learned in and from archaeology.

1. The Context for Collaborative Practice: A Sea Change in Archaeology

Archaeology is undergoing a fundamental sea change. Indigenous peoples have long insisted that the sites and cemeteries and cultural material of their ancestors are part of a living heritage, not only or primarily a scientific resource to be exploited by archaeologists. Recent activism has brought these claims to the fore, and in many contexts they are now backed by law. One high-profile but by no means unique example is the Native American Grave Protection and Repatriation Act (NAGPRA), signed into law in the United States in 1990. The impact was immediate. Museums were required to inform tribal groups of any material they held that might be subject to repatriation, and archaeologists found themselves subject to regulations that require them to consult with, to get consent from, and to practise in ways that respect the traditional values of Native Americans. With this, the ground rules for archaeological practice decisively changed: archaeologists could no longer assume privileged access to and control over material they regarded as essential data, and long-standing conventions of disciplinary autonomy and self-determination were now very publicly contested.

In raising these challenges, Native Americans and a great many other descendant communities world-wide call into question a set of assumptions that had informed archaeological research for well over a century: that indigenous peoples were disappearing, or had disappeared, and that the cultural history and traditions to be salvaged are significant not to a living community but as an element of world history or, often enough, as part of natural history. Confronted with descendant communities whose cultural traditions are very much alive, outspoken critics of repatriation legislation argued that the interests of scientific investigation should take precedence as a matter of principle. David Hurst Thomas details this debate in *Skull Wars* (2000), quoting a physical anthropologist who makes these claims explicit: 'ancient skeletons belong to everyone'; they are 'the remnants of unduplicable evolutionary events [about] which all living and future peoples have the right to know'; by extension, no 'living culture, religion, interest groups, or biological population' have the right to restrict the research mandate of scientific experts who have the necessary skills and knowledge to make the best use of surviving 'remnants' as evidence (Thomas 2000: 209–10). These arguments recapitulate a set of ideals that have been widely presumed to define the enterprise of science in the post-Second World War era: that scientific inquiry is a quest for truth that transcends local interests and beliefs; it is accountable only to standards of justification shared, in principle, by all rational inquirers, however they may be situated; and, in this, it is an intrinsically (and universally) valuable pursuit. On this account, the authority of the sciences depends upon ensuring that its practice and its practitioners are insulated from the influence of external, contextual values (as discussed by Montuschi, Crasnow, and Douglas in Part III): if a field like archaeology is to be scientifically credible, its autonomy must be protected at all cost.

The debate about 'who owns the past' has thus been cast as an intractable conflict between science and religion or, more generally, between science which has universal import and culturally specific ways of understanding the world that arise from traditional (non-scientific) belief systems limited, in their salience, to particular local contexts. Not surprisingly, in this era of 'science wars' (mentioned in the Introduction), this has been the stuff of breaking news. And, from the outset, the cases that have grabbed headlines are ones in which the most uncompromising reactions against any interference with the autonomy of archaeology are on vivid display. One of the most widely discussed has been the protracted legal struggle over 'Kennewick Man' in which the plaintiffs, eight prominent archaeologists and physical anthropologists, sued for the right to study a 9,400-year-old skeleton that had been exposed by erosion in the banks of the Columbia River near the town of Kennewick (Washington State). The US Army Corps of Engineers control the land where Kennewick Man was found and determined that his remains should be repatriated, without further scientific study, to a consortium of local tribes led by the Umatilla. This decision was immediately challenged, as it exemplified exactly the kind of worst-case scenario feared by critics of NAGPRA. Human remains of this antiquity are extremely rare in North America, and to repatriate them without study would be a terrible loss to archaeological science. The legal case brought by the plaintiffs turned on the claim that no affiliation with specific contemporary Native American tribal groups could be established for remains of such age and, in any case, that the interests of scientific research should take precedence over those of the tribes. The plaintiffs won access in a 2005 court ruling that sharply limits the scope of Native American claims of affiliation and in many quarters has reinforced

Native Americans' long-standing mistrust of science in general and of archaeologists and anthropologists in particular.

Reflecting on cases like Kennewick one especially forthright archaeological critic of NAGPRA, Geoff Clark, denounced repatriation legislation as pandering to the interests of 'various pseudo- and anti-scientific constituencies'. 'We all lose,' he argues, 'if for reasons of political expediency, Indians rebury their past.' What's at issue here, on Clark's account, is not just the loss to archaeologists of crucial data but, more broadly, a fundamental challenge to the scientific worldview. To accede to repatriation puts the religious beliefs of Native Americans 'on an equal footing with science' and this, he insists, threatens to roll back all the accomplishments of Enlightenment rationality, science having been instrumental in 'achieving the modern world'; it legitimates superstition and ignorance, returning us to a 'demon haunted world' (Clark 1998: 22, 24; see also Clark 1996). More immediately, Clark fears that it threatens the autonomy and integrity of archaeology, opening the door to the influence of parochial, politicized interests and to non- or anti-rational values that are anathema to scientific inquiry.

These underlying epistemic worries are taken up in a philosophical context by Paul Boghossian, who opens his recent book, *Fear of Knowledge* (2006), with discussion of a *New York Times* story about the NAGPRA controversy (Johnson 1996). He characterizes it much as Clark had done, as a conflict between science and a fundamentally different (non-scientific) worldview, and is chiefly interested in the stance taken by two archaeologists—Roger Anyon and Larry Zimmerman—who figure as advocates for a more conciliatory stance. They resist the polarized positions that dominate public debate, insisting that Native Americans have interests and insights that archaeologists should take seriously. In this they are a prime example, for Boghossian, of well-meaning practitioners who end up embracing a muddle-headed, self-undermining relativism that he finds pervasive in the humanities and social sciences. Boghossian's worry here is that, if we accept that different worldviews or systems of knowledge have their own distinctive 'norms of justification'—i.e. if we do not assume that there are universal standards determining what we should count as knowledge regardless of context—then there can be no basis for choosing between claims generated by different systems. They can only be assessed in terms of the standards set by the worldview in which they originate, and in this sense they are context-relative. In the selection of quotes that Boghossian reproduces from the *New York Times* article, Anyon and Zimmerman seem to endorse such a view: Anyon concedes that 'science is one of many ways of knowing the world'—the 'Zuni world view is just as valid as the archaeological viewpoint'—and Zimmerman that, 'personally, I do reject science as a privileged way of seeing the world'. Boghossian objects that this 'doctrine of equal validity' entails a relativism that undercuts any claim to epistemic authority and is, in this, patently untenable.

Boghossian doesn't consider the archaeological debate in any more detail but it's clear that, on the 'classical picture of knowledge' he endorses, Anyon and Zimmerman have no reason to give any quarter where the authority of archaeological science is concerned. He argues that, however appealing it may be to take a relativist stance and accord credibility to alternative worldviews, in the end 'we have no option but to think there are absolute, practice-independent facts about what beliefs it would be most reasonable to have under fixed evidential conditions' (2006: 110). Moreover, on Boghossian's view, the 'norms of justification' characteristic of contemporary science are a good approximation to these facts. There is no reason to question these norms, he argues, unless an alternative worldview can be shown to have a 'proven track record' of epistemic success that has produced 'more advanced science and technological abilities' than our own, based on genuinely different 'norms of justification'—and none has been presented (2006: 101). The goals of inquiry as well as what counts as success are thus assumed to be given: a timeless and absolute set of standards that all rational inquirers would recognize if they could transcend the specifics of context and take the stance of a 'view from nowhere'. The implication seems to be that Anyon and Zimmerman should not take Native American ways of knowing seriously unless they can be shown to deliver scientifically credible results, and if these embody non-scientific goals and standards of epistemic success, then by definition they have no bearing on archaeological inquiry.

What's lost in this debate, structured as it is by stark oppositions between science and non-science, is a whole range of cases that never make the headlines, ones in which, far from being shut down or compromised by taking seriously Native American interests and beliefs, archaeological research is thriving in the context of collaborative partnerships. One that Thomas discusses in *Skull Wars* as a counterpoint to Kennewick Man is a project that was undertaken jointly by archaeologists and Native Alaskans when human remains were found in a cave in Tongass Forest on Prince of Wales Island, Alaska (Thomas 2000: 268–76). These remains, which were discovered just a few weeks before Kennewick Man in 1996, proved to be 9,200 years old—just as significant as Kennewick scientifically and of intense interest to local Tlingit and Haida communities. By contrast, however, there was no high-profile drama: no headline news, no legal battle but rather a long-term research project grounded in respectful exchange between Native Alaskans and archaeologists that continues to bear fruit. A crucial condition for the success of this project that was missing in the case of Kennewick Man is that there already existed an infrastructure for collaboration: archaeologists based in the region had long-established working relationships with Native Americans. This is, in fact, the most often cited factor that makes a difference to the viability of collaboration and is a feature of the case I will shortly consider in more detail.

This is just one example of many that fall along a broad continuum of positive responses to the demands for accountability that are reshaping archaeological practice. At the conservative end of the continuum are cases in which the archaeology itself is little changed but research is conducted in ways that respect the values and sensibilities of stakeholders; archaeologists negotiate terms of access, engage in ongoing consultation, and in various ways give back to the communities that have a stake in or are affected by their research. Scientific and non-scientific belief systems coexist, not always easily but no longer with priority granted automatically to scientific interests. In other cases of more proactive engagement, the process of meeting obligations of respectful practice gives rise to more robust forms of collaboration: various forms of partnership with Indigenous communities that do affect the substance of the science, sometimes in transformative ways.

In all cases traditional authority structures are reconfigured but, rather than signalling a crippling compromise, the archaeologists involved in these collaborations routinely argue that there are any number of ways in which their understanding of the past has been enriched by taking seriously other 'ways of knowing the world'. The *New York Times* article cited by Boghossian includes a number of telling statements along these lines that he doesn't discuss. For example, Zimmerman's statement about science not being privileged is followed by this observation: 'that's not to say [science] isn't an important way that has brought benefit. But I understand that, as a scientist, I need to constantly learn'; what's needed is 'a different kind of science, between the boundaries of Western ways of knowing and Indian ways of knowing' (Johnson 1996).

The philosophical question this raises is: how can an openness to exploring 'a different kind of science' enrich, rather than fatally compromise, a social science like archaeology? And what are the implications for conventional views of scientific knowledge—the Enlightenment ideals defended by Clark, the 'classical picture' of knowledge endorsed by Boghossian, the conviction that autonomy and impartiality are a necessary condition for genuinely scientific inquiry—that, in their various forms, still have a powerful grip on the social sciences? To address these questions, consider a recent example of collaborative practice in archaeology that begins with formal consent and consultation but then mobilizes intellectual engagement between archaeologists and descendant communities that creatively pushes epistemic boundaries.

2. Kwaday Dän Ts'inchi

Like Kennewick Man, Kwaday Dän Ts'inchi is a case of unanticipated discovery that began when the frozen remains of a young man were discovered by sheep hunters in August 1999 melting out of a high elevation glacier in northern British Columbia near the Yukon border, in the traditional territory of the Champagne and Aishihik First Nations, the CAFN. But like the Tongass Forest project, this is a case in which a political and legal infrastructure for resource management was already in place that put the CAFN in a position of full partnership with archaeologists and provincial officials (Beattie et al. 2000). The CAFN council of elders decided at the outset that 'efforts should be made to learn something about this person' whom they named 'Long-Ago Person Found'—Kwaday Dän Ts'inchi—and they worked out an agreement with provincial authorities which would 'ensure [that] cultural concerns are respected while recognizing the significant scientific considerations inherent in a discovery of this nature' (British Columbia Ministry 2011). A news story published in the *Yukon Times* echoes Zimmerman: 'the project became a blend of traditional values and modern science; rather than claiming ownership, the First Nations shouldered the responsibility for stewardship of this remarkable discovery' (Gates 2009).

In the course of a decade, the CAFN worked with provincial authorities and the team of researchers they assembled, setting the research agenda, jointly reviewing and approving all proposals for scientific study of the human remains and associated artefacts, and ensuring that local, Indigenous values were respected in the treatment of the deceased. It was especially important to the CAFN to determine, if possible, whether Kwaday Dän Ts'inchi had any living family or clan descendants so the appropriate members of the community could handle his memorial and return to a final resting place. This collaboration made a wide range of scientific work possible, including destructive testing and a DNA study, both types of research that are, for good reason, often unacceptable to Indigenous communities. Crucially, the agreed-upon research programme included the questions about clan and family affiliations that were of interest to the First Nations but were not on the agenda for the scientists who made up the research team, in part because it seemed implausible that DNA testing, or other tools of archaeological science, would make it possible to identify descendants of such a long-deceased individual.

So what was done, and what's been learned? The CAFN approved radiocarbon and collagen dating which established that Kwaday Dän Ts'inchi lived some time between AD 1670 and 1850, and a full autopsy provided the data necessary for a pathology workup and food residue analysis, which made it possible to reconstruct what he had ingested in the three days before he died, in roughly six-hour increments. Isotope and trace element analysis of hair, dentition, bone core, and muscle tissue produced longer term dietary profiles, and analysis of the associated artefacts—Kwaday Dän Ts'inchi's spruce root rain hat and squirrel skin robe, tool kit, and cache of food—and of the various pollens, microbes, parasites, and insects lodged in the traveller's hair, skin, clothing, and equipment, suggested cultural affinities and provided further environmental clues to the specifics of his last trip.

The upshot is that Kwaday Dän Ts'inchi was 18–20 years old and had travelled roughly 100 km in the three days before he died, likely in the summer and originating on the coast where, early in his trip, he had eaten salmon, shellfish, mosses, and flowering beach asparagus, and been exposed to chenopodium pollen. Mineral deposits in the water he'd consumed on his trip reinforce these conclusions: two to three days before he died he drank brackish water that occurs in coastal marine environments, and in his last hours he drank glacial melt water. His lifetime dietary profile indicates that he lived predominantly on the coast, eating a marine diet. However, hair composition analysis makes it clear that, in the last year of his life, he had shifted to terrestrial inland foods. His clothing and tool kit likewise incorporate both coastal and interior elements. His rain hat was woven of sitka spruce that grows only on the coast while his robe was made of arctic ground squirrels that live only in the interior. Finally, the community DNA study initiated by the CAFN, for which close to 250 community members volunteered blood samples, is reported to have identified some seventeen living matrilineal relatives of the deceased, most members of the Wolf Clan, with both interior and coastal connections.

The significance of these results lies in the fact that these multiple lines of evidence bear witness to extensive family and clan affiliations that link coastal and interior communities. This calls into question a set of assumptions about ethnic identity that underpin much conventional ethnography and archaeology: that tribal identities are spatially defined—they are social groups (communities) that are tied to a specific region—and that these geographically localized affiliations take precedence over kin or clan identities. This reflects an imposition of social categories familiar within Euro-American traditions and informed by theories of cultural evolution—a set of framework assumptions that are at odds with community understanding and oral tradition. As reported in the local news: 'the DNA research has been a scientific confirmation of something that the people have long known, that the traditional ties between the coastal Tlingit and the people of the Southwest Yukon transcend artificial political boundaries' (Gates 2009). In short, the research agenda set by the CAFN generated key insights about social organization, cultural history, and identity that have broad implications for the archaeology and ethnography of the region, and for entrenched framework assumptions of much wider import.

3. What's Gained by Collaboration?

The Kwaday Dän Ts'inchi project is an example of collaborative research that illustrates how 'the incorporation of Aboriginal worldviews, histories, and science... [can] inform and broaden understanding and interpretation of the archaeological record' (Nicholas 2010: 11). This is exactly the kind of collaborative partnership that a growing number of archaeologists advocate in response to the sea change I described at the outset. But it is, of course, the very idea that archaeological inquiry might be in any way influenced by, or held accountable to, Indigenous/Aboriginal understanding of their own history and cultural traditions that raises the hackles of those who defend conventional ideals of epistemic integrity and disciplinary autonomy. This throws into relief two philosophical questions to which I now turn.

- What exactly does this kind collaborative project contribute to archaeology? What are its epistemic benefits?

- How are we to understand the epistemic advantages that, counter-intuitively for some, seem to accrue to collaborative archaeology?

Where the first question is concerned, Kwaday Dän Ts'inchi illustrates three key epistemic contributions that are common to many forms of collaborative practice in the social sciences. First, the terms of collaboration enlarged the research agenda, raising a set of questions about cultural affiliation that particularly concerned the CAFN but were not high on scientists' research agenda. Central among these were the questions about lineal descendants that led to the DNA testing project. Second, pursuing these lines of inquiry directed attention to types of evidence and interpretive resources that had not gotten uptake in conventional research. For example, the CAFN partners to the project brought to bear considerable depth of knowledge about local ecology and regional subsistence practices that made it possible to interpret the dietary profiles generated by analysis of Kwaday Dän Ts'inchi's remains and the various items of material culture found with him. Combined with the resources of oral history that testify to long-standing family and clan connections spanning the region, this background knowledge was crucial in establishing that Kwaday Dän Ts'inchi had ties to and had lived in both coastal and interior communities. Third, this enlargement of the scope of inquiry and expansion of the resources on which it drew was not just a matter of adding detail to an existing body of archaeological understanding. The evidence of cross-region connections poses a significant challenge to framework assumptions that had long informed research in the region. These include assumptions about the subject of inquiry—the presumption that tribal communities are spatially defined—as well as methodological assumptions about what counts as evidence that had discounted insights from oral tradition.

This last point is especially crucial, illustrating one of the key benefits of bringing the critical distance of an outsider's perspective to bear on disciplinary conventions. Time and again the archaeologists involved in collaborative practice report that, when they engage seriously with descendant communities, the contrast with other ways of thinking throws into sharp relief the contingent, evolving nature of their own, taken-for-granted disciplinary goals and 'norms of justification'. It forces the question of whether entrenched modes of practice—the standards that define what counts as evidence and what it is to do (good) archaeological science—actually serve stated goals and whether these goals themselves exhaust the range of questions archaeologists could or should be asking. The result is a process of critical appraisal that opens up creative alternatives that might never have arisen through internal deliberation.

4. What's the Philosophical Rationale?

Finally, then, the second of the two questions I posed at the outset: how is it that these collaborations enrich rather than compromise archaeological science? The central principle at work here is articulated by the archaeologist Larry Zimmerman when he observes that, as a scientist, he has to be prepared constantly to learn. I understand him to be taking a stance of openness not just to learning new facts but to learning about and continuously refining the science he practises. From within the perspective of this stance there's a great deal to be gained by mobilizing, rather than categorically denying the relevance of the resources afforded by context and interest-specific standpoints that lie outside archaeology.

Within philosophical contexts this point is captured by the liberal democratic conviction that more ideas, diverse voices, and angles of vision are inherently a good thing where the production and evaluation of knowledge is concerned—as discussed in Part III and by Solomon in Chapter 13. The wider the range of perspectives brought to bear on a question, or in the assessment of prospective knowledge claims, the more likely it is that error and bias will be exposed, that the full complexity of the subject and all relevant implications will be appreciated. There is, of course, the risk that inviting critique from all directions will reduce inquiry to a cacophony of voices, undermining the kind of single-minded focus and ease of communication that facilitates the smooth functioning of a productive research community; this is a problem that afflicts interdisciplinary collaborations as well, as discussed by Sophia Efstathiou and Zara Mirmalek in Chapter 12. But, as we see from Crasnow, the risk of insulating research communities from external criticism is that like-minded peers, who share common cognitive goals and conventions of practice, will also share significant cognitive lacunae; they may be the last to recognize the limitations of their research programme, especially those inherent in framework assumptions and 'norms of justification' that they take for granted. So the wisdom from democratic theory is that, even though research communities must sometimes suspend critical self-examination of framework assumptions to move forward with a research programme, it is crucial to ensure that there are mechanisms in place which can counteract 'group-think' dynamics, bringing the resources of diverse perspectives to bear on claims made within this framework and securing the possibility that background assumptions and taken-for-granted standards of practice can, periodically, be subjected to critical scrutiny.

Taking this insight seriously requires a fundamental shift of focus where the goals and defining ideals of scientific knowledge are concerned. Rather than seeking universal 'norms of justification' that promise approximation to a 'view from nowhere', it suggests that the point of departure must be recognition that current research goals, conventions of good practice, and what counts as epistemic success are purpose-built and have a history; they have all evolved and continue to evolve in the context of ongoing practice. This, in turn, suggests that what's required is a proceduralist approach to specifying what will count as credible knowledge: a set of best practice guidelines that define in general terms the processes of critical appraisal by which a well-functioning research community will determine which claims to endorse as ones we can trust for specific purposes, ones we can take as a guide to action in specific contexts. Helen Longino offers such an account, arguing that the beliefs we should 'ratify as knowledge' are those that arise from the right kind of process of critical scrutiny, and the 'right process' is one which ensures that contending beliefs are subject to 'criticism from multiple points of view'. Crucially, these community practices must have the potential to expose error or distortion not only in specific beliefs but also in framework assumptions and entrenched norms of practice: this is what Longino means by 'transformative criticism' (2002: 129).

Longino posits a set of four jointly social and cognitive norms that, together, characterize the kinds of institutions and processes she believes are necessary to ensure a broad spectrum of critical engagement within a research community. They include, for example, the requirements that there be established venues for and uptake of criticism, that the evaluation of knowledge claims be subject to shared standards which are themselves open to critical scrutiny, and that research communities should recognize the value of critical input from all its members, regardless of social status. This last principle, a norm of 'tempered equality of epistemic authority', is especially relevant here. It specifies that mechanisms be in place to counteract exclusionary practices within scientific communities: 'not only must potentially dissenting voices not be discounted, they must be cultivated'; to fail to do this is 'not only a social injustice but a cognitive failing' (2002: 131–133).

Although Longino recognizes that this fourth norm raises 'complex questions of community membership'—it 'makes us ask who constitutes the "we" for any given group'—her formulation articulates 'duties of inclusion and attention' that primarily apply internally, to the members of a community of scientists (2002: 132, 134). The need to widen the circle is well illustrated by the cases I have described of collaborative practice in archaeology and by many other examples of participatory action research (PAR) and community-based participatory research (CBPR) in the social sciences. I argue for an extension of Longino's norm, motivated by arguments drawn from critical race theory and feminist standpoint theory. Well-functioning research communities should not only take steps to counteract exclusionary bias internally, among fellow scientists; they should actively seek out external communities that hold relevant expertise and critical insight, and extend the norm of 'tempered equality of epistemic authority' to them so that they can play an active role in critically assessing the credibility of knowledge claims and the epistemic norms that underwrite them.

The rationale for reframing the norm of 'tempered equality of epistemic authority' in this way is two-fold. First is the point already made: insiders who share the defining goals and norms of a research community will often be the last to recognize problems inherent in the framework within which they work and possibilities for inquiry that lie beyond it. The second complementary thesis is that key epistemic insights and resources often arise on the margins, inverting standard (socially inflected) appraisals of credibility: those who are socially marginal—and whose expertise is therefore discounted or misrecognized—have to navigate dimensions of the social and natural world with which the comparatively privileged rarely engage (or are invested in avoiding). They may, as a result, draw on a distinctive range of experience and set of conceptual resources. More specifically, the experience of exclusion or marginalization may itself be a source of insight, generating a critical, sometimes oppositional awareness of the conditions under which knowledge is conventionally ratified, as when survival as an insider-outsider requires that you understand conventions that are taken for granted within a dominant culture as well as those that structure your own subdominant community. This point is ubiquitous in critical social science. It was articulated in influential terms early in the twentieth century by W. E. B. Du Bois in *The Souls of Black Folk* in which he argued that, under conditions of racial oppression, African Americans develop a 'double consciousness', a capacity to see themselves and the social world as the dominant white community does as well as in their own terms. This complex identity comes with considerable cost but is also a source of critical and creative insight that has inspired successive generations of standpoint theorists. It gives rise, for example, to the methodological recommendation that researchers should take the situated knowledge and experience of those who are marginal as their point of departure (Harding 1991); it is from these standpoints that what remains tacit for the comparatively privileged becomes visible. The history of feminist research and critical race studies is replete with examples in which this has proven to be highly productive; I argue elsewhere that they are a primary motivation for contemporary standpoint theory. The upshot is that, depending on purpose and circumstance, those who are outsiders to a research community may be uniquely well situated to mobilize 'transformative criticism'.

Given this standpoint theory rationale for extending the scope of Longino's norm of 'epistemic authority', I propose the following principle as an answer to my focal question 'Why does collaboration matter epistemically':

> If well-functioning epistemic communities are to counteract the risks of dysfunctional group dynamics that insulate their established standards of justification from critical scrutiny and revision, they must seek out critical, collaborative engagement with those communities that are most likely to have the resources— not only to fill lacunae and correct specific errors in their substantive beliefs but also to generate a critical standpoint on their own knowledge-making and ratifying practices.

The rationale for extending duties of 'attention and response' to collaborative partners in archaeology thus arises not only from moral obligations to descendant and affected communities but also from an epistemic obligation rooted in norms of critical scrutiny that are at least as fundamental to our flourishing traditions of scientific inquiry as the ideals of autonomy and the quest for a view from nowhere invoked by the critics of collaborative practice.

As I noted at the outset, these insights about the advantages of collaboration are by no means unique to archaeology. They resonate with arguments for socially engaged research in the traditions of PAR and CBPR that have taken shape over decades in a number of other contexts. The standpoint theory rationale for such practice was articulated with particular clarity thirty years ago by sociologists Elizabeth Petras and Douglas Porpora (1993), who made the case that the poor and oppressed bring significant epistemic resources to the table when they are engaged as partners in research projects; they are in a position to generate genuine insights—theoretical, methodological, and empirical—that represent an important contribution to disciplinary sociology as well as providing a crucial basis for interventions designed to address poverty and oppression. More recently, Louise Fortmann, a rural sociologist and advocate for community forestry, makes the case for recognizing the value of what she calls 'civil science', in its own right and in partnership with 'professional science':

> I have worked for decades with farmers in east and southern Africa and with rural communities in the U.S., coming to respect their expertise just as I do knowledge produced by scientists...Over time I have come to understand that scientists can answer some questions, people with other kinds of knowledge answer other equally important questions, and that some questions are best answered in collaboration, what is called here interdependent science. (2008: 2)

This brief for recognizing that valuable expertise, methodological wisdom, and critical and constructive insight are to be found outside the boundaries of scientific communities powerfully captures the rationale for collaborative practice that is illustrated by but extends well beyond the archaeological examples I have considered here: that it is not only morally, politically, and sometimes legally the right thing to do, but that it has substantial capacity to improve the research, sometimes as measured in quite conventional terms against established goals, and sometimes through a process that involves critically reassessing these goals and standards and the aligned conventions of established disciplinary practice.

References

Beattie, O., Apland, B., Blake, E. W., Cosgrove, J. A., Gaunt S., Greer, S., Mackie, A. P., Mackie, K. E., Straathof, D., Thorp, V., and Troffe, P. M. (2000). 'The Kwäday Dän Ts'inchi Discovery from a Glacier in British Columbia', *Canadian Journal of Archaeology,* 24(1): 129–48.

Boghossian, P. (2006). *Fear of Knowledge: Against Relativism and Constructivism.* Oxford: Oxford University Press.

British Columbia, Ministry of Forests, Lands and Natural Resource Operations, Archaeology. (2011) *Kwäday Dän Ts'ínchí Chronology.* British Columbia Provincial Government 2000. Available from: <http://www.for.gov.bc.ca/archaeology/kwaday_dan_tsinchi/chronology.htm>. Accessed Dec. 2011.

Clark, G. A. (1996). 'NAGPRA and the Demon-Haunted World', Society for American Archaeology Bulletin, 14(5): 3.

Clark, G. A. (1998). 'NAGPRA: The Conflict between Science and Religion, and Political Consequences', Society for American Archaeology Bulletin, 16(5): 22.

Du Bois, W. E. B. (1993). *The Souls of Black Folk.* New York: Alfred A. Knopf. Original edition 1903.

Fortmann, L., ed. (2008). *Participatory Research in Conservation and Rural Livelihoods: Doing Science Together.* London: Wiley-Blackwell.

Gates, M. (2009). 'Kwäday Dän Ts'ìnchí Teaches us How to Work Together', *Yukon News*, 20 Mar.

Harding, S. (1991). *Whose Science? Whose Knowledge? Thinking From Women's Lives*. Ithaca, NY: Cornell University Press.

Johnson, G. (1996). 'Indian Tribes' Creationists Thwart Archaeologists', *New York Times*, 22 Oct.

Longino, H. E. (2002). *The Fate of Knowledge*. Princeton: Princeton University Press.

McLean Petras, E., and Porpora, D. V. (1993). 'Participatory Research: Three Models and an Analysis', *The American Sociologist*, 23(1): 107–26.

Nicholas, G., ed. (2010). *Being and Becoming Indigenous Archaeologists*. Walnut Creek, CA: Left Coast Press.

Thomas, D. H. (2000). *Skull Wars: Kennewick Man, Archaeology, and the Battle for Native American Identity*. New York: Basic Books.

Further Readings

Atalay, S. (2013). *Community-Based Archaeology: Research with, by, and for Indigenous and Local Communities*. Berkeley, CA: University of California Press.

Koskinen, I. (2010). 'Seemingly Similar Beliefs: A Case Study on Relativistic Research Practices', *Philosophy of the Social Sciences*, 41(1): 84–110.

Longino, H. E. (1990). *Science as Social Knowledge: Values and Objectivity in Scientific Inquiry*. Princeton: Princeton University Press.

McLean Petras, E., and Porpora, D. V. (1993). 'Participatory Research: Three Models and an Analysis', *American Sociologist*, 23(1): 107–26.

Nicholas, G. P., and Wylie, A. (2009). 'Archaeological Finds: Legacies of Appropriation, Modes of Response', in J. Young and C. Brunk (eds), *The Ethics of Cultural Appropriation*. Oxford: Blackwell, 11–54.

Wylie, A. (2005). 'The Promise and Perils of an Ethic of Stewardship', in L. Meskell and P. Pells (eds), *Embedding Ethics*. London: Berg Press, 47–68.

Wylie, A. (2012). 'Feminist Philosophy of Science: Standpoint Matters', *Proceedings and Addresses of the American Philosophical Association*, 86(2): 47–76.

Zimmerman, L. J. (1989). 'Made Radical by my Own: An Archaeologist Learns to Understand Reburial', in R. Layton (ed.), *Conflict in the Archaeology of Living Traditions*. London: Unwin Hyman, 60–7.

Part II
Ontological Issues

5

Social Ontology

Deborah Tollefsen

1. Introduction

Suppose that an alien race from a far off planet sends a few of its researchers to Earth to study the human world. These aliens have a unique perceptual capacity to read the minds of human beings and identify their intentions, beliefs, and desires better than any human psychologist. Indeed, they know our minds better than we know them ourselves. They are able to predict our behaviour with stunning accuracy and offer explanations of human behaviour that go far beyond current psychological theories.

Now assume that these alien super psychologists visit Wall Street. If *we* take a stroll through the financial district in New York City, *we* might see two business women working on a financial report for a major corporation, a committee of shareholders deliberating the merits of a certain joint investment strategy, the effect of the buying and selling of stocks on the Dow Jones industrial average. *We* are able to see that certain corporations are faring better than others in the stock market. Will the aliens see everything that we see?

In an effort to explain the various things we witness on Wall Street we might attribute attitudes such as intentions, beliefs, and goals to corporations and to the smaller groups that comprise them. For instance, we might find the following statement, or something like it, in a newspaper: 'The Bank of America is unhappy with the Federal Reserve's decision to reduce rates, but the Federal Reserve believes this is the best course of action to curb the recession.' After reading this the aliens might respond, 'Where are these entities called "Bank of America" and "Federal Reserve"? All we see are individual human beings and their thoughts and actions!'

This thought experiment is designed to get you to think about the relationship between the individual and the collective—the psychological and social worlds—and raises a number of interesting questions. Are social entities like corporations anything 'over and above' the individual human beings that comprise them? If we know all the facts about individual psychology, will we understand social processes, relations, and entities? If we went about counting all the things in the world—people, chairs, leaves, snails—would groups be added to the list? Do groups really have attitudes such as belief and intention?

Questions regarding the nature of social reality and how one ought to go about explaining social facts, relations, and processes are the main subject of social ontology. Because the social sciences often appeal to social groups, social processes, and social relations, and because social scientists often attribute causal powers and properties to social groups, social ontology and the philosophical debates within social ontology are of great importance to the social sciences. In this chapter we will consider whether groups exist 'over and above' their members (section 3), the notion of shared or collective intentionality and the construction of social reality (section 4), and the possibility of group minds (section 5). Focusing the chapter in this way necessarily leaves out a vast number of developments in social ontology that might well be useful for the social sciences, but forgoing breadth will, I hope, provide more depth.

2. Historical Debates

One way to view current philosophical discussions regarding social facts, entities, and processes is to see them as a continuation of the social scientific debates between collectivism and individualism that occurred during the early part of the twentieth century. Max Weber and Emile Durkheim, for instance, spilled a great deal of ink over the proper methodology of the social sciences. The sides in this debate were often marked by the terms 'collectivism' and 'individualism'. Unfortunately, these terms have been used in such varied ways in the literature that it has led to a great deal of confusion. The discussion has now become so voluminous that it is difficult to ascertain clearly what the respective positions in the debate actually are. Nonetheless, the core idea of both collectivism and individualism is still present in many of the current debates.

For our purposes we can distinguish between an ontological and a methodological version of both collectivism and individualism. 'Ontological collectivism' is the view that there are social entities that exist, and these entities are on par with individual human beings. 'Ontological individualism' is the view that there are no non-reducible social entities—only individuals exist.

'Methodological individualism' is the view that individual actions and individual intentional states are the basis of all explanations of social phenomena. 'Methodological collectivism' is the view that social phenomena cannot be explained solely in terms of individuals and their intentional states. One must appeal to other social facts. The methodological collectivist will often appeal to certain structural or functional characteristics to explain social phenomena.

The ontological and methodological versions of individualism may be related in various ways depending on how one defines these positions. According to the definitions given, ontological individualism and methodological individualism might plausibly go hand in hand. If only individuals exist then one might insist that they must be the basis of explanation of any social phenomena. Further, it seems likely that, if one is an ontological collectivist, they will also be methodological collectivists. If there are social wholes that cannot be reduced to a mere aggregate of persons then structural or functional features of groups are likely to play a role in social scientific explanation.

There is a third position one might adopt here that represents a sort of methodological compromise. One might argue that individuals are ontologically prior and that groups are nothing 'over and above' the individuals that comprise them (and so adhere to an ontological individualism) but also argue that the relations between individuals give rise to certain properties and events that wouldn't otherwise exist apart from these relations. 'Interrelationism' is the idea that social groups, processes, and relations are to be explained by reference to individual human agents and the relations between them. To the extent that interrelationism advocates a methodology that utilizes explanations that go beyond the individual human agent, it avoids strict methodological individualism.

One last point of clarification before we move on: the word 'holism' has sometimes been confused with what I am here calling 'collectivism'. 'Holism' is the view that human agents depend non-causally on their social relations with one another for the possession of distinctive human capacities. They only have these capacities (for instance, the capacity to think) as social beings. 'Atomism' defends the opposite view. According to atomism, it is possible for human beings to develop all the capacities characteristic of human beings in complete isolation from other humans. There is no incoherence, according to the atomist, in the possibility of a solitary thinker or a language that is private. Holism and atomism are theories about the capacities of individual human beings. Collectivism and individualism (of both the ontological and methodological form) are theories about social groups and the relationship between social groups and the individual.

3. Types of Groups and the Reality of Social Groups

Consider the many different types of groups we might find the subject of social scientific research: cultural and ethnic groups, families, organizations, clans, governments, committees and teams, among others. Is there anything that unites these groups such that we can call them all 'social'? At a minimum a social group involves more than one individual. But consider the group of all red-haired men. This is clearly a group of more than one person but is it a social group? Social groups appear to be more than simply classes of individuals that share the same physical trait. What makes a cultural or ethnic group a social group, for instance, goes beyond the fact that they share a common biological origin or geographical location. Cultural and ethnic groups are collections of people that interact with one another and share beliefs, customs, and goals.

We might define a social group, then, as a collection of people that interact with one another on the basis of shared attitudes. No doubt there are various distinctions to be made between types of social groups. Some social groups might be fleeting and relatively short-lived—a jury that meets to deliberate about a case and never meets again, or two people that unite to perform an action (e.g. moving a table) and then quickly disperse. Others might have a relatively stable structure that persists despite a change of membership—sports teams and corporations, for instance.

There are a variety of positions one could take regarding the reality of social groups. There are at least two approaches open to the ontological individualist: eliminativism and reductivism. The eliminativist argues that social groups do not exist and talk of social groups and their properties refers only to individuals and their properties. The eliminativist might go so far as to argue for the elimination of group concepts such as 'nation' or 'team'. Given the prevalence of this language and its explanatory power in the social sciences eliminativism has not had many defenders.

Another approach is to acknowledge the existence of groups but try to identify them with their members. On this account the Democratic Party is to be identified with its members; the school board with its members. But this raises the following difficulty. On a standard theory of identity, if A is identical to B, then A and B are not distinct things. But if a group is identical to its members, and there is more than one member, then the group (a single thing) is identical to many things (its members). Thus, we can hold this simple identity thesis only at the expense of violating a standard theory of identity.

One might avoid this problem by identifying a group with the *set* of its members. But this approach runs into difficulties as well. Some social groups seem to retain their identity despite their change in membership. Whereas sets are individuated by reference to their members, not all groups are. Consider, for instance, sports teams. The New York Yankees remain the same baseball team over time even though many of its players, owners, and managers have changed over the years. Therefore, we cannot identify the Yankees baseball team with a particular set of individuals. If we did, every time the Yankees lost or gained a player it would be a different team. But that certainly doesn't accord with our practice. We speak of the *Yankees* losing a player, not a new Yankees team coming into existence when a player is traded.

The problems facing reductive and eliminativist strategies regarding the reality of social groups are similar to those faced by certain theories of the relation between the mind and the body (or brain). An eliminativist about the mind believes that only the brain exists and all talk of mental states should be replaced by talk of neurons or whatever concepts the brain sciences identify as relevant to psychological phenomena. But eliminativism about the mind is not a popular view precisely because it seems to be counter-intuitive to our daily experience and our rich practice of attributing and making sense of others and ourselves in terms of beliefs, desires, and intentions. Likewise, the eliminativist about social groups has a tough row to hoe. We certainly talk about groups and social groups as having causal powers not had by their members. Eliminativism regarding social groups seems to be asking us to radically revise our everyday explanatory practice.

Those who argue for an identity between mental states and brain states run into the problem of multiple realizability. It seems plausible that a type of mental state, say a belief, can be realized by various types of brains (animal, human, alien) and hence there is no strict type identity. Likewise, if we try to reduce a group to the set of specific individual members we find that different sets can still remain the same group. Groups seem to be multiply realized—by different sets of people.

Given these similar problems we might approach the social ontological issues as some philosophers of mind have approached the mind and talk about groups in structuralist or functionalist ways. A functionalist account of mental states is one in which a mental state is defined in terms of its function within a complex system of inputs and outputs. Beliefs, for instance, are caused by certain sorts of inputs, cause other internal states, and function in certain ways to produce certain outputs. My belief that it is snowing is caused by certain perceptual inputs (e.g. the perception of snow and the feeling of cold, for instance), it causes certain other states (e.g. the desire to stay warm), and causes certain behaviours (e.g. the donning of hat, scarf, and mittens). Whatever plays that functional role is a belief about snow, regardless of whether it is played by a neuron or a computer chip.

We might develop a similar approach to the ontology of social groups. On this account, a social group is a certain functional structure and individuals play a role in helping to instantiate that structure. A soccer team is defined in terms of its structures and roles (player positions, coach, manager) and the rules that govern the actions within the structure. The particular players help to instantiate these structures and roles and act in accordance with the rules. To adopt a structuralist or functionalist account of social groups, however, is to give up on a strict ontological individualism and adopt a form of collectivism.

4. Shared (Collective) Intentionality

Recall that what makes a social group a *social* group has to do with the way the members interact and share attitudes and actions such as beliefs, intentions, goals, rituals, and activities. Indeed the ability of human beings (and some animals) to engage in joint action (doing things together) and to share attitudes such as intentions and goals has seemed to many philosophers, such as Margaret Gilbert, John Searle, Raimo Tuomela, and Michael Bratman, to be the heart of sociality. These philosophers have argued that collective or shared intentionality is the 'social glue' that binds individuals together and serves as the basis for many social groups, relations, and processes. But what does it mean to share intentionality and in what sense could intentionality be 'collective'?

Intentionality refers to the ability to represent or be 'about' something in the world. Our mind has the ability to represent the environment and the states that represent the environment are said to be 'intentional' in the sense that they are 'about' things in the world. Intentional states come in a variety of forms. Beliefs are intentional states that, in standard cases, represent states of affairs. They have what University of California, Berkeley philosopher John Searle (1983) describes as a mind-to-world fit. They attempt to get the mind to fit to what the world is like. My belief that it is snowing outside my window will 'fit' the world to the extent that it is indeed snowing outside my window. Desires, on the other hand, are states that have a world-to-mind fit. They represent the way that an agent would like the world to be. My desire for sunshine will be fulfilled only if the sun shines. Beliefs, desires, and intentions are all examples of intentional states. In addition to intentional states, philosophers often talk of intentional agency. Intentional agency refers to the ways in which individual intentional states guide and direct action. It refers to actions done on purpose or with an intention. When a person engages in intentional agency they are *doing something* rather than having something done to them or doing something accidently. They are acting rather than merely moving their body. The action they perform can be attributed to them as the source and in some cases moral responsibility is attributed to the agent on the basis of intentional agency. Human beings clearly have intentional states and engage in intentional agency. Shared intentionality or collective intentionality refers to the ways in which groups of individuals can share intentional states and engage in joint intentional actions (i.e. engage in purposeful action together).

There is a rather obvious way in which individuals share beliefs and other intentional states. It is probably the case that the readers of this text share a number of beliefs and intentions in the sense that they have them 'in common'. Each reader might believe that this is a textbook and they might each intend to read this chapter. These common beliefs are not the sorts of 'shared beliefs' that distinguish mere classes from groups. After all, each red-haired man might have the belief that red hair is charming and yet this wouldn't make the set of red-haired men a social group in the sense we are discussing. So, there has to be more to shared intentionality than merely having the same intentional states in common (see Figure 5.1).

Having an intention in common also seems insufficient to explain the ways that we act together. Suppose Bill and Judy are shopping together. Can we explain this joint activity by appeal to Bill's intention to shop and Judy's intention to shop? These individual intentions could be present in a case where Bill and Judy are shopping at different stores in different towns. Appeal to these common intentions doesn't seem to help us to understand how Bill and Judy's actions could be coordinated in a way that brings about their shopping together. Even if Bill and Judy know of the other's intention to go shopping they might very well be shopping alone.

This suggests that whatever individual attitudes Bill and Judy have regarding shopping must be somehow related to one another or linked in some way. The use of the first person plural 'we' often marks a distinction between mere collections of people engaged in individual actions and social groups engaged

Figure 5.1. Shared intentionality is more than having the same intentional state.

in joint actions. Consider a soccer team whose members chant: 'We will win! We will win!' Surely they do not mean that each individual will win or that they intend for each individual player to win the game. When attributions of intentional states are made to groups, there is often a sense of togetherness or sharing that goes beyond a mere commonly held belief. But if we-intentions and we-beliefs are not always to be reduced to beliefs or intentions held in common, how are we to understand them? Is it the group itself that has these intentional states?

Philosophers have answered this question in a variety of ways. Those committed to methodological and ontological individualism answer it in the negative. They argue that, although we-intentions or we-beliefs cannot be reduced to a set of I-intentions or I-beliefs, we-intentionality (or collective intentionality) can be reduced to individual intentional states of a special type. For instance, John Searle (1990) has argued that in order to make sense of how groups can engage in joint actions we need to appeal to states of individuals of the form 'we intend to win the game'. Just as an individual can intend from the first person singular perspective ('I intend to win the game'), humans (and animals) can form intentions from the first person plural perspective or we-mode ('we intend to win the game'). These 'collective beliefs' cause joint actions by informing the individual actions that comprise the joint action. This capacity to form beliefs and intentions from what might be called the 'we-mode' is, according to Searle, a biologically primitive capacity shared by human beings and animals alike (Figure 5.2).

The ability of human beings (and perhaps animals) to share intentionality (in the form of shared intentions and beliefs) is thought to be foundational for social reality in general. Consider money. Bits of paper are exchanged under various conditions and such exchanges count as monetary exchanges. But how does this happen if all we are exchanging are bits of paper? According to Searle, money is money and has the value it does because we collectively

Figure 5.2. Forming intentions in the 'we-mode'.

believe and accept it as such. This shared or collective acceptance is a form of shared intentionality and is the basis of all social reality. Human beings have the ability to ascribe functions to material objects. I can make a rock a paperweight. But groups of individuals can also ascribe functions to objects via we-intentionality. Social institutions such as money, marriage, economic systems, and even corporations are a function of collective beliefs and intentions. Because Searle's we-intentions and we-beliefs are states of individuals, he is able to give an account of social reality that starts from the biological basis of human consciousness and maintains both ontological and methodological individualism.

Others have argued that believing or intending from the 'we-mode' is a bit mysterious. Michael Bratman, a philosopher of action theory at Stanford University, has argued that we ought to understand shared intentions as a state of affairs consisting of individual intentions of the form 'I intend that *we* J' (where J is an action type) that are interrelated in specific ways (Bratman 1993). Each individual has the intention 'I intend that we J' and the existence of these intentions is common knowledge (each knows of the existence of the other's intention). Their individual intentions are formed in response to a similar intention had by their partner. It is because Judy has formed the intention 'I intend that we go shopping' that John has formed the intention 'I intend that we go shopping' and vice versa. Further, the means by which John and Judy plan to accomplish their intention to shop together must somehow mesh as to allow for the coordination of individual subplans. According to Bratman, this set of mutually referring intentional states *is* the shared intention. When we say 'John and Judy intend to shop together', we are referring to this complex state of affairs made up of their individual intentional states in appropriate relation to one another. We might view this approach to shared intention as exhibiting a form of methodological interrelationism (Figure 5.3).

Bratman (2007), like Searle, denies that there is some supra-agent that is the appropriate subject of mental state ascriptions. Shared intentions refer to states of affairs consisting of facts about individual mental states and their interrelatedness. It would be an ontological mistake, according to Bratman, to think that shared intentions are literally the intentions of the group.

Bratman appeals to shared intentions and shared values to develop an account of practical rationality. Human beings are often constrained not only by what they individually intend but by the shared intentions they form with others. Shared values are the backdrop against which shared intentions are formed. If, for instance, a group of individuals share the value of a good education, this may lead them to form shared intentions regarding the ways to increase educational opportunities for themselves and others.

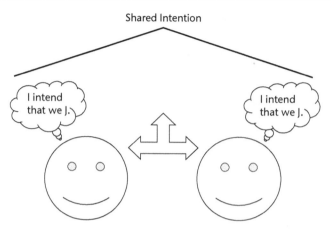

Figure 5.3. An illustration of Bratman's methodological interrelationism.

On the face of it, our everyday ascriptions of beliefs and intentions to groups seem to take the group to be the subject of these states. It seems that what makes an intention a group's intention or a belief a group's belief, as opposed to an individual belief or intention (even suitably interrelated), has to do with the way the individuals come together to become a *unified* subject. Ascriptions of attitudes to groups presuppose a unification of agency. This idea is present in the work of University of California, Irvine philosopher Margaret Gilbert.

According to Gilbert social groups are *plural* subjects. Plural subjects are any population of people committed in a certain special way—what Gilbert (1989) calls 'jointly committed'—to act, intend, or believe as a body or as a unit. A set of individuals can jointly commit, for instance, to shop as a unit or to believe that 'shopping is fun' as a body. What is it to jointly commit to doing something 'as a unit' or believe something 'as a body'? To jointly commit as a body to believing something is to avoid saying things contrary to the group belief and to act in accordance with the group belief. In effect, to act or believe or espouse a goal 'as a body' is to act as if one were part of a single body, to work in unity with others in order to create a unified subject. If John and Judy form a joint intention to go shopping together, John and Judy will avoid doing things that are contrary to that intention. John won't, for instance, continue to sit on the couch in front of the TV.

According to Gilbert joint commitments are formed when all parties express their readiness to be jointly committed and do so under conditions of common knowledge. Expressions of readiness to be jointly committed with others need not be overt verbal expressions. In some cases there will be an explicit agreement, while in other cases people may just 'fall into line' and doing so express their willingness to be jointly committed with others to doing something as a body. Consider Gilbert's example of taking a walk together. You might accidently meet up with a friend on the sidewalk and start to walk together to class. There is no overt joint commitment made in this case but an implied one. In all cases, however, there is some awareness that the joint commitment is in place and some understanding of the obligations and entitlements that ensue because of it. If after walking with your friend you dash away unannounced, it would seem reasonable that your friend would be puzzled by your behaviour, even upset. 'Hey,' she might call after you, 'weren't we just walking together?'

Unlike individual or personal commitments, joint commitments are 'had' by groups. The subject of the joint commitment is responsible for both the forming of it and the rescinding of it. That is, one person alone cannot make a joint commitment and joint commitments cannot unilaterally be rescinded. An individual may 'walk away' from a group and even have very good reasons for doing so, but doing so does not eliminate her obligation to others to behave in a way that achieves that to which the group is committed. She has a prima facie reason to behave in ways that achieve that to which the group is committed but her 'all things considered' judgement may lead her to violate the joint commitment.

The fact that joint commitments are plural commitments—commitments of a group, rather than any individual—makes Gilbert's theory closer to a form of collectivism. Joint commitments cannot be reduced to individual commitments. When joint commitments are in place, group intentions and groups beliefs are appropriately attributed to the group rather than simply to each individual. In fact, Gilbert argues that there could be cases where no one individual believes that p but because of a joint commitment to believe p as a body, it is appropriate to attribute the belief that p to the group. Consider, for instance, a committee of artists that is charged with judging which work of art is the best. There might be a serious disagreement among individual artists as to the merits of a certain work of art (call it x). But they might jointly commit to believing as a body that x is the best work of art. This joint commitment gives rise to a 'we' which can be attributed distinct beliefs and intentions (Figure 5.4).

Gilbert has appealed to her plural subject theory to explain a variety of social phenomena including social convention, culture, and political obligation (2008). Although Gilbert's theory is developed from reflection on cases of small groups, she explicitly extends her account to larger ones. The basic mechanism for doing so is to think of larger social groups as having joint commitments regarding the mechanism by which other joint actions and decisions will take place. So, for instance, the members of a society might jointly agree to allow others (either individuals or smaller plural subjects) to

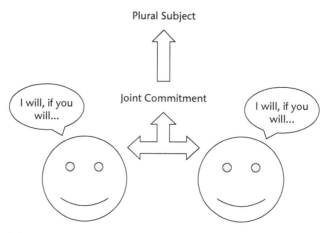

Figure 5.4. Joint commitment giving rise to a plural subject.

make decisions regarding the placement of troops during a war. Plural subjects will be embedded within larger plural subjects.

5. Group Minds?

If we acknowledge the existence of groups and acknowledge that groups can, at times, be the appropriate subject of mental state attribution, are we committed to the idea that groups have minds?

The idea of group cognition or group minds was prevalent in the early days of social psychology. The earliest texts in social psychology, Le Bon's (1896) *Psychology of Crowds* and McDougal's (1920) *The Group Mind*, espoused the view that group behaviour could not fully be understood by studying individual behaviour. Instead, one must appeal to group- or aggregate-level properties and forces. To this extent they were in agreement with sociologists and social philosophers such as Herbert Mead and Emile Durkheim. The development of behaviourism in psychology all but banished the idea of the group mind, however. Although interest in group-level phenomena has waxed and waned over the decades, the focus has been primarily on individual cognition in a social or group context.

Social psychology, however, has witnessed a resurgence of interest and research on cognition at the group level. The backdrop for much of the research is artificial intelligence. For instance, some social psychologists and organizational theorists have adopted the use of connectionist networks to make sense of group cognition. A connectionist network is a computational model that involves synchronous parallel processing among many interrelated unreliable and/or simple processing units. The basic idea is that knowledge in very large networks of very simple processing units resides in patterns of connections, not in individuated local symbols. Any unit's activity is dependent upon the activity of neighbouring units, connected to it by inhibitory or excitatory links whose strength can vary according to design and/or learning. In a connectionist network, any one unit can represent several different concepts, and the same concept in a different context may activate a slightly different network of units.

Edwin Hutchins (1991) has used connectionist networks such as the 'constraint satisfaction network' to model how groups arrive at interpretations or judgements. A constraint satisfaction network is a network in which each unit represents a hypothesis and in which each connection between the units represents constraints among the hypotheses. For instance, if feature B is expected to be present whenever feature A is, there will be a positive connection from the unit that represents the hypothesis that A is present to the unit that represents the hypothesis that B is present. If constraints are weak, then the weights assigned to the connections will be small. If the constraints are strong, the weights assigned to the connections will be large. The inputs to this network can be viewed as evidence from the world. Positive input to a unit means that a particular feature is present. Negative input provides evidence that the feature is not present. Each unit will adjust its activation on the basis of the activation of the units connected to it and the strengths of the connections to those units. The network will then eventually settle into a state in which as many constraints are met as possible. A constraint satisfaction network models, among other things, the ways in which a person might arrive at an interpretation or judgement.

Hutchins's work reveals how the constraint satisfaction network model can be used to understand the way that groups arrive at decisions or judgements. A group-level constraint satisfaction network will involve many sub-networks. These sub-networks represent individuals in the group. The individuals are then connected in various ways and these connections are given weights depending on whether the connection is one that inhibits or excites. The connections between individual networks represent communication between individuals in the group. There are several communication parameters including: the pattern of interconnections among networks (who talks with whom), the pattern of interconnectivity among the units of communicating networks (what they talk about), the strengths of connections between the networks that communicate (how persuasive they are), and the time course of communication (when they communicate). Altering these patterns has significant consequences for how quickly and efficiently groups arrive at judgements and decisions.

In 'The Social Organization of Distributed Cognition' (1991) Hutchins argues that confirmation bias, the propensity to affirm prior interpretations and to discount, ignore, and reinterpret counterevidence to an already formed interpretation, occurs at the level of groups. But, by manipulating the communication parameters, his connectionist network models have shown that confirmation bias can be mitigated. For instance, when individual networks have overlapping rather than mutually exclusive task knowledge, they have less of a tendency to ignore counterevidence. When individuals are aware of each other's expertise and their responsibilities within the group, there is less of a tendency to stick to an interpretation and more discussion of alternative interpretations.

Another line of research that supports the view that cognition can take place outside the individual mind is work on collective memory. Although memory is usually viewed as a process that occurs within individuals, recent research by social psychologists strongly suggests that memory is also a process found in groups. One of the most intriguing and well-developed accounts of collective memory can be found in the work of Daniel Wegner, a psychologist at Harvard University.

At the individual level, memory involves three different stages: encoding, storage, and retrieval. Information is encoded and stored in long- or short-term memory so that it may be retrieved at a later time. Items are not stored independently, however. Whole sentences may be stored or connected with other items. Bananas, for instance, may be stored with the colour yellow. Retrieval of one item is often accompanied by retrieval of many other items. Recalling that I have a dinner party to go to, for instance, might also retrieve the information that I need to purchase a new dress.

Wegner has argued convincingly that certain types of groups engage in processes that are identical to the stages of memory found at the individual level. At the individual level, information is stored both internally and externally. Indeed, many of our everyday activities and tasks would be much more difficult if we did not rely on external storage. 'Our walls are filled with books, our file cabinets with papers, our notebooks with jottings, our homes with artifacts and souvenirs, our floppy disks with data records, and at times, our palms with scribbled answers to a test. Quite simply, we seem to record as much outside our minds as within them' (Wegner 1986: 187). It is important to note that external storage is not simply an aid in retrieving information that is stored internally. Although we might leave a note on the fridge that says 'garbage' in order to aid us in retrieving the information that today is the day the garbage must go out, external storage is not simply about triggering retrieval. It is often the central storage area for large bodies of information. Consider, for instance, the way we rely on the internet in recalling information and events.

Externally stored information is retrievable only if we know where to retrieve it. The successful retrieval of something from external storage requires that we encode a retrieval cue or label for the item and a notion of the location of the item. For instance, I will not be able to retrieve the things my son said when he was 2 unless I encode and store internally the information that I wrote down these things in the leather journal and where that journal is at the present time. The necessity of having a label and information about location suggests the external storage is very different from internal storage. But the notions of a memory item, its label, and location have analogues at the level of individual memory. We can retrieve items from internal storage only if they are labelled as well. I cannot recall Mary Lou's phone number unless I label it such. The cues or labels are often very broad. I may be reminded of the number simply by thinking of Mary Lou, rather than having the label 'Mary Lou's number' in mind.

The processes of encoding, retrieval, and storage, then, have both internal and external manifestations. We can encode and store information either internally or externally. Successful encoding of either type requires that we label the information or associate it with some cue and that the label itself be encoded and stored internally. In the case of internal encoding, the item itself must be encoded with the label. In the case of external encoding we need not encode the item itself, we need only to internally encode the item label and the location of the item.

Just as notebooks, computers, journals, etc. can be external storage areas, so too can people. I might tell my husband that I have an appointment on Tuesday, knowing that this information will be retrievable on Monday night. I have access to information in his memory in virtue of knowing that he is the location of an item with a certain label. As Wegner suggests, this interdependence often produces a 'knowledge-holding' system that is larger and more complex than either of the individuals' own memory.

A transactive memory system involves the operation of individual memory systems and the interaction between them. This system goes through the same stages that occur at the individual level: encoding, storage, and retrieval. Encoding at the collective level occurs when members discuss information and determine the location where it will be stored in the group and in what form it will be stored. Retrieval involves identification of the location of the information. Retrieval is transactive when the person who holds an item internally is not the person who is asked to retrieve it. Full retrieval may come only after various sources are checked.

Transactive memory, then, provides us with another example of cognition at the group level. Transactive memory is a group process, not simply something individuals do in a group. It is not to be found in any particular individual but is a result of individual memory systems interacting in various ways. It involves the same stages of encoding, storage, and retrieval found at the individual level. Thus, it is functionally analogous to individual memory.

The extension of theories of mind, cognition, and mental states to groups is likely to be met with scepticism. The extension of connectionism, for instance, may seem to be unjustified given connectionists' claims that their work is grounded in the brain's microanatomy. But connectionists themselves admit that their models are merely theoretical models. Although neural networks are modelled after networks of neurons in the brain, connectionists are open to the possibility that neural networks are multiply realized. Indeed, they must be in order to acknowledge the possibility of artificial intelligence.

The use of individual cognitive models to understand group cognition is no more problematic than using computational models to understand the way that the human brain processes information. The computational model is, in the first place, a description of how computers process information. It has been adopted in the last seventy years or so as a model for understanding how humans think and process information. The description of how a computational machine processes information is at a very abstract level of description, and these models were adopted, in part, because they allowed for multiple realizability. As in the case of transactive memory, there are functional analogues of individual-level processing at the collective level. It may have seemed odd at the infancy of the computational approach to mind to think of the human mind as a computer, but the approach has been explanatorily fruitful. Likewise, it may seem odd at first to think of certain groups as connectionist networks or information-processing units, but for the social scientist such approaches must be judged on the basis of their explanatory fruitfulness. If we think of a mind not as a thing or substance (physical or immaterial) but as a collection of processes, then the idea that groups have minds may seem more plausible.

6. Summary

This chapter has explored some ideas on the reality of social groups, the notion of shared (or collective) intentionality, and the possibility of group minds. The social sciences often appeal to the existence of groups and their attributes. Consider the economist who appeals to governments and economies; the political scientist who appeals to political parties and voting blocks; the historian who references social processes and relations involving small committees, teams, or factions; the organizational theorist who analyses corporate goals and intentions. Recent work on collective intentionality (be it shared or had by the group itself) promises to provide a theoretical framework for these discussions and further our understanding of the social world in which we live. Research in the social sciences may, in turn, provide support for philosophical theories of the nature of social groups and their attributes.

References

Bratman, M. E. (1993). 'Shared Intention', *Ethics,* 104(1): 97–113.

Bratman, M. B. (2007). *Structures of Agency: Essays.* New York: Oxford University Press.

Durkheim, E. (1953). *Sociology and Philosophy.* Tr. from French by D. F. Pocock. Glencoe, IL: Free Press.

Gilbert, M. (1989). *On Social Facts.* New York: Routledge.

Gilbert, M. (2008). *A Theory of Political Obligation.* New York: Oxford University Press.

Hutchins, E. (1991). 'The Social Organization of Distributed Cognition', in L. B. Resnick, J. M. Levine, and S. D. Teasley (eds), *Perspectives on Socially Shared Cognition.* Washington, DC: American Psychological Association, 283–307.

Searle, J. (1983). *Intentionality: an Essay in the Philosophy of Mind.* Cambridge: Cambridge University Press.

Searle, J. (1990). 'Collective Intentions and Actions', in P. Cohen, J. Morgan, and M. E. Pollack (eds), *Intentions in Communications.* Cambridge, MA: Bradford Books/MIT Press, 401–16.

Wegner, D. M. (1986). 'Transactive Memory: a Contemporary Analysis of Group Mind', in B. Mullen and G. R. Geothals (eds), *Theories of Group Behavior.* New York: Springer Verlag, 185–208.

Further Readings

Gilbert, M. (1996). *Living Together: Rationality, Sociality, and Obligation.* Lanham, MD: Rowman & Littlefield.

Searle, J. (1995). *The Construction of Social Reality.* New York: Free Press.

Tuomela, R. (2007). *The Philosophy of Sociality: The Shared Point of View.* New York: Oxford University Press.

List, C., and Pettit, P. (2011). *Group Agency: The Possibility, Design, and Status of Corporate Agents.* New York: Oxford University Press.

6

Individuals or Populations?

Helen Longino

1. Scale Matters

When confronting a social phenomenon, such as the prevalence of criminal behaviour, rates of addiction, variations in sexual behaviour, prevalence of altruism and cooperation, extent of religiosity, novelty-seeking, and so on, we frequently ask whether the behaviour is a result of nature or nurture, of our (inherited) biological makeup or of our social environment. Another contrast used to mark roughly the same distinction is that between innate and learned. The biological makeup or innate factors in question can include genes, hormones, neurosystem structures and processes; social environment or learning can include parental influence, school, media exposure, peer relations, and larger 'macro-social' factors such as socio-economic status (SES). The question is partly encouraged by the rapid developments in genetic research and the media attention directed to studies that purport to show or suggest that some interesting human behaviour pattern is genetically influenced. Such a report in mass media is usually 'balanced' by report of critics or doubters who suggest the behaviour has social, learned roots as much or more than biological ones.

Such representation of a scientific disagreement, one that pits biologically oriented researchers against socially or environmentally oriented ones, is misleading in several respects. First, it can suggest that all biological researchers are committed to the nature side of the debate and all sociological researchers are committed to the nurture side of the debate. In fact, one can find biologists arguing for the role of social and environmental factors in the inculcation of behaviours and psychologists and sociologists arguing for the role of biological factors. Second, it suggests that the question requires that causation be either biological or social. In fact, most researchers in the fields of human behaviour agree that biological *and* environmental factors are involved in the development and expression of complex human traits, and the real debate has to do with relative degree or strength of causal contribution. So the debate concerns a how-much question, rather than a whether question.

I want to focus on a third respect in which this representation is misleading. As described, it suggests that causal questions about social problems involving human behaviour are answered by understanding what factors operate causally on individuals, activating processes internal to individuals that cause them to behave as they do. This tendency is sometimes called 'methodological individualism' (as also mentioned in Chapter 5) and is understood in the world of social research as the equivalent in social and behavioural research of 'methodological reductionism'. Methodological reductionism is an approach to research that tries to understand the features of a phenomenon, whether a galaxy or an atom, in terms of constituents of the phenomenon. That is, the research strategy is to understand the behaviour of a phenomenon by representing it as the effect of the behaviours of the (smaller) parts of the phenomenon. In the world of human social behaviour, this means the research strategy is to understand a social behaviour, first, by understanding it as the effect of the behaviours of individuals and, second, by understanding the behaviours of the individuals as the effect of factors internal to them, whether those are understood biologically or psychologically. Phenomena at one scale are transformed into (expressions of) phenomena at a lower scale. Phenomena at the scale of the social are understood as the expression of phenomena at the scale of the individual. I should stress that the use of 'methodological' is intended to restrict the individualism or reductionism in question to investigative strategies. *Methodological* individualists or reductionists are not making metaphysical claims about what there is but epistemological claims about how to gain knowledge of what there is. Furthermore, strictly speaking, methodological individualism is a view that treats the reasoned choices of individuals as the fundamental level of explanation, not the causes of those choices in biology or social experience. The approaches to be discussed here are better thought of as examples of methodological reductionism, as they are concerned with the causal roots of the choices as much as the roots of the behaviours.

To take an example, crime, especially violent crime, is in the methodological individualist/reductionist strategy understood as the expression of aggressive dispositions on the part of individuals. Questions about crime then become questions about the individuals who commit crimes, such as what accounts for the development of aggressive dispositions in individuals. Is it a result of biological factors, like genes or hormones or brain structures? Is it a result of environmental factors, such as the experience of abuse as a child, exposure to media violence, or exposure to local actual violence? Is there, as one headline alarmingly put it, a 'murder gene'? I want to suggest that there are some questions about social phenomena, such as crime, that cannot be answered by employing the methodological individualist strategy, and that the kind of question we seek to answer and the problem we seek to solve determine the appropriate scale at which to conduct our investigations. I will first show that some standard ways of thinking about the relations among the various approaches focused on individual differences are not sustainable upon closer examination of the presuppositions of those approaches. They cannot be seen as empirical competitors, nor can they be integrated in the forms in which they currently exist. This demonstration suggests that there is something wrong with the nature–nurture question, however it is understood. Then I will show that the nature–nurture debate is incomplete as it ignores research approaches that do not focus on individuals. Finally, I will suggest that, in some cases, the differences are not merely academic but inform deep attitudes about how we should live with each other.

2. Studying Individual Differences and Similarities

The research approaches most embroiled in the nature–nurture debate include classical and molecular genetic approaches, social-environmental approaches, neuroanatomical and neurophysiological approaches, and several approaches that attempt to integrate the factors studied in these approaches. If we examine their evidential structures, we can see that incompatible presuppositions underlie their collection and analysis of observational data. Given that each of these approaches can produce knowledge, the incompatibility I demonstrate supports taking a philosophically pluralist stance towards them. Let me first briefly describe these approaches.

'Classical' or 'quantitative, behaviour genetics' analyses phenotypic variance (the degree of variation in a trait) in a given population by correlating measured behavioural variation with measured biological relatedness and unrelatedness. What is sought is the frequency with which biologically related individuals are consonant for the trait or its absence as against the frequency with which biologically unrelated individuals are consonant for the trait or its absence.

So, quantitative behaviour geneticists will measure the variation in some index of a trait (starting playground fights is an index of aggression, for example) observable in a given population. The population could be children born in a particular time frame in a particular region, or the students in a particular school district. They will then plot the expression of the trait against the biological relatedness or unrelatedness of the subjects. When the correlation of relatedness and behaviour is higher than would be expected if the association were random, researchers have evidence for what they term 'heritability'. For example, if biologically related individuals are more likely to share the behaviour of starting fights on the playground than are biologically unrelated individuals, and this difference is great enough, researchers will take this as evidence for the heritability of the trait (aggression) for which starting fights is taken to be a measurable index. (See Chapter 14 for a discussion of indicators like this.) One of the challenges that such research faces is establishing that the conditions of the study population are sufficiently similar to the conditions of the general population to warrant extrapolating the results from the study population to the general population (a challenge encountered by much other research in the social sciences, as pointed out in Chapters 3 and 16).

'Molecular behaviour genetics', by contrast, takes advantage of the phenomenal strides that have been made in molecular biology in recent decades to try to identify particular regions of the genome that can be associated with a trait. Rather than seeking evidence that there is some heritable biological component shared by individuals expressing a particular trait, molecular geneticists attempt to identify just what that component, if genetic, is. One of the first studies to try to find a specific genetic basis for aggression was conducted in the Netherlands (Brunner et al. 1993). Those researchers found that the men in an extended Dutch family who expressed high levels of various forms of aggressive behaviour also shared a mutation on a gene related to the production of the enzyme monoamine oxidase (MAOA), which is in turn related to the regulation of the neurotransmitter serotonin. This first study both raised concerns about eugenic applications and catalysed many more studies of that gene region and its possible effects on behaviour.

What I label 'social-environmental approaches' seek to identify determinants of behaviour within the social environment. The methods employed involve both observational research, correlating traits of interest with environmental conditions, and experimental research, intervening on social-environmental conditions. For example, Cathy Widom (1989) correlated higher incidence of antisocial behaviour with documented abuse as a child. Suzanne Lavigueur and colleagues (1995) intervened in interactions in families of delinquent boys. By comparing correlations, researchers can show that a given social-environmental factor is more highly correlated than another with a given behavioural pattern in the population under study. Interventions on elements of the social environment can support conclusions that the factor intervened on plays a causal role in the development or expression of the behaviour. Social-environmental approaches discriminate among different environmental factors, rather than trying to show that environment rather than genes accounts for behavioural variation.

'Neurobiological research on behaviour' seeks to identify the neural structures and processes involved in behaviour (both behavioural dispositions and behavioural episodes). The methods, including post-mortem examination of neural structures, study of brain damage, use of imaging technologies, biochemical analysis of neurotransmitters and neuroactive hormones, and analysis of physiological concomitants of types of experience, are each sufficient to discriminate hypotheses within the scope of what is measured. Research is directed to such matters as whether receptor activity or neurotransmitter synthesis is the physiological correlate of a given trait or whether a given behavioural trait is controlled by some specific brain area. Researchers have linked such neurobiological phenomena as variation in serotonin metabolism or frontal lobe size with variations in aggressivity.

'Integrative approaches' are interested in the interactions among components studied in these research programmes. They include both approaches that, like 'Development Systems Theory' (DST), argue that the totality of factors, internal and external, must be considered and those that focus on some subset of factors—a particular gene and a type of environmental factor, for example, a mutation in the gene involved in MAOA production and experience of abuse as a child.

3. Comparing the Approaches

As I have noted, the question of causation has moved far beyond the simple nature–nurture dichotomy, as it is recognized that nature *and* nurture are causally implicated both in the evolution of particular behaviours and behavioural dispositions and in their expression in individuals and populations. And while the different approaches differ on the precise implications of this for research, they do agree that, for any causal factor, one can only think in terms of its contribution to (a) behaviour relative to that of others. While a certain amount of popular press reporting is sensitive to this fact, it still presumes a context in which the first question, the question about accuracy, is pre-eminent. Reports thus tend to frame the issue as a competition: which approach is ahead in the race to understand a given behaviour? The scientific disputes, however, are about the weight or strength of one type of factor vis-à-vis that of others, about the degree to which certain types of factor can be ignored, about the relative strength of investigative methods, about the relative value of different kinds of knowledge.

Furthermore, each approach has methods capable of discriminating among a distinctive range of hypotheses—with surprisingly little overlap. Basically, except for quantitative behavioural genetics (about which more later), approaches employ methods for discriminating causal factors only within their sphere of investigation. (For more on testing causal claims, see Chapter 16.) For example, research in neurophysiology can discriminate among competing neurophysiological hypotheses but not among members of a set that includes neurophysiological hypotheses and non-neurophysiological ones. If it showed no correlation between the factor under study and the behaviour of interest, all that could be concluded is that something other than the factor was responsible but not what. A study design that attempts to isolate one factor must employ methods that can measure it and the behaviour under investigation. This requires stabilizing and neutralizing other contributory factors. Suppose researchers are trying to understand the contribution of reduced MAOA function to aggressive behaviour. They must have a standard way of identifying and measuring the behaviour, a standard way of measuring MAOA function, and they must eliminate the possibility that other physiological or environmental factors could be influencing the behavioural effect. This means varying only MAOA and holding everything else constant. Similarly, research on environmental factors that might account for variation among individuals, such as experience of abuse as a child, or loss, or not, of a parent, must employ standard measurement protocols and find ways to eliminate the influence of confounding causal factors.

Even then, there are limitations to what can be concluded. The most important limitation comes from the research itself. In no case has research in any of the approaches found a complete correlation between a (human) behaviour of interest and whatever causal factor is investigated. Instead what researchers can claim at best is that the factor they study accounts for some percentage of the variation in or expression of the trait. Thus each approach can generate knowledge about a given behavioural phenomenon. The knowledge, however, is partial knowledge: in environment E, when all other factors are held constant, variation in Y in population P contributes (to some specified degree N) to the expression of X in population P. Nothing about what Y might do with respect to the expression of X in other populations or in other environments can be concluded from investigation in the population or environment selected for study. This echoes the problem of external validity, discussed more fully in Chapter 3, which is endemic across social science studies.

Quantitative behaviour genetics gives even less knowledge than some other approaches. It tries to parse how much of the variation in a trait in a population is due to heritable variation and how much to environmental variation. Even if it does successfully parse the variation, its methods are not adequate to indicate what the heritable factors are or what the environmental factors are. So, while it does promise knowledge of how much variation in a trait measured in a specific population in a specific environment can be correlated with heritable factors and how much with non-heritable ones, it does not have the methods to discriminate among the particular factors within these categories.[1] And, additional research of a very different kind would be required to establish the similarity in population structure and environment that would support generalizing to populations other than the one under study.

One additional point is worth emphasizing here. Popular representations of genetic research have tended to treat those approaches as more scientifically promising than social-environmental approaches. Even some of the researchers suggest that genetics will be more informative about the bases of behaviour than the environment, because environmental causes are so much more various and environmental influences so diffuse. This attitude is expressed in reporting such as that describing the low-MAOA genotype as 'the warrior gene' or a 'murder gene'. But what molecular genetics has really taught us is that, while single genes in a given environment may increase the likelihood of expression of a behaviour by some small amount, genetic influence is multi- rather than single-genic. Genetic influence is as diffuse in the genome as environmental influence is in the environment.

This privileging of genetics, however, helps keep the focus on alternatives that also attempt to understand variation among individuals in a population: why Johnny is given to fighting to solve problems while Jimmy is given to negotiating. But approaches focused on individual variation are not the only approaches developed to understand patterns of human behaviour. Take crime, for example. We might want to know why one city or country has higher rates of assault than another. It's hardly credible that patterns of genetic variation or childhood abuse or neurosystem development and function would vary systematically from city to city or country to country. There's no evidence that patterns of variation in factors that causally contribute to variation in individuals are not pretty similar from region to region. To find out about regional differences in frequency or distribution of patterns of behaviour, a different kind of approach is required and available. An ecological study of human populations looks at population-level properties or processes in understanding variation among populations. Such a study might look at physical factors such as the rate of increase or decrease of resources and variation and shifts in other physical variables, such as climate, that impact availability of resources, and at social factors, such as variations in age distribution, kinship structures, distribution of access to resources, distribution of wealth and of income, patterns of ownership. Here the effort is

---

[1] Traits that are linked with others do permit some localization claims but, without molecular analysis, do not permit specific allelic identification.

to correlate patterns of frequency and distribution of a given behaviour in populations with these other population-level factors.

Just as there are a variety of approaches that focus on individual variation, there are a variety of approaches that focus on social or population variation. Jeffrey Fagan and colleagues studied rates of arrest and incarceration in New York City neighbourhoods between 1985 and 1997 (Fagan et al. 2003). They found, first of all, that these rates were highest in the poorest neighbourhoods. They further found a disparity between the drop in crime rates in 1990–1996 and incarceration rates in the same period. Incarceration rates fell much more slowly than crime rates, and the excess incarceration was concentrated among non-white males living in the city's poorest neighbourhoods.[2] Given the brutalizing effects of incarceration, the lack of re-entry programmes for released convicts, and the high proportion of young men from the poorer neighbourhoods who are in jail at any given time, Fagan proposes that incarceration simply begets more incarceration, i.e. that in these neighbourhoods a flow in and out of incarceration has become established. The different structures of opportunity and constraint in New York City neighbourhoods, including housing and employment availability, policing patterns, age structures, and so on, and not features internal to the individuals living in those neighbourhoods, account for the differences in incarceration rates (or as we might say, following Fagan's metaphor, the rates of flow from neighbourhood to prison to neighbourhood and back to prison).

Other approaches reflecting such ecological thinking include the 'broken windows' theory, which proposes that the accumulated uncorrected evidence of small, unpunished acts of vandalism or law-breaking morphs into higher rates of criminal activity, and the 'collective efficacy' theory, which proposes that different rates of collective community engagement can account for different rates of criminal activity in different neighbourhoods. And, focusing on a later stage of the crime cycle, the Justice Mapping Center has developed strategies for constructing city or regional maps that identify areas of higher and lower rates of incarceration and recidivism and correlate those with a variety of other socio-demographic variables, including income, home-ownership rates, unemployment rates, social-service expenditures, parole caseloads, and so forth. These maps provide the basic data for developing explanations of crime and for informing possible interventions at the population level, rather than at the individual level.

Whatever the merits of these different approaches, they are not about why some individuals differ from other individuals in their manifestation of a particular behaviour, but rather about distributions of interactions among

---

[2] Neighbourhoods in which average annual household income was below $8,000 in some cases or $15,000 in others.

populations, whether the subpopulations (neighbourhoods) of a given population (all of New York City) or larger populations and the relation of those
distributions to the distribution of other population-level factors. The difference is a difference in scale, where by scale we mean not only orders of magnitude but level of factors among which correlations are sought. This manifests
in different ways of understanding population-level differences. Applying
approaches that focus on individual variation to population-level variation
requires treating properties of populations in an aggregative manner, as the
additive effect of properties of their constituent members. Differences in crime
rates in two localities are treated as a function of the numbers of individuals engaged in crime in those localities, and the resources to explain those
numbers have to be the distribution of factors that drive individual variation, such as prevalence of genetic configurations or of child-rearing patterns.
The ecological approaches, by contrast, treat properties of populations in a
non-aggregative manner, as the effect of other population-level properties.
They offer different ways of thinking about causality and about classification,
about what explains and what is explained in the sciences of behaviour.

4. A Pluralist Analysis

Can these research approaches be compared empirically? Empirical comparison would require a single body of evidence against which hypotheses
from the different approaches could be evaluated. However, research pursued
under the aegis of any of the individually focused approaches pushes them in
non-reconcilable directions. Refining and improving the methods of a given
approach enables researchers to produce better knowledge within that particular framework but does not produce tools—either in the form of data or
of methods—for cross-approach empirical evaluation. Even though there is,
from one point of view, a common phenomenon to be understood—behaviour or rather, specific behaviours or behavioural patterns such as aggressivity or choice of sexual partners—each approach brings with it a prior and
distinctive representation of the domain of investigation. Researchers and
most observers see the causal factors as existing in some kind of vertical and
thus hierarchical relation, with genes at the lowest level and social factors
at the highest level. This may represent their ontological relations, but their
epistemological status is better appreciated by a more neutral representation.
At the outset of investigation, we don't know the causes of a phenomenon or
which among a set of possible causal factors is more influential. A horizontal
array that assigns each type of factor to a box, as in Figure 6.1, enables us to
see how their respective roles are understood without incorporating assumptions about which are more basic.

Genotype 1	Genotype 2	Intrauterine environment	Physiology	Non-shared environment	Shared (intra-family) environment	Socio-economic status
[allele pairs]	[whole genome]		[hormone secretory patterns; neurotransmitter metabolism] Anatomy [brain structure]	[birth order; differential parental attention; peers]	[parental attitudes re discipline; communication styles; abusive/ non-abusive]	[parental income; level of education; race/ethnicity]

Figure 6.1. A representation of the potential causal space.

Let us suppose that Figure 6.1 includes all the factors that can bear on individual variation and similarity. We can call it a representation of the potential causal space. Each approach parses this potential causal space in different ways: some attend only to factors in one block, treating the others as inactive; others try to assign portions of variance to different blocks, treating one subset as active and the complementary subset as inactive. Except for Developmental Systems Theory (DST), each approach reduces the universe of potential causes in some way. So, for example, molecular genetics has methods that enable it to explore a causal universe that looks like Figure 6.2, while quantitative genetics has methods that enable it to explore a universe that looks like Figure 6.3. Social-environment oriented approaches have methods that enable them to explore a universe that looks like Figure 6.4. In each case, there is an unlabelled catch-all box for whatever accounts for the portion of the phenomenon not correlated with the factor investigated.

Thus, each approach measures variation in a differently construed causal space. Rather than developing strategies for simultaneously sampling each portion of the potential causal space, each develops new investigative strategies to improve its exploration of the causal space as it has parsed it. Since each must distribute the assignment of causal weight to the factors in the

Genotype 1 [allele pairs]	Genotype 2 [whole genome]	Other

Figure 6.2. The causal universe of molecular genetics.

Genotype 2 [whole genome]	Non-shared environment [measured by non-heritable trait variation unaccounted for by environmental variation]	Shared environment [includes socio-economic status, parental attitudes, other shared features]	Other

Figure 6.3. The causal universe of quantitative genetics.

Non-shared environment [birth order; differential parental attention; peers]	Shared (intra-family) environment [parental attitudes re discipline; communication styles; abusive/non-abusive]	Socio-economic status [parental income; level of education; race/ethnicity]	Other

Figure 6.4. The causal universe of social-environmental methods.

causal space as it construes it in a way that sums to 100 per cent and the combination of factors considered varies from approach to approach, there is no common measurement of potential causal factors.

These different construals mean that the approaches are evidentially incommensurable. Each approach can show, as long as other factors are kept or assumed constant, that variation in the space it explores influences variation in the trait under investigation. Each approach can evaluate hypotheses about different factors within the part of causal space it explores: one set of alleles as opposed to another set; one neurophysiological process as opposed to another; one socio-environmental factor as opposed to another. But even while a given approach only measures variation in the values of the type of causally influential variable on which it is focused, the phenomenon under investigation is affected by factors in all the boxes of Figure 6.1, even if they are held constant. Whether constant or varying, their status is contributing to the measurements turning out the way they do.

Furthermore, the same factor can appear in different categories (boxes) depending on the approach. Parental divorce can be part of the non-shared environment for behaviour geneticists, if the offspring differ in the trait under investigation, while it is part of the shared environment for social-environment oriented researchers. Uterine factors, if not directly measured, will affect the measurements of genetic and social-environment researchers differently, counting as genetic for one and environmental for the other.

These differences in what gets counted in what category obviously affect the correlational data generated. Because the approaches work in differently constituted and incongruous causal spaces, their measurements of putatively the same factors are not comparable. The lack of comparability means that they cannot be taken to be empirical competitors in any significant way. That they are each able to generate results that are replicable and can be put to use in either cognitive or practical projects, however, means that they cannot be dismissed. These two aspects of the individually focused approaches support taking a philosophically pluralist stance towards them. A pluralist stance neither demands that they be combined into one comprehensive theory, nor that one be demonstrated to be empirically superior to the others. From a pluralist perspective, they constitute incommensurable and incompatible, but nevertheless productive, efforts to understand the same phenomena.

The argument so far in this section concerns relations among the approaches exploring the roles of one (or at most two) of the kinds of factor. Integrative approaches, at least those so far developed, do not overcome the incommensurability problem. DST holds that all the factors that are potentially causally relevant are actually at all times not just causally relevant but interacting and that efforts to research the contributions of any single type of factor, as molecular genetics does, will end up misrepresenting the causal relationships.

The difficulty for DST is that it has not yet devised strategies for empirically discriminating among different possible DST hypotheses. One of the principles of DST is that all causes are on a par with one another. The theory has not yet developed empirical strategies to demonstrate this principle, so it is better understood as a commitment rather than an empirical hypothesis. Experimental work performed under the aegis of DST tends to demonstrate the necessity of factors from two or more types for the expression of some behaviour. Such demonstration is generally presented as a way to disconfirm or refute single factor or additive approaches. (Additive approaches are those that recognize different types of causal factor influencing some outcome but treat them as acting independently.) One experiment focused on hypertension in rat pups. Pups bred to be spontaneously hypertensive (SHR) only developed hypertension if also suckled by the SHR mothers. They did not develop hypertension if suckled by non-SHR mothers, nor did non-SHR pups develop hypertension if suckled by SHR mothers; both having been birthed *and* suckled by an SHR mother were necessary. (Whether this result reflects differences in behavioural interactions between mother and pup or substances in the milk is not clear.)

This kind of experimental work shows that two kinds of factor are necessary for the development of some trait, so it can show the inadequacy of any single factor approach. It also shows that their relation is not additive. It's not the case that each factor independently adds a bit to the outcome, as without the other each has no effect. This kind of work does not, however, have the means of demonstrating whether one is more contributory than another, nor does it have strategies for measuring all the (potential) factors simultaneously. Varying one factor at a time, as advocated by one prominent advocate of this approach (Gottlieb 1991), shows the necessity (or not) of the factor so intervened on, but it does not show *how* all the factors are interacting. Moreover, its preferred experimental strategies are neither practically nor ethically feasible with human subjects. One might say that DST is ontologically integrative but not epistemologically or experimentally integrative. It remains more of a metaphysical position, effectively cautioning against reductive analysis rather than supporting alternatives.

Another integrative approach, the *GxE* or *GxExN* model proposed by the two American psychologists Avshalom Caspi and Terrie Moffitt (2006), has proceeded by showing that for some traits, such as depression or some indices of aggression, the frequency of the trait is higher in subpopulations characterized both by a particular genetic mutation and histories of some social/environmental trauma than in subpopulations characterized by the genetic mutation alone or the social/environmental trauma alone. But this integrative model is developed explicitly to address behavioural or psychic disorders and still captures not only just a portion of the expression of the trait in whatever population is under study (that portion attributable to a disorder) but only a portion of that portion. It does not purport to offer a comprehensive account of the aetiology of behavioural traits.

While not comprehensive, each of these approaches produces some knowledge of processes generating phenotypic behavioural traits. The survey leaves us with a plurality of approaches generating accounts of the aetiology of individual behavioural dispositions that are not reducible to some fundamental level of causation, not integrable into a single comprehensive account, and not empirically commensurable in a way that would permit the elimination of rivals. Integrative approaches are either not empirically tractable or reduce the phenomena to be explained to disorders.

In the context of the nature–nurture debate, the plurality among individually oriented approaches is competitive to the extent that each is trying to address a common question. The plurality among these approaches is different from the plurality that results from asking questions posed at different scales. The causal factors to be investigated belong to different causal spaces to be sure, but the real difference is generated by the phenomena being explained: traits of and variation among individuals, in the one case, and properties of and variation among populations, in the other. Using an individually focused approach to population-level questions would imply an aggregative, or methodologically individualist, investigative strategy. It would imply that one thought that population differences were a result of different frequencies or distributions of the factors involved in generating differences among individuals. Success of the aggregative approach would require that distribution of the causal factors affecting individual traits (genes, school and family environments, neural structures and processes) vary in parallel with the behavioural distributions.

Consider, for example, a study that sought to understand if there is a sex difference in heritability of aggression, using data from the UK and Sweden (Eley et al. 1999). The data indicated that there was no sex difference in heritability of aggressive behaviour, but there was such a difference in heritability of non-aggressive antisocial behaviour. This result concerning sex differences in heritability held in both national cohorts. But one of the most interesting features of the data generated in the study (which the researchers note but do not analyse, as it lies outside the scope of the study) is the difference in frequency of aggressive behaviour between the two, the British population showing a higher frequency of interpersonal violence than the Swedish one. If one were to explain this disparity with an aggregative approach, the Swedish and British populations would have to differ genetically, neurally, or with respect to patterns of child-rearing (or in some combination of these factors) in a way that tracks the different frequencies of aggression in those populations. Whether two northern European populations would differ systematically enough in any of these factors to support a methodologically individualist explanation of the noted behavioural difference is a matter for research, not assumption.

Population-level approaches are neutral about the factors that operate at the individual level. Although one might hold that population-level factors interact with those that impinge directly on individuals to produce specific differences, any of the accounts of individual difference and similarity will be compatible with population-level accounts of population differences, as long as the individual-focused accounts are not attempting to explain population level differences as well.[3] A population approach is also compatible with a view that eschews seeking any specific causal explanations of individual behaviour, seeing individual behaviour as a (reasoned or chosen) response to the opportunities, rewards, and constraints afforded by one's immediate and distal environment. An ecological or population-level investigation of the difference in frequency of aggressive behaviour between UK and Swedish populations, such as that found in the study mentioned, would look to differences in population-level variables, such as different structures of opportunity, reward, and constraint. A population approach neither affirms nor denies that individual behaviours are the outcomes of some combination of genetic, environmental, and physiological factors or that variation among individuals within a population, when physical resources and structural factors are uniform, is ultimately accounted for in such terms. It does reject the suggestion that differences in distributions among populations are the same as differences in distributions within populations. This point was made repeatedly in the context of debates over group differences in performance on IQ and other standardized tests, but was not then situated in the kind of pluralist analysis this chapter advocates. One further point to remember is that 'population' does not have a fixed reference: What counts as one population for one purpose may count as several populations for another purpose.

If we set aside the aggregative approach to population differences, the plurality evinced by approaches focused on individual traits and those focused on population differences is of a non-competitive or compatible sort. The two types of approach can be understood as being directed at different scales, and while phenomena proper to the different scales might theoretically interact, there is not the confounding of measurement within the same scale that characterizes the relation of the various approaches directed at individual traits. A deeper study of population-level research may well reveal the same kind of plurality among approaches focused on population-level factors as

<hr/>

[3] And, as noted, the accounts of inter-individual variation hold for individuals in a specified population or environment, not across environments.

I contend characterizes individual trait approaches, but that will have to be demonstrated in a different study.

5. Science in the World

Up to this point I have argued that these scientific approaches to the study of human behaviour exhibit two forms of plurality. Those sciences focused on individual differences and similarities that fuel the nature versus nurture debate are in an important sense incommensurable. By this I mean that, because they parse their domains of investigation differently and incompatibly, the measurements on which they base their claims cannot coincide in a way that makes empirical comparison among them possible. This doesn't invalidate those measurements as grounds for pursuing further investigation within the approach, but it does undermine the basis of nature/nurture debates. The world does not come to us in neat packages to which we can simply apply our measuring instruments (as discussed in Chapter 14). Instead we develop categories for the task of identifying and then measuring aspects of the world in a way that will enable us to track those sequences or flows of change that are important to us. In order to get started on genetic or physiological or psychological investigations, researchers have to start with some kind of correlation and then find ways to refine their measurements and correlations within the domain. The results that emerge in one line of investigation are not invalidated because other approaches are similarly refining the information obtainable through their methods. In all cases so far, only a portion of the phenotypic variation will be accounted for by the explanatory factors specific to any of the current lines of research, whether focused on single or multiple interacting factors. This kind of plurality is ineliminable.

There is a second kind of plurality, however, that characterizes the relation between approaches focused on individual differences and similarities and those focused on population differences. These more ecological approaches seek connections among population-level variables and focus on differences and similarities among populations. They are compatible with any of the intra-population approaches, so long as these stay focused on intra-population variation. If we understand the individual and population approaches to be asking different questions, this plurality is of the compatibilist or eliminable sort. The point is to see that the questions that arise at different scales are very different in character, so there is no need to see the individual and population approaches in the same kind of competition that animates (and is animated by) the nature–nurture debate. Here the question is not about what moves individuals but about the structures within which individuals move, whatever the motors of their movement. Thus it is not about individual praise or blame or excuses; it is about relations at a higher scale than those among individuals.

Why is it important to attend to these matters of scale? In the last century and a half, since the biological study of behaviour was initiated by the publication of Darwin's *Origin of Species* and his subsequent writings, such as *The Descent of Man*, there have been efforts to understand social differences in terms of biological differences among individuals. Socio-economic class differences were thought by the so-called Social Darwinists (following Herbert Spencer's interpretation of Darwin's theory of natural selection) to be the outcome of innate and inherited differences among individuals. Anthropology was rife with theories of racial difference that not only attributed racial difference to intrinsic differences but that treated some racial groupings as superior to others. The development of genetics, after the discovery of Gregor Mendel's research (the founder of genetics) and of statistics, in the work of Ronald Fisher and Egon Pearson, fostered the study of human differences. These included not only such matters as eye colour and height but intelligence, gender differences, and anti- and prosocial behaviour. The nature–nurture debate emerged as researchers sought to emphasize environmental factors as offering alternative explanations to the biological ones suggested by the advances in genetics.

This debate was particularly acerbic with respect to putative racial differences. In the early part of the twentieth century, many American intellectuals and politicians were worried that an influx of immigrants from southern Europe would contaminate the American gene pool. This worry fuelled the passage of legislation restricting immigration. In the second half of the twentieth century, the poorer, on average, performance of African-American students compared to that of Euro-American students on tests of intellectual aptitude prompted speculation that, because individual variation in intellectual aptitude had a genetic component, the racial differences were also genetically based. The idea in both cases was that cognitive and behavioural differences between human groups, such as intellectual aptitude, were biologically based as much as biological differences such as skin coloration. Such suggestions were met with outrage by African-American scholars and by biologists and social scientists who argued instead for the roles of racism and poverty in impeding intellectual development. Genetic research, they could argue, showed greater within-group genetic variation than between-group variation, thus undermining the case for a genetic base for group differences in performance on tests of intellectual aptitude or in any other behavioural trait. And new research focusing specifically on differential test performance, whether by race or by gender, has shown the effect of environmental factors. Reminding test takers of the stereotypes associated with their racial or gender identity affects their test performance. This phenomenon is known as stereotype threat.

In the mid-1990s, the genetic research on aggression began to be put to use to explain crime. While researchers did not make the explicit link to racial differences, they did not need to. It is no secret that African-American men are highly over-represented and Hispanic men increasingly so in the US prison population. Furthermore, researchers on stereotyping and implicit bias, such as the American social psychologists Philip Goff, Jennifer Eberhart, and their colleagues, have found that subjects in the United States associate African-American physiognomies with crime and danger more frequently than they do Euro-American physiognomies (Goff et al. 2008). These two features of American society, along with the media's emphasis on advances in genetics and neuroscience, provide fertile ground for the racializing of crime along lines similar to the racialization of intelligence. Whether the focus is on research seeking genetic bases or on research seeking to understand the effect of single-parent households on children, it effectively blames racial factors for poorer intellectual or social performance. It becomes ever more important, therefore, to attend to the scale at which a phenomenon can be identified.

Questions about differences between groups are questions about population-level differences. Questions about differences between individuals are questions about the difference in factors that affect individuals. If we are trying to affect the outcomes for individuals, for example, if we seek to alleviate afflictions such as depression or paranoia, we need to understand how factors such as genetic configuration, neural function, parental interaction, and so on affect development. And, if we are concerned with blame and degrees of responsibility, we need to understand factors impinging on individual behaviour. But, if we look only to research on individual differences for answers to questions about population-level differences, we will miss the population-level structures of opportunity and constraint within which individuals, no matter what combination of causes makes them who and what they are, navigate. As was the case with differential performance on tests of intellectual aptitude, those structures are much more likely to correlate with group differences in behaviour than are genetic, neurological, or socialization factors. Scientific research ought to be used to counter prejudice, not strengthen it. In this, scale matters.

References

Brunner, H. G., et al. (1993). 'Abnormal Behavior Associated with a Point Mutation in the Structural Gene for Monoamine Oxidase A', *Science,* 262: 578–80.

Caspi, A., and Moffitt, T. (2006). 'Gene-Environment Interactions in Psychiatry: Joining Forces with Neuroscience', *Nature Reviews: Neuroscience*, 7: 583–90.

Eley, T., Lichtenstein, P., and Stevenson, J. (1999). 'Sex Differences in the Etiology of Aggressive and Non-aggressive Antisocial Behavior: Results from Two Twin Studies', *Child Development*, 70(1): 155–68.

Fagan, J., West, V., and Holland, J. (2003). 'Reciprocal Effects of Crime and Incarceration in New York City Neighborhoods', *Fordham Urban Law Journal*, 30: 1551–1602.

Goff, P., Eberhardt, J. L., Williams, M. J., and Jackson, M. C. (2008). 'Not Yet Human: Implicit Knowledge, Historical Dehumanization, and Contemporary Consequences', *Journal of Personality and Social Psychology*, 94(2): 292–306.

Gottlieb, G. (1991). 'Experimental Canalization of Behavioral Development: Theory', *Developmental Psychology*, 27(1): 4–13.

Lavigueur, S., Tremblay, R., and Saucier, J. (1995). 'Interactional Processes in Families with Disruptive Boys: Patterns of Direct and Indirect Influence', *Journal of Abnormal Child Psychology*, 23(3): 359–78.

Sampson, R. J., Raudenbush, S. W., and Earls, F. (1997). 'Neighborhoods and Violent Crime: A Multilevel Study of Collective Efficacy', *Science*, 277: 918–24.

Widom, C. (1989). 'Does Violence Beget Violence?' *Psychological Bulletin*, 106(1): 3–28.

Further Readings

Bechtel, W., and Richardson, R. (1993). *Discovering Complexity: Decomposition and Localization as Strategies in Scientific Research*. Princeton: Princeton University Press.

Kellert, S., Longino, H., and Waters, C. K., eds (2006). *Scientific Pluralism*. Minneapolis: University of Minnesota Press.

Longino, H. E. (2013). *Studying Human Behavior: How Scientists Investigate Aggression and Sexuality*. Chicago: University of Chicago Press.

Ostrom, E. (2007). 'Challenges and Growth: The Development of the Interdisciplinary Field of Institutional Analysis', *Journal of Institutional Economics*, 3(3): 239–64.

Plaisance, K., and Reydon, T., eds (2012). *Philosophy of Behavioral Biology*. Dordrecht: Springer.

Part III
Questions about Objectivity

7

Scientific Objectivity

Eleonora Montuschi

The question over the objectivity of the social sciences was framed from the start in a comparative form: 'can the social sciences be as objective as the natural sciences?' The comparison, in its turn, was premised on the belief that the natural sciences are the better 'sciences'. This explains why the social sciences have fallen prey to debates that only partially focus on issues appropriate to their own ontology and epistemology.

Both the comparison and its premise have a historical grounding and a philosophical motivation behind them. Historically, modern science emerges in the seventeenth century as natural science, with figures like Francis Bacon first and then Galileo and Descartes. Its image and status derived essentially from physics and astronomy. The social sciences followed much later, in the nineteenth century, when the natural sciences had already established their reputation and secured publicly acknowledged results.

Philosophically, the modern image of science associates science with method, and the idea of method was conceived by the so-called natural philosophers (Bacon, Galileo, Descartes) as a set of rules of reasoning completely separate from either individual judgement or social context. Only a method conceived in this way was believed to deliver objective knowledge when applied to natural facts.

Much later, in the nineteenth century, the behaviour of society and of individuals started being looked at as objects of scientific inquiry in their own right. However, it was taken for granted—as, for example, the empiricist philosopher John Stuart Mill made clear—that scientific knowledge of any social phenomena could only be pursued (though with due readjustments) by adopting the method and logic of natural science. Social inquiry was then presented from the start as a territory to add to the domain of scientific method and explanation, and its comparison with the 'better sciences' has since affected the way social science has disposed its own theoretical and practical resources in achieving objective results.

Against this backdrop, the call for objectivity in social science focused on three main demands, articulated in comparative form:

1. *Grabbing only onto real objects and real facts.* It is generally believed that the natural sciences deal with real natural facts. Just as they struggled to get rid of ambiguous categories such as vital forces, or entities such as caloric or the ether, so too the social sciences should do away with objects and categories that are not 'really there'. To be 'really there' for a social fact is, however, less intuitive than for a natural fact. Marriage, money, crime, political refugees are 'really there' because of man-made activities and categorizations. Take those activities and categorizations away (indeed, take humans away) and those facts would cease to exist in a way that does not seem to apply to molecules and genes and chemical elements. In reflecting on the objectivity of their inquiries then, the social sciences must take into account this peculiar question: can there be an objective reality that exists partly because of human agreement (or by virtue of the fact that we believe that it exists—as in the case of the social norms and conventions discussed in Chapter 11)?

2. *Driving out values from descriptions and explanations.* As Chapter 9 explains in more detail, according to the received view values might be present in science, yet they should not be employed in establishing scientific results. Equally, it is argued, in social science we should try to separate facts and values and keep values at bay as far as possible. Suppose, though, a case like that discussed in Chapters 6 and 9: in support of the hypothesis that different races are intellectually unequal some intelligence theorist might adduce: (1) evidence coming from IQ tests performed on different racial groups, showing racially consistent differences in scores; (2) some theory about the genetic, inherent basis of human intelligence; (3) some racially motivated belief concerning certain groups of people. In this case, it might well be that (3) is as involved in reaching the conclusion that a certain race is more intelligent than another as (1) and (2) are. Even more worryingly, it might be that (3) informs and encourages a certain reading of the results offered by purportedly 'objective' measurement in (1), or else it might be part of the background assumptions of the theories on human intelligence in (2). Of course this would make the objective credentials of the conclusions reached on the basis of such 'evidence' controversial. Indeed the debate on race and intelligence starting in the early twentieth century is a very instructive case of how questionable value judgements might affect the course of social scientific inquiry (Jacoby and Glauberman 1995). Value freedom then faces a special challenge in the social domain where it proves more difficult to keep values from interfering with factual descriptions, and where in some

cases they simply can't be eliminated, as they are so finely engrained in theories and background assumptions concerning people and human nature.

3. *Using only methods likely to secure true outcomes.* It is commonly believed that this is achieved in natural science by the use of quantitative methods, so social science should as far as possible follow the same path. The divide between quantitative and qualitative, despite being the object of ongoing fierce debates, has had profound effects on the image and status of social science—with disciplines such as economics being taken more prominently as 'sciences' than other social sciences precisely because of their quantitative methodological orientation. Moreover, recently in areas such as education, crime, child welfare, and development economics, the belief in the objectivity of numbers has led to favouring procedures that are deemed 'mechanical' over those that require judgement or background knowledge—so, for example, leading to a demand for using randomized control trials (as discussed in detail in Chapter 3) wherever it seems possible, though with questionable, sometimes highly contentious results.

In the face of these three demands social science had then to prove its credentials as an objective domain of inquiry, often borrowing a style of reasoning and of investigation which did not do justice to its subject matter and to the questions it pursued. It must be said though that such a blunt comparison between domains of science does not do much service to the natural sciences either. In the call to imitate 'science', the image of science adopted as a paradigm of inquiry appears in many respects misleading for the natural sciences themselves. First, the reality of natural facts has become less intuitive because more attention has been given to the role theories have in 'constructing' models of the facts they refer to rather than in 'discovering' facts in a world where these simply pre-exist theories. Second, value-ladenness is a feature that has become more and more recognized as being part of scientific inquiries in the natural sciences too (as discussed in Chapter 9). Third, separating out quantitative and qualitative techniques and favouring 'mechanical' procedures of inquiry have recently become contentious strategies across the whole board of science. So the comparison with the natural sciences has proved penalizing in a double sense. It made the social sciences 'lesser' sciences, but also it made them victim of a skewed, ill-conceived comparison.

Unfailingly though, the three demands cursorily described appear at the forefront of any discussion concerning scientific objectivity. Therefore, in what follows I will analyse each of the three demands, keeping an eye both on what the received view asks social science to comply with and on how the actual practice of social research achieves its best results in terms of objectivity *pace* comparison.

1. The Ontological Demand: 'Only Real Facts'

In the 1960s heated discussions over the scientific status of psychoanalysis called into question the ontological credentials of categories such as *id/ego/superego* and of the very entity that Freud had invested with fundamental causally explanatory power, i.e. 'the unconscious'. In order to show that there is a correlation between types of childhood experience and types of adult behaviour, as well as to show that remembering childhood situations might alter adult behaviour, we hardly need any psychoanalytic theory, let alone any reference to an unobservable entity called 'the unconscious', the philosopher Alisdair MacIntyre once famously argued. A couple of decades on, the philosopher of science Adolf Grunbaum published a provocative book called the *Foundations of Psychoanalysis*, which stirred up the debate once again by arguing that the causal inferences drawn by psychoanalytic theory on the basis of clinical evidence are not cogently tested, and because of the very nature of the so-called 'data' gathered by means of psychoanalytic method they can perhaps never be so tested. In the absence of real data that allow rigorous testing, psychoanalysis cannot be considered a 'science'.

Several of the debates concerning the objectivity of the social sciences indeed called into question the very existence of their subject matters. Take another broad example: 'society'. From the start, i.e. from when 'society' came into being as the object of a science (sociology, social science, science of society), its existence had to be argued for. In one of the early debates (mid-nineteenth century), Robert von Mohl—a professor of political science at Tubingen and Heidelberg (1824–45)—was confident that something entirely new had come into being in the last fifty years during his life, the 'particular being' of society; whereas his opponent, the historian and political writer Heinrich von Treitschke, rejected altogether the idea that 'society' existed as an independent entity. For von Treitschke, all the relations and elements purportedly constituting this new 'object' had essential, reducible links to the state, making the case for the existence of society as a separate entity redundant. And so the debate developed. Does society exist as separate from the state? Does it exist as separate from individuals? Does society have causal effects? Does it exist as an organism? And so on. It is interesting that in the 1934 *Encyclopaedia of the Social Sciences* T. Parson and R. MacIver suggest a far-reaching genealogy for the concept of 'society', going as far back as Plato and Aristotle, although—they admit—in those early days when sociology did not exist, society lacked the status of an 'independent reality'.

More examples come to mind. Does 'alcoholism' exist before it becomes the phenomenon that sociological studies of substance abuse have identified? Does 'suicide' exist before the nineteenth-century emergence of the medicine of insanity? Do 'inflation' or 'productivity growth' exist before a particular economic machinery for measuring them is put in place? Do 'cultural representations' exist before cognitive science accounts for their hypothetical existence in the context of anthropological research? While in natural science it seems intuitive that gases, molecules, and heat exist before science sets out to investigate them, this appears less intuitive for the objects investigated by the social sciences.

Still, although there is an intuitive distinction between 'brute' facts (those that would exist even if humans do not exist) and 'constructed' facts (those that owe their existence to human activity and belief), the facts that science, any science, deals with are rarely 'brute'. They are always partly 'made real' by the theories, the explanations, the categories, the experiments that different scientific investigations resort to in dealing with those facts. The objects of science (gases, molecules, heat, dreams, inflation, culture) belong to the world studied by working scientists, namely a world that includes those special categories that scientists employ to refer to the phenomena they study. Becoming a referent of scientific inquiry largely depends on the scientists' interests, lines of questioning, and techniques of salience and embeddedness in research practice. This does not mean that scientific objects are created by the scientist but that they become 'more or less' real depending on how much and how deeply they are embedded within scientific practices and scientific interests (the idea of so-called 'working objects' is discussed in Chapter 8). The historian of science Lorraine Daston shows, for example, how in the sixteenth and seventeenth centuries so-called 'preter-natural philosophy' studied phenomena such as 'images found in agates or marbles, comets presaging the deaths of kings, a Medusa's head found in a hen's egg in Bordeaux, the power of flax seeds to inspire prophetic dreams'—phenomena that were natural and yet unusual, 'beyond (preter-) nature' (2000: 15ff.). These very phenomena then faded away when preter-natural philosophy was supplanted by natural philosophy in the late seventeenth and eighteenth centuries. When scientific interest abandoned these objects, agates and marbles with strange images, comets, flax seeds, etc. stayed where they were. They only ceased to be *scientific* objects.

Accepting that both natural and social facts are partly real and partly constructed makes it mandatory to ascertain what interplay occurs between the two categories (real/constructed) when applied to each type of fact. The philosophers John Searle and Ian Hacking have addressed this particular issue.

As we see in Chapter 5, Searle reflects on the divide between natural 'brute' facts and social 'institutional' facts (as he calls them) at the ontological level: the latter, unlike the former, can only exist if they are 'represented' as being those facts (by the agreement of a community of speakers). 'X counts as Y in C' (X = a piece of green paper counts as Y = a one-dollar bill in C = the American/global financial market) is meant to express the logic by which specific functions or meanings (Y = being money) are attributed to specific things (X = pieces of paper) in specific contexts (C = economic transactions) and from within these contexts the X in question becomes what the functions or meanings say that they are (Y). They 'represent' X as a Y (Searle 1995). Thus, social facts appear to be partly real and partly constructed, though it is the constructed part that makes them exist at all as 'social' facts. Representing an individual (X) as the president of the United States (Y) is necessary to that individual's existence as president. By contrast, the top of a mountain exists independently of whether it is represented by us as such.

Ian Hacking argues not only that social facts require representations, but more specifically he identifies what type of representations are required and with what consequences for social facts and for social scientific inquiry (Hacking 1999). There is a remarkable difference, Hacking claims, between atoms, molecules, and quarks on one side, and criminals, political refugees, and children TV viewers on the other. A quark—even when it reacts to experimental manipulations—does not behave in certain ways as a consequence of how we classify it. Quarks are indifferent as to whether they are called quarks. The situation changes when we shift from natural kinds to social kinds. Social kinds are, according to Hacking, *interactive* precisely in the sense that individuals knowingly interact with the ways they and others are classified—and often their behaviour is affected as a consequence.

Distinguishing between indifferent and interactive kinds is important, for more than one reason. First, it makes us realize that forcing comparisons between natural and social sciences and expecting some substantial similarity in return is a faulty move. Second, Hacking does not recommend a strict divide between natural and social sciences—surprising as it might sound, given the distinction in classifying kinds he argues for. The objects of knowledge that social science deals with might well be classified at the same time as indifferent and as interactive kinds. For example, an autistic child can be both the bearer of a specific pathology and the recipient of a socially constructed disease—i.e. one classification does not exclude the other. This means, though, a fortiori that an epistemology built only on indifferent types is inadequate for social science. Third, and most important, there are consequences for the way research is carried out in social science. A mixture of quantitative and qualitative methods of analysis (hard and soft, general and local in a way that will be qualified later) might well prove appropriate in the social domain. This would though at the same time raise the pressing issue of how to combine procedures and results coming from different methods. Even more, this has consequences for whether and how the outputs of those combinations can be labelled 'objective'. These two issues will be addressed in the third and the final sections.

2. The Epistemological Demand: 'No Values'

A typical philosophical distinction, first formulated by the eighteenth-century empiricist philosopher David Hume, is that between the way things are (factually) and how we would like them to be, or how we think they 'ought' to be (normatively). To be objective, it has often been argued since Hume, entails both that we ought to stick only to facts and that we ought actively to pursue ways to prevent values interfering with facts. Further, it is commonly argued that science in order to be objective should only describe facts. This does not mean that scientists make no value judgements. It does mean though that the objectivity of the results they achieve in science is independent of those judgements.

Social science immediately faces a challenge: a commonly held claim is that social science is value-laden through and through. Values appear both at the level of the results of social inquiry and at the level of the means and resources of this inquiry. We see a number of examples of this in Chapters 9 and 14. For this reason, when we enter the domain of social inquiry the distinction between what is factual (or descriptive of facts) and what is evaluational (or prescriptive of facts) is difficult to draw. However, the pervasive value-ladenness of social science is not necessarily damning. Max Weber, often labelled the father of sociology and a strong supporter of objectivity in social science, engineered a strategy for relating factual research to value-laden practice while propounding a 'value-free' social science. The strategy entailed a distinction between 'value judgements' and 'value relevance' (Weber 1949). Value judgements are practical, subjective evaluations based on ethical ideals, worldviews, opinions, or standpoints. Value relevance refers to the domain of cultural and social values which attribute significance to, and reveal our interest in, what we investigate— namely those values that make segments of reality significant, or 'relevant' for us to enquire about. Social scientists, says Weber, should avoid making value judgements in teaching social science and in making claims in social science; they can instead allow value relevance in scientific inquiries. For example, the object of sociological investigation that goes under the term 'capitalism' is an object identified by a set of features which the investigator considers 'relevant' to analyse. What makes the emergence of capitalism in Europe an interesting 'object' for sociological investigation is, according to Weber, 'internal rationalisation', namely the fact that capitalism has become a systematic attempt to organize human activities in an efficient, calculable, and impersonal way. However, says Weber, once values have helped in the selection of an object for study, values have completed their job. The investigation can proceed in a scientific manner—i.e. by looking for empirical causes, evidence, laws, etc.

Weber's strategy is interesting for a number of reasons, besides that of being a precursor for positions to come. First, Weber is among the first to make us realize that not all values are alike: some are merely biases and prejudices, others might be instrumental to carrying out research. Second, he also makes us reflect on the fact that the presence of values in scientific research does not necessarily make research unscientific. It is just a matter of finding an appropriate role for the values to play. Values should be as far as possible acknowledged in social research (arguably, in any type of research) and be given a strategically relevant position in the conduct of an investigation—be it as selectors of research programmes (as in Weber himself), or as aids in deciding the acceptability of results in contexts of uncertainty (as discussed in Chapter 9) or in choosing methods (as in standpoint theory discussed in Chapter 8 and in community-based archaeology discussed in Chapter 4), or as indicators of how scientific terminology is used (as pointed out by the philosopher of biology John Dupré and discussed in Chapter 9).

A value-sensitive social science is not to be viewed as a type of inquiry that is endlessly contested or at the mercy of the most disparate interests. Quite the contrary, it is a type of inquiry that makes the facts it refers to socially accountable and open to value assessment. To see how this is possible (in a direction that takes its cue from Weber's perspective and yet makes it all the more encompassing) let us look at a contemporary example.

In Chapter 2 Parker recalls the controversy concerning the so-called 'discount rate' in economic analyses of climate mitigation. This is an instructive case of how values enter the domain of scientific analyses and drive them in specific directions, raising questions about the objectivity of the outcomes of the analyses themselves.

How much should we invest today in reducing carbon emissions to save future generations? On the basis of a cost–benefit analysis, the 2006 *Stern Review* (so-named for the British economist Nicholas Stern who was commissioned to write it) shows that the long-term benefits of reducing carbon emission immediately would be far greater than the costs of reducing them. The magnitude of these costs, we are reminded in the introduction to the *Review*, is of a scale similar to that of the Great Depression at the beginning of the twentieth century.

Those who agree with Stern were then for immediate and substantial action. However, not everybody agrees with Stern's analyses. Some argue that Stern's calculations proceeded by taking into account only the most pessimistic risk scenarios (that's the reason why the *Review* urges immediate action). There are other economic analyses, also by distinguished economists, that draw different conclusions by arguing from different premises (e.g. work by the American economist from Harvard William Nordhaus or by Richard Tol from Carnegie Mellon falls within this camp). The more or less tacit view of many

of Stern's critics is that economic conclusions should proceed from only factual considerations. Stern was accused of having imported value judgements
into his analysis: the high figure he attached to the costs of reducing emissions, it was suggested, depends on the fact that he makes use of ethical premises—very particular ethical premises—to reach his conclusions. Stern did not
stick only to 'the lore of the market'. By so doing he made his assessments
biased.

One of the central issues of dispute revolves around the values used in the
Review for the 'discount rate' for future generations. Before addressing what
is at stake I want to clarify the basic terminology. Said in simple and general
terms, the value that we attribute to the utility of future goods (goods = bread,
cars, savings, etc.) is generally less than the value we attribute to present utility. That is what it means to say that the future utility is 'discounted'. The
'rate' of discount measures how quickly utility gets discounted. What are
the reasons for discounting? And in our specific example, why discount the
utility of future generations? In answering these questions two scenarios are
envisaged by the *Review*, both entailing the resort to values.

Here is the first scenario. The *Review* employed an *expected utility* model,
which is typical in this kind of economic analysis. Utility, as we learn in
Chapter 10, is an abstract notion that stands for whatever the study at hand
deems valuable to have—with money conventionally taken as a surrogate for
this in economic analyses. The idea is to calculate how much total utility is
rational for an individual to expect from one course of action versus another.
However, whose utility? The *Stern Review* does not make calculations about
each and every individual but instead looks at different generations (present,
future). So the calculation starts with a formula that looks like this:

$$U(\text{total}) = \Sigma w(i) U(i)$$

where each *i* represents a different generation and *w* the controversial discount factors.

The *Stern Review* treated every generation (present, future) almost equally
(except for a small discount to take into account that a catastrophe might
occur and future generations not be here). So, for this purpose all the *w*s are
more or less equal (low discount rate). It is more conventional in economics
to use formulae that discount the future far more heavily. Why? It can be
just a ham-fisted device to deal with the fact that we have less knowledge
about the future, but there are also more principled reasons that arise, for
instance, from studying savings rates (the model normally used in this kind
of analyses).

It seems that in general people do not save at a rate that suggests they
value their future states as much as they value their current states. These
rates can be read from market behaviour. Stern instead seems to make his

choice of treating everybody equally on the basis of moral considerations (human beings have the same rights independently of their birth certificate). So the *Stern Review* is criticized for using a value-based rate rather than the objective observable market savings rate. This explains the large discrepancy in calculating how much future generations are to be discounted: 1.4 per cent according to Stern as opposed to, for instance, 6 per cent according to Harvard economist Nordhaus. Stern and others argue in reply—with a mix of ethical, logical, and factual distinctions and claims—that it would be a conceptual mistake to use the observed savings rate, for several reasons:

1. What is at stake is social policy and not one's own feelings about one's own future. So it should be settled by what we ought to do, not what we do do.

2. Savings rates do not express what the savers think they ought to do for future *generations*, only for future *selves*.

3. The rates don't even do this since they at best measure what savers do do for their own future, not what they think they ought to do. We know that people are prey to wishful thinking, weakness of the will, error of calculation, etc.

4. The savings rates reflect only what those whose rates are measured do, and the measured savers are nothing like a representative sample of all of us even alive now.

5. Even if they did reflect in a representative way what all of us alive think is owed to future generations, they do not take into account the views of future generations.

In the end, and most importantly, there is no way to get around making an ethical judgement. Some $w(i)$ needs to be put into the formula—not writing it down is just equivalent to setting it to 1. Whether to decide according to a moral view, or to put it to a vote by Parliament or by some other group, or to choose to use the rate at which the savers in the US or Europe save for their futures, this itself is an ethical decision.

There is though also a second, different scenario for discounting future generations (Broome 2008). Economic theory tells us that, assuming a tendency for global economy to grow (in itself a big 'if'), on average future generations will possess more goods than the present one. The more the goods, the less the value of their utility; and the quicker the growth, the higher the discount. This consideration appears at another place in the Stern model—namely, in a part of the model that considers discounting future generations not simply because they are in the future (the 'pure time discount rate' which we have been considering so far) but because they are expected to be richer. So the richer future generations are, the more discounted is the utility.

Here we face the issue: when it comes to distinctions between the rich and the poor, in calculating overall utility for policy about global climate change, should a unit of utility contribute the same, regardless of whether it is a unit for the rich or the poor, or should it contribute differently, and if differently, how exactly? So here again, in explaining one choice over another, it seems there is no avoiding a value judgement. In the service of objectivity, value judgements, like all other steps in the modelling process, can be subjected to open critical debate and probing investigation. As a start in this direction it is helpful to compare two moral theories:

1. Prioritarism: the benefit that goes to a rich person has less value than it would have were it to go to a poor person.
2. Utilitarianism: the value of a benefit is indifferent vis-à-vis who receives it (the goal of society is to maximize total utility, independently of how this is distributed among its population).

How can these two theories help us in understanding the different choices of discount rate? Assuming economic growth, future populations will possess more goods, they will be richer vis-à-vis present populations, therefore they should be discounted more—so would a prioritarian reason. Some alternative models to Stern's set a discount rate much higher than Stern's (as recalled above, Nordhaus's 6 per cent is not untypical, versus Stern's 1.4 per cent). Supposing that the overall discount for the future is primarily due to trade-offs between the rich and the poor and not to a pure time factor, then it seems that the rate in the *Stern Review* reflects a utilitarian moral theory whereas the higher rates are more prioritarian.

The two scenarios just outlined show us that it is not only economic and social facts, theories, and practices that mould models of the economics of climate change. Differences in ethical views—utilitarianism versus prioritarianism and the rights to equal treatment or not across the generations—may be invoked to explain the difference in how specific models calculate their discount rates. The *Stern Review*, by assuming an egalitarian perspective, adopts a rate consistent with what generous democratic societies seem willing to pay in taxes to redistribute wealth; whereas his opponents, by adopting an apparently more liberal and enlightened moral perspective, end up somehow paradoxically to be less generous and more conservative vis-à-vis future generations. This observation would challenge the views of some economists, such as those held by the Nobel laureate Robert E. Lucas. He claimed at the 2010 Annual Meeting of the American Economics Association: 'What disciplines economics, like any science, is whether your work can be replicated. It either stands up or it doesn't. Your motivations and whatnot are secondary.'[1] As the two scenarios here discussed outline, and despite what economists like Lucas might think, the results of the application of any scientific tool (in the case discussed, a cost–benefit modelling) are indeed informed by a value-laden choice. Nonetheless, as should appear clear by now, this does not make economic calculations of the sort here discussed subjective, arbitrary, and impossible to evaluate rationally. They certainly raise contentious questions and difficult issues of choice. Nonetheless moral philosophy is equipped to address them by analytic argument.

To conclude our discussion of this example, the task of understanding the economics of climate change for purposes of policy deliberation seems to call for an expected utility framework: we want to know at the very least what overall utility can be expected given various policy choices. But once this basic framework is settled on, there is no alternative to choosing *whose utilities* will be counted and how much they will weigh. The task requires some decision or other. If economists carrying out the investigation are to make this decision, and if this entails ethical considerations, how should they proceed? One of the central standards generally demanded of good science, whether it be natural or social, is that all aspects of the process should be open to critical scrutiny, as for instance recalled by Wylie in Chapter 4 in discussing Helen Longino's position. According to Longino, critical scrutiny is regulated by publicly acknowledged criteria, as for example recognized avenues for the criticism of evidence, methods, assumptions, and reasoning; or by intellectual authority shared equally among qualified practitioners. Acknowledging these criteria should allow for an open dialogue to take place concerning hypotheses and theories, as well as the background assumptions that frame them.

Applying this standard for good science across the board—whether it is a question of values introduced into the modelling or a more purely scientific issue—seems to require that economists be prepared to engage in an open, informed debate. It could also be argued that social scientists should feel the responsibility to consider the possible repercussions that the facts they claim to establish might have on society and public welfare. This would arguably turn their expertise into the best, most 'objective' way to offer results that meet the requirements of good governance and to inform political/social action in a democratic society.

3. The Methodological Demand: 'Follow the Best Method'

Can some methods be objective in principle—i.e. can they secure objective results because of the way they are designed? In order to be considered

---

[1] Robert E. Lucas, quoted in *New York Times*, 31 Dec. 2010; reported in Earle 2011: 230.

objective a method of analysis must normally prove to be valid. Validity is first of all characterized *internally*: on the basis of agreed upon premises the conclusions drawn must consistently follow from the application of the method in question (true conclusions).

This view has produced two strong parallel beliefs in science. First, internal validity is best identified by a number of formal requirements, which are taken to secure the consistency of results (the reasons why they obtain and why they are considered valid). Internally valid methods are normally couched in operationalized/probabilistic/statistical language. Second, internally valid methods, in the way they have just been described, are the best methods in principle and can be successfully and widely applied quite independently of context of application (or at least *ceteris paribus*, i.e. all things being equal). Let us see what each belief amounts to vis-à-vis objectivity.

3.1 *Numbers as the Route to Objectivity*

Rigorous formal methods are normally opposed to qualitative methods such as interviewing, focus groups, ethnographic observation, and content analysis, that are considered vague, subjective, opinion-laden, etc. by contrast with the more quantitative methods. For this reason, or so it is argued, qualitative methods ought to be kept at bay in good scientific research. By subscribing to this view the social sciences, where qualitative methods find a natural home, often resort to translating them into quantitative formats, as for example in case study analysis (discussed in Chapter 15), where cases and stories might be divided up in sub-units of analysis, which can then be treated according to statistical or probabilistic criteria; or in cultural anthropology, where millions of pages of ethnographic reports might be turned into patterns of coded data and then statistical analyses are done on the patterns, or elements and features in different narratives are extracted to be ranked and scored. All this entails turning words or images into numbers. Ethnographies, political speeches, television ads, are turned into a matrix—the rows being the units of analysis and the columns the variables—and by means of such transformation quantitative testing becomes possible.[2]

By prioritizing quantity over quality it is believed that bias and judgement are contained, and differences of opinion between individual researchers, as well as between different schools of thought, are minimized. For this reason, particularly in the social sciences, the demand for objectivity has often driven a preference for quantitative methods over qualitative, or more generally for

---

[2] Sometimes data are analysed in parallel by using mixed procedures. For example, quantitative methods are used to measure levels and changes of impacts in evaluation analysis and qualitative methods are used to understand the processes behind a particular observed impact.

quantification—even when this meant sacrificing rich concepts in order to promote rigour and clarity, as the historian of science Ted Porter reminds us in his book *Trust in Numbers* (1996).

Trust in the objectivity of numbers is deeply rooted in our society and in our social history. Numbers exude objectivity, Porter claims. Quantification is a safe 'technology of distance'—distance from judgement, distance from subjectivity, distance from bias. For this very reason the role of quantitative expertise in the making of public decisions has been an ever growing phenomenon in our society. Between the subjectivity of individual competence and experience and the intersubjective, public acceptance of claims to knowledge stand reassuring impersonal or mechanical forms of evaluation and communication of data. From social statistics to randomization to the composition of rates (of crime, unemployment, suicide) the route pursued via numbers is our best shot at objective assessment, so it is claimed.

Let's take a classic example. The nineteenth-century French sociologist Emile Durkheim attempted to explain the incidence and distribution of suicide in certain socio-geographical areas. To achieve this explanation he did not proceed by considering single cases of suicide and the full array of individual circumstances leading to the act. An objective explanation, claims Durkheim, should emphasize what is typical about a series of cases that display resemblances to one another and from here set out to discover the causes of each type of suicide. This is what distinguishes a properly sociological explanation from psychological ones. Psychological features change from one person to another, they 'fluctuate' depending on the very specific circumstances of each suicide (Mr X was bullied as a child for his chronically bad breath, he was abandoned by his wife who preferred an itinerant fire eater to him, his beloved Egyptian Mau cat scratched him every time he tried to feed him and did so the day he killed himself) and they cannot be generalized from purportedly similar cases of suicide.

An objective sociological explanation should target suicide as a collective social phenomenon; it should look at *rates of occurrence* of suicide: rates display enough stability and enough variability to show that suicide is a recurrent phenomenon in every society but also it shows that within each society unequal distributions of occurrences among, say, different racial, religious, or professional groups cannot be accounted for simply by referring to psychological traits of individuals. So we read in Durkheim:

> The suicide rate constitutes a single and determinate order of facts—as is shown both by its permanence and its variability. For that permanence would be inexplicable if it were not related to a cluster of distinct characteristics associated with one another and simultaneously effective despite different attendant circumstances; and the variability proves the concrete and individual nature of those

same characteristics, since they vary with the society's individual character. In short, what these statistical data express is the tendency to suicide with which each society is collectively afflicted. (1951: 51)

Why is suicide more frequent among certain groups than others (e.g. Protestants vs. Catholics)? Why does frequency vary with age, or levels of occupation, or of social integration? These are the types of questions that an objective sociological explanation should try to answer.

However, are rates such an unproblematic basis for answering them? Rates are often collated with the help of official statistics. Doubts apply both to whether official statistics are well assembled (not only in practical terms, but in principle) and to whether rates calculated on the basis of statistics of, say, suicides might take for granted questionable aspects regarding 'suicide' as a social category. As has been effectively summarized by Sacks:

'Suicide' is a category of the natural language. It leads to a variety of practical problems, such as, for example, explaining particular suicides or explaining the variety of suicide rates. To say that Durkheim's error was to use official records rather than for example studying the variation in the reporting of suicides is to suppose that it is obvious that events occur which sociologists should consider 'really suicides'. (1963: 8)

Indeed, as J. Douglas (1967) illustrated, the first problem in analysing official statistics on suicide rates is one of *definition*. A suicide is not simply a case of death. Describing a death as a 'suicide' entails attributing a particular *meaning* to that death, and the attribution of meaning is itself a complex social practice. There are also different possible ways for a death to be described as a suicide (e.g. is drinking yourself to death a case of suicide?). Therefore a statistic of 'suicides' can seem to presuppose what in fact needs to be explained or established in the first place, i.e. what counts as a suicide. Durkheim would object that the actions or phenomena that we put together share similar features. But similarity is not a given; it cannot be simply and plainly observed. It implies methods of categorization, and any such method requires decisions as to how, for example, we might restrict the boundaries of the category (e.g. including only overt cases of suicide rather than less overt cases, such as death by alcoholism, heroin addiction, and smoking, or also the category of attempted suicides). These decisions cannot be taken for granted since the choices made by the compiler(s) of the statistics affect the interpretation of the work that the sociologist does with them.

Another pressing concern involves the evidential grounds these statistics are based on. In order to issue their numerical data statisticians rely on a number of sources of evidence: coroners' reports, death certificates, interviews with the deceased's relatives and/or friends. None of these sources are neutral providers of evidence. For example, if families have been interviewed they may have lied, for they may be reluctant to discuss the fact that their loved ones have brutally ended their own lives, or they want to be kind to the memory of their beloved deceased. Reconstructing a victim's biography goes far beyond producing a plain record of his/her past. Coroners, in deciding upon a verdict of suicide, will often have to rely on their common sense in order to give meaning to very circumstantial evidence; or to endorse the evidence offered by some other expert, for example a pathologist, trained to draw certain conclusions on the basis of the available medical information (Douglas 1967).

By taking all these problems on board, we can in the end hardly agree with Durkheim when he claims: 'By proceeding in this way from the outset the sociologist is immediately grounded firmly in reality. Indeed, how the facts are classified does not depend on him...but on the nature of things' (1982: 76). Of course, pointing out the problems associated with assembling official statistics (as well as rates, scales, scores, ranks, etc.) is not meant to discourage their use in social scientific inquiry. It is meant to discourage the belief that quantitative procedures can be taken for granted, namely that they are methodologically best equipped on their own to guarantee a most objective representation of social phenomena.

Let's also briefly take the example of randomization in experimental or field trials (there will be more on this in the next section). Randomization assigns participants to the comparative groups of an experimental research on some treatment or intervention 'by chance rather than choice'. The rationale is that the participants are treated fairly (each of them has an equal chance of allocation) and the researchers avoid bias (no individual decision regarding allocation interferes with the design of the experiment). Randomization normally relies on tables of random numbers to allocate participants. The best experiments are also expected to be 'blinded': nobody knows, not even the researchers, who ends up where.

Is all this enough to secure objectivity to the methodology used? For example, it has been pointed out that randomization implies some uncertainty and individuals differ regarding their attitude towards risk. Given that in social experiments subjects are free to participate (as well as to drop out) it might be that whoever stays in the experiment is either the least risk averse (he/she does not mind ending up in the group where a powerful potentially harmful drug is administered) or, despite being risk averse, have an incentive to stay (e.g. a show-up fee) (Harrison et al. 2009). Although there are ways to treat risk attitude, or even to marginalize so-called 'sample selection bias', we ought nonetheless to reflect on the fact that no numerical procedure can secure objective results by virtue of its mechanical—in this case 'chancy'— deployment. Numbers are not objective by their very nature but are made so by practice, context, and use. What makes numbers speak in favour or against a certain hypothesis, correlation, or random selection goes well beyond the numbers themselves.

3.2 Best Methods in Principle

Between 1998 and 2001 a randomized clinical trial (RCT) was authorized by the Minister of Health in the Netherlands to deal with a staggering number (24,000) of heroin users who would not overcome their addiction by participating—as about half of them did—in some methadone programme or other. The RCT was intended to test whether additional provision of heroin would improve the medical, psychological, and social condition of these 'therapy resistant users'. The implementation of the trial came after years of debate and opposition, as well as endless discussions concerning the design of the experiment (number of participants, number of control groups, the possible benefits of a preliminary pilot study, etc.) but eventually an argument prevailed that a randomized clinical trial would be the truly scientific approach to the problem and the best method to achieve 'objective' results.

Did the RCT live up to promises? As the social psychologist Trudy Dehue points out, a series of troubling problems appeared almost from the start, emerging from trying to make the design protocols of the experiment cope with practical obstacles (Dehue 2002). For example, it was expected that the prospect of free drugs would attract large numbers of participants, so that there would not be any problem in meeting the agreed upon requirements for composing the control groups. Quite the opposite, even the minimum number required to make up the groups proved difficult to assemble. It soon became clear that the initial estimates were not going to be met and numbers had to be reconsidered in the light of the practical response. The experiment, Dehue argues, failed to take into account that addiction, besides being a physical condition, is for drug users a way of life, the expression of an alternative culture. The experiment set out an artificial culture of drug taking, far remote from what drug users are acquainted with. The participants in the trial soon started complaining that the government's heroin 'tasted differently', that there was probably something wrong with it. Unsurprisingly so, comments Dehue: 'Which wine buff would enjoy the finest glass if it were handed out through a window in a maintenance station' (2002: 90) at set times and days, after passing a metal detector door (to avoid smuggling) and with the prospect of being randomly selected for urine tests and undergoing a thorough medical and psychological assessment every month? Heroin on prescription is nothing like free heroin: it comes at a high price for individuals used to a completely different drug-taking scenario.

Besides, the design of the clinical trial pre-*ordered* the 'reality' of drug abuse into categories and classifications purposefully chosen to meet the formal requirements of the experiment. So for example, those who took part in the trial were dealt with as if they were 'patients' and this partly explains the difficulties in recruiting them for the experiment and in avoiding defections. Only those capable and willing to accept the rules and the protocols of the experiment stayed in, and many left before it ended, inducing further self-selecting strategies within the already selected groups. The problems with the execution of the trial had then little to do with whether its methodology was followed accurately, or whether infringements in the protocols of experimental research were responsible for its shortcomings. 'Even in perfect RCTs, in which each collaborator or participant fully keeps to the experimental protocol, the results cannot *represent reality as it is*' (Dehue 2002: 86). The politicians and their scientific advisers had promoted the RCT as being descriptively impartial and unambiguous, the 'best route to discover the truth'. Instead, the experiment could only represent the 'reality' allowed by the limits and constraints of its own design—which do not necessarily allow us to see what ought to be seen, or what is relevant to see in and of the phenomenon under investigation.

Would other methods deliver better results? It has been pointed out (Carlson et al. 1995) how an ad hoc ethnography could be used to develop a methodology sensitive to the complex behaviour (individual as well as social) related to drug use and HIV infection. This methodology would entail observing natural groups rather than artificial ones, participating in and interpreting drug culture rather than experimenting with clinical trials. We should not though be led to believe that participant observation is a more 'objective' way of portraying the reality of drug abuse, by simply being the better method. There are not better/best methods in principle in view of achieving objective results. The objectivity of a method is often the consequence of how a method responds to the questions posed by a specific context of investigation. Besides, best answers often come from a combination of methodologies, rather than expecting one single method to have all the answers or all the tools required in the circumstances. There is no 'golden rule', no 'one size fits all' strategy able to offer 'the most objective' assessment and to guide us confidently in making decisions on what works and what does not in real situations. In particular, we should never expect too much even from our best statistical results, our best experiments, or our best formally conceived outcomes.

The example just discussed is also a good illustration of a well-established methodological prejudice. Since we trust things labelled 'scientific', we can easily slip into the belief that anything scientific offers better solutions to any problem than anything else. We are inclined to expect objective outcomes more from the use of some methods rather than others. This is a prejudice that lurks behind much of social intervention. As it has been put, 'we know what works'[3]—i.e. in terms of best technology, best methods, best science—but *'how do we know that what we know is what needs to be known in context?'* (Seckinelgin 2008).

Adopting the 'we know what works' strategy has led—to give another example—to extended medicalization of the HIV/AIDS problem in Africa and a consequent preference for undertaking policy actions which subscribe to this view. Medicalization is an overarching process which goes as far as defining and treating non-medical problems as if they were medical problems. No doubt HIV/AIDS is a medical condition, but that is only part of the story. As in the previous examples, sufferers are not only 'patients', but also mothers, sons, husbands, members of social communities guided by rules and mechanisms that might 'interfere' with the way in which these 'patients' behave (or we expect that they behave) once they are made acquainted with their health condition. This is indeed one of the major problems in dealing with the disease in Africa, as Seckinelgin claims: most of the models of behaviour assumed by policies in developing countries are based on behavioural expectations which have little, sometimes nothing, to do with real behaviour (or else they are extrapolated from typically Western courses of conduct or models of expectation). It is not surprising, then, that the actual impact of such models is limited. However other sources of potentially useful knowledge could help—for example, so-called 'anecdotal evidence', made up of individual stories and biographies of affected people. This type of 'local' knowledge is often difficult to appraise, or systematize, but this is not a good reason for simply leaving it behind. It might indeed help contextualize what we do know and make what we know more effective.

What the cases discussed in this section seem to point out is that 'mixed' methodologies should be devised to give outcomes a wider objective basis on which to stand. Claiming objectivity for results that we obtain only on the basis of what we consider to be rigorous, or established knowledge, neglecting issues of application and context, and failing to consider how these results combine with other potential sources of knowledge, will translate not only into a restrictive, inadequate view of what to count as objective. More worryingly, all this might inform courses of action which prove inefficient, ineffectual, or detrimental. Striving for objective knowledge in social science is not an exclusively epistemological pursuit, as we are going to discuss in some final remarks.

---

[3] Repeatedly said at the African Union Summit, World Forum on Health and Development, 10 July 2003; quoted by Seckinelgin 2008: 96.

4. Conclusion

Social science, as pointed out in Chapter 1, was from the very start in the nineteenth century valued for its practical, applied implications. Producing scientific knowledge concerning society was justified by the aim of attaining a kind of understanding and control over emerging social problems similar to the understanding and control that the natural sciences possess over the world of nature. More specifically, control meant prediction: if our knowledge of social issues is predictive, then the problems surrounding those issues can be taken into account fairly in advance and possibly be solved before they become detrimental or dangerous.

Social science was meant to be the provider of data, statistics, and factual knowledge for decision-making and for social action. If, arguably, social science is to be of any use in the solution of social problems, objective facts are to be brought to bear on the solutions themselves. How can we trust social science in its applied role? There was a naïve idea that there is a fairly direct route from factual information and empirical research to theory and social knowledge, and then onto social choice and change through policy programmes. The best way to construct this route is via quantitative methods. If such a route is followed, so the argument goes, then social decisions and public policies will be 'objective'.

In this chapter we have gathered reasons to disbelieve that such a picture is adequate. Factual information, it seems, is value-laden in a plurality of ways. This is not said necessarily in a derogatory sense that tags all factual information (or whatever is presented as being factual) as essentially biased and therefore unreliable. It is instead meant to point out that value-ladenness is an aspect of factual information that cannot simply be set aside. We have also rehearsed arguments that quantitative methods should not be kept separate from qualitative ones, and even that a sharp divide between the two is untenable. Contemporary versions of socially useful research models (which you learn more about in Chapter 3), when they are not used as tools of political propaganda, have grown out of a new awareness of the conditions and limits for using the results of research and science (in fact, any science) in view of the public good.

In this arguably less naïve picture, how can we still make sense of objectivity as a regulatory principle of social scientific inquiry and of social practice—i.e. a principle that makes us 'trust' the results of that inquiry and the solutions pursued on the basis of those results? To answer this question a list of pointers or recommendations can help in identifying some of the issues that cannot be neglected in assessing the objectivity of social science research.

1. Don't think that objectivity in social science is precluded by the fact that the phenomena it deals with are—unlike in the natural sciences—partly man-made.

There is a sense in which the objects of any science are partly real and partly constructed, so comparing natural and social science in terms of a rigid divide between what is 'really' there and what is not appears ill-conceived from the start. We should rather be aware of how facts are identified in the course of inquiry, how they are described, classified, and used as relevant empirical tools of inquiry.

2. Don't think that values necessarily detract from objectivity. Value can drive research to adopt objective decisions by exposing decisions to intersubjective evaluation and by being themselves open to rational, justifiable assessment. The presence of values in scientific inquiry is not 'bad' in principle, it becomes so when values are ignored, or when tacitly adopted.

3. Take into account the ways and contexts whereby methods are put to work, under what conditions, by means of what auxiliary factors, etc. and keep in mind that the objectivity of their results (even when pursued by the most formalized techniques) is not guaranteed when shifting from the ideal (e.g. the design of an experimental setting) to the applied (a real life situation), or from one real setting to another.

4. Learn how to question the objectivity of claims to knowledge in the context of the demands posed by the problem situations under investigation, or when confronted by the needs and strictures of practice, without giving precedence in principle to particular methods (e.g. quantitative over qualitative); and be open to using a plurality of methods if the phenomena under study so require.

5. Consider that a more inclusive concept of objectivity in social science, or a more contextual one, sensitive to details and circumstances of application, need not lose its grip on reality. Understood in this more inclusive, more contextual way, objectivity might become a more realistic, yet not less satisfying, goal to pursue.

References

Broome, J. (2008). 'The Ethics of Climate Change', *Scientific American*, 298: 96–102. <www.SciAm.com>.

Carlson, R. G., Siegal, H. A., and Falck, R. S. (1995). 'Qualitative Research Methods in Drug Abuse and AIDS Prevention Research: An Overview', *National Institute on Drug Abuse Research Monograph Series: Qualitative Methods in Drug Abuse and HIV Research*, 157: 6–26. <http://corescholar.libraries.wright.edu/aids/6>.

Daston, L. (2000). *Biographies of Scientific Objects*. Chicago: University of Chicago Press.

Dehue, T. (2002). 'A Dutch Treat: Randomized Controlled Experimentation and the Case of Heroin Maintenance in the Netherlands', *History of the Human Sciences*, 15(2): 75–98.

Douglas, J. (1967). *The Social Meaning of Suicide*. Princeton: Princeton University Press.

Durkheim, E. (1951). *Suicide: A Study in Sociology*. Glencoe, IL: Free Press.

Durkheim, E. (1982). *The Rules of Sociological Method*. London: Macmillan Press.

Earle, W. J. (2011). 'Jon Elster and Economics', *Philosophical Forum*, 230.

Hacking, I. (1999). *The Social Construction of What?* Cambridge, MA: Harvard University Press.

Harrison, G. W., Lau, M. I., and Rutström, E. E. (2009) 'Risk Attitudes, Randomization to Treatment, and Self-Selection into Experiments', *Journal of Economic Behavior and Organization*, 70(3): 498–507.

Jacoby, R., and Glauberman, N. (1995). *The Bell Curve Debate*. New York: Times Books.

Porter, T. M. (1996). *Trust in Numbers: The Pursuit of Objectivity in Science and Public Life*. Princeton: Princeton University Press.

Sacks, H. (1963). 'Sociological Description', *Berkeley Journal of Sociology*, 8: 1–16.

Searle, J. (1995). *The Construction of Social Reality*. London: Allen Lane.

Seckinelgin, H. (2008). *The International Politics of HIV/AIDS: Global Disease, Local Pain*. London: Routledge.

Weber, M. (1949). *The Methodology of the Social Sciences*. Tr. E. A. Shils and A. Finch. Glencoe, IL: Trade Cloth.

Further Reading

Daston, L., and Galison, P. (2007). *Objectivity*. New York: Zone Books,

Grunbaum, A. (1984). *The Foundations of Psychoanalysis: A Philosophical Critique*. Berkeley-Los Angeles and London: University of California Press,

Montuschi, E. (2003). *The Objects of Social Science*. London and New York: Continuum Press.

Stern, N. (2006). *The Economics of Climate Change: The Stern Review*. Cambridge: Cambridge University Press. <http://webarchive.nationalarchives.gov.uk/+/http://www.hm-treasury.gov.uk/independent_reviews/stern_review_economics_climate_change/stern_review_report.cfm>. Accessed Dec. 2011.

8

Feminist Standpoint Theory

Sharon Crasnow

1. Science, Social Science, and Feminist Critiques

On 26 May 2009, United States President Barack Obama nominated Judge Sonia Sotomayor of the 2nd US Circuit Court of Appeals to fill retiring Justice David Souter's seat on the Supreme Court. In announcing the nomination, Obama (2009) remarked, 'For as Supreme Court Justice Oliver Wendell Holmes once said, the life of the law has not been logic, it has been experience; experience being tested by obstacles and barriers, by hardship and misfortune; experience insisting, persisting, and ultimately overcoming those barriers. It is experience that can give a person a common touch and a sense of compassion, an understanding of how the world works and how ordinary people live.' Eight years earlier, when Sotomayor had delivered the Judge Mario G. Olmos Memorial Lecture at the University of California Berkeley School of Law she might have been making reference to just these sorts of experiences. The title of her speech was 'A Latina Judge's Voice' and the bit of her speech that drew the most attention after Obama's 2009 nomination of her was the following: 'I would hope that a wise Latina woman with the richness of her experiences would more often than not reach a better conclusion than a white male who hasn't lived that life' (Sotomayor 2001). In the months leading up to Sotomayor's confirmation, this quote became a centre of controversy. The traditional ideal of justice as 'blind' is generally interpreted to mean that an individual's different experiences should not influence her judgements—that all good judges, using objective standards, should and will come to the same conclusions. Sotomayor's claim, and perhaps the sentiments expressed by Obama as well, suggests that individual characteristics often thought to result in bias could, in some cases, have a positive effect, contrary to the traditional view.

There are strong similarities between the debate over Sotomayor's remarks and debates that have surrounded feminist philosophy of science. As we have discussed in Chapter 7, science, like the law, has been thought of as achieving its desired goal (knowledge) through the objective use of method based in reason. This ideal has included the belief that the characteristics of individual scientists (knowers) and communities of scientists are not relevant to the successful use of scientific method and, in fact, if such social, political, and cultural characteristics do come into play, they are believed to be a danger-ous source of bias and so detrimental to the pursuit of scientific knowledge. For this reason, some have claimed that feminist philosophy of science is 'incongruous', since either to have feminist values or to think, as many femi-nist philosophers of science do, that political, cultural, or social factors, such as gender, might be relevant to knowledge challenges this ideal of scientific objectivity. But feminist social scientists in the last thirty years have advo-cated methods that do require attending to features (such as gender, race, and class) of both the knower and those whom they hope to know. They argue that the impact of the incorporation of such features into research does not always affect knowledge in a negative way but may often have positive results, i.e. produce better knowledge. Sorting out how and why this might be so has been one focus of feminist philosophy of science. This chapter investigates one influential feminist social science methodology—feminist standpoint theory—and considers several philosophical accounts that have been given to explain its success.

Feminist standpoint theory is one of three alternatives to traditional phi-losophy of science proposed by Sandra Harding, in her 1986 *The Science Question in Feminism*. Feminist standpoint theory has its roots in Marxism and takes as a starting point the idea that people in different social/political locations (different classes in its Marxist version) sometimes have access to information that those in more socially/politically privileged positions do not. Furthermore, feminist standpoint theory includes the idea that whatever access of this sort they have as individuals accrues to them in virtue of their group identity. Among the sorts of evidence that members of such groups may have this privileged access to is evidence that is relevant for hypoth-esis development and theory choice. Both the social location (social group or groups to which they belong) of the researcher and the social location of those who are the subjects of social science research are thought to be relevant to good science. These views challenge the traditional ideal of the objectivity of science, as discussed in Chapter 7.

Early feminist critique of the social sciences revolved around the recogni-tion that women had been missing from the social sciences both as research-ers and as subjects of research. It seemed plausible that androcentric bias in these disciplines could be corrected through the inclusion of women in both capacities. However, by the second half of the twentieth century, deeper critiques emerged as it became clear that some of the key concepts of the social sciences were inadequate to accommodate features of the social reality of gender. Feminist sociologists Judith Stacey and Barrie Thorne (1985: 302) describe the change:

> The initial period is one of filling in gaps—correcting sexist biases and creating new topics out of women's experiences. Over time, however, feminists discover that many gaps were there for a reason, i.e., that existing paradigms systematically ignore or erase the significance of women's experiences and the organization of gender. This discovery leads feminists to rethink the basic conceptual and theoretical frameworks of their respective fields.

An example is the need for a reconceptualization of women's work. Traditionally the analysis of labour looked only at paid work in the public sphere. A consequence of this understanding of labour is that domestic labour is invisible. Labour is reconceptualized first by including women as subjects of research, since without doing so domestic labour may not even be noticed, and then recognizing that such work is indeed labour, thereby altering the category. Another example is the emergence of the concept of 'sexual harassment'. Until the individual humiliations experienced by working women are grouped together as falling under one concept and seen as the result of the social location (gender) that women in the workforce occupy, the individual 'bad experiences' are believed to be private injustices and not an object for social science research.

Feminist standpoint theory can be characterized as being committed to some version of the following three theses: the situated knowledge thesis, the thesis of epistemic privilege, and the achievement thesis. The thesis of situated knowledge is the idea that knowledge is local in a profound way—knowledge is knowledge *for* and *by* a particular set of socially situated knowers. It can best be understood in contrast to a modernist or traditional view of knowledge—that there is one viewpoint from which the truth about reality can be discerned. The situated knowledge thesis denies the possibility of 'the view from nowhere' (as philosophers call it) and includes the claim that knowledge is relative to cultural/social/political location. Knowledge embraced by the dominant culture is not *by* those who are in the social location of 'others'—those who are at the margins (i.e. women, African-Americans, Latinos, the poor), and frequently it is not *for* them either in the sense that it does not help inform solutions to their most pressing concerns. Feminist standpoint theory is most specifically focused on cultural/social/political aspects of location and the power relations that those aspects reinforce.

In part because of the differential distribution of power, the situated nature of knowledge derives from the fact that those who are in different social locations may, and usually do have, different interests. As the sociologist Dorothy Smith puts it, 'From the point of view of "women's place" the values assigned to different aspects of the world are changed. Some come into prominence while other standard sociological enterprises diminish' (2004: 21). Among the differences that are most salient for standpoint theory are those that are in conflict with the interests of the dominant group. Thus the metaphors of situated knowledge and social location give rise to one of the key methodological tropes of feminist standpoint theory—the insider/outsider who has 'double-vision'. This double-vision is the ability to see the world both through the categories of the social scientist and through the experiences of the marginalized group. Thus the assumptions of the dominant group that are incorporated into social science may be visible *as assumptions* to the insider/outsider but not to those who lack the outsider experience. Patricia Hill Collins (1986), for example, discusses how Afro-American women sociologists might have insights that other sociologists do not. Collins says

> traditional sociological insiders, whether white males or their non-white and/or female disciples, are certainly in no position to notice the specific anomalies apparent to Afro-American women, because these same sociological insiders produced them. In contrast, those Black women who remain rooted in their own experiences as Black women—and who master sociological paradigms yet retain a critical posture toward them—are in a better position to bring a special perspective not only to the study of Black women, but to some of the fundamental issues facing sociology itself. (2004: 121)

Thus the woman who is a social science researcher may see that many of the concepts and methods that are taken for granted by those working in the field are problematic—the assumption that domestic labour does not count as work, for example.

The second thesis, epistemic privilege, has been one of the most contentious components of feminist standpoint theory. It has been misinterpreted as a claim that *all* women have access to evidence that it is not available to others. On this mistaken understanding, epistemic privilege is imagined to be automatic—merely in virtue of being a woman one would have access to information (evidence) that those who are not women do not have access to. If feminist standpoint theory is making the claim that epistemic privilege is automatic in this sense then the claim would be either trivial or false. The thesis of (automatic) epistemic privilege would be trivial if it were the claim that those who have particular experiences are the only ones who know what it is like to be the subjects of such experiences. The thesis would be false if it were the claim that all women have the same knowledge in virtue of being women, since it is clear that they do not. Women's experiences differ depending on many factors, including but not limited to aspects of their social location other than gender (race, socio-economic status, sexual orientation, etc.). But this highlights another worry about epistemic privilege. If it does not presuppose a *sameness* of women and if it acknowledges that gender is only one aspect of social location, it appears to lead to a proliferation of identities and hence many kinds of knowledge based on a myriad of different social locations. But how many social locations are there and how should they be identified and counted? Social locations seem to proliferate very quickly as we identify characteristics that enable finer distinctions within categories. Thus, misunderstanding the thesis of epistemic privilege leads to believing that it either commits us to an unacceptable relativism defined through an infinite number of social locations in combination with the thesis of situated knowledge or to ignoring real difference among women.

To understand what feminist standpoint theorists intend by the thesis of epistemic privilege, the situated knowledge and the epistemic privilege theses need to be understood in conjunction with each other and standpoint must be differentiated from a similar concept with which it is often confused—perspective. If standpoint is interpreted as perspective, we get the trivialization of the thesis of epistemic privilege and social locations multiply. According to Harding, standpoint differs from perspective in four ways. First, feminist standpoint theory

> intends to map the practices of power, the ways the dominant institutions and their conceptual frameworks create and maintain oppressive social relations. Secondly, it does this by locating, in a material and political disadvantage or form of oppression, a distinctive insight about how a hierarchical social structure works....Third, the perspectives of the oppressed cannot be automatically privileged....Finally, standpoint theory is more about the creation of groups' consciousness than about shifts in the consciousness of individuals. (2004a: 31–2)

Harding's final point emphasizes the third element of feminist standpoint theory—the achievement thesis—the process of coming to have a group consciousness that is political. Thinking of social location as *perspective* de-emphasizes the crucial political element in feminist standpoint theory. The final section of this chapter explores the importance of the political understanding of the achievement thesis in more detail.

2. Epistemic Relativism and Objectivity

Epistemic relativism—the idea that there is no set of beliefs that can properly be described as knowledge, but rather that knowledge is always relative to a particular group or perhaps even to a particular individual—is probably the most worrisome of the issues raised for feminist standpoint theory. Given that feminist philosophers of science generally argue that feminist social science is *better* science, they appear to need to appeal to a standard by which to evaluate science in order to support that claim. Since feminist standpoint theory rejects the traditional notion of scientific objectivity, which is discussed in Chapter 7, advocates of feminist standpoint theory who agree that relativism is problematic have offered alternative accounts of objectivity as part of their efforts to explain its success as a feminist social science methodology. Three such approaches are explored here.

2.1 Sandra Harding: Strong Objectivity

Sandra Harding argues that feminist standpoint theory produces 'strong objectivity' which she contrasts with 'objectivism', her characterization of a traditional notion of objectivity as disinterested, impartial, impersonal, and value-free. According to Harding, the problem with objectivism is that, because it denies that contextual values (social, cultural, and political) should have any epistemic role, the positive role that they do sometimes play cannot be explained. For example, Harding argues that democratic values are more conducive to good science than non-democratic values and that strong objectivity shows why this is so. According to Harding, strong objectivity requires that the subject of knowledge be placed on the same critical plane as the objects of knowledge. Strong objectivity requires 'strong reflexivity'— the knowers need to reflect upon the processes through which they acquire knowledge. They are to question the process of coming to know, including the nature of the knower and the context in which the knowledge is acquired. These contextual elements play a role in the determination of what counts as evidence. They shape research programmes, the formation of hypotheses, the design of research, the organization of research communities, the collection, interpretation, and categorization of data, as well as decisions about when to stop research and how results of research are reported.

Harding argues that feminist standpoint theory provides ways of achieving strong objectivity because it highlights the role of contextual factors (social location and values) in producing good science as well as bad. It does this by focusing on the subject as crucial to knowledge, explicitly identifying the subject, her perspective, and interests, and reflecting on the role the subject plays in knowledge production. The conscious identification of these factors makes it possible to evaluate which subjects and values produce better knowledge. Harding acknowledges that this account involves relativism, but she claims that it is a sociological, not epistemic relativism and so not the sort that prevents us from evaluating alternative scientific accounts. Specifically, she claims that it possible to make judgements about whether a standpoint facilitates attaining the goals of those whose standpoint it is. Does the achieved epistemic privilege of a particular group allow them to understand better and in ways that promote their ability to change their world? Does it provide knowledge *for* as well as *by* them? Such judgements provide measures of the strong objectivity of the theory.

> [A] maximally critical study of scientists and their communities can be done only from the perspective of those whose lives have been marginalized by such communities. Thus strong objectivity requires that scientists and their communities be integrated into democracy-advancing projects for scientific and epistemological reasons as well as moral and political ones. (Harding 2004b: 136)

However, Harding's strong objectivity leaves questions unanswered. For instance, by what criteria are we to judge which values are more conducive to good science than others? The example that Harding offers is that democratic ideals have been shown to result in better science. But she offers only a thin account of what it might be about democratic values that contributes to the epistemic goals of science. Democratic values might be conducive to feminist standpoint projects, which are presumably egalitarian and liberatory, but there are egalitarian and liberatory projects that are not necessarily feminist knowledge projects. How are we to decide which among such possibly competing projects is the best and so which should be pursued? The standard of feminist standpoint theory is that the better science is that which better serves the interests and goals of those seeking the knowledge. Knowing this does not answer the question, however, but only returns us to an evaluation of potentially competing standpoints. Harding argues that, rather than being an impediment to knowledge, multiple and competing standpoints are a resource for feminist epistemology. Our awareness of the different standpoint projects generated from race, class, sexuality, physical ability, and/or their intersections constrains our ability to universalize in ways that would reinforce or reproduce the power relations of the status quo. But it is difficult to see how to reconcile this pluralism with the claim that a virtue of standpoint theories is strong objectivity, which would seem to require making judgements about which standpoints are better.

2.2 Alison Wylie: Rehabilitating Objectivity

Alison Wylie's understanding of feminist standpoint theory—which we can see reflected in the discussion of collaborative archaeology in Chapter 4—is more clearly grounded in traditional standards of theory assessment. Wylie notes that 'objectivity' is frequently used to indicate a particular relationship between theory and the world and consequently is identified as a property of knowledge claims. Rather than attempting to analyse this property, she proposes that the judgement that such claims are objective is really a judgement that they conform to a standard set of epistemic virtues, such as empirical adequacy, explanatory power, internal coherence, and consistency with other established bodies of knowledge (and perhaps some others). Feminist standpoint theory provides a way of understanding how these various virtues are to be weighted as we choose among theories. They can rarely, if ever, be actualized at the same time and so we must decide which virtues are most important in any particular context. Even empirical adequacy, sometimes identified as being the most crucial of these virtues, is ambiguous. It might be either 'fidelity to a rich body of localized evidence (empirical depth), or ... a capacity to "travel" (Haraway) such that the claims in question can be extended to a range of domains or applications (empirical breadth)' (Wylie 2004: 345). In any particular context the question of whether we should maximize breadth or depth can arise. While, according to Wylie, objectivity consists in nothing more than meeting the standards that these virtues codify, some virtues could be more useful to maximize than others depending on standpoint. Standpoint theory appears to challenge the objectivity of science since, as a methodology, feminist standpoint theory advocates interestedness and partiality. But, in fact, standpoint theory might be thought of as increasing objectivity because it sheds light on the sort of empirical adequacy, explanatory power, or other virtues that are relevant for a particular knowledge project.

Standpoint theorists argue that those in positions of subordination have an epistemic advantage regarding some kinds of evidence, special inferential heuristics, and interpretative or explanatory hypotheses. Wylie affirms this epistemic privilege, though she notes that such advantage is contingent—for some knowledge projects the insights of the insider/outsider provide crucial leverage—though this need not be the case for every knowledge project. Some examples from feminist sociology are helpful for understanding what she means. Marjorie DeVault (1999), a sociologist who uses and has written about feminist methodology, gives several examples that show how the standpoint of women can reveal evidence that might have otherwise gone unnoticed. One case she describes is from the work of Elizabeth Stanko, a criminologist who has done research on the various strategies women employ to avoid assault. By asking women to give an account of 'things that we do to keep safe' Stanko elicited descriptions of a variety of activities that had not previously been seen as 'self-defence': choosing a place to live, deciding when and where to walk, choosing a time to go to the laundromat or grocery store, deciding what to wear, and so on (Stanko 1997). The descriptions women give of these activities become evidence for an account of women's strategies to avoid assaults. In conducting her interviews, Stanko functioned as an insider/outsider. As a woman, she is aware that there are many things women do that are associated with 'keeping safe' but are not strictly self-defence. As a sociologist, she recognized both the role that such behaviours play in shaping the daily lives of women and the way these behaviours are shaped by the societal structures in which women live. As an insider/outsider, she was able to put this information together to see that these behaviours can be relevant evidence for understanding how citizens defend themselves against crime. Her feminist standpoint includes awareness of how power relations shape social structures. Her results suggest the need for stretching the concept of self-defence in ways that lead to the identification of a broader range of evidence.

DeVault discusses another way that evidence can be revealed through the use of standpoint theory. In her interviews she came to see that the 'messiness' of the everyday speech of her interview subjects frequently revealed emotional attitudes that were relevant to her research project. Traditional interviewing and transcribing methods call for the interviewer to 'smooth out' these features of speech and record only the content of the respondent's remarks as data, and so as a sociologist this is how DeVault first transcribed her interviews. But as a woman, DeVault believed that the hesitations—the 'you knows' and other such features of conversational speech—were meaningful, and so as an insider/outsider (as a researcher starting from the standpoint of her subjects) she saw these normally discarded bits of conversation as evidence, since they revealed the respondent's emotional attitudes towards the topics discussed. Paying attention to them served both as a heuristic for pursuing related avenues in the interview and as evidence for claims that she made in her research. Wylie's account explains these sorts of examples. DeVault trades one sort of empirical adequacy for another. In the case of the interviews, she prefers depth of empirical adequacy rather than breadth. In the case of Stanko's investigation of behaviour women engage in to avoid assault, the research provides greater breadth in order to capture an account that will be empirically adequate to women's experience.

Although Harding's and Wylie's accounts differ, Harding's knower appears to be less stable—the multiplicity of social locations (sites for situated knowledge) threatens to dissolve knowledge all together. On the other hand, Wylie's knower is an individual whose contingent social location provides a means for recognizing that some evidence or types of evidence are more relevant than other potential evidence. For Wylie, while political values (feminism) play a role, the role is contingent. But, though the specifics of particular power relations may be contingent, *that there are power relations* in social structures is not. Although Wylie's account acknowledges this, her account is not deeply political since the account relies on contingency only in this first sense. She notes:

> ... [W]herever structures of social differentiation make a systematic difference to the kinds of work people do, the social relations they enter, their relative power in these relations, and their self-understanding, it may be relevant to ask what epistemic effects a (collectively defined) social location may have. And whenever commonalities of location and experience give rise to critical (oppositional) consciousness about the effects of social location, it may be possible to identify a distinctive standpoint to which strategic epistemic advantage accrues, particularly in grasping the partiality of a dominant way of thinking, bringing a new angle of vision to bear on old questions and raising new questions for empirical investigation. (2004: 348–9)

The qualifications that Wylie includes in this summary indicate her focus on the more general contingency—that there are power relations in social structures, not specifically what they are. Wylie's account does not do justice to the fundamentally collective and political nature of knowledge, but rather treats the political as subject to epistemic requirements that are weighted depending on values, rather than describing the epistemic requirements as being brought to bear in service of the political. For Wylie, a particular social/political location *may* allow one access to evidence that is not available from other locations but it is not a fundamental starting point for knowledge projects.

Both Harding's and Wylie's accounts provide insights into how standpoint theory might work as a successful methodology; however, each results in (different) worries. In Harding's case, she holds out strong objectivity as an alternative to both objectivism and relativism, but because of the potential proliferation of standpoints it is not clear how judgements about strong objectivity are to be made. On the other hand, Wylie ultimately bases her account in traditional empiricist epistemology and so de-emphasizes the political aspect of standpoint. Both of these criticisms are based on the view— yet to be defended—that there is something *political* that is crucial to understanding standpoint. The account of feminist standpoint theory in the next section is an attempt to follow through on that promise.

2.3 *Interest-Based Objectivity*

Another way we might think about objectivity is to begin with a recognition that the objects of scientific research are not the complex objects of the world but are instead what we might think of as conceptual models of those objects. Lorraine Daston and Peter Galison have called the objects of scientific research 'working objects'. 'All sciences must deal with this problem of selecting and constituting "working objects", as opposed to the too plentiful and too various natural objects' (Daston and Galison 1992: 85). Scientific research is always concerned with significant features of our world—i.e. features that are significant relative to the goals of the research. Consequently not every feature of reality is relevant—we do not need to pay attention to everything that we potentially could pay attention to. In order to get at the 'working objects', the objects of scientific knowledge, researchers make choices about which features of the multivarious social world are important (relevant) and in doing so 'construct' or model the objects of (social) scientific knowledge. While the objects of knowledge are not strictly speaking the same as the objects of the world—for our discussion, specifically of the social world—these working objects (modelled objects) are constrained by the actual world. They are constrained by the world in at least two ways—while we do not model all of the properties of the actual objects, the properties that we do model must also be actual properties, and the properties that we select to model must indeed be properties that are relevant to our goals. The modelled objects have to provide us with knowledge that will work to achieve those goals.

Just as in choosing features to measure and/or constructing ways to measure them, as Chapter 14 describes, for modelling too researchers choose characteristics that they have reason to believe will facilitate finding answers to the questions that are most pressing at any given time. These questions are expressions of interests and it is because of those interests that some features of the world are seen as more significant, or relevant to the knowledge project at hand, than others. While, as Chapters 7 and 9 discuss, questions are generated by our values (interests), which features of the world are relevant for answering these questions is subject to empirical constraint. Do the models constructed enable us to do what we want to do in the world? Are we able to successfully meet our goals and address our interests? We find this out by interacting with the world through our model. When these interactions are not successful we revise and adjust our models. It is not surprising, when we think of understanding the world in this way, that sometimes the interests of one group might not be met through a model that successfully meets the interests of another.

To make this clearer, consider some examples from the previous section. In Stanko's study of how women keep safe, one way of describing what she does is that she models self-defence differently than it is standardly understood. As it is traditionally modelled in criminology it would not include the ways in which women organize their lives to avoid assault, but when modelled as 'what we do to stay safe', behaviours that might not seem relevant, such as where one walks and what time of day one goes to the laundromat, become relevant. This way of thinking about self-defence challenges the traditional understanding of what the security needs of a community are. An organization of public spaces that is perceived as serving security needs might come to be seen as more obviously serving the interests of men but failing to serve the interests of women. For example, decisions about lighting in public areas might be different depending on consideration of these interests.

The assumption that domestic labour does not count as work makes the domestic tasks that are done predominantly by women invisible to social scientists investigating work. Feminist critique calls into questions such assumptions. Starting research from the everyday lives of women can reveal that the model of society that makes the daily tasks that (mostly) women undertake irrelevant does not produce an understanding of social reality that serves the interests of women in such social change. The work that (mostly) women do preparing meals, getting children ready for school, seeing that their homework is done, packing their lunches, and sending their husbands off to work in the visible economy is real work. However, it remains invisible in part because it sustains and perpetuates an institutional structure which requires the invisibility of women's work and hence the invisibility of women. Beginning from the reality of the daily lives of women makes the work visible and reveals the discrepancies that exist between their experiences and the concepts of work, leisure time, individual choices, and other conceptual models of the social world that social scientists had been using.

A philosophy of social science that considers the way that the working objects of science (modelled objects) are shaped by interests provides another way to understand what feminist standpoint theorists mean when they say that the approach provides knowledge *for* women. Feminist standpoint theory calls for an explicit awareness of women's interests as they are used in constructing models of the social world and legitimizes the role of such interests. The social science produced is thus *for* women, in the sense that it uses models that pick out the features of the empirical world that are *relevant* for women's lives. The idea that knowledge is a tool and serves some group's collective interests is explicit. Feminist standpoint theory highlights the collective and, hence, political interests of women, and so those features of the social world that contribute to maintaining the power relations that keep women in subordinate positions are relevant given the goal of transforming those power relations. The examples presented thus far serve as cases in point. Social expectations about participation in public life may not be sensitive to the understanding that women have that they need to do certain things to stay safe and so women may experience a world in which they seem to have fewer choices about where and when they may move in the public sphere than men do. If the model of the social world is not challenged then their interests may not be addressed—the liberatory and egalitarian (feminist) interests of women may not be met.

Feminist standpoint theory embeds social science in political interests and goals and so challenges the traditional ideal of objectivity described in Chapter 7. But requiring that interests themselves be acknowledged as playing a role in delineating the object of research suggests another way of thinking about the objectivity of feminist social science research. Although conceptual models are constructed, preferred, and selected relative to interests and the political values that shape those interests, it is the empirical constraint on those values that ultimately supports maintaining some aspects of the traditional meaning of objectivity. Interests are subject to empirical constraints in two ways. First, which values, actions, and social structures actually do promote liberatory goals is an empirical matter—some will work and others will not; second, which coalitions are actually formed and which interests are shared is a contingent and empirical matter. While knowledge may be relative to the interests of one or more community of knowers, that knowledge serves their interests and that those are indeed the interests of that community is not relative. Some interests are fairly easy to identify as central to the broader human community. Humans all need food, shelter, and companionship, for example. But other sorts of more specific collective interests are negotiated and require discovering (or uncovering) shared interests and forming coalitions around those interests. This is an inherently social and political activity. Minimally, when our models of social objects are constructed within the confines of fulfilling such needs then the resulting social science is objective in the sense that the modelled objects must be empirically adequate and must actually support the fulfilment of shared interests. This is interest-based objectivity.

3. Conclusions: Achieving Standpoint

Interest-based objectivity comports with the situated knowledge thesis and the epistemic advantage theses. Because the way that objects are conceived reflects interests, the differences in interests give rise to different models. To have epistemic advantage relative to those social locations results from modelling the social world in ways that are more successful for serving those interests than the available alternatives. While both Harding and Wylie give accounts in which knowledge is situated and at least some knowers have epistemic advantage, the interest-based account has the virtue of offering a better way to conceptualize why feminist standpoint theory is a successful feminist social science methodology. It provides a means of understanding how knowledge is situated and improved through the epistemic advantage of knowers. In what follows, how it can help understand what it means for standpoint to be achieved will also be explained. In giving an account of the achievement thesis other outstanding questions still need to be addressed, specifically questions about disagreements over interests and problems with the multiplicity of identities that threaten to fragment the knower and define competing standpoints. Understanding the political nature of shared interests may provide a better understanding of how feminist standpoint is a methodology that incorporates the political. In order to explore this possibility we return to the achievement thesis.

Gaile Pohlhaus criticizes Harding's explication of standpoint, claiming that it depends too heavily on the spatial metaphor of social *location*. Pohlhaus provides the following example: 'She [Harding] states "one must be engaged in historical struggles—not just a disembodied observer of them—in order to 'occupy' social locations"' (2002: 285). Although Harding puts 'occupy' in scare quotes, the force of the metaphor is to individualize the knower, since only one individual can occupy a place at one time. The location—a place occupied by an individual—does not combine well with the idea of the myriad of social factors that might intersect in any one individual, thus producing as many social locations as there are individuals and creating an untenably fragmented knower. Pohlhaus's critique thus converges with the concerns raised earlier in the discussion of Harding. Harding's knower is unstable because the categories of the social are unstable. What is needed is an account of what it is to 'occupy' a standpoint that does not depend on understanding the knower as an individual knower who shares characteristics with all other knowers in virtue of which she knows (such as depersonalized and impartial reason, on the traditional account) or portrays knowers as so fragmented that there is no basis for shared knowledge.

Pohlhaus argues that Harding's account really requires a more social conception of the knower(s). A similar point about Wylie's account was developed in section 2.2. It is important to note that a social conception of the knower is also a political conception of the knower(s), given that the social structure is structured by the distribution of power. Pohlhaus argues that in explicating standpoint theory Harding identifies 'knowing as a struggle-against and knowing as a struggle-with'. But Harding focuses primarily on knowing as a struggle-against since standpoint is seen as coming about through struggling *against* the dominant understanding of the social world. Pohlhaus notes, 'defining myself against someone or something does not necessarily facilitate my relations with someone else' and '[t]o struggle-with would involve building relations with others by which we may come to know the world and understand one another, that is the project of building knowing communities' (2002: 291–2). Understanding how knowing communities are built provides the key political element of standpoint theory and makes the achievement thesis clearer.

Pohlhaus's insight puts in place one piece of the puzzle—to achieve standpoint involves struggling-with. Worries about the multiplicity of social locations and the fragmentation of the knower still need to be addressed. A full recognition of diversity, one that allows for overlapping identities and interests but avoids the fragmentation that makes political (feminist) solidarity (shared interests) impossible, is required to complete an account of achievement and hence of feminist standpoint theory. The political process of coalition building and understanding how shared interests are forged should be part of a complete account of feminist standpoint theory since political communities are built on shared interests and forged through finding ways to adjudicate among interests when they are not shared. A feminist standpoint does not derive from some essential feature of women that allows for the postulation of a universal woman, nor is it one that is impossible because there is no one category that corresponds to the designation 'woman'. It is created out of shared interests that are built or negotiated through struggling-with.

This brings us back to interest-based objectivity. Our conception of the parts of the social world we are studying—the way we model social objects—should serve those shared interests. By starting with the lives of those she studies ('studying up') and so by working with them, the feminist standpoint theorist forges shared interests with research subjects and creates a knowledge community. Somewhere between the individual woman and the 'women's standpoint' are communities that become seized with problems that impinge on women's lives: constraints that limit their options and oppress them. Women who are engaged in social research or knowledge projects form communities around those questions because they are real questions for women, and thus the objects—the objects of research—get defined around the process of identifying what aspects of the world matter for the broad goal of eliminating oppression and striving toward an egalitarian polis. The specific forms these projects take vary locally. Such communities are not stable in the sense of being permanent; however their success depends in part on the stability that they are able to build as a community around a particular liberation project and the knowledge that they will need to achieve that end.

Thus feminist standpoint theory provides a resource for feminist epistemology in a variety of ways. It directs us to take seriously the epistemic differences that result from social location and so to include as evidence the experiences of the lives of women. One of the reasons why feminist standpoint theory prescribes that researchers start from the lives of women is because women have epistemic privilege as a result of their social location. However, that privilege is not automatic. It does not stem from merely being women but requires that the standpoint through which epistemic privilege is acquired be achieved—i.e. the result of negotiated or otherwise identified shared interests of a particular knowledge community. Wylie and other feminist epistemologists have been able to describe ways in which particular women and even groups of women at particular times might have epistemic privilege,

159

but these accounts do not entirely capture what it is for standpoint to be achieved. Interests must be collective interests, arrived at through negotiation, 'struggle-with', and engagement both among the community of knowers and with the dominant social structure.

The challenge to the ideal of the impartiality of science that feminist standpoint theory presents is indeed much like the challenge to the ideal of the dispassionate judge that appears in Sotomayor's 2001 speech. Both challenges direct us to examine the positive—not merely the negative—role played by social, cultural, and political interests that inform our judgements about the world. This chapter offers three attempts to understand how such socially located epistemic insights might work to produce political informed knowledge.

References

Daston, L., and Galison, P. L. (1992). 'The Image of Objectivity', *Representations*, 40: 81–128.

DeVault, M. L. (1999). *Liberating Method: Feminism and Social Research*. Philadelphia: Temple University Press.

Harding, S. (1986). *The Science Question in Feminism*. Ithaca, NY: Cornell University Press.

Harding, S. (2004a). 'A Socially Relevant Philosophy of Science? Resources from Standpoint Theory's Controversiality', *Hypatia: A Journal of Feminist Philosophy* 19: 25–47.

Harding, S. (2004b). 'Rethinking Standpoint Epistemology: What is "Strong Objectivity?"', in S. Harding (ed.), *The Feminist Standpoint Reader: Intellectual and Political Controversies*. New York: Routledge, 49–82.

Hill Collins, P. (2004). 'Learning from the Outsider Within: The Sociological Significance of Black Feminist Thought', in S. Harding (ed.), *The Feminist Standpoint Reader: Intellectual and Political Controversies*. New York: Routledge, 103–26. Previously publ. in Social Problems, 33 (1986): S14–S32.

Obama, Barack (2009) Remarks on the nomination, 26 May <http://www.msnbc.msn.com/id/30943237/ns/politics-white_house/t/obamas-sotomayor-nomination-remarks/#.UCAp28hYvUA>. Accessed Aug. 2012.

Pohlhaus, G. (2002). 'Knowing Communities: An Investigation of Harding's Standpoint Epistemology', *Social Epistemology*, 16(3): 283–93.

Smith, D. (2004). 'Women's Perspective as a Radical Critique of Sociology', in S. Harding (ed.), *The Feminist Standpoint Reader: Intellectual and Political Controversies*. New York: Routledge, 21–34.

Sotomayor, Sonia (2001) 'A Latina Judge's Voice', Judge Mario Olmos Memorial Lecture. In *La Raza Law Journal* (Apr. 2002). Repr. 'Lecture: "A Latina Judge's Voice"', New York Times, 14 May 2009 <http://www.nytimes.com/2009/05/15/us/politics/15judge.text.html?_r=2&pagewanted=all>. Accessed Aug. 2012.

Stacey, J., and Thorne, B. (1985). 'The Missing Feminist Revolution in Sociology', *Social Problems*, 32: 301–16.

Stanko, E. A. (1997). 'Safety Talk: Conceptualizing Women's Risk as a "Technology of the Soul"', *Theoretical Criminology*, 1: 479–99.

Wylie, A. (2004). 'Why Standpoint Matters', in S. Harding (ed.), *The Feminist Standpoint Reader: Intellectual and Political Controversies*. New York: Routledge, 339–52.

Further Readings

Anderson, E. (2012). 'Feminist Epistemology and Philosophy of Science', in E. N. Zalta (ed.) *The Stanford Encyclopedia of Philosophy* (Fall 2012 Edition). <http://plato.stanford.edu/archives/fall2012/entries/feminism-epistemology>.

Harding, S. G. (1991). *Whose Science? Whose Knowledge?* Ithaca, NY: Cornell University Press.

Hartsock, N. C. (1983). 'The Feminist Standpoint: Developing the Ground for a Specifically Feminist Historical Materialism', in M. B. Hintikka and S. Harding (eds), *Discovering Reality*. Dordrecht: Kluwer Academic Publishing, 283–310.

Intemann, K. (2010). 'Twenty-Five Years of Feminist Empiricism and Standpoint Theory: Where are we Now?', *Hypatia: A Journal of Feminist Philosophy*, 25(4): 778–96.

Smith, D. (1987). *The Everyday World as Problematic*. Boston: Northeastern University Press.

Wylie, A. (1992). 'Reasoning about Ourselves: Feminist Methodology in the Social Sciences', in E. D. Harvey and K. Okruhlik (eds), *Women and Reason*. Ann Arbor: University of Michigan Press, 225–45.

9

Values in Social Science

Heather Douglas

1. Introduction

The social sciences have long had an inferiority complex. Because the social sciences emerged as distinct disciplines after the natural sciences, comparisons between the mature and successful natural sciences and the fledgling social sciences were quickly made. One of the primary concerns that arose was over the role of values in the social sciences. There were several reasons for this. First, the social sciences did not have the clear empirical successes that the natural sciences did in the seventeenth and eighteenth centuries to bolster confidence in their reliability. Some postulated that an undue influence of values on the social sciences contributed to this deficit of empirical success. Second, social sciences such as economics and psychology emerged from their philosophical precursors gradually and often carried with them the clear normative trappings of their disciplinary origins. Third, although formal rules on the treatment of human subjects would not emerge until the second half of the twentieth century, by the time the social sciences emerged, it was obvious there were both ethical and epistemic challenges to experimenting on human subjects and human communities. Controlled settings were (and are) often difficult to achieve (or are unethical to achieve), making clear empirical success even more elusive. Finally, there is the additional complication that social sciences invariably study and/or comment upon human values. All of these considerations lent credence to the view that social sciences were inevitably more value-laden, and as a result less reliable, than the natural sciences.

While there were clear motivations for raising such a concern, many social scientists and philosophers of social science have resisted the conclusion that social science is inevitably or inherently more value-laden and thus less reliable than the natural sciences. Nevertheless, the concern over values in science has been a core element in numerous debates, including debates over what the possibilities are for unifying the sciences, whether the social sciences should be funded in the same way as the natural sciences, and whether the knowledge produced by the social sciences is generally as reliable as that produced by the natural sciences. It is around this issue, of whether the social sciences are distinctive from the natural sciences with respect to values in science, that this chapter will be framed. Rather than provide a chronology of these debates, I will organize it into three main areas of concern with respect to values in social science.

The first area concerns the role of values in the direction and selection of research, the decision about which research to do. The second concerns the role of values with respect to inference in science, the decision about what to infer from the evidence. And the third concerns the role of values with respect to language in science, and the way in which values permeate the words we use to describe things. I will examine each of these areas to survey the arguments for whether social science is distinctive with respect to the role values play in science. We will find that it is surprisingly hard to make the case that the social sciences have a distinctive problem of value contamination. Indeed, we will find that, contrary to common wisdom, the practice of science, whether natural or social, is shot through with values. We will attempt to tease apart where and how values influence social science and examine whether natural sciences are free from the same kinds of challenges as are found in the social sciences. Where values influence science, and how those values influence science, is crucial to understanding the role of values in science. By looking at the various ways in which values influence science generally, we can assess the arguments that social sciences are the same or different from natural sciences in this regard.

First, a word about values. Values here are meant to indicate normative or emotive commitments people hold. Such commitments may be tacit or explicit. They can also concern a wide variety of things, from commitments to ethical principles, communal patterns of being, or even to qualities one wants to have in one's knowledge about the world. Philosophers have carved up the possible space of values in various ways, but one common distinction is between values that concern epistemic/cognitive practices and values that concern moral and social life. Examples of cognitive values include concern for simplicity, explanatory power, theories with broad scope, and predictive accuracy. Caring about these attributes in one's science makes these considerations values, but few have suggested that these values thereby corrupt science. Indeed, these values are generally considered wholly acceptable in science, and when scientists and philosophers refer to the value-free ideal for science (whether natural or social), they do not intend to exclude these particular values from science. Instead, it is social/ethical/moral values that are thought to be the problem.

Although this distinction between cognitive and moral/social values has intuitive appeal and many adherents, it has also come under scathing criticism. Some philosophers have noted how the character of the cognitive values can be heavily influenced by social factors. For example, Phyllis Rooney has pointed out that the cognitive value of simplicity is often a reflection of the cultural context in which it is employed. A scientist tends to look for the kind of simplicity that reflects their cultural beliefs about the way the world is, perhaps a world created by a powerful and caring designer or a world in which social gender roles are a reflection of the natural order (Rooney 1992). As we see in Chapter 8, feminists and others have gone further, proposing alternative sets of epistemic virtues to show the non-obviousness of the supposedly standard canon. If cognitive values can be so heavily influenced by the social context in both their selection and their particular meaning, then it is unclear why we should be sanguine about their role in science.

But this debate over which and whether some values are acceptable gains its pointed salience when we think that understanding values in science involves deciding which ones should be in and which ones should be out. In this chapter, we will see that this is not the only, or even most interesting, question to ask about values in science. Just as important are where in the scientific process values are having an influence and what that influence is. We will now turn to three important entry points for values in the scientific process: (1) the direction of research, (2) scientific inference, and (3) scientific language.

2. Values and the Direction of Research

Whether a scientist is interested in studying humans or non-human aspects of the world, scientists have to make choices about which areas of study to pursue and how to pursue those areas. Many factors are involved in such choices. Scientists' disciplinary training will focus their attention on some aspects of the world (particularly those that they believe they have a good way of measuring) rather than others. A scientist will also be influenced by the sources of funding available. If there is more funding for research on a particular topic or in a particular area, scientists will often shift their focus to that topic, if they are unable to gain funding for their initial preferences. In addition to the influence of training and funding, there are values that influence a scientist's choice. Some of these influences have been long thought unproblematic, and even laudable. Others have been a source of concern and criticism.

2.1 *Legitimate Roles*

One way in which values influence scientists' choice in the direction of their research has long been held to be uncontroversial. Scientists can and should study that which interests them, and what drives their interest can be a range of values. They may pursue the study of butterflies because they find them to be beautiful (an aesthetic value), because they believe there are endangered species that demand our protection (a moral value), or because they find their lifecycles fascinating (a personal epistemic value). Similarly for social scientists, they may be interested in human communication on social media sites because they find the patterns of interaction beautiful (an aesthetic value), because of the need to understand a powerful force in modern culture (a moral value), or because they find the area of research intrinsically interesting (a personal epistemic value). Often some combination of these kinds of values shapes and directs the attention of scientists.

That scientists' decisions on what they research should be so deeply influenced by such a wide range of values has long been thought unproblematic. In 1904, Max Weber noted that human culture and behaviour was so complex that a scientist had to have an idea of what was significant in that complexity in order to pick it out as worthy of study (Weber 1949: 81). Many thinkers in the second half of the twentieth century agreed, noting that the problem of deciding what research questions to pursue, of deciding what is significant enough to study, is a problem for both natural and social scientists. For this decision, social, ethical, personal, aesthetic, and epistemic values all converge to shape what it is scientists choose to pursue, within a disciplinary and funding context. Indeed, scientists' choices of which discipline to pursue as a student, and thus in which disciplinary context they pursue their work, reflects an earlier value judgement which then structures their later choices.

As we see in Chapters 7 and 13, many philosophers have also noted the importance of having a diversity of views on what is valuable and interesting to pursue in science. They have argued that maintaining epistemic diversity, even fostering dissent in science, is crucial to ensuring that a sufficiently rich range of research agendas are actually pursued within the scientific community. As such, having a range of different values influencing what scientists find interesting and choose to pursue is important for the epistemic health of science. Given the complexity with which the social sciences grapple, a diversity of interests and efforts will be just as crucial as in the natural sciences.

Once scientists have chosen a particular focus for their research efforts, they must then decide which methodological approach they should use when studying their subject. Here again social and ethical values are essential, particularly because of the social scientist's focus on human behaviour and society.

Concerns over the treatment of human research subjects punctuated the last century. In the medical sciences, the brutal treatment of concentration camp victims by Nazi scientists horrified the world and led to one of the first articulations of principles for human research, the Nuremberg Code (1949). Despite the broad nature of these principles, some scientists continued to conduct unethical research into the 1960s. In the US, the revelation of the infamous Tuskegee experiments (in which African-American men were left untreated for syphilis by public health workers from 1932 to 1972 in order to track the full course of the eventually fatal disease even after the development of penicillin, a clear cure), of involuntary use of patients at the Brooklyn Jewish Chronic Disease Hospital (in which twenty-two patients were injected with live cancer cells without consultation or consent), and of the numerous additional ethical lapses disclosed by Henry K. Beecher in 1966 (Beecher 1966) led finally to the passage of the National Research Act of 1974. The Act required the ethical review of research proposals using human subjects through the mechanism of Institutional Review Boards at all research-conducting universities which decide upon the ethical acceptability of research utilizing human subjects.

While much of the public furore over the ethical lapses regarding human subjects centred on the medical sciences, the social sciences also presented cases of concern. Two experiments in particular became focal points for ethical reflection: Stanley Milgram's obedience experiment and Philip Zimbardo's Stanford prison experiment. Neither experiment physically harmed the research subjects, both used volunteers, and both produced scientifically valuable and interesting results. But both raised serious ethical worries.

In Milgram's obedience experiment, deception of the subject was key to the nature of the experiment. The subjects were told they were participating in an experiment on pain and learning, when in fact they were participating in an experiment on obedience to authority. Subjects were brought into a laboratory context, where an actor in a white lab coat told them to administer increasingly intense electric shocks to another actor, who pretended to suffer mightily as a result. (The second actor was pretending to fail at improved learning that was supposed to be motivated by pain avoidance.) Milgram was interested in the extent to which the average person would cow to the authority of the 'scientist' with the clipboard, inflicting suffering in ways they would never do normally. Disturbingly, most subjects proved quite obedient (Milgram 1963).

Although the subjects were told of the nature of the experiment after it was over, and met with the actors so that they could understand that they actually had not harmed anyone, great concern was raised over both the psychological harms such an experiment might produce in the subjects and the general inability to have fully informed consent for the subjects. Research subjects could not be informed about the nature of the experiment because the experiment depended on deception. Without the subjects believing that the actor actually was receiving painful shocks, the experiment would not have been able to get at the phenomena of interest: the extent to which ostensibly ordinary and good people will cow to authority, even when their own safety is not at risk.

Were the risks of harms to the subjects (from the stress of having participated, and of the changed self-conception they could have as a result of their participation) worth the knowledge produced? Milgram defended these experiments on the basis that the information gleaned was very valuable to society—both so that the phenomena of authority could be better understood and so that individuals might be made aware of the powerful effect authority figures can have and of the importance of one's own moral compass. Social scientists have debated these issues ever since the Milgram experiments. Many insist that some deception of the subject is worth the knowledge that can be so produced, and that as long as a reasonable person would agree to the risks of the experiment, it is not necessary to inform every subject of the precise nature of the experiment before conducting it (although most agree that coming clean afterwards is essential). Others argue that informed consent is impossible in deceptive research, and thus any deceptive research violates basic human autonomy.

Zimbardo's Stanford prison experiment was far less dependent on deception but still raised ethical concerns. Philip Zimbardo was a social psychologist interested in the social conditions that produced pathological behaviour and in the problems of the American prison system. Participants in the study, largely white middle-class males, were recruited in a transparent way, informed that they would be signing up for a study of prison life, which would include 'an invasion of privacy, loss of some civil rights, and harassment' (Zimbardo 1973: 254). After preliminary screening to remove potential participants with pre-existing psychopathology, the researchers divided the participants randomly into 'prisoners' and 'guards' (Haney et al. 1973). Prisoners were picked up by the local police, who assisted in making the study realistic, processed in the usual way, and then turned over to Zimbardo's mock prison, built in a basement at Stanford University (Haney et al. 1973). The one deception in the study was that guards were led to believe that they were not subjects in the study, that the study was primarily interested in the effect of imprisonment on the prisoners. But in fact, the behaviour of the guards was of equal interest. Although the study was slated to run for two weeks, Zimbardo ended the study early, after only six days, because of the disturbing behaviours that emerged and concern for his research subjects.

Subjects were told that they would not be subject to physical abuse (or be allowed to utilize physical punishment), but verbal harassment was allowed. Despite the fact that the participants all knew the assignment to 'prisoner' or 'guard' was arbitrary, the guards and prisoners took their roles all too well. As the study reported, 'Despite the fact that guards and prisoners were essentially free to engage in any form of interaction (positive or negative, supportive or affrontive, etc.), the characteristic nature of their encounters tended to be negative, hostile, affrontive, and dehumanizing' (Haney et al. 1973: 80). The prisoners became passive and withdrawn; the guards became aggressive and controlling. The stress on the prisoners was clearly too much (one developed a psychosomatic rash). Zimbardo closed the study, to the delight of the prisoners, but apparently to the chagrin of the guards, some of whom enjoyed wielding power over the prisoners (Haney et al. 1973: 81, 88).

The Stanford prison study became one of the most important social psychology studies of the twentieth century, demonstrating to many the power of social contexts and cues, even when we know that our place in these social contexts is entirely arbitrary. Like the Milgram experiment, the Zimbardo experiment provides insight into the roots of tyrannical and abusive behaviour for some contexts. But it also provoked a great deal of criticism. Zimbardo was surprised by the strength of the reaction and thus did not fully anticipate what would happen in the study. Participants clearly suffered during the study but apparently did not suffer from long-term psychological damage (Haney et al. 1973: 88; Zimbardo 1973: 249, 254). But the disturbing nature of the study and its results have caused ethical soul-searching over whether such research can and should be done.

Indeed, social psychologists Stephen Reicher and Alexander Haslam have argued that Milgram's and Zimbardo's experiments, and the subsequent ethical concerns, effectively blocked similar research for nearly thirty years, particularly research concerning the social psychology of tyrannical or unethical behaviour, greatly hampering theoretical understanding of social roles and their impact on ethical decision-making (Reicher and Haslam 2006). Without the stomach to subject human participants to controlled social contexts where we can see under what conditions tyrannical human behaviours might be produced, we have been left with underdeveloped theory and evidence about such social contexts, and focused more on neurological and individual cognitive factors. This dearth Reicher and Haslam find unacceptable and distorting.

Rather than try to settle the debate over deceptive and/or disturbing research here, it is important to note the importance of values in the debate over methods in research. In the methodological judgement of whether to proceed with a deceptive experiment, the social scientist must decide which is more important: the value of human autonomy and fully informed consent of research subjects or the value of the knowledge that might be produced. The two values must be weighed against each other, and both have a legitimate role in directing how research should be done. In the case of disturbing research, like Zimbardo's, we face a similar difficult weighing of values. Here, one must decide whether the knowledge produced is worth the distress that will likely be caused to the subjects. Now that we know social group situations can cause such behaviour, should we open human subjects to this kind of disturbing experience, where subjects might be forced to confront the fragility of their identity? Will the knowledge of how social context can create unethical behaviour be worth the even temporary distress caused? This is obviously a difficult judgement to make, and one the researcher (who will likely be biased in favour of the value of their research) should not make on their own. This is one reason why an independent review of research methods is needed. (Zimbardo's study was indeed approved by Stanford's research ethics oversight committee. Zimbardo himself argued after the fact that such studies should have independent continuous oversight: Zimbardo 1973.) Values on both sides of the argument have a clear role to play in deciding what a scientist should do.

Concerns over deceptive or disturbing research are not the only place where competing values in social science methodology legitimately arise. In the information age, ethical concerns over the privacy of human subjects are an increasing locus of attention. Social scientists often collect large multi-attribute datasets, with information arising from surveys, records, or online activity. While social scientists take care to anonymize such information, several studies have suggested that it is relatively easy to de-anonymize the dataset with just a few specific pieces of information. The extent to which privacy must be protected, and the extent to which the very gathering of information to study human behaviour can place those being studied at risk of losing their privacy even if anonymizing techniques are used, will require our attention and deliberation in the coming years. We will need to weigh the various risks, considering the extent to which we value privacy and the extent to which we value the knowledge that might be produced.

It is clear that ethical and moral values are needed to place restrictions on how research is conducted and how data are handled. In cases where a methodology violates a basic human right, such as the Nazi medical experiments where people were tortured and killed, ethical and moral values rightly forbid pursuing such research. Because we value human rights more than the value of knowledge that might be produced were we to violate human rights, prohibitions on such research prevail. It is better not to know, or to have to use a less than ideal methodology (one which does not involve rounding people up and doing research on involuntary subjects), than to pursue knowledge despite these moral concerns. The moral concerns trump the epistemic value, the value of knowledge.

But in cases where it is less clear that a basic human right has been violated, such as in cases of deceptive research, disturbing research, or concerns over privacy, we need to decide on a case-by-case basis whether the pursuit of the research agenda is worth the risks posed to individuals who are either subjects of the research or whose personal details are central to the research project. Here, both the social/ethical values and the value of the knowledge must be considered carefully. Both have a legitimate place on the table.

2.2 Illegitimate Roles

In addition to these proper roles for values in the shaping of methodology, there is another way in which values could influence methodological choice that is more fraught. Instead of running roughshod over human rights or creating moral concerns over the method of producing knowledge, a scientist could be tempted to produce a methodology that will ensure a particular result. Here, the value of knowledge itself, that it is produced in a genuine attempt to gain understanding, is violated in favour of a preferred societal outcome. An example will help to illustrate why this is not acceptable.

Suppose a social scientist is convinced that, if society believed a particular claim was true, that society would be better off. For example, suppose the claim was 'Caring for a dog is good training for being a parent'. Now, this claim might be true, but what is important to us is what grounds we have to believe it is true, and in what contexts. Suppose our social scientists already strongly believe the claim (perhaps because of personal experience) and they want to generate the empirical evidence to show that it is true in order to support general public policies such as encouraging people considering becoming parents to adopt dogs to see whether they are cut out for parenting. Suppose our social scientists proceeded to attempt to gather evidence for the claim by doing things like collecting evidence on the rates of child abuse among parents who raised dogs prior to parenting vs. parents who did not. And suppose they tended to throw out cases where clearly sociopathic or psychopathic tendencies could be surmised in the parents because they were 'outliers'. And in cases where parents had raised dogs and also abused kids, the scientists presumed sociopathic tendencies. Notice what the social scientists have done—structured their study so that a particular outcome is nearly assured: dog training makes one a better parent.

The scientists in this case may have the best of intentions. They may truly believe raising dogs makes one a better parent and they may truly believe that convincing others of this will produce a better society. (And it may be true!) But the scientists are violating the value of doing science, of attempting to produce genuine empirical evidence, which may or may not support one's preferred theory. The value we place on science rests on the fact that it is empirically supported knowledge and that it is always challengeable based on new empirical information. But this means that scientists, when developing their specific methodological approaches, must have methods which can produce empirical surprises—which are open to finding out that the world is not the way they thought it was.

There is a subtle tension between moral and epistemic values in the methodological choices of scientists. As I have noted, some moral values place clear restrictions on what scientists can do with or to human subjects. The value of knowledge is outweighed by the moral value. But the value of the knowledge is not undermined or violated by the moral value. It is rather that we have decided that the knowledge is not worth the moral costs. If there is another way (even if less epistemically ideal) to pursue that knowledge without going against these strong moral norms, the scientist is free to do so. In cases such as the Milgram experiment, the moral concerns about deception compete with the value of the knowledge to be gained. If the knowledge is particularly valuable, we might allow some deception, even some psychological distress, to be inflicted, as long as it is not too severe or harmful, and as long as key basic human rights (e.g. the right to depart an experiment and the right to know what was going on afterwards) are fully respected. Social and ethical values can compete with and outweigh the value of knowledge in methodological choices.

However, one value outweighing another value is not equivalent to undermining a key value. This undermining (or violation of) the other value is precisely what happens with illegitimate uses of values in the direction of research. When the scientist jerry-rigs their methodology to ensure the production of a particular empirical result, the value of knowledge is *damaged* by moral or social values, not just outweighed by them. To pursue a method with no possibility of genuine discovery is to harm the value of knowledge itself. Methods should enable us to investigate the phenomena of interest, not produce predetermined results. Respect for the value of knowledge must remain intact and on the table even if at times it is outweighed by other values.

Values are crucial for directing our attention and for reminding us of the limits of what we should do when pursuing scientific knowledge. But the value of knowledge itself must also be respected. Even when outweighed by potent moral and ethical values, the fact that we do value scientific, empirical knowledge, and the basis of that value (genuine empirical discovery) means that scientists should not make choices which undermine or damage that value. At the same time, the value of knowledge can be outweighed by moral and ethical values, which means scientists cannot pursue every possible means of producing new knowledge. Values thus play a pervasive and important role in determining the direction of social science research, as they do in natural science research.

3. Values and Inference

The importance of values in shaping the direction and methodologies of the social sciences is widely acknowledged and uncontroversial. What is of greater concern is the role of values in scientific inference. There have been cases in the history of science where scientists' societal values have badly distorted how they have viewed the available evidence and what inferences they have drawn from it. There have even been cases where it seems that scientists have allowed their values to trump the available evidence, causing them to ignore it, or to fabricate evidence more to their liking.

One of the most famous cases involved a scientist named Cyril Burt. A psychologist convinced of the strong hereditability of intelligence, Burt was having difficulty finding good evidence to support his claims, particularly as his views came under increasing criticism in the 1950s. Because human behaviour was known to be influenced by both genes and the environment, studying differences in intelligence among families was not enough to establish the genetic basis of intelligence. Smart parents having smart children could be due as much to the intellectually rich and challenging environments in which the children were raised as to the genes the parents passed onto their children. And switching children at birth to different environments would be obviously unethical. To get around these methodological difficulties, Burt claimed to study identical twins separated at birth and raised in different households, comparing them to identical twins raised together. If the twins raised apart had as strongly correlated IQs as twins raised together, and if the environments for separated twins were substantially different, Burt could claim to show that IQ was strongly genetically determined (Fancher 1985).

Unfortunately for Burt (although perhaps fortunately for the children), there were not many twins separated in this way. But Burt was so convinced of the accuracy of his views, he was so sure he was right, that he manufactured the data to support his belief. Disturbingly, his fraud went unnoticed for decades, and his fabricated studies were widely cited as a key source of evidence on the genetic component of intelligence. It was only when some careful observers noticed that the statistical patterns in Burt's data were too perfect that his deceit was uncovered and his reputation destroyed (Fancher 1985). As Fancher notes, other legitimate studies of twins showed a much messier picture, because of the selectivity of adoptive homes and because of the very small numbers of twins raised separately. In short, there is no good evidence from such studies on the genetic hereditability of IQ.

Although the case of Cyril Burt is extreme, wherein sets of twins were invented out of thin air, this pattern—a pattern of such deep conviction of one's views that one comes to believe the correctness of one's claims *despite* the available evidence—is a deep worry about the role of values in science. The more recent case of fraud involving Marc Hauser at Harvard shows that the concerns over cases like Burt's are still with us. Hauser was a world-famous cognitive scientist who studied primate behaviour in order to understand the nature of animal (and human) cognition. In his studies, he would expose primates to various stimuli and record their resulting behaviours. Officially, tapes of the behaviours were to be coded 'blind', i.e. without knowledge of what the stimuli for the particular tape were. Yet Hauser's coding did not match those of his research assistants (Gross 2011). When the discrepancy was discovered, Hauser attempted to force his research assistants to use his assessment of the primates' behaviour. Worried about the integrity of the study, the assistants reviewed video tapes of the monkeys' behaviour and did not see what Hauser claimed he saw. As the case unfolded, other examples of fraudulent assessment of evidence by Hauser became apparent. It now appears that Hauser regularly fudged data to produce the desired results. Hauser has since resigned from Harvard University.

One way to read such cases is to see Burt, Hauser, and similar fraudsters as selecting a methodology guaranteed to produce a particular result—namely that they make up the data so that such a result is produced! The value of getting the desired result is driving their choices, determining what it is they will do. As discussed in the previous section, this violates the value of knowledge and is thus unacceptable.

Another way to read such cases, particularly if the scientist is genuinely attempting to collect and interpret data, is not that their methods are deeply flawed but that at the moment when they must decide what to make of the evidence, when they must decide what to write in their lab notebook or how to interpret what they see, strongly held values are distorting how they view the evidence so much that the results are dictated by the values rather than the evidence.

That values could play such a role in our reasoning is deeply worrisome to scientists. If, at the moment when we interpret a complex set of evidence, our values are determining what we see in that evidence, or even what comes to be seen as evidence, then we are merely reproducing our own wishful thinking rather than investigating the world. It is because of such worries that many scientists and philosophers of science have argued that the internal reasoning of science should be 'value-free', in the sense that ethical, social, and personal values should not influence such reasoning. It is also because of such worries that scientists use blinding where they can when characterizing evidence, as we see in the discussion of randomized control trials in

Chapters 3 and 16. If they do not know what the particular case 'should' look like (in order to support their theory), they are less likely to describe it using wishful thinking.

The picture of values in scientific reasoning gets more complex, however, when we realize that values can play two different roles in scientific inference. In the examples just discussed, values are playing a direct role in the reasoning. The values are determining what is made of the evidence, directly shaping its characterization and interpretation. The value serves as the reason (often implicitly) for the choices of the scientist. This is clearly unacceptable if we are to respect the scientific process and the value of knowledge properly. But this is not the only role values can play.

There is also a more subtle role values can play in science. This role, what I have called an indirect role, operates only through the uncertainty in the claim being made (Douglas 2008). In any case of evidence interpretation, of deciding what to make of a set of evidence, there is some uncertainty. This uncertainty can be avoided only if the claim follows deductively from the evidence, which would require that the claim be very limited and usually uninteresting. For example, suppose a group of scientists gathered evidence on the handedness of a group of people. They found that eighty people in the group were right-handed and twenty were left-handed. From this, it can be concluded deductively that 80 per cent of the people in the group are right-handed. But this is really uninteresting. The interesting claims come from expansions on what this sample group means for a larger group. If the group was properly sampled from a population, should one draw the conclusion that in the larger population, we should expect 80 per cent of the people to be right-handed?

Notice two important points. The first is that, while the evidence clearly supports the broader claim about the population, it cannot definitively support it. There is still substantial uncertainty on whether the broader claim is true. Perhaps our sample was not sufficiently representative or perhaps, despite careful sampling techniques, we unluckily drew a skewed sample. In every case of scientific inference where the conclusion does not follow deductively from the evidence, we have some uncertainty. The second point is that we must invariably decide what we should do in the face of that uncertainty. We must decide whether, in our judgement, the evidence is sufficient to support the claim we want to make. It is in making this judgement that values play an invaluable role, the indirect role.

How do values help us make this judgement of whether the evidence is sufficient? One crucial way is in helping to assess the importance or significance of making an incorrect choice. There are often clear and problematic consequences of mistaken judgement. It is most important to scientists to avoid accepting claims as well-supported before they are. Such early acceptance could lead to lots of problems in science, of building complex theoretical edifices with scant support, of doing research on what one thinks is a sound foundation only to find it thoroughly eroded later. It is because of these concerns over the potential consequences of making a mistake that scientists usually demand statistical tests to see how likely the pattern of evidence would be if the hypothesis were not true and demand that the probability be low.

Indeed, one can read some of the value of the traditional cognitive values as hedges against premature acceptance of a claim based on evidence. If the claim is simple, and thus easy to test, or has broad scope, and thus has many venues of potential testing, or has explanatory power, and thus again can produce many possible tests, scientists might be willing to see the evidence as sufficiently supportive of the claim, with the idea that further tests are readily forthcoming and will be assiduously pursued. A complex, narrow, or limited claim often requires stronger evidential support, if further evidence to support it is likely to be hard to come by. But note that the values here are only valuable to the extent that they indicate the range of testing options and the extent to which those testing options are actually pursued. The presence of such values are not indicative in themselves of the reliability of the claims.

Concerns over importing a false claim into the body of scientific knowledge are not the only important consequences of error. There are also societal concerns to consider, over possible consequences of accepting a claim as well supported when it is not, or conversely, rejecting a claim as insufficiently supported when it is in fact true. Such societal impacts can be crucial for when we should think a claim is sufficiently well-supported, particularly when that claim is relevant to social policy.

Consider, for example, whether or not Zimbardo's Stanford prison experiment provides sufficient evidence that human beings in the right social settings will tend toward tyranny. Does the Stanford prison experiment show us that prisons are hopeless, that the power imbalance will necessarily produce widespread and egregious abuse? Should we give up on prisons as inhumane as a result of the experiment? Clearly, Zimbardo's study raises concerns about how social context can bring out the worst in us. But the study has been criticized as not being quite as straightforward as it first appeared concerning whether the prison system per se is likely to produce the worst behaviours. In addition to Reicher and Haslam's concern over the lack of further study, they suggest that it was not just the prison structure that produced the behaviours so disturbing to Zimbardo. Just as important may have been Zimbardo's leadership role in shaping the sometimes extreme behaviour of the guards. Zimbardo apparently briefed his guards that they were to 'take away [the prisoner's] individuality in various ways' and produce 'a sense of powerlessness' (Reicher and Haslam 2006: 4). If Zimbardo primed his guards in this way, it is less clear that the social role of guard spontaneously produces aggressive and tyrannical behaviour. Zimbardo was possibly instrumental in that transformation. Reicher and Haslam thus ran a similar study, creating a mock prison with the help of the BBC, with different results (Reicher and Haslam 2006). Although roles were taken on by prisoners and guards, the guards were less oppressive and the prisoners more assertive of their rights.

So the implications of Zimbardo's experiment are not quite as clear cut as one might initially think. There is some uncertainty concerning both what one should conclude and what further inferences should be drawn from the available data. Whether the evidence is sufficient for a particular claim depends in part on what we think the consequences of error are for the inference we are considering. Should one conclude that social contexts determine behaviours in prisons? Probably not. There is not enough evidence, and if we conclude that incorrectly, we could undermine the sense of individual responsibility people have, with harmful effects resulting. In addition, if the prison context necessarily results in dehumanizing behaviours, it seems we should abandon wholesale our penal system (and perhaps we should). But doing so erroneously would impose high costs, which should warrant further study. Holding off on such a conclusion until the issue is better studied imposes a potentially inhumane system on current prisoners, if it turns out the prison context is irredeemable. Given our value-laden assessment of the consequences of error and the available evidence, it seems such a strong conclusion would be premature. More plausible is that we should conclude that the nature of a social context does shape human behaviour—while not determining it. There seems ample evidence for that, and ignoring that possibility if it is true would lead to ignoring ways in which we could alter social contexts to bolster ethical behaviours. Indeed, pursuing social psychology to understand how to improve ethical responses and how to forestall dehumanizing tendencies through altering social cues seems a promising research agenda.

Such weighing of the consequences of premature or late inference (or false positives and false negatives) to assess whether the evidence is sufficient is a common issue in social science. One can think of examples from education policy (do standardized tests properly assess student learning? would a longer school year help students?) to economic policy (would lowering interest rates help the economy? what measures would help get people out of poverty?) where the issue of the sufficiency of evidence is a central part of the debate. Ethical and social values on the potential consequences of getting it wrong are needed to weigh the sufficiency of evidence across these cases.

Thus, societal and ethical values are important for deciding which consequences of error we might be willing to accept in the face of uncertainty, and which we would not. If our values—whether due to concerns over the body of scientific knowledge or concerns over the societal impact of knowledge—tell us that given the uncertainty present the risk of a false positive is too great, we need to do further research before seeing the available evidence as adequately supporting the claim in question. On the other hand, if our values suggest that given the uncertainty present and the current strength of evidence, the risk of a false negative is too great, then we should accept the claim as sufficiently well-supported (for now). Both decisions can of course be overturned as the research process proceeds. But when we need to make a decision on what to infer, and on whether the evidence is sufficient at a point in time, values of all kinds have an important role to play.

This 'indirect' role is important for both the social and the natural sciences (Douglas 2008). For just as the social sciences make inferences about the available evidence in the face of uncertainty, so too do the natural sciences. Natural scientists face judgements about how to best characterize their evidence and whether that evidence is sufficient to support the hypothesis of interest. Even in a controlled laboratory setting, the scientist must decide whether the experimental run was a good one, whether other interfering factors mean it should be thrown out, and precisely how it should be characterized. Scientists work to reduce these points of judgement, but they are not eliminable. And the scientist must still decide what counts as sufficient evidence.

One might wonder, however, whether the subjects that social science tends to study might make performing scientific inference properly more challenging. That is, because social science often studies things that are valued in a culture, or by the scientists themselves, that they might have greater difficulty in maintaining values in the indirect role at the heart of scientific inference, or that even within the indirect role, their strong value commitments could distort their inferences. Given that social scientists often address powerful human concerns, from criminality and punishment, to gender roles, to the causes of poverty, to the roots of violence, this is clearly a worry.

But, given the powerful impact and relevance of the natural sciences on human societies, we should be sceptical that this problem is particular to the social sciences. Natural scientists have produced some (although not all) of the most profoundly societally disturbing results of the past century, challenging our conception of ourselves and of the way in which our society functions. The discoveries of the persistence of human chemicals in the environment (such as DDT or CFCs) and of the impact of human activity on the planet have made it quite clear that our natural environment is not an unlimited resource for our use, but rather has limits we would be unwise to push beyond. We have also learned of our profound physical dependence on natural systems, such as water purification systems in wetlands, flood control in forests, and the oxygen production of plants and algae. Neither the natural nor social sciences can claim to study that which is not of great import to, or even constructive of, what humans value.

Given the crucial role of values in shaping what we study we should be surprised if it were otherwise. At the same time, the importance of not seeing the world the way you might want it to be, of not allowing values (through a direct role) to distort inference about the world, should be held in the forefront of the scientist's mind. Even if the scientist uncovers uncomfortable results, such as a link between animal abuse and human abuse or the difficulty of predicting certain kinds of economic recessions from past data or in the case of natural science, of discovering ozone thinning, problematic ecosystem effects of chemical use, or climactic change, it is better to confront the evidence as it stands than to wish it to indicate something other than what it does. We can have legitimate debates over how much evidence is enough for any given claim, or how well-characterized the evidence needs to be. But we should not ignore or neglect evidence because we should prefer it to be otherwise. Nor should we construct evidence because we want or will the world to produce such evidence. Such uses of values in inference devastate the value of science itself, whether natural or social.

The pervasiveness of the indirect role for values in scientific inference does have an important policy implication for social scientists. Because the scientist must use values to decide when the evidence is sufficient, they should be clear about which values are shaping their decision in any given study. That is, they should be clear about why they think the evidence is sufficient in their work. Such clarity means that scientists must culturally abandon the value-free ideal, eschewing the image of themselves as interchangeable inference makers. Different scientists will have different values and thus see different inferences as warranted. But with the value-free ideal set aside, this source of rational disagreement can be brought out into the open and become a source for robust discussion both within and beyond the scientific community.

4. Values and Language

Values thus have a pervasive, yet limited role to play in social science inference. But there is a more subtle influence on scientific knowledge that has long been of concern in the social sciences. This influence arises because much of our language carries with it value inflection, and scientists are invariably bound to use language when doing their work. While scientists often invent new terminology as their work develops, they just as often use existing language, whether as a metaphor or a direct import, to aid with clarity in understanding phenomena. When the language carries with it value connotations, those meanings get imported into the heart of the science.

To see how this can be a problem, consider the following examples. Philosopher John Dupré has discussed the way in which scientists studying animal behaviour have used the term 'rape' to describe a behaviour in animals that they see as similar to the human crime of rape, namely copulation that appears to be against the wishes or will of one of the participants (usually the female) (Dupré 2007). In utilizing the term 'rape' the scientists seek to provide a term that gets clear on what the behaviour is, but the scientists also seek to provide an explanation for the behaviour in reproductive terms: namely that rape is a strategy employed by males who are unsuccessful at attracting mates through other means. The scientists who develop such explanations are not seeking to 'justify' or legitimize the behaviour in humans, but their use of the term often has that effect. Even more pernicious, the use of the term tied to the idea of a reproductive strategy obscures many of the actual facts about human rape—that it often has little to do with reproductive urges (as many of the victims are clearly not reproductively fertile, being children or beyond child-bearing years) and that human rape is more about power, violence, and control of the victim. The importation of the term 'rape' to animal behaviour obscures this, even as scientists attempt to illuminate (poorly) the animal behaviour they seek to describe and explain. The value connotations of 'rape' create distortions in our understanding that reverberate back to the original meaning of the term.

In the case of 'rape', clearly a better term is needed, one that does not draw parallels with a human crime. But other cases of the importation of language with value connotations have produced clarification rather than distortion. As Michael Root has argued, the use of the terms 'spousal abuse' and 'wife battering' by sociologists in the 1970s helped to illuminate general patterns of behaviour in the abuser and general patterns of harm in those who were abused (Root 2007). The term, with its value-laden connotations of something that should not be done and that is harmful, allowed an area of human behaviour to be conceptually organized in an illuminating way, and led to changes in policies (such as the establishment of women's shelters). Thus, sometimes the use of a value-laden term can reveal rather than obscure.

Finally, some terms used in social science become contested because their normative content is unavoidable. Consider, for example, the term 'involuntary unemployment'. Someone is involuntarily unemployed when they cannot find employment, as opposed to being voluntarily unemployed when one does not wish to work despite available employment. Clearly, involuntary unemployment is an economic problem, whereas voluntary unemployment is not. But what should count as involuntary unemployment? Does involuntary unemployment actually exist? If one cannot find work suited to one's skills and abilities, and thus keeps searching for a job, despite more boring, dangerous, or menial work being available, is one's unemployment truly involuntary? As Hausman and McPherson (2006) have noted, it depends on what one considers voluntary. If all the choices before a person seem truly awful, the choice context may seem so coercive that any choice seems involuntary. Should people in such a context be put together with the (very rare) situation of not having any choices at all? The decision on how to categorize job seekers is clearly a moral decision, not just a value-free empirical decision by economists. At the heart of the debate over involuntary unemployment is the question: should the autonomy of the individual to decide when a job-seeking context is so bad it feels coercive be respected? Or should economic experts decide when someone should have been willing to take a job, and thus the expert decides when the unemployment is voluntary or not? Such debates show how value judgements, moral judgements, play a role in shaping language, and the characterization of empirical phenomena, deep in social science.

Because of the social science's focus on human behaviour and society one might think that such challenges of value-laden language are unique to the social sciences. But this would be a mistake. As Kevin Elliott has shown in analysis of language choices in the assessment of chemical contaminants in his debates over what is known as 'hormesis' or in the debate over whether a particular medical syndrome should be called 'multiple chemical sensitivity' or 'idiopathic environmental intolerances', language choices are fraught and sometimes value-laden in the biological and medical sciences as well (Elliott 2011). Given the complexities of human language and the widespread use of it in the sciences, we should be surprised if it were otherwise.

What norms should guide the use of language, often value-laden, in science? A blanket prohibition on the use of natural-language terms would be unwise, given the potential for clarity and even discovery such terms can bring (as the 'spousal abuse' example shows). Instead, scientists should (1) be aware of the value-laden aspect of the terms they use, to avoid fiascos like the 'rape' example, (2) watch to see if the language choice proves illuminating or obscuring in practice, and (3) note the limitations of the analogies, metaphors, and connotations created. Scientists can and should draw upon human language but need to do so with awareness of the potential problems that comes with that use.

5. Conclusion

Do the social sciences have a special problem with respect to values? At first glance, it might seem so. The complexity of the human realm to be studied, the ethical restrictions on generating controlled contexts for many behaviours of interest to social scientists, and the value connotations of human language used by scientists seem to create a particular challenge for social scientists.

However, if we examine the natural sciences carefully, we see similar structural challenges. The natural world is extremely complex too, and philosophers of science have been calling for a clearer recognition of this, in both the pursuit of understanding and the use of scientific knowledge in the policy realm. Ethical concerns over the treatment of animals in experiments is on the rise, and some experiments in ecological settings, such as experiments in geoengineering, are also raising ethical worries. And both natural and social scientists use value-laden language in their work.

Delving deeper, we have seen that values play important roles throughout the scientific process, whether natural science or social science. Values are important for deciding what is of interest to the scientist. Values are essential for placing ethical restrictions on methodologies. At the same time, the value of knowledge itself must be respected, such that scientists pursue methods that are aimed at genuine discovery rather than a predetermined result. Values must not direct the results inferred from the evidence but are crucial for determining when the evidence is deemed sufficient. And value-laden language can help illuminate phenomena, even as sometimes it can obscure it. All of these roles occur in both natural and social science, so there does not seem to be a particular qualitatively unique problem of values in social science.

The question of the reliability of the social sciences for public decision-making thus becomes a problem of assessment for each area of science, for each study pursued. How carefully was the evidence gathered? How strong is the support for the claims made? What alternative explanations are available for the evidence? Have they been developed or pursued? And, as we see from Chapter 3, does the study provide evidence relevant for the policy issue in question, or are its results only indicative for the particular local context in which the study was conducted? Given the complexity of both social science and the social world on which we desire policy guidance, these are not easy questions.

Yet the value saturation of science becomes a useful resource in policy-making as well (as discussed in Chapter 7). With values openly on the table as part of the scientific process, scientists and policy-makers can include both evidence and values, in their legitimate roles, as part of the public discussion.

References

Beecher, H. K. (1966). 'Ethics and Clinical Research', *New England Journal of Medicine*, 274(24): 1354–60.

Douglas, H. (2008). 'The Role of Values in Expert Reasoning', *Public Affairs Quarterly*, 22(1): 1–18.

Dupré, J. (2007). 'Fact and Value', in H. Kincaid, J. Dupré, and A. Wylie (eds), *Value-Free Science? Ideals and Illusions*. New York: Oxford University Press, 27–41.

Elliott, K. C. (2011). *Is a Little Pollution Good for You? Incorporating Societal Values in Environmental Research*. New York: Oxford University Press.

Fancher, R. E. (1985). *The Intelligence Men: Makers of the IQ Controversy*. New York: Norton.

Gross, C. (2011). 'Disgrace: On Marc Hauser', The Nation, 21 Dec.

Haney, C., Banks, C., and Zimbardo, P. G. (1973). 'Interpersonal Dynamics in a Simulated Prison', *International Journal of Criminology and Penology*, 1: 69–97.

Hausman, D., and McPherson, H. (2006) *Economic Analysis, Moral Philosophy, and Public Policy*. New York: Cambridge University Press.

Milgram, S. (1963). 'Behavioral Study of Obedience', *Journal of Abnormal and Social Psychology*, 67(4): 371–8.

Reicher, S., and Haslam, S. A. (2006). 'Rethinking the Psychology of Tyranny: The BBC Prison Study', *British Journal of Social Psychology*, 45(1): 1–40.

Rooney, P. (1992). 'On Values in Science: Is the Epistemic/Non-Epistemic Distinction Useful?', *Proceedings of the Biennial Meeting of the Philosophy of Science Association* (1992): 13–22.

Root, M. (2007). 'Social Problems', in H. Kincaid, J. Dupré, and A. Wylie (eds), *Value-Free Science? Ideals and Illusions*. New York: Oxford University Press, 42–57.

Weber, M. (1949). *The Methodology of the Social Sciences*. Tr. E. A. Shils and A. Finch. Glencoe, IL: Trade Cloth.

Zimbardo, P. G. (1973). 'On the Ethics of Intervention in Human Psychological Research: with Special Reference to the Stanford Prison Experiment', *Cognition*, 2(2): 243–56.

Further Readings

Douglas, H. (2011). 'Facts, Values, and Objectivity', in I. Jarvie and J. Zamora-Bonilla (eds), *The SAGE Handbook of the Philosophy of Social Sciences*. London: Sage Publications, 513–29.

Part IV
Using Formal Models

10

Choice Models

Katie Steele

1. Introduction

Adequate explanation and prediction of human behaviour often requires understanding the beliefs and values that motivate action. In this way, we gain a deeper understanding of the behaviour in question, beyond just noting that it has some regularity. For instance, the hypothesis that Dave goes to church weekly is prima facie less informative than the hypothesis that Dave goes to church primarily because he is in love with another member of the congregation. Likewise, the hypothesis that many voluntary public goods projects fail is prima facie less informative than the hypothesis that certain projects fail because individuals do not place positive value on their own participation and believe they can free ride on the efforts of others. In short, the social sciences involve special kinds of models that track our notions, based on common sense or 'folk' psychology, of the causes of human behaviour. These are models that depict the choices/behaviour of persons as resulting from what philosophers call, as we learn in Chapter 5, the persons' 'intentional attitudes'—their beliefs and values.

Formal choice models are used to represent these subjective beliefs and values in a concise way. The field is commonly divided into three domains: *decision theory, social choice theory*, and *game theory*. Decision theory concerns the intentional attitudes and choices of a single person or *agent*. This is of intrinsic interest in psychology and cognitive science. In fact, decision theory has wide reach as it is a building block of the other two domains of choice models as well, which concern groups of agents. *Social choice theory* models a group of agents who must reconcile their attitudes in order to act as a single agent with 'shared' attitudes (think of voters who must settle on a choice of leader); social choice theory is employed in political science and public economics, amongst other areas. Finally, *game theory* models strategic interaction amongst individuals—all choose their own course of action, but they strategize because the combination of choices affects the outcomes of all involved. Game theory is used extensively in (micro)economics, and increasingly in sociology and other social science disciplines.

All of these domains of choice theory—decision, social choice, and game theory—are also used to explore normative questions, i.e. questions about how things *should* be done, rationally and/or morally speaking. Philosophers and other normative theorists appeal to choice theory to answer questions like 'What constitutes *rational* choice attitudes?' or 'What group attitudes *justly* represent the attitudes of its constituent members?' or 'How should public institutions be designed to deliver *adequate* outcomes, given the attitudes that citizens are likely to have and the strategic behaviour they are likely to engage in?' These are all interesting questions, but they are not the focus in this chapter; here I am primarily interested in the use of choice models in the empirical sciences. I concentrate just on decision and game theory, in the interests of space, and also because social choice theory arguably has more normative than descriptive applications. In any case, we shall see, however, that the normative and descriptive perspectives on choice theory are intimately linked, for better and worse reasons.

The chapter is organized as follows. In section 2, the basics of individual decision and game models are introduced. I will then, in section 3, address criticisms of the deployment of these models in the social sciences. My general position is that, while there is ample scope for criticizing particular applications of choice models, this should not be taken as an argument against choice modelling in the social sciences *tout court*.

2. Introducing Choice Models for the Social Sciences

This section introduces the basic notation for choice models in the social sciences. I consider, in turn, individual decision and game models. The two are not entirely distinct. It will come as no surprise that game models involve individuals. But game theoretic considerations also impact on individual decisions, so neither is obviously the more general choice model. To some extent, it is simply the case that the two kinds of models are useful in different contexts.

2.1 *Individual Decision Models*

I shall first introduce individual decision models. The main components of these models are *prospects* and *preferences*. Prospects may be further divided into *acts, states,* and *outcomes*. In this way, the complexity of an agent's attitudes towards the world is reduced to a relatively simple model.

In short, the agent has preferences over prospects. That is, there are various 'items' or 'states of affairs' (the prospects) that the agent compares and ranks in terms of which ones he/she likes better than others (the preferences). The core prospects are acts, which, as the name suggests, are things that an agent can do of their own volition, like 'pick the orange from the fruit bowl', or 'go to the park', or, at a slightly grander level, 'pursue graduate studies in psychoanalysis'.

Let us denote a *weak preference* for act A_i over act A_j as $A_i \geq A_j$: either the agent *strictly prefers* A_i to A_j (written $A_i > A_j$), or the agent is *indifferent* between A_i and A_j (written $A_i \sim A_j$). Acts may be decomposed in terms of states of the world and outcomes. The states of the world are the possible (mutually exclusive) ways the agent thinks the world may be; this is the locus of the agent's uncertainty about the world. The uncertainty at issue may concern a very local and mundane issue like the result of a coin toss (where the states are 'heads' and 'tails'), or, for more worldly decisions, the uncertainty may concern the economic prospects of a country (where e.g. the states may be 'permitted to stay in the Eurozone with large debt repayments until 2020', and so on). Associated with each act and state is an outcome, which is what will come about, at least from the point of view of the agent, if the act is performed and the state in question is the true state.

The relationship between acts, states, and outcomes is best appreciated by considering the typical tabular representation of a decision problem, as per Table 10.1.

For instance, we might be interested in Mary, who is very conscientious and prudent; we want to know what she will do when confronted with various health insurance options. The acts $A_1 \ldots A_r$ are possible insurance packages she could purchase. The states $S_1 \ldots S_n$ represent the relevant possible scenarios that Mary envisages. For example, S_1 might be the state where she has only minor ailments during the next ten years, while S_2 is the state where she has some significant but not critical health problem, like reduced eyesight. The outcomes $O_{1,1} \ldots O_{r,n}$ are the various possible outcomes that Mary

Table 10.1 Tabular representation of decision problem

	S_1	S_2	...	S_n
A_1	$O_{1,1}$	$O_{1,2}$	...	$O_{1,n}$
A_2	$O_{2,1}$	$O_{2,2}$	...	$O_{2,n}$
...	...	...	...	...
A_r	$O_{r,1}$	$O_{r,2}$	...	$O_{r,n}$

anticipates, given the insurance benefits and her health prospects. For example, $O_{2,2}$ might be the outcome that Mary loses much vision yet her insurance gives her free access to consultations and glasses, etc.

The agent has preferences over the acts of the decision problem of interest, but we presumably need to work out/predict what these preferences are. This is done by making assumptions, perhaps based on past observations, about the agent's beliefs and desires. Shortly I shall expand on the basis for these assumptions; for now, note that, standardly, the agent's beliefs about the states of the world are represented by a probability function, Pr, over these states, and the agent's relative desires for the basic outcomes are represented by an *interval-valued* utility function, U, over these outcomes (to be explained shortly). For example, the strength of Mary's belief that she will have only minor ailments in the next ten years might be 0.7, and in this case, by the rules of probability, the strength of her belief in the contrary is 0.3. A utility function is *interval-valued* or *cardinal* just in case the differences between the utilities are meaningful in the following way. If, say, the decision outcome for minor ailments under package A_1 has utility 10, the outcome under package A_2 has utility 4 and the outcome under package A_3 has utility 1, then Mary prefers the A_1 outcome to the A_2 outcome twice as much as she prefers the A_2 outcome to the A_3 outcome. By contrast, if Mary's utility function were only *ordinal*, then the differences in utilities would be meaningless and all we could infer from the specified values is that Mary prefers the A_1 outcome to the A_2 outcome to the A_3 outcome.[1]

The standard calculus for deciding between options or acts is the *expected utility principle*, which claims that a (rational) agent's preference ranking tracks expected utility, or the average utility for a prospect given the probabilities and utilities for each of the possible outcomes, such that:

$A_i \geq A_j$ IF and only IF

$$\sum_n \Pr(S_n) \times U(O_{i,n}) \geq \sum_n \Pr(S_n) \times U(O_{j,n})$$

In other words, one act is preferred to another act just in case, for the first act, the sum over all the states of the world of the probability of the state multiplied by the utility of the outcome of the act in that state is greater than this

---

[1] Note that an interval-valued utility function is more formally described as a utility function that is *unique up to positive linear transformation*. In general, the uniqueness conditions associated with a mathematical measure tell us what information is given by the measure. To say that the utility function is *unique up to positive linear transformation* is to say that, if e.g. chocolate ice-cream has utility 5 while vanilla has utility 2, then this very same information is represented by utilities $5m + c$ and $2m + c$, for any positive m and any c. In other words, no conclusions should be based on the utility values 5 and 2 that do not also hold for utility values $5m + c$ and $2m + c$.

same sum for the second act. In the case of indifference, the sums for the acts are equivalent. Note that the utility function, U, must be interval-valued or cardinal, otherwise it is not meaningful to multiple utilities with probabilities and then sum these terms.

If we can characterize Mary in terms of her probabilities for states and her cardinal utilities for outcomes, then we can work out her preferences for health insurance packages, provided we also assume she is an expected utility maximizer. But one might well ask what justifies characterizing Mary in this way. Indeed, this is a significant part of the scientist's task. Recall Mary's example utility function, where the outcome for minor ailments under package A_1 has utility 10, the outcome under package A_2 has utility 4, and the outcome under package A_3 has utility 1. How could we know that this is Mary's utility function? That is, how could we know that she prefers the A_1 outcome to the A_2 outcome twice as much as she prefers the A_2 outcome to the A_3 outcome?

In the 1920s Frank Ramsey proposed an ingenious way to determine, at least in theory, a person's utility function over outcomes *and* their probability function over states of the world. It involves asking the person to rank a large number of bets. One must also assume that the person is an expected utility maximizer, i.e. they rank bets according to the rule just stated. Sometime later in the 1940s von Neumann and Morgenstern developed a similar method for measuring a person's utility; on their account we need to know the person's preference ranking over a large number of lotteries. By way of example, here is a very simple construction of a cardinal utility scale for the three holiday destinations Rome, Paris, and Barcelona. Assume the agent has the following preference ranking over the destinations: Rome > Barcelona > Paris. Now there is some lottery over Rome and Paris with objective probability p, i.e. a lottery that has chance p that the agent will go to Rome, and chance $1 - p$ that the agent will go to Paris, such that the agent is indifferent between this lottery and Barcelona. The probability p for this lottery is the utility for Barcelona, if the utility for Paris is set at 0 and the utility for Rome at 1, since then the expected utility calculations are in keeping with the claim that the agent is indifferent between Barcelona and the lottery. (Note that the expected utility for the lottery is $p \times 1 + (1 - p) \times 0 = p$). We can check that this makes sense by considering a couple of cases. If going to Barcelona is only marginally worse than going to Rome, then the agent would require a very high probability for Rome to be indifferent between Barcelona and the lottery. After all, the lottery might land the agent in Paris. In this case, the utility for Barcelona matches this high probability. On the other hand, if Barcelona is just a bit better than Paris, then the agent would require only a small probability for Rome to be indifferent between Barcelona and the lottery; this small probability is then the utility for Barcelona. So we see that lotteries enable a utility representation of an agent's preferences over prospects. We could use this construction of the agent's utility function (in addition to the probabilistic measure of their beliefs) to predict the agent's preferences in other more complex decision problems. In Mary's case, we might test how she ranks a number of lotteries involving her basic health outcomes, and so determine her utility function over these outcomes. We could then use this utility function to predict what she would choose in the 'real-life' decision of choosing a medical insurance option.

Even if a person's utility and probability functions may be determined from their preferences over bets/lotteries, there is still the large question of how to elicit these preferences. It is difficult to ascertain a person's preferences over just a few prospects, let alone the many required for detailed measures of belief and desire. The key question is: what sort of data serve as evidence for an agent's current preferences? The answer depends on how preference is to be understood, and in particular, what is the presumed relationship between preference and choice behaviour, and between preference and other psychological traits. I can only touch the surface of this issue here. An extreme yet surprisingly mainstream position, particularly in economics, is the so-called theory of *revealed preference*, which holds that preference simply *is* choice, or perhaps choice disposition, rather than some deeper psychological attitude. In that case, we cannot look further than a person's choice behaviour in order to determine their preferences because these preferences are constituted by the choice behaviour and have no deeper grounding. It follows that decision models are reduced to mere descriptions of an agent's choices, where the probability and utility functions are just mathematical constructs and not properly representative of belief and desire at all.

The revealed preference interpretation offers little by way of explanation and prediction of choice behaviour. It does not have the resources to express what *particular* features of a prospect an agent finds (un)desirable and therefore (un)choiceworthy. There is thus no way to determine whether some current/future choice situation is relevantly similar to a past choice situation, such that one would expect an agent to behave similarly. In short, revealed preference theory has no inductive (predictive) power. Moreover, the view does not countenance an agent having irrational preferences or choosing contrary to their preferences, due to impulsiveness or weakness of will.

The more fruitful position is surely that preference is distinct from, but plays some kind of motivating role with respect to, choice behaviour. As such, choice behaviour is still important *evidence* for preferences. This might be choice behaviour in the laboratory, or in the wild, so to speak. Indeed, one could yet argue that choice behaviour and preferences are inextricably linked, whether on metaphysical or evidential grounds or both. For instance, some hold that preference, which is a psychological attitude, completely determines choice behaviour, even if it is not identical to it. This is to say that it is impossible for a person to choose contrary to their preferences, and so phenomena like weakness of will would need some alternative explanation. Others maintain a 'causal gap' between preference and choice, filled by strength of will, habits, urges, instincts, and the like. Either of these views may or may not be coupled with the evidential claim that choice behaviour is the *only* reliable evidence for preferences. Even if that were true, experimenters must do much inferential work in deciphering choice behaviour if they want to construct appropriate utility functions for agents—the experimenters must make assumptions about how the agents perceive the options available to them, whether the agents have sufficiently reflected on their choices, and what are the agents' relevant background beliefs. Alternatively, or in addition to observing choice behaviour, experimenters could ask agents outright what their preferences are over some prospects, or ask agents various questions that are deemed relevant to their preferences. Different techniques will be more or less successful in different contexts; indeed, the appropriate way to conceive of and elicit preferences in particular settings is a topic of debate amongst social scientists.

2.2 Game Models

Game models are intended to capture the special situation of strategic interaction between agents. 'Strategic' here does not necessarily mean conniving or in some way dishonest; it simply means that, when choosing a course of action, agents consider what others are likely to do and how this bears on the possible outcomes. There are many such situations in social life, from political manoeuvring during an election campaign to simple coordination problems like choosing to drive on one side of the road rather than the other. This section serves to introduce and interpret game models and to outline the standard ways of 'solving' games; section 3 discusses the usefulness of game models in the social sciences.

There are some basic components to the *description* of a game. First, there are the *players*—in the simplest case, two players. These players have a set of available *acts* or *strategies*, and we ultimately want to know which of these the players each choose. The rules or procedures of the game specify the *outcomes* for each player, given each possible combination of players' strategies. Players have preferences over these outcomes, represented by a utility function that may be cardinal or ordinal. (Recall that for the former kind of utility function, unlike the latter kind, the distances between utility values are significant and represent strength of preference.) As already alluded to, the players may well be entirely self-regarding, but they need not be. As with individual decisions, in terms of preferences, agents in a game come in many stripes and colours.

Table 10.2 A literal prisoners' dilemma

	Cooperate (confess)	Defect (don't confess)
Cooperate	(light sentence, light sentence)	(very harsh sentence, go free)
Defect	(go free, very harsh sentence)	(harsh sentence, harsh sentence)

Table 10.2 depicts a *normal-form* (tabular) game model for two players; let us call the players 'row' and 'column'. The table shows that both players have two possible strategies: 'cooperate' and 'defect'. (The strategies of the 'row' player can be read off the rows of the table, while the strategies of the 'column' player can be read off the columns.)

The table describes a well-known type of game; it in fact depicts the original narrative used to illustrate this type of game. The story goes like this: there are two prisoners accused of a crime. The prisoners are told that if they each cooperate (i.e. confess), they will both get a light sentence. If they each rather defect (i.e. fail to confess), they will both get a harsh sentence. If one confesses but the other does not, the one that confesses will get a very harsh sentence while the other goes free. The convention is for the utility payoff to 'row' to be specified first in the appropriate cell of the table, followed by the utility payoff to 'column'. Take the case where both players cooperate. That is, 'row' plays 'cooperate' and 'column' plays 'cooperate' as well. Here they both get light sentences, which for each of them is the second-best possible outcome. In the case that 'row' cooperates whereas 'column' defects, 'row' gets the worst outcome—a very harsh sentence—while 'column' gets the best outcome of going free. The reverse situation occurs if 'column' cooperates while 'row' does not. The paired outcomes associated with each pair of strategies constitute the rules of the game.

I have here described a literal prisoners' dilemma, but the reason Table 10.2 describes what is known as a *Prisoners' Dilemma* (PD) game, in the technical sense, is simply the pattern of outcome utilities associated with the pairs of strategies. This pattern can be seen more clearly if we replace the literal outcomes with utilities as in Table 10.3. To characterize the PD game, the utilities need only be ordinal, i.e. only the ordering of the utilities matters and not the differences in their values. One can check that the ordering of the utility values reflects the preference ordering of the outcomes in Table 10.2.

There are many social scenarios involving two players (and many more involving more than two players, if we were to generalize) that have the pattern of outcomes given in Table 10.3. The situation is one where free-riding, or defecting when the other cooperates, gives the most utility for the defector and the least utility for the cooperator. It is better that both cooperate, however, than both defect. An infamous example of the PD, at least according to some, is the arms race of the Cold War, where cooperating is pursuing disarmament and defecting is continuing to stockpile weapons. Of course, it is questionable whether the PD model accurately characterizes the Cold War scenario, but it is not implausible that the players' ordinal utilities (players here being national governments) were in line with those in Table 10.3. Other prime examples of PD games concern environmental protection. Here the agents may be national governments with a common interest in, say, global fish stocks or forestation or climate stability, or, at the other end of the spectrum, they may be individual citizens with a common interest in local air or river pollution. These are PD games just in case all prefer a sufficiently clean environment where everyone does 'their bit', to a polluted environment, and yet all players most prefer that the others refrain from polluting while they pollute and still enjoy a sufficiently clean environment. (It must also be the case that all players least prefer doing their bit when others don't do theirs, presumably because this makes the do-gooders' efforts futile.) Here again, it is questionable whether any particular environmental protection problem does in fact have the form of a PD game rather than another type of game. For one thing, it may be that polluting while others preserve the environment is not most preferred, perhaps because all players value helping the cause, or because even a small amount of pollution is damaging enough to be undesirable. In short, whether or not a scenario can be represented as a PD game as per Table 10.3 depends on the players' preferences, and also the way the world is, both in terms of natural laws and social institutions, as these structures dictate the rules of the game.

Beyond the description of a game, there is the *solution concept*, which specifies how the agents eventually settle on their respective strategies and associated payoffs. The central solution concept in game theory is the *Nash equilibrium*, formulated by its namesake John Nash in the early 1950s in his graduate thesis. A Nash equilibrium is a combination of strategies such that each player's strategy is the *best response* to the other player's strategies. That is, each player's strategy affords them the highest possible utility given what the other players do. A simple way to identify Nash equilibria in a two-player game model is to circle the row player's maximum values for each column (i.e. row's best response to each of the strategies that column might choose), and likewise circle the column player's maximum values for each row. Remember

Table 10.3 The general prisoners' dilemma

	Cooperate	Defect
Cooperate	(3,3)	(−1,4)
Defect	(4,−1)	(0,0)

that, for each strategy pair, the value for row is given first in the table cell, followed by the value for column. The Nash equilibria are the cells that have both row and column utility payoffs circled.

The PD game has only one Nash equilibrium: the strategy combination where both players defect, which yields the utility payoffs (0, 0) by the representation in Table 10.3. Note that if 'row' chooses to defect, then 'column' does best by also defecting, thereby gaining utility 0 rather than -1. Likewise, if 'column' chooses to defect, 'row' does better by also defecting, thereby gaining utility 0 rather than -1. That is why both players defecting is a Nash equilibrium; neither player can do better by switching to another strategy. None of the other strategy pairs are Nash equilibria. Consider the potential case where both 'row' and 'column' cooperate. This is not a Nash equilibrium because either player would do better by switching to defection, thereby gaining utility 4 instead of 3. In fact, the combination of both players defecting is a particularly robust kind of Nash equilibrium because it is a *dominant solution* for both players: for each player, the defect strategy is best, not just on the assumption that the other player is also playing their Nash equilibrium strategy, but *no matter what the other player does*. Even if 'row' is irrational and does not choose to defect, it is still better for 'column' to defect, and vice versa.

In a Nash equilibrium (including the special case of a dominant solution), no player can do better by *unilaterally* switching to a different strategy. It is possible, however, that all players could do better by *simultaneously* switching to a different strategy, i.e. a Nash equilibrium is not necessarily *Pareto optimal*. A Pareto optimal strategy set is optimal in this sense: there is no other strategy set such that shifting to this strategy set would result in at least one player being better off and no player being worse off. The tragedy of the Prisoners' Dilemma is that the one Nash equilibrium (here dominant solution) is the *only* strategy combination that is not Pareto optimal. Indeed, *both* players would be better off if they both cooperated. (Even the strategy pairs where one player defects and the other cooperates are Pareto optimal, because a shift to another strategy pair would result in at least one player—the one getting the maximum utility of 4—becoming worse off.) This is why the Prisoners' Dilemma is said to illustrate the 'failure of collective rationality'.

One might wonder what is so special about Nash equilibria, especially if they can in a sense yield inferior outcomes, as per the Prisoners' Dilemma. The logic is as follows: when reasoning about what strategy to opt for, an agent knows the set-up of the game, including the utilities of all players, and they also know that other players know the set-up of the game, and that these other players know that the agent knows they know the set-up of the game, and so on. Some claim that it is this *common knowledge assumption*—the cycle of 'I know you know I know you know etc.' reasoning—that leads to the privileging of Nash equilibria, which are joint best responses to each other's strategies. Others disagree that common knowledge leads players to reason their way to Nash equilibria; there is simply an additional assumption that the players each believe their opponents will choose the/a Nash equilibrium strategy, perhaps due to the history of plays of the game. In any case, game theory rests on the assumption that players make 'intelligent' choices that lead them to settle on Nash equilibria. Either the players reason intelligently all the way to Nash equilibria, in which case it is necessary that they have rational preferences and are aware of the game description, or, at the other end of the spectrum, the players do not reason at all but are subject to environmental or 'selective' pressures that favour players who at least *act* as if they intelligently choose Nash equilibria after repetitions of the game.

Note that it may be desirable to treat the selective-pressure/evolutionary interpretation of Nash solutions explicitly. Indeed, this has given rise to *evolutionary game theory*, which finds application in biology as well as social science. The games in these models can even be 'played' by unconscious entities like bacteria that pursue strategies in an automated fashion. Strategies are replicated according to their success. The solution concepts of evolutionary game theory are in many ways similar to those of regular game theory, but there are differences, and of course the set-up and interpretation of the models differ (Alexander 2009). This chapter does not explore evolutionary game theory, but rather sticks to games with genuinely intelligent players.

Nash equilibria are central in this way: it is widely regarded a *necessary* condition of a game solution that it be a Nash equilibrium. Some games have multiple Nash equilibria, however, and this raises the question of what are *sufficient* conditions for something to count as *the* game solution. Game theorists refer to this as the 'refinement program'.

A number of games with multiple Nash equilibria arguably feature in social life. In many such cases, the question of what is the unique equilibrium 'solution' of the game is pressing. For example, the game in Table 10.4 represents a typical coordination problem; provided agents play the same strategies, the outcome is good. The game is commonly known as the 'driving game' because the choice of two players of whether to drive on the left or the right side of an isolated country road is a simple coordination problem that fits the pattern. We see that the top left and the bottom right entries in the table, corresponding to both players choosing 'left' and both choosing 'right' respectively, result in each player receiving (ordinal) utility 1. Both of these strategy combinations are Nash equilibria: if one player opts for 'left' then the best response of the other player is also 'left', and likewise if one player opts for 'right', then the best response of the other player is also 'right'. Note that these two Nash equilibria are also Pareto optimal. The question then arises: what if the players shoot for different Nash equilibria?

Table 10.4 Multiple Nash equilibria: the driving game

	Left	Right
Left	(1,1)	(−1,−1)
Right	(−1,−1)	(1,1)

This will yield bad outcomes. If one player plumps for the 'left' Nash equilibrium while the other player plumps for the 'right' Nash equilibrium, then we are in the top right or bottom left entries of the table, where the players receive -1 utility apiece. So in this game, it is important that the players aim for the same Nash equilibrium. (In other games, it may not be important that the players aim for the same Nash equilibrium, if their utility payoffs are in any case unaffected.)

The question of what Nash equilibrium players will/should aim for arguably depends on principles that go beyond game theory proper, like which equilibrium is more salient for all players. For instance, in a literal driving game on an isolated country road, presumably the salient equilibrium is the one that accords with the driving rules of the nearest municipality, whether this be 'always drive on the left' or 'always drive on the right'. Note that there are many coordination problems that have the formal structure of a driving game, as given in Table 10.4, and the conditions for salience will differ in these different applications. For instance, consider the case where two complementary NGOs can achieve good outcomes if they each target the same community, but there will be no good result if they divide their efforts. How should they each proceed? Presumably, if the NGOs were able to come to an agreement on which equilibrium to aim for (i.e. which community to direct their efforts at), this equilibrium would be very salient indeed. The NGOs would have no reason to deviate from such an agreement. Other game situations, however, may not lend themselves to straightforward negotiations regarding multiple equilibria; a major obstacle is when different equilibria are better for different players.

Indeed, the 'driving game' is just one example of a simple game structure with multiple Nash equilibria. There are other similar kinds of games, and moreover, these sorts of games are arguably more prevalent in the social world than the tragic Prisoners' Dilemma. Indeed, as we can see in Chapter 11, Cristina Bicchieri argues as much, by appeal to social norms; in brief, she claims that we internalize social norms, like 'one must do one's bit for community projects rather than free-riding on the efforts of others', such that satisfaction and thereby utility is gained from obeying the said norms, or otherwise lost by disobeying the norms. This phenomenon of *norm-internalization* serves to 'convert' a scenario that would otherwise be a PD game, for instance, into a more benign game with better collective equilibria. Of course, for multiple equilibria, there remains the issue raised of whether agents can coordinate effectively.

There are many more facets to game theory, and its applications are much richer in variety than have been touched upon here. For instance, there are game models for any number of players, not just two. There are game models that distinguish the order in which players choose their strategies, and the amount of information they each have about the prior choices of the other players. There are special considerations that apply to repeated plays of the same game. And, as mentioned earlier, there is the burgeoning area of evolutionary game theory, which increasingly finds application in the biological and social sciences, and which can accommodate players that merely *act* as if they are intelligent upon repetitions of a game. These are just some of the further dimensions to game theory. The most powerful contributions of game theory to the social sciences are arguably the more basic ideas, however, which I have introduced here.

3. Ideal Type and its Discontents

Having introduced formal choice models for the social sciences, we now consider criticisms of their deployment. The critics have two main targets: the idealized characterisation of individuals in choice models, and the fact that individuals and not societies are the primary building blocks of models of social interaction. I discuss these in turn. My general point is that standard criticisms of choice models tend to overshoot; one must bear in mind the general limitations of scientific modelling and also appreciate that choice models come in a variety of forms.

3.1 *Standard Decision Theory: Unfalsifiable or Simply False?*

There is a temptation to reject wholesale the project of generalizing and predicting human motivation and behaviour. But this is surely too pessimistic and casts doubt on the social sciences as a whole. Indeed, Max Weber (1864–1920), claimed to be one of the 'principal architects of modern social science', started from a more optimistic position. Weber argued that the social scientist's aim, unlike the historian's, is not to represent the vagaries in attitudes of some particular persons, but rather to represent attitudes and behaviour that can be generalized across people and/or across time and which therefore have explanatory value. To use Weber's terminology, the social scientist explains and predicts on the basis of *ideal types*.

According to Weber himself, a key ideal type for the social sciences is the agent who rationally furthers her own ends, or who, in other words, has rational preferences over prospects. Weber's claim then is that, when studying human behaviour and social interaction, it is useful to depict agents as making choices on the basis of rational preferences. This assumption is indeed borne out in the social sciences, and particularly in economics; while we know that people sometimes act irrationally or have inconsistent preferences, it is assumed that such cases of irrational behaviour are temporary deviations that in some sense 'cancel out' in large groups or in the long run. Consequently, the ideal type in economics as well as other disciplines is commonly in line with the standard theory of rational choice outlined in the previous section—expected utility (EU) theory. As such, EU theory is the locus of criticism with respect to formal choice models in the social sciences. Oddly, however, EU theory is criticized on two opposing fronts: some argue that the theory is unfalsifiable, i.e. that it cannot be proven wrong and so is vacuous, while others argue that it is outright false. How could both of these views have gained purchase? I claim that it is due to different understandings of the flexibility of choice models.

Start with the charge that EU theory is descriptively false, even as an approximation. Consider standard economic models—typically, the outcomes that agents are supposed to care about are bundles of consumer goods, or money, and the more of these goods the agent procures for him or herself, the better. In other words, it is standardly assumed that the only relevant distinction between decision outcomes is the amount of goods or money that will accrue to the agent. So, for example, $50 is always worth the same, no matter how this amount was procured, whether by hard labour or by cheating one's friend, and two sacks of potatoes are better than one, regardless of these products' provenance. It is easy to see that a real agent, and a perfectly rational one at that, may not be well described by an expected utility model constructed in this way. To begin with, the agent may not be indifferent between outcomes that are supposedly identical, like $50 procured by hard labour and $50 procured by cheating.

This point is perhaps more vivid when it comes to game models. To give an example: a classic game for characterizing and testing the bargaining behaviour of agents is the 'Ultimatum Game'. In this game, there is some pot of goods, often just a sum of money that needs to be divided between the two players. The rules of the game are as follows. One player—the dealer—selects a split of 'the pot', and the other player—the receiver—decides whether or not to accept the split. So, for instance, the dealer might recommend a 50:50 split (the fair strategy), or she might recommend, say, an 80:20 split (an unfair strategy), which is to say that she keeps 80 per cent of the pot and gives 20 per cent to the receiver. If the receiver accepts, then each gets what the dealer

Table 10.5 Ultimatum game with monetary outcomes

	Accept	Reject
Fair	($5, $5)	($0, $0)
Unfair	($8, $2)	($0, $0)

decreed, but if the receiver rejects the offer, neither gets anything. A simple version of this game, where the dealer has just the two strategies stated and where the pot is $10, is given in Table 10.5.

The outcomes of the game are specified in monetary amounts, and moreover, these amounts are assumed to track the agents' utilities. This is typical of game models in economics. But the Nash solution of ($8, $2) is not very compelling in this case, and indeed laboratory experiments and real-world observations suggest that agents in this kind of scenario overwhelmingly settle on the 'fair/yes' strategy pair, i.e. the dealer offers 50:50 and the receiver accepts. Furthermore, it seems entirely rational for these agents to reject the apparent Nash solution: they care not just about money but also about whether justice has been done.

There are further limitations of EU models that distinguish outcomes only in terms of personal holdings of goods/money. Besides having altruistic tendencies, many agents are sensitive to the menu of available options, and to what might have happened if they chose differently or if things turned out differently. So, for instance, an agent's preference for relaxing at home over a luxury holiday might switch depending on whether a third option of an adventure holiday is available. (The latter might make the 'stay-at-home' option seem like the timid choice rather than the modest choice.) To give a different example: losing a gamble and receiving nothing may be better or worse depending on whether one might otherwise have won $10 or $1,000 dollars. A decision problem developed by the late French economist Maurice Allais received much attention for exposing such attitudes of regret and its effect on agents' evaluations of outcomes. These sorts of preferences are not consistent with an EU model that distinguishes outcomes only in terms of money/material goods.

Is expected utility theory then false, both descriptively and normatively? There is an obvious argument to the contrary: EU models must simply be sufficiently detailed such that outcomes include all properties that agents care about, including the well-being of others and unrealized possibilities that inspire feelings of regret/envy/self-critique. (Decision theorists use the term *comprehensive outcomes*.) Then there are no obvious conflicts between EU theory and reasonable choice behaviour. For instance, returning to the

Table 10.6 Ultimatum game with comprehensive outcomes

	Yes	No
Fair	$(5 + \delta, 5 + \delta)$	$(0, 0)$
Unfair	$(8 - \theta, 2 - \theta)$	$(0, 0)$

Ultimatum Game, the monetary amounts apparently do not represent typical agents' utilities for outcomes. The 'right' characterization of the game is plausibly as per Table 10.6. The δ and θ amounts here represent the utility and disutility associated with fair play and unfair play respectively. In this case the 'fair/yes' strategy pair may well be a Nash equilibrium. Likewise, if outcomes in decisions include the properties that inspire regret or risk attitudes, then EU theory may well capture common choice behaviour amongst risky options.

This brings us to the other critique of expected utility theory: that it is unfalsifiable. The charge here is that EU theory is not false precisely because it *cannot* be proven false. Perhaps in avoiding one problem we run into another: if outcomes are so comprehensive that they include everything that an agent cares about, it would seem that EU and game models could be fitted to any choice behaviour and social interaction whatsoever. This would suggest that the theories in fact have no empirical/descriptive content; there is no substance to the claim that an agent is an expected utility maximizer, or chooses Nash equilibrium strategies, because the agent could not fail to have preferences of this sort.

For instance, I mentioned the phenomenon of regret that Maurice Allais saw as a challenge to EU theory, at least from the descriptive point of view. Allais showed that people seem to value possible outcomes differently depending on what are the other possible outcomes that they might have received instead. To give a new example, consider someone who values the outcome 'win travel scholarship' differently, depending on whether the other possible outcome was 'win nothing' or 'win travel scholarship plus living expenses'. These different evaluations of the same outcome, depending on what are the other chancy outcomes, are not consistent with EU theory. There is, however, a way to accommodate such regret phenomena within EU theory. At the extreme, we can simply include in the description of an outcome what else might have, but did not, occur. The following could then be regarded as two distinct outcomes: 'win travel scholarship when the other possibility was nothing' and 'win travel scholarship when the other possibility was a better scholarship'. Distinct outcomes can of course be evaluated differently by the lights of EU theory. But at what cost do we 'save EU theory' in this way? If, whenever an agent appears to care about more than just the *expected utility* of options, the attitudes in question, such as regret, can simply be accounted for by enlarging the description of outcomes, it is unclear whether maximizing expected utility has any substantial meaning. Indeed, a number of theorists have debated this issue. A similar worry applies to game models. If, whenever agents appear to strategize at odds with Nash equilibria, we can simply redefine the game so that the utility functions track everything the agents seem to care about (as per my treatment of the Ultimatum Game), the theory is apparently unfalsifiable, i.e. it cannot be proven wrong.

So we see that the question of whether EU/game theory is false or unfalsifiable depends on the level of detail in which we may describe decision outcomes. The trouble is, it is very difficult to justify any particular level of detail, or any particular list of properties that may be used to distinguish the outcomes. This is a very pressing question for normative inquiry—it would be worrying indeed if our theories of rational choice were wrong or vacuous. The question is not so relevant for empirical uses of choice models, however, and this is our interest here. Note that there is an important difference between EU *theory* being unfalsifiable, and any particular EU *model* being unfalsifiable. In the former case, the key issue is whether it is only *rational* preferences/choice behaviour that can be represented by *some* EU model, or whether in fact *all* preferences/choice behaviour can be represented by *some* EU model. The arguments in the literature and my comments concerning regret attitudes are directed at this issue. This need not concern us as social scientists however. The important question for us is whether *particular* EU/game models that describe acts/states/outcomes in a specific way are adequate or inadequate for given descriptive, explanatory, or predictive tasks. For instance, does an EU model with utility increasing linearly with net family income adequately describe the impact on Bangladeshi families of a microfinance scheme? To give another example: is it useful, for the purposes of explaining international climate action to date and predicting future prospects for cooperation, to characterize national governments as playing a Prisoners' Dilemma game with respect to controlling their carbon dioxide emissions?

It is worth noting that it may well be empirically useful to treat EU *theory* as unfalsifiable. Francesco Guala has recently (2008) argued that EU theory is often used as a measuring instrument; we assume that an agent maximizes EU, and this allows us to measure her preferences in a given context and thereby characterize her with a particular EU *model*. The utility function (and/or the belief function) is determined by what model best 'fits' observed choice behaviour. Indeed, I noted earlier that using betting behaviour to infer an agent's probabilistic beliefs and/or utilities for outcomes has a long pedigree in decision theory that can be traced at least to Ramsey. Game theory can similarly serve as a measuring instrument. Under the assumption that agents maximize expected utility and opt for Nash equilibria, if both players settle on the 50:50 split in the Ultimatum Game, for instance, we can infer that they care about fairness and not just monetary outcomes. In this way we come to understand the agents' psychology and we have principled reasons for including fairness properties, over and above monetary outcomes, in models intended for further predictive purposes.

There may be good reasons, however, to restrict the content of choice-model outcomes. Perhaps the model must achieve a certain amount of generality, or perhaps, if the model is to be practically viable, the identifying properties of outcomes must be measurable by independent means. This would presumably rule out subtle risk and fairness attitudes. In some applications, at least, it is surely the case that the best balance between simplicity and predictive power involves distinguishing outcomes only in terms of money/material goods.

In the case of crude outcomes, it should not be taken for granted that agents are best represented as expected utility maximizers. Indeed, once we acknowledge some slippage between empirical choice models and rational choice theory, the question arises as to whether non-EU models may be more adequate for at least some empirical purposes. One might argue that the ideal type in the social sciences need not be the rational type. Alternatively, one might argue that the ideal type *is* the rational type, and yet, *when model outcomes are crudely described*, the rational type need not correspond to expected utility maximization. The properties of preferences that are linked to maximizing expected utility theory are plausibly self-evident requirements of rationality *only if* the preferences are interpreted as expressing an agent's all-things-considered attitudes of approval. But this interpretation rests on outcomes 'containing' everything that an agent cares about. This is not typical of outcomes in empirical models—they are generally cruder or more restricted than this—and thus the corresponding preferences must be interpreted differently, and need not conform to the expected utility principle.

So-called *behavioural* decision theories may be understood in this light. These are proposed alternatives to EU theory, and include prospect theory, regret theory, satisficing theory, and various choice *heuristics* or shortcuts (see, for instance, Kahneman et al. 1982). Prospect theory, for example, deviates from EU theory in this way. Instead of assessing acts in terms of the sum of the probability of each state multiplied by the utility of the outcome associated with that state, the probability term (which, recall, represents belief) is transformed or converted according to the agent's risk attitudes. The comparison of two acts A_i and A_j can then be written as follows:

$A_i \geq A_j$ IF and only IF

$$\sum_n r(\Pr(S_n)) \times U(O_{i,n}) \geq \sum_n r(\Pr(S_n)) \times U(O_{j,n})$$

This is very similar to the expected utility rule described earlier, except that the utility of outcomes is multiplied by $r(\Pr(S_n))$ instead of simply $\Pr(S_n)$, where r stands for the agent's (personal) risk function and is subject to the constraint that $r(0) = 0$ and $r(1) = 1$. The idea is that people tend to overweight or give extra importance to low probabilities, and underweight or give lesser importance to high probabilities. So, for instance, a probabilistic belief of 0.01 (that, say, one's house will burn down) might be converted by the r function to 0.10, i.e. $r(0.01) = 0.10$, and a probabilistic belief of 0.99 (that, say, one will win a million dollars) might be converted by the r function to 0.90, i.e. $r(0.99) = 0.90$.

There are various criticisms of basic prospect theory that have led to a refined version known as 'cumulative' prospect theory. But these details need not concern us here. The point is simply that prospect theory is one amongst a number of behavioural or *non-expected utility* decision theories. These theories are varied in form and motivation. Moreover, they are understood in different ways. Some consider their favoured behavioural decision theory to be a challenge to EU theory as an account of *rational* choice. Others simply consider these decision theories to be better suited to empirical tasks because they represent the irrational agents that we mostly are. There is, however, a third way. The theories may, in specific contexts, be better for empirical tasks because they represent rational choice given a limited or crude interpretation of outcomes. Prospect theory, for instance, may be considered useful because it can accommodate varying risk attitudes and yet still confine the description of outcomes to monetary amounts or material goods.

3.2 Game Theory: The Reductionist Critique

Some of these points have bearing on a further criticism of game theory: that it is inappropriately *reductionist* in its representation of social interaction, given that the basic units of game models are individuals, and specifically, their preferences. Indeed, game theory is paradigmatic of *methodological individualism*, a term first used to describe the Weberian programme of explaining group-level phenomena in terms of the attitudes and behaviour of the individuals who constitute the relevant groups. It is a form of explanation whereby groups are *reduced* to their constituent individuals. As we see in Chapter 6, some argue, however, that depicting individuals as basic is grossly misleading, given the way individuals themselves are shaped by social norms and shared institutions. In other words, the charge is that game theory has the arrow of explanation going the wrong way—from individual attitudes to social arrangements rather than from social arrangements to individual attitudes.

There is both a negative and a positive response to this charge. Let us begin with the negative or defensive line, and that is that the critics are confusing their targets. They are arguing against *atomism*, where individuals are conceived as asocial entities that interact but do not influence each other's psychology. But atomism neither implies nor is implied by methodological individualism. To begin with, as already emphasized, there is no reason to take a narrow view with respect to the outcomes that individuals care about; the agents in a game model may be sensitive to each other's plights and to all sorts of social factors that go beyond material goods. Furthermore, the provenance of agents' attitudes is left open; it may well be that agents' preferences were socially conditioned or in other words simply reflect the dominant attitudes of the group.

More generally, the existing social and institutional arrangements act as constraints on individuals, and play a corresponding role in game models. Beyond the agents' preferences, the prevailing social setting determines what strategies are actually available to agents, and the sorts of outcomes that result from combinations of strategy choices. For instance, the institutional setting of scientific publishing constrains scientists' options with respect to project funding and submission of work, and also influences the outcomes associated with the various players' choices of projects and submissions. When choosing an avenue of work, the scientist must take into account the competition of her peers and also their expected assessment of her work, as this, together with the procedures of journals and grant agencies, partially determines her outcomes. The social setting, in other words, shapes the 'rules of the game', and this is expressed in the parameters of a game model. In other words, game theory need not be blind to the fact that individuals are embedded in a social/ institutional context!

The critic might nonetheless push further and argue that the real explanatory task is to explain these social forces and institutions that constrain individuals, and not simply to posit them in a model. To some extent, however, this argument misses the mark. A scientific model can only represent/explain some limited aspect of the world. In one model, particular social norms or institutions may serve as boundary conditions or constraining assumptions, but this is not to say that the emergence and/or persistence of these institutions cannot be explained via a different game model. Presumably, in such a model, 'higher-order' or more basic institutions will serve as the background constraints. Returning to our scientific publishing example, a different game model could be used to explain the procedures of the publishing business that served as the institutional context in the model alluded to; the players in the new model might be competing journals or grant agencies, rather than scientists themselves. The 'higher order' institutions will presumably amount to the broader economic and educational setting which shapes the possibilities and outcomes for the scientific journals.

The appeal to different orders of game models goes some way towards answering the critic's charge that game theory does not explain what we most want to understand: social forces and institutions. There remains the problem, however, of explaining the mechanisms by which social forces shape individual preferences. We can describe ever richer layers of game models, but these models are still underpinned, at bottom, by fixed individual preferences. Indeed, this must be acknowledged as a limit of standard game theory (if not evolutionary game theory); it does not elucidate the process of preference change, since a basic ingredient of any game model is the set of players with their fixed preferences over prospects.

So much for the negative argument—what game models need not be. In short, they need not assume asocial agents. The positive argument is that the insights afforded by game models can be very valuable. In fact, Weber claimed that individualist explanation is what distinguishes the social sciences from other sciences: a key role of the social sciences is to offer an interpretative explanation of action in terms of *subjective attitudes*, and only individuals, as opposed to groups, are the locus of subjective attitudes. The basic idea is that we do not properly understand what people do unless we understand *why* they do it, and to answer such questions we must inevitably appeal to the beliefs and desires of individuals.

Furthermore, some striking cases highlight that we ignore individual attitudes at our peril. We need not look further than games like the Prisoners' Dilemma, introduced earlier. This game shows that, even if there is a collective goal or a common preferred outcome within a group, this outcome may nonetheless not be realized due to the structure of individual incentives. (Recall for the Prisoners' Dilemma that both agents value the fruits of cooperation, but, alas, both have an incentive to 'free-ride'.) The contemporary social and political theorist Jon Elster makes much of these game-theoretic insights in arguing for the acceptance of methodological individualism. If a common goal is salient in a group, we may make hasty predictions that the goal will be achieved, when a closer examination at the level of individuals would reveal otherwise. Elster (1985) appeals to a striking example in political science to make this point vivid: Marxist theory. He argues that Marxists appealed to the general will of the proletariat as the predicted driver of social change and failed to appreciate the more subtle motivations of individual workers. These individuals may well be sympathetic to the end-result of revolutionary change but nonetheless have an incentive to free-ride on the revolutionary efforts of others.

Some decades earlier in the twentieth century, and prior to the popularization of games like the Prisoners' Dilemma, the economist Friedrich von Hayek made similar cautionary remarks about the realization of social ideals. Hayek did not stress free-riding so much as the different frames of motivation of individual citizens versus policy-makers. While policy-makers may be keenly aware of society-level variables like inflation, citizens going about their regular lives do not generally respond to these factors but rather have a more local set of concerns. The upshot is that the connection between macroeconomic variables and individual behaviour is not straightforward. The best-laid plans for the collective may be difficult to orchestrate at the individual level. (This is, in a sense, the flip-side of the *invisible hand* phenomenon, where unorchestrated individual activity leads to the appearance of planning at the collective level.)

Hayek's message is that we should be sceptical of social planning initiatives. We need not accept his conclusion, but we should take heed of Hayek's worries. Indeed, the conclusion one might draw is that social planning proposals may be better understood through careful game-theoretic modelling!

4. Concluding Remarks

One major conclusion to draw from this chapter is that we should not ask whether choice models, *in general*, are true/false or unfalsifiable in the social sciences, but rather whether *particular* choice models are useful. To be useful, a model must be true enough, and it must yield insights or predictions that justify the trouble of modelling in the first place. Furthermore, the question of how we can *permissibly* construct choice models, and, in particular, define outcomes, is misguided in the empirical setting, even if the question is important in the normative setting. What are the appropriate properties of decision outcomes in empirical models simply depends on what facilitates adequate explanation and/or prediction.

A consequence of these points is that we cannot take for granted that the best empirical models are expected utility models. Having said that, the expected utility principle has a powerful simplicity, and it underlies much analysis in game theory, so should not be dismissed too hastily.

References

Alexander, J. M. (2009). 'Evolutionary Game Theory', in E. N. Zalta (ed.), *Stanford Encyclopedia of Philosophy* (Fall 2009 Edition) <http://plato.stanford.edu/archives/fall2009/entries/game-evolutionary>.

Elster, J. (1985). *Making Sense of Marx: Studies in Marxism and Social Theory*. Cambridge: Cambridge University Press.

Guala, F. (2008). 'Paradigmatic Experiments: The Ultimatum Game from Testing to Measurement Device', *Philosophy of Science*, 75: 658–69.

Kahneman, D., Slovic, P., and Tversky, A. (1982). *Judgement Under Uncertainty: Heuristics and Biases*. Cambridge: Cambridge University Press.

Weber, M. (1978). *Economy and Society*, ed. G. Roth and C. Wittich. Berkeley, CA: University of California Press.

Further Readings

Binmore, K. (2007). *Game Theory: A Very Short Introduction*. Oxford: Oxford University Press.

Broome, J. (1991). *Weighing Goods: Equality, Uncertainty and Time*. Oxford and Cambridge: Basil Blackwell.

Hausman, D. M., and McPherson, M. S. (1996). *Economic Analysis and Moral Philosophy*. Cambridge and New York: Cambridge University Press.

Heath, J. (2011). 'Methodological Individualism', in E. N. Zalta (ed.), *Stanford Encyclopedia of Philosophy* (Spring 2011 Edition) <http://plato.stanford.edu/archives/spr2011/entries/methodological-individualism>.

Resnik, M. D. (1987). *Choices: An Introduction to Decision Theory*. Minneapolis: University of Minnesota Press.

11

Norms, Conventions, and the Power of Expectations

Cristina Bicchieri

What is the difference between a chair and a social norm? Both are human artefacts, existing for human use. Yet think for a moment what would happen if, like in an old episode of *The Twilight Zone*, all life on earth was wiped out. All life but one. You alone remain, wandering around in a world now horribly silent. You stumble on a broken chair, unusable. You may not look at it ever again, you will never sit on it, and will soon forget about that broken chair, but until time wipes it out, that chair will exist in its corner of the world. In your previous life, you were a student, a family member, a friend. Each group had its own norms, and some, like reciprocity or truth telling, were very general, spanning across all groups. You were a norm follower; not always, but most of the time. Now there are no norms to speak of. Truth telling makes no sense if there is nobody to talk to, and so it goes for every other norm you can think of. To exist at all, norms need people who collectively believe they exist. You suddenly realize you have followed norms because you thought other people were following them, and also trusted that all those people believed that everyone should obey those norms. You thought of norms as having an independent existence not unlike that broken chair, an existence in the world beyond what people thought and believed about them. You were wrong: these beliefs are no more, and all norms have therefore ceased to exist.

What is the point of being honest and trustworthy, cooperative and fair, if there is nobody to appreciate and reciprocate it, not to mention to interact with? You used to be the proud member of the 'Red bandanna group', a group of motorcycle enthusiasts who met every Sunday to compete with other groups in reckless speed races. That red bandanna was a sign of distinction and belonging, and your pals would have taken offence seeing you without it. They all wore it, and thought it should be very visible on the head of every group member, to signal the privilege of being part of a gang that had won innumerable races. That group is no more, gone are the motorcycles and the red bandannas. You still have one in your pocket, though; should you wear it? You might, if you get nostalgic, but its signalling power is gone. There is nobody to signal anything to, and nobody will get offended and reproach you if you stop wearing it.

Norms are social constructs, like tables and chairs, but much less permanent and independent of our thinking about them. Though norms are expressed in prescribed or proscribed behaviours, actions we can observe or at least describe, these actions would be senseless, or at best lose their original meaning, without the collective beliefs that support them. So the most important question to ask about norms is what system of beliefs supports and defines norms. Once we understand these beliefs, we can tell whether the behaviours that we observe are norm-driven or not, measure the consistency between beliefs and behaviour under different conditions, and make predictions about future behaviours. Before we come to define the kind of beliefs that support and define social norms, however, we shall briefly look at the most common, ubiquitous definitions of social norms, their advantages and shortcomings, and what can we learn from them.

Social norms have been extensively studied in the social sciences, though different disciplines have stressed different features of norms. Yet a shared, common understanding of what a social norm is can be traced across all fields: *a norm refers to a behaviour that is collectively approved or disapproved in a group or population and is enforced by sanctions.* It is also tacitly implied that social norms are very different from moral or legal norms, though this difference is not often articulated in detail. Although legal norms in particular seem to fit the collective approval/disapproval/sanctioning description, there are important differences between legal and social norms. First and foremost, a legal norm is an explicit, mandatory rule of behaviour formally established by the state. It usually proscribes behaviour, whereas social norms often also prescribe. Social norms are often unspoken and informal, and their origin is not clearly identifiable with a particular moment in time. They have evolved out of protracted social interactions, but we cannot usually tell exactly how they have evolved and in which circumstances. Whereas a legal norm explicitly indicates the conditions of its implementation, the subjects whose actions it regulates, their mutual rights and duties, and the sanctions for failure to obey one's duty, a social norm is much less specific. This difference is particularly evident in employer–employee relations. Such relations are formally regulated by contracts, but the greatest influence is usually exerted by non-legal incentives and sanctions, such as reputational concerns and relationship-specific advantages. The social norms that regulate work relations are much less specific than legal contracts, and the sanctions for non-compliance, such as blacklisting or negative gossip, are entirely informal.

Social norms often engender expectations of compliance that are felt to be legitimate, and close in a sense to 'having a right' to expect certain behaviours on the part of others, who therefore are perceived as 'having an obligation' to act in specific ways. This is because we have an ingrained tendency to move from *what is* to *what ought to be*, and conclude that 'what is' must be right or good. Yet, apart from our long-standing habits of performing and expecting others to perform certain actions, there is no deeper foundation to these presumed 'rights and obligations', however intensely felt they might be. Whereas violation of legal norms elicits formal negative sanctions and there is no formal reward for complying with the law, the positive and negative sanctions that attach to social norms are quite different. With a social norm, the approved behaviour is buoyed up by informal positive sanctions (tangible rewards, praise, status, reputation, etc.) and the censured behaviour is discouraged by means of negative sanctions (punishments, shaming, ostracism, ridicule, etc.).

Note that informal sanctions are also used to discourage or support moral norms. It is debatable whether we can draw a sharp distinction between social and moral norms, but we usually refer to norms as 'moral' when they have a universal content—such as norms against harming others without reason—and when our allegiance to them tends to be independent of what others do. As we shall see later, a distinguishing feature of social norms is that they are conditionally followed, whereas a moral norm is unconditional. This does not mean that we always obey moral norms. We may be tempted to perform 'immoral' acts, but an excuse such as 'I did it because others did it' is not deemed to be acceptable. In the case of a social norm, however, this is a perfectly reasonable justification. So it is reasonable to state 'I did not pay my dues because I know nobody pays', but few would accept 'I raped and killed the prisoners because all my fellow soldiers did it' as a good reason to perform such a horrific act.

Sometimes social norms can get internalized to the extent that they do not need social enforcement and are spontaneously adhered to by individuals. In this case we say that individuals are directly motivated to comply with the norm, whereas the use of sanctions is a form of indirect motivation. Sanctions, however, keep playing a role, since 'direct motivation' may be tied to feelings of guilt and shame that the mere thought of transgression evokes. In this case an internal monitoring mechanism has taken the place of social monitoring and sanctioning. The sociologist Talcott Parsons was one of the main proponents of norm internalization. In his view, we form lasting dispositions to conform to our society's norms through a process of socialization that starts within the family (Parsons 1951). This view has been criticized on two counts. The first refers to the long-standing debate between methodological individualism and holism. Since the Parsonian view accords priority to social value systems and views individuals as bearers of social values, individual actors can no longer be the basic units of analysis. This has major consequences for the study of social institutions. In many a sociologist's view, social institutions cannot be explained as resulting from individual actions and interactions, since actions are not a primitive unit, independent of those very institutions they are supposed to explain. Institutions and their relations are the primitive units of analysis, irreducible to the microsphere of the individuals that act within their scope. This stands in sharp contrast to the individualist's view, according to which all social institutions can be explained as resulting from, and being reducible to, individual agency. (You can read more about this issue in Chapter 6.)

The second and more damaging criticism of Parsons's view of internalization has to do with the empirical adequacy of what can be inferred from it. Norms that are internalized will be very resistant to change, and we should observe a positive correlation between *personal* normative beliefs and action. Yet history is full of examples of rapid norm change (think of smoking and sexual mores), as well as swift norm emergence. As to the positive expected correlation between personal normative beliefs and behaviour, there are many studies in social psychology that fail to find it. Even personal normative beliefs that are typically acquired during childhood, such as honesty, tend to be uncorrelated with behaviour. The more secure positive correlation that is regularly observed is one between *social* normative beliefs and behaviour. Whenever individuals think that the relevant group holds certain normative beliefs, they will be inclined to act according to them even if, personally, they may be indifferent or even opposed to those actions. Indeed, the existence of a social norm usually leads to actions consistent with it, provided it demands behaviour that a reference group defines as appropriate and desirable; this fact, however, militates against the internalization view of norms as a *general* account of conformity.

There are, however, two alternative interpretations of internalization that do not stand in sharp contrast to these empirical observations about usual norm compliance. One interpretation is moral, the other cognitive. We cannot deny that there exist norms that we have internalized to the point that almost no variance exists in norm-induced behaviours. Such norms are typically proscriptive, and as such not likely to be correlated with observable behaviour. Take, for example, norms that proscribe inflicting unwarranted, gratuitous harm. By and large, harming someone for no reason is not even conceived as an option, as the mere thought of performing a destructive, unjustified act spawns revulsion and guilt in most of us. Such norms are internalized to the point that we become aware of their force only when faced with a violation, and our allegiance is perceived as unconditional. What we usually call moral norms, insofar as we understand them to be internalized, unconditional imperatives, fit this description. It is an open question whether we are born with a 'moral organ' shaped by evolution or it is society that shapes our moral sensibilities. In any case, social norms are not unconditionally followed and are not internalized in this sense, unless we want to blunt the boundaries between the moral and the social.

The second interpretation of internalization is my own cognitive one. Many of the norms we follow are *learned*, often through repeated interactions in a variety of situations that we come to categorize as typical cases to which the norm applies. So we learn to accept and return favours and gifts, but not bribes; to share equally, but also reward merit and make allowance for need. We learn when and how to greet, how to behave at a party, and what to say at a funeral. When we find ourselves in one 'typical' situation where a learned norm applies, we tend to conform in automatic ways. The norms we learn we uphold as 'default rules', ready to apply them to similar cases until it becomes evident that conformity has become too costly. It is well known that, in repeated social dilemmas of the kind discussed in Chapter 10, players start by cooperating but cooperation precipitously declines as soon as someone defects; the players adopt cooperation as a default rule, but are ready to abandon it when they realize it has significant costs. Internalization in this sense means we economize on thought, not that the norms that society has imposed on us are so deeply entrenched as to be inflexible and unchangeable.

The very generic definition of norms as socially approved behaviour supported by sanctions tells us two important things. First, social norms are closely tied to *sanctions*; without sanctions (internal or external), they may not exist. Second, part of the very definition of norm is that it refers to behaviours and patterns of behaviour that are collectively approved or disapproved, hence such behaviours *matter* to people. A lot of attention has been paid to the question why certain behaviours matter so much that people will go to great lengths to make sure they are adhered to, and engage in costly sanctioning to support them. An obvious answer is that norms perform critical social *functions*, such as maintaining social order and coordinating useful collective action, or even help one group to exclude or discriminate against another group, thus keeping vital resources within the group. Yet saying that a norm performs an important social function does not explain how it originated, or why we keep obeying it. A norm may have evolved to smooth social interactions, and it may keep doing so quite efficiently, but we would be hard pressed to say that this is the reason why it came about.

Take reciprocity. It is certainly important to live in a social environment where people reciprocate valuable, beneficial actions. Without reciprocity there would be no trust, and without trust we would have no markets or modern political systems: Markets and democracy rely on people trusting their business partners, as well as their elected representatives. Recognizing the social importance of trust, we care for and support norms of reciprocity, and in this sense we may say that their *stability* is linked to the social functions they fulfil. Their *origin*, however, cannot be explained in this way. A social function a norm comes to play is not the cause of its spontaneous emergence. Take, again, a norm of reciprocity. A society may have evolved *several* strategies that promote reciprocation of trust; all these strategies involve some punishment for non-reciprocators, from mild to harsh, and they can exist alongside each other. Taken together, all these strategies result in observationally equivalent behaviours: almost all individuals trust and reciprocate, but the norm itself results from many different strategies. The individuals who adopt one of these strategies do so because it is in their long-run interest to reciprocate trust, not because society at large benefits from it.

Yet the social function a norm plays may, and often does, explain its stability within a population. This statement needs qualification. A norm is stable if it is durably obeyed by great part of the population (or group) in which the norm exists. Transgressions occur, but they do not challenge the norm's permanence. This does not mean that compliance with a norm is mainly due to our being conscious of the social functions it performs, so that knowing its beneficial function gives us an overriding *reason* to obey it. Often we are not fully aware of the social benefits of a particular norm, but even if we are, our reasons to obey it are often much less worthy. If knowing the benefits of cooperation were a sufficient reason to cooperate, there would be no free-riders, i.e. people who do not cooperate with others but benefit from the fact that others cooperate. Think of taxpayers; we have public services that anyone can use because people support them by paying taxes. Someone who does not pay, however, can still use and benefit from these services. We have norms precisely because there is often a tension between what we would like to do (skirting a common task, avoiding paying our dues, being less than fair) and what is socially beneficial.

To explain a norm's stability, as well as its existence, we have to look further into the reasons why individuals conform. If we are less than fully aware of the benefits a norm may bestow upon society or, even if aware, we are not fully motivated by them, why do we conform? Many believe the answer lies in the existence of sanctions. They may be internal, as when we say that a norm has been *internalized*, by which we mean it has become part of our value system. Or, more often than not, external sanctions are at work to keep people in line. In this case, we say that there is a *rational* motivation to obey a norm: we want to reap the benefits of conformity or avoid the costs of transgression. If we think of individuals as rational decision-makers, we can see the appeal of this view of norm compliance. Norms are exogenous, external constraints we have to take into account when we make a choice. Economists are particularly fond of this view; a norm is, not unlike a budget constraint, a constraint on the set of possible actions one may take. The constraint, in fact, is not the norm per se, but the expected consequences of disobeying it. In this view, if the expected benefits of transgressing a norm are greater than the expected punishment, people will not conform. A main point to notice about the cost–benefit view of conformity is that it disentangles conformity from attribution of value, i.e. one may conform to a norm even if, for that individual, the norm has no value. We shall come back to this important point later.

Yet most of our actions do not stem from a cost–benefit calculation, at least not a conscious one. As I mentioned, norms are more often than not like default rules that we mindlessly follow in the appropriate circumstances. We are not *aware* of the possible sanctions, even if it is hard to deny that sanctions often do play a role in driving conscious compliance, especially in those cases in which people do not care much about what the norm stands for (think of foreign women having to cover their heads in a Muslim country). Since the cost–benefit model can be thought of as a *rational reconstruction* of norm conformity, we can disentangle awareness from rational choice. The cost–benefit model specifies when and why norm compliance is rational, but it does not profess to be a realistic, precise description of the way we in fact deliberate. It just says that, were we aware of the presence of sanctions, we would choose the course of action that minimizes costs. Even a rational reconstruction, however, has its constraints. A cost–benefit model must require that, were sanctions clearly absent, behaviour would change in predictable ways. A good model, however abstract, must make testable predictions.

Another, more important objection to the cost–benefit view of motivation has to do with interdependent expectations. In that view, avoidance of negative sanctions constitutes a decisive reason to conform, *irrespective of what others do*. The only expectations that matter are those about the sanctions that will ensue. What others do or do not do is irrelevant to motivation. The traditional rational choice/cost–benefit model depicts a decision-maker who stands alone in the face of uncertainty and a measurement problem. All that matters is how one should assess the present and future costs and benefits of incurring or avoiding sanctions, the severity of these sanctions, and the probability of being monitored and caught.

In reality we are embedded in a thick network of relations, we constantly interact with others, and what they do and think matter a great deal to us. Game theory (that, as we see in Chapter 10, studies interactive decision-making) provides a framework for understanding social interactions and the mutual expectations that accompany them and thus provides good, if incomplete, models for the kind of decisions involved in following a norm. It allows a micro-level analysis of how the incentives to behave in specific ways are influenced by others' behaviour, and in what way behaviours are interdependent.

From social psychology we know that only *some* expectations are positively correlated with norm-abiding behaviour; only those normative beliefs that people perceive to be collectively shared and put into practice matter to action. Casting aside for the moment the issue of how to differentiate among types of expectations, we want to know how a game-theoretic model can broadly represent how individuals' expectations converge and prompt individuals to behave according to them. To see what I mean by convergence of expectations, let's suppose we all believe, for whatever reason, that within a month there will be a market crash. We act on those beliefs and immediately sell our stock positions. This sudden sale depresses stock prices and, indeed, the market tanks. The market expectations were by no means normative, but they give us a vivid example of how collective expectations can bring on actions that make those expectations true. These are what we call *self-fulfilling expectations* and I want to argue that they have a lot to do with how norms persist. As you learn from Chapter 10, game theory is a good tool if we want to model the interaction of beliefs (expectations) and behaviour, and several authors have used it to give an account of norms and conventions. However, as we shall see, game theory falls short of producing a satisfactory account of the *role* different kinds of expectation play in conformity.

Norms as Equilibria: The Game Theory Connection

Various authors, including myself, have proposed a game-theoretic account according to which a convention or a norm is broadly defined as a *Nash equilibrium*. As Chapter 10 explains, a Nash equilibrium is a combination of strategies, one for each player, such that each individual's strategy is a best reply to the others' strategies, were one to take them as given. This means that a Nash equilibrium is an outcome of the game from which no individual player has any incentive to diverge. This outcome, however, is not necessarily the most efficient (think of the mutual defection equilibrium in the prisoner's dilemma described in Chapter 10); it is just one on which the players will converge, if they are acting rationally on the basis of their beliefs.

Most of these authors were interested in conventions, but social norms, too, can be thought of as equilibria. Since it is an equilibrium, a norm is supported by self-fulfilling expectations, in the sense that in equilibrium players' beliefs are mutually consistent, and thus the actions that follow from those beliefs will validate them. Characterizing social norms as equilibria has the advantage of emphasizing the role that expectations play in upholding norms. On the other hand, this interpretation of social norms does not prima facie explain *why* people prefer to conform if they expect others to conform.[1] After all, if everyone else cooperates the defector will reap great benefits, so the mere expectation of universal cooperation may not be enough to induce good behaviour.

When I mentioned the stability of norms I said that, in order to explain stability, we have to understand why people conform. The game-theoretic account gives a clear answer in the case of conventions. Take for example conventions such as putting the fork to the left of the plate, adopting a dress code, using a particular sign language, or blowing one's nose with a handkerchief. In all these cases, my choice to follow a certain behavioural rule is usually conditional upon expecting most other people to follow it. I say 'usually' because one may have other, overriding reasons to follow a rule. Take dress codes: for a very religious person, wearing a yarmulke/skullcap may represent one's compact with God and be completely independent of expecting others to do the same. In this case we cannot say that that person is following a convention. In a convention, on the contrary, mutual expectations are everything. Once my expectation about others' behaviour is met, I have every reason to adopt the behaviour in question. If I do not use the sign language everybody else uses, I will not be able to communicate, and if I blow my nose in my hands when everybody else uses handkerchiefs, I will send out the wrong signal about who I am. It is in my immediate interest to follow a convention, if my main goal is to *coordinate* with other people. So if I expect others to act in a certain way, and I want to coordinate with them, I will adopt that behaviour. *Why* one may want to coordinate with others is another issue. All the examples that are typically employed to illustrate conventions, like driving or language, rely on the idea that one's goal can only be achieved by doing what others do. So if I want to be safe on the road or just communicate, I will have to coordinate my actions with those of other people.

In the case of conventions, there is continuity between individual's self-interest and the interests of the community that support the convention. It is an example of harmonious interests: we all want to drive safely and speak the same language. This is the reason why David Lewis (1969) represented conventions as equilibria of *coordination games*. Such games have multiple equilibria, in the sense that—to communicate—we need a language, but which one among many is irrelevant. (See Chapter 10 for more discussion of multiple equilibria.) The same goes for driving: to be safe, we need to all drive

---

[1] The numbers (or letters) we put in the cells of a game matrix represent 'utiles' that illustrate how much a player likes a particular outcome of the game. *Why* a player has those 'utiles' is not a question game theory can answer.

to the right or to the left, but which we coordinate upon is irrelevant. Any of these coordination points is, from the viewpoint of achieving our common goal, an equally plausible outcome. Once one of the possible equilibria has been established, players will have every incentive to keep playing it, as any deviation will be costly for the deviant.

Social norms are a different story. For one, the fact that sanctions do play a role in compliance suggests that following a norm may not be in the individual's immediate interest. Behaviours that are socially beneficial, when not mandated by law, are normally supported by social norms that involve sanctions, both positive and negative. Social dilemmas, such as overpopulation, pollution, or energy conservation are examples of situations in which each individual profits from free-riding, but the group is better off if everyone contributes. Pro-social norms such as norms of cooperation or reciprocity have evolved to solve such dilemmas, and we often refer to them as unambiguous examples of the discontinuity between individual and collective interests. Not all norms have evolved for this reason, however. Norms of honour killing (murders of women by family members that are justified as removing some imputed stain on the family's honour) do not seem to be related to the provision of any collective good, even if honour is the highest valued virtue in some cultures.[2] Conforming to an honour code confers or restores status to those who comply with it, and not conforming is severely sanctioned by the community. Strict honour codes are costly to enforce (you may have to kill your own sister or daughter), but the temptation to evade the norm is tempered by the presence of positive (status, honour) and negative (stigma, ridicule, lack of trust) sanctions. In the words of Middle East media analyst Yotam Feldner,

> The honour of the Arab family or tribe, the respect accorded it, can be gravely damaged when one of its women's chastity is violated or when her reputation is tainted. Consequently, a violation of a woman's honor requires severe action, as Tarrad Fayiz, a Jordanian tribal leader, explains: 'A woman is like an olive tree. When its branch catches woodworm, it has to be chopped off so that society stays clean and pure.' The murder of women to salvage their family's honour results in good part from the social and psychological pressure felt by the killers, as they explain in their confessions. Murderers repeatedly testify that their immediate social circle, family, clan, village, or others expected them and encouraged them to commit the murder. From society's perspective, refraining from killing the woman debases her relatives. (Feldner 2000)

---

[2] Men are occasionally killed, but the large majority of victims are women. In the honour killing culture, a man who refrains from 'washing shame with blood' is a 'coward who is not worthy of living...as less than a man' (Feldner 2000).

We still have a tension between the individual and the collective, albeit one that is less transparent than what we see in a social dilemma. The point to be made is that social norms, as opposed to conventions, do not arise out of situations of harmonious interests but out of situations in which a potential or open conflict exists between individual and group interests.

You learn about game theory in Chapter 10 and I will presume here that you are comfortable with some of the ideas and language from there. The typical game that represents a state of affairs in which following a pro-social norm would provide a better collective solution than the one attained by a rational, selfish choice is a *mixed-motive game*. In such games the unique Nash equilibrium represents a suboptimal outcome, but there is no way to do better within the confines of the game. I have argued that pro-social norms, as opposed to conventions, are never born as equilibria of the mixed-motive games they ultimately transform. Whereas a convention is one among several equilibria of a coordination game, a norm can never be an equilibrium of a mixed-motive game (such as e.g. a prisoners' dilemma or a trust game). When a norm exists, however, it *transforms* the original mixed-motive game into a coordination one. As an example, consider the prisoners' dilemma game (Figure 11.1), where the payoffs are B = Best, S = Second, T = Third, and W = Worst. Clearly the only Nash equilibrium is for both players to defect (D), in which case both get (T,T), a suboptimal outcome.

Suppose, however, that society has developed a norm of cooperation: Whenever a social dilemma occurs, it is commonly agreed that the parties should privilege a cooperative attitude. Should, however, does not imply 'will', therefore the new game generated by the existence of the cooperative norm has two equilibria: either both players defect or both cooperate (Figure 11.2).

Self \ Other	Cooperate	Defect
Cooperate	**S, S**	**W, B**
Defect	**B, W**	**T, T**

Figure 11.1. Prisoner's dilemma.

Self \ Other	Cooperate	Defect
Cooperate	**B, B**	**W, T**
Defect	**T, W**	**S, S**

Figure 11.2. A coordination game.

Note that in the new coordination game created by the existence of a cooperative norm, the payoffs are different from those of the original prisoners' dilemma. Now there are two equilibria: if both players follow the cooperative norm they will play the optimal equilibrium and get (B,B), whereas if they both choose to defect they get (S,S), which is worse than (B,B). Players' payoffs in the new coordination game differ from the original payoffs because their preferences and beliefs will reflect the existence of the norm, which has affected players' incentives. More specifically, if a player knows that a cooperative norm exists and has the right kind of expectations, then she will have a preference to conform to the norm in a situation in which she can choose to cooperate or to defect. In the new game generated by the norm, choosing to defect when others cooperate is not a good choice anymore (T,W). The existence of sanctions for non-compliance explains the lower payoff.

The honour killing norm is quite different. This is not a pro-social norm in the sense cooperation or reciprocity norms are. We do not have a social dilemma to start with, so casting the norm as arising from a mixed-motive game would be a mistake. It does not arise from a coordination problem either, since it is difficult to imagine a situation in which there are many equipossible 'honour codes' people can end up adopting, and what matters to them is just to collectively pick (or stumble upon) one. In cultures in which the reputation and honour of the family are the most important attributes, failure by a member to follow adequate moral conduct weakens the social status of the family. The unwed girls of a shamed family will not find a husband, and male relatives will be scorned and ridiculed. The only way to restore honour and reputation is to 'cut away' what brings shame. Since in these cultures honour is often linked to the 'purity' of women, the duty to restore the lost honour is to 'cut away' the lost woman by killing her.

	Others All H	All not H
H	S, S	T, T
Not H	W, T	B, B

Figure 11.3. A game for the honour killing norm.

Yet *when the norm is in place*, we do have a coordination game, since a player can decide to obey/disobey the norm, but in this case, unlike the case of a norm of cooperation, the honour killing norm may be an *inferior* equilibrium. As I already mentioned, keeping the honour code is costly (you will have to kill your straying daughter/sister or be forever dishonoured), and all would benefit from some other arrangement. To see that, let's look at the matrix in Figure 11.3, where the payoffs go from B (best) to W (worst) and we assume for simplicity that Others are all choosing the same strategy, i.e. to embrace the honour killing code (H) or to abandon it (Not H).

Observe that for H to be a strict equilibrium, it is necessary that the action of a single player (Self alone chooses to stick to the honour code H) imposes *costs* on all the others who have chosen a different path (Not H). For example, if the whole community has rejected honour killing in favour of a more humane and respectful treatment of women, they will be shaken by the brutality of the act and will have to punish the deviant as a human rights violator. The worst case scenario for Self is still one in which he flaunts the honour code when it is still adopted by the group. So Self is punished if he disobeys the norm, as he imposes a cost on the others who instead follow it (W,T) by giving women a bad example of leniency, but Self is also punished if he sticks to the norm when others have changed their ways. These two sanctions will significantly differ. In the disobedience case, the group would ridicule and ostracize Self as well as his family; if instead Self keeps following the (costly) honour code when others have abandoned it, he would bear a significant personal cost without reaping any status benefits.

The two off-diagonal boxes have asymmetric payoffs for Self because I am assuming that the direction of collective change is from honour killing (the original norm) to no honour killing. When a norm is abandoned, the curmudgeon that won't change his ways loses out. The story (and the pay-offs) would be very different if a new norm is created, as people move from no honour killing to honour killing. In this case, the trendsetter who suggests that honour killing is a way of showing family devotion and protecting purity may be offering other people something compelling that induces them to join in. And he would benefit from being in the vanguard and innovative. Unfortunately, the matrix representation is a poor tool to characterize the asymmetry between building and abandoning a norm, because it cannot represent temporal direction.

The simple matrix representation tells us just one thing: any social norm, however generated, *creates* a coordination game of which it is an equilibrium. This simply means that, in the presence of any norm, there are always two possible equilibria: either all follow the norm, or nobody does.[3] Note, however, the profound difference that exists between norms and conventions in this respect. A convention is characterized as one of many possible equilibria of a coordination game. Once players converge to one of them, deviating has a cost for the deviant, but not for the group. With norms instead, deviations always involve *negative externalities*, which means that the deviation of one individual impacts in a negative way all others. A typical example of a multi-person coordination game would be Figure 11.4.

I am assuming here that Others (All) are all playing the same strategy, so that their payoffs are not changed in a perceptible way by Self's deviation.[4] Suppose that A, B, and C represent alternative ways of greeting strangers. Strangers being introduced may bow, shake hands, or put the palms together in front of the chest (as in India). Assume all members of a specific population coordinate on one of these greetings. Self is clearly better off by following the existing convention. Doing otherwise may lead to confusion and to being perceived as uncouth and inappropriate. Failing to coordinate with Others is just Self's loss. All the others who follow the convention will not suffer a perceptible loss if Self deviates from it; however, if a greater number of 'deviants' were to be present in the group, the loss may become significant (and perceived as such), as coordination may be lost. This example could represent any convention adopted by a large group. It is in everyone's interest to keep following it, and the lone deviant will pay a price, but she will not be sanctioned by the community, since Others incur no perceptible cost.

---

[3] Note that the simple game theoretic representation given here could also represent situations in which, for a norm to be followed, it is sufficient that a majority follows it. In that case, Self will have to believe that the majority of Others are norm-followers and that his deviation is not critical, i.e. it will have no effect on the number of followers.

[4] In fact, the change is insignificant and not perceived (it lowers the payoff of everyone else by ε, where ε is close to zero). However, were many players to deviate, a tipping point may be reached, where the payoff of the convention followers would be diminished in a significant way.

Self \ Others	All play A	All play B	All play C
A	**1, 1**	**0, 1-ε**	**0, 1-ε**
B	**0, 1-ε**	**1, 1**	**0, 1-ε**
C	**0, 1-ε**	**0, 1-ε**	**1, 1**

Figure 11.4. A multi-person coordination game.

A more ambiguous story would be that of two parties who have to coordinate on a particular signalling code. Suppose Self and Other have two possible signalling systems available, Red and Blue, each most preferred by one of them. The matrix in Figure 11.5 represents this situation, as well as the fact that both players want to communicate and prefer that outcome to following their particular inclinations (i.e. Self will not choose Blue, her most preferred code, unless she is sure Other also chooses it). Clearly *both* players lose by mis-coordinating.

Now imagine that the players happen to converge, by trial and error, communication, or any other reason, on Red as their common signalling code. A unilateral deviation will still damage *both* players but, depending on the costs imposed on the party that sticks to the convention, the damage may be greater for one of them. For example, if Red is the conventional code, and Other deviates, Self will feel doubly damaged: she is not coordinating with Other *and* she was 'sacrificing' by choosing a code that she did not much like to start with. The matrix would thus look like the one in Figure 11.6.

In this case it seems reasonable to assume that some form of sanction might be put in place to discourage even 'innocent mistakes'. For example, the players may decide to impose a monetary penalty on the distracted party (Figure 11.7).

Has the original convention morphed into a norm? Is Other sticking to the Red code because he fears the punishment that will surely follow a deviation, or still chooses Red because, irrespective of the possible punishment, he badly wants to communicate with Self? I think the answer lies in assessing

Self \ Other	Red	Blue
Red	1, 2	0, 0
Blue	0, 0	2, 1

Figure 11.5. Coordinating on a signalling code.

Self \ Other	Red	Blue
Red	1, 2	−1, 0
Blue	0, −1	2, 1

Figure 11.6. Deviating from an accepted signalling code.

Self \ Other	Red	Blue
Red	1, 2	−1, −2
Blue	−2, −1	2, 1

Figure 11.7. Sanctions for deviating from a signalling code.

the *reason* a player has for behaving in a particular way. In the case of a norm of cooperation, the shadow of external sanctions may be the main or even the sole reason why one chooses to cooperate, otherwise cooperation would not be in one's best interest. Following an honour killing code, too, may be chiefly motivated by the sanctions that a transgression brings about. Killing one's daughter or sister presumably has a high psychological cost, so one should be 'pushed' to do it.[5] In a convention which is usually followed by many people (as in Figure 11.3), the main reason to adhere to it is the desire to coordinate with others in order to fulfil one's goals, which happen to coincide with others' goals. The only sanction that matters is one's failure to coordinate, which presumably has a cost. Even in a two-person convention, when the aim is mutual coordination, there is no tension between what one wants to do and what one is expected to do, regardless of the sanctions that the parties may want to impose on each other to discourage reckless deviations. In a convention, players may experience a form of what is called *moral hazard*: since I know that you still want to coordinate with me and that a small 'distraction' will not harm me too much, I may become cavalier in my behaviour. To avoid this form of moral hazard, players may want to impose heavier sanctions.

The Power of Expectations and Epistemic Traps

A game theoretic account proves too limited to permit a meaningful discrimination in many ambiguous cases. The numbers (or letters) in the cells of the matrix represent 'utiles' or preferences; we model choices as more or less costly or beneficial and rank choices according to the costs/benefits they confer on the decision-maker, but we have no tools to say, as in the ambiguous case of Figure 11.7, what costs (lack of coordination or external punishment) matter most to the players. Saying that a norm or a convention is an equilibrium just says that, if a player expects conformity, she will have no reason to deviate and, if *everyone* expects conformity, these expectations will be self-fulfilling. Such equilibria are self-perpetuating: the belief that the norm/convention is (almost) universally endorsed generates widespread conformity, and observation of conformity further confirms expectations of universal endorsement. In other words, game theory, while it stresses the importance of interdependence and mutual expectations, does not convey any information about the *nature* of such expectations. Yet it is precisely the types of expectation that guide us that distinguish a norm from a convention.

---

[5] Typically the killing occurs after a period of warnings and is decided by the whole family.

Let's go back for a moment to the two games of Figures 11.1 and 11.2. For a player who is playing a regular prisoners' dilemma, being informed that her partner is an altruist who always cooperates is not sufficient to induce reciprocal cooperation. It will instead strengthen the temptation to defect. But if a norm of cooperation exits, things have changed. Now if one expects the other to cooperate, reciprocal cooperation has become the best choice. Why? Because defecting triggers negative sanctions. The same happens with a norm of honour killing (Figure 11.3). If one expects others to follow it and also expects to be punished for not conforming (and be rewarded for compliance), there is every reason to obey. In both cases there is something else, beyond expecting others to conform, that motivates conformity: a *normative* component that is absent in a convention. To understand this important point, let us define more explicitly the two kinds of expectation that support norm compliance:

(a) *Empirical expectations:* individuals believe that a sufficiently large part of the relevant group/population conforms to the norm.[6]

(b) *Normative expectations:* individuals believe that a sufficiently large part of the relevant group/population believes they ought to conform to the norm and may sanction behaviour.[7]

If having both types of belief buttresses norm compliance, it follows that one may follow a norm in the presence of the relevant expectations, but disregard it in their absence. To be more specific:

(c) *Conditional preference*: individuals will prefer to conform to a social norm on condition of holding the relevant empirical and normative expectations.

Note that conditional preferences for conforming to a norm are different from a preference for what the norm stands for. For example, my reason to

---

[6] Note that the 'sufficiently large part' clause tells us that universal compliance is not usually needed for a norm to exist. A few transgressions are a fact of life. However, how much deviance is socially tolerable will depend upon the norm in question; small group norms (think of a youth gang's rules) and well-entrenched social norms (think of reciprocating favours) will typically be followed by almost all members of a group or population, whereas with new norms or norms that are not deemed to be socially important greater deviance is usually accepted (think of the bride wearing a white dress). Furthermore, as it is usually unclear how many people follow a norm, different individuals may have different beliefs about the size of the group of followers and may also have different thresholds for what 'sufficiently large' means. What matters to individual conformity is that an individual believes that her threshold has been reached or surpassed.

[7] It is important to emphasize that sometimes we obey norms just because we recognize the legitimacy of others' expectations (Sugden 2001). In this case, it is not so much the external sanction that matters but an internal one. Transgressions are avoided precisely because one feels others have a 'right' to expect a certain kind of behaviour, and one has an 'obligation' to fulfil others' expectations.

engage in honour killing or cooperate in a given situation does not mean I have a general motive to cooperate or kill to save my honour as such. Having conditional preferences also means that, were my expectations to change, my behaviour would change too.

The triad of empirical and normative expectations and conditional preferences is what, in my view, *defines* social norms. It is a richer definition than the game-theoretic one, since it allows for a clearer distinction between norms and conventions based upon which expectations matter to choice. We can now say that a convention is defined by a simpler dyad: empirical expectations and conditional preferences. In order to adopt a signalling code convention, I only need to believe that almost everyone has adopted it. My preference for using that specific code is conditional upon having certain empirical expectations of group compliance and nothing else. On the contrary, my preference for carrying out an act of honour killing depends on believing that this is the customary behavior in my community, that I am expected to perform such an act, and that my whole family will be dishonoured and ostracized if I do not perform as I should.

It is worthwhile to point out that, whereas empirical expectations are first-order beliefs (I believe others will do so and so), normative expectations are *second-order beliefs*: they are beliefs about the beliefs of other members of the collective (I believe others believe I should do so and so). One's personal inclination to support, like, or dislike a particular social norm is not the most relevant variable in determining one's allegiance to it. Normative expectations do matter, and they may significantly differ from personal normative beliefs. A personal normative belief that, say, a family should ensure their daughters are married as soon as they reach puberty may agree with the normative expectation about what one's community believes is appropriate behaviour, but it also happens that individuals dislike behaviours mandated by a shared norm. When personal beliefs and normative expectations disagree, I predict that normative expectations, not personal normative beliefs, will guide behaviour. This is in line with what social psychologists have observed: beliefs that are perceived to be shared by a relevant group will affect action, whereas personal normative beliefs often fail to do so, especially when they deviate from socially held beliefs.

If we come back to the issue of norm stability, we can now see that a social norm is stable insofar as a majority of followers are motivated to conform. Since conforming to a social norm is *conditionally* preferred (otherwise we are dealing with moral norms or values), a norm's stability will be a function of the stability of the expectations that support it. Let us look at a simple case of two different social norms, N_1 and N_2 that are present in a group G. In both cases, we have that

1. All members of G believe that all other members of G follow N_1 and N_2.

2. All members of G believe that all other members of G believe one ought to follow N_1 and N_2.

However, in the case of N_2, it is not true that 'all members of G believe one ought to follow N_2'. In fact, a majority of individuals dislike N_2 and do not think for a moment one ought to follow it. Yet they observe compliance, or what they think are the consequences of compliance, and have no reason to believe that those who conform to the norm dislike it as much as they do. So they do not dare speak out or openly transgress, and a norm nobody likes keeps being followed or, if transgressions occur, they are kept secret. This is a case of what is known as *pluralistic ignorance*, a cognitive state in which each believes her attitudes and preferences are different from those of similarly situated others, even if public behaviour is identical (Miller and McFarland 1987). The ensuing set of conditions is a fertile ground for pluralistic ignorance:

(a) Individuals engage in social comparison with their reference group. We constantly observe what others do and get clues as to appropriate behaviour, others' preferences, etc. In the case of norms, we are influenced by the preferences of other group members, but we do not know the true distribution of preferences, which we try to infer from observing their behaviour.

(b) Others' behaviour is observable. If not, the consequences of such behaviour are observable. For example, compliance with norms that regulate sexual behaviour or other unobservable behaviours can be assessed by observing the presence or absence of the consequences of such behaviours. In the case of norms that prohibit pre-marital sex, teen pregnancies would be a sign that the norm has been flouted.

(c) No transparent communication is possible. Because of shared values, religious reasons, or simply the fear of being shunned or ridiculed as a deviant or just different, we do not express views that we think will put us at a disadvantage.

(d) It is assumed that, unlike us, others' behaviour is consistent with their attitudes and preferences. There are several possible reasons why this might occur. Fear of embarrassment or the desire to fit in are not easy to observe, so we may come to believe that we experience these emotions more strongly than others do. Another possible cause of the self/other discrepancy is what is called the *attribution error*: we tend to overestimate the extent to which others act on private motives (beliefs, preferences) and instead attribute our own behaviour to external factors (social pressure in this case).

(e) It is inferred that all but us endorse the observed norm. We discount our personal evidence in favour of what we observe and take it at face value.

(f) All end up conforming to the public norm, oblivious to the possibility that they are participants in a group dynamic in which all pretend to support the norm but in fact all dislike it.

In a state of pluralistic ignorance, individuals are caught in an epistemic trap and will keep following a norm they deeply dislike. How long can this last? One may suspect that a norm that is so much disliked would not be stable, since even small shocks to the system of beliefs that support it would lead to its demise. Once the frequency of true beliefs is conveyed to the relevant population, a change would occur. This is only partially true. When actions are strongly interdependent, it is not sufficient to know, and possibly reach common knowledge, that most group members dislike N_2. Since a norm is supported by normative expectations, the participants must also be sure that its abandonment will not be followed by negative sanctions. People face a double credibility problem: they must believe that the information they receive about the group members' true beliefs is accurate, and they must also believe that everyone else is committed to change their ways. There are many ways to achieve these goals, and there are several examples in the literature of successful change of negative norms by means of information campaigns, public declarations, and common pledges.

I have stated that a norm that is beneficial to society is *in principle* more stable than one that is not, or that is even secretly disliked by its followers. Stability, however, is not a *direct* function of the social benefits a norm confers upon its followers. It must be the case that this beneficial function is recognized and expressed in the beliefs of those who conform to the norm, i.e. there must be a shared belief that the norm is valuable for the group that embraces it. Since mutual beliefs support social norms, a norm's stability is a direct function of the stability of those beliefs.

Conclusion

I have presented a view of social norms that, though it encompasses the traditional understanding of what a social norm is (e.g. behaviour that is collectively approved or disapproved and is enforced by sanctions), goes well beyond it. Norms exist because of the expectations of those who follow them. These expectations are not just empirical, as in the case of conventions; they are normative, too, and may include the belief that transgressions will be punished and compliance rewarded. The cost–benefit model of conformity is right in pointing to the importance of sanctions, but its limit is that it does not grasp the importance of mutual expectations. Game theory is a good modelling tool if we want to highlight the interdependence of actions and mutual expectations; yet it does not offer a language specific enough to discriminate between descriptive (empirical) and normative expectations. That distinction is crucial to understanding the difference between social norms and other concepts, as normative expectations are part of what motivates compliance with norms. Finally, a definition of norms in terms of conditional preferences and expectations is *operational*, in that it allows us to make predictions about how changes in expectations will trigger behavioural changes, as well as measure norms and what determines our compliance.

References

Feldner, Y. (2000). '"Honor" Murders—Why the Perps Get off Easy', *Middle East Quarterly*, 7(4): 41–50.

Lewis, D. (1969). *Convention: A Philosophical Study*. Cambridge: Cambridge University Press.

Miller, D., and McFarland, C. (1987). 'Pluralistic Ignorance: When Similarity is Interpreted as Dissimilarity', *Journal of Personality and Social Psychology*, 53: 298–305.

Parsons, T. (1951). *The Social System*. New York: Routledge.

Sugden, R. (2001). 'The Bond of Society: Reason or Sentiment?', *Critical Review of International Social and Political Philosophy*, 4(4): 149–70.

Further Readings

Bicchieri, C. (2006). *The Grammar of Society: The Nature and Dynamics of Social Norms*. New York: Cambridge University Press.

Bicchieri, C., and Muldoon, R. (2011). 'Social Norms', in E. Zalta (ed.), *The Stanford Encyclopedia of Philosophy* (Spring 2011 Edition) <http://plato.stanford.edu/archives/spr2011/entries/social-norms>.

Coleman, J. (1990). *Foundations of Social Theory*. Cambridge, MA: Belknap Press.

Wikan, U. (2008). *In Honor of Fadime: Murder and Shame*. Tr. from Norwegian by A. Paterson. Chicago: University of Chicago Press.

Part V
Methodological Perspectives

12

Interdisciplinarity in Action

Sophia Efstathiou and Zara Mirmalek

Interdisciplinarity. You are in the midst of it—or soon will be. Whether in an interdisciplinary programme or not, you will find yourself working with people who view problems from different angles than you and use different tools to solve them. You will be in conversation with academics, industry, or government collaborators with special approaches to identifying, analysing, or evaluating issues. Mutual respect is needed but not sufficient for such collaborations to flourish.

This chapter gives you some keys for meeting the challenges of interdisciplinary work. We look at interdisciplinarity in action: how its challenges and rewards play out in practice. Social science is especially touched by interdisciplinarity as addressing social science issues often relies on the collaboration of many different experts in academia, government, and policy. Indeed our approach in writing this chapter is 'interdisciplinary' and offers a perspective from the field of 'Science Studies'.

Science studies, or science and technology and society (STS), joins social science approaches with philosophy and history to study the production of scientific knowledge about the world. Philosophical questions about science examine ethics, methods, and deeper assumptions; history examines the dynamics of change in scientific practice; social and cultural approaches include analysis of social structures and power relations shaping and shaped by science. STS brings together such questions and methods in an array of studies of how scientists work together and cooperate with government and industry; cases that provide information and ideas about the common problems you face in an interdisciplinary workplace.

Here we select some examples from our own work and others' to focus on three challenges: figuring the 'whats', the 'hows', and the 'whys' of interdisciplinary work. The first case examines how dealing with racial health disparities relies on deciding what is at stake in this complex phenomenon. The second case discusses how responding to population ageing involves coordinating how people work, in real time. The last section shows that doing 'good' interdisciplinary science involves combining different reasons why to pursue this work. But before we go on, what is it to be 'interdisciplinary'?

1. Discipline, Doctrine, Ethos: Interdisciplinary How, What and Why?

Interdisciplinarity is an approach to academic learning, research, and teaching that is juxtaposed with mono-disciplinarity and to multidisciplinarity. The term 'discipline' is commonly used to define the academic backgrounds or learned skills of professionals. Discipline comes from the Latin *discere*, 'to learn'. In the Catholic Church discipline outlined the rules one had to follow to behave in the ways desirable, while doctrine corresponded to the theory or belief guiding and realized by discipline (Cunningham 2002). Doctrine was what a disciple (a student) learned from a doctor (a teacher) through discipline.

Universities began their existence as places where Catholic monks and nuns were educated, so it is no surprise that we still call the training of university students into various professions 'disciplines' and give our experts 'doctorates'. The thing to remember is that disciplines are fundamentally practices with rules and methods for imparting doctrine, applied and upheld with a certain rigour or force—for instance examinations, and penalties for failing these.

Multidisciplinarity involves many disciplines working side by side, each on the questions it is expert on, with a strict division of labour for addressing different aspects of a challenge. Interdisciplinarity, on the other hand, involves a stronger form of disciplinary mixing. Consider the etymology of the connective 'inter-' which means 'in between' or 'among', as in international, or 'mutually', as in interrelated or interacting. This is strictly speaking different from multidisciplinarity, which would rather involve 'multi-', many or multiple, disciplines, but would not necessarily mix them (Alvargonzález 2011; Klein 2010).

Interdisciplinarity must by default involve some sharing or mutuality in disciplinary practice and theory, shaping joint questions and joint answers to them. Such an integration of disciplines could lead to the development of new questions and domains of practice.

This brings up the question of interdisciplinary ethos. Ethos comes from Greek, where it has a dual meaning: 'habit' or 'custom', and 'character'. Ethos comprises habits that build and define (moral) character. Character, also a Greek word, comes from the verb *charaso*, which means 'to carve'. Our character is built from habits, repeatedly carving us out.

234

When we examine the ethos of science, or do 'science ethics' we are asking: how do our science habits and practices carve out people, and the world? Different disciplines, different practices, carve out the world differently. They have and form different characters for people, and for the research produced. As we see in Chapter 9, the visible moral character of research, what 'good' it drives to uphold or attain, can motivate people to become part of a discipline. The ethos of an interdisciplinary effort is thus also up for mutual negotiation and formation, along with its ways of raising and addressing questions.

Using these distinctions between discipline, doctrine, and ethos we can think of being interdisciplinary as responding to three main challenges:

- Finding a common basis for understanding *what* is at stake (doctrine)
- Deciding and coordinating *how* to deal with issues at stake (discipline)
- Justifying *why* we should pursue shared research on these matters (ethos)

The first challenge is sharing a starting point from which to develop shared understanding and knowledge of an issue. It includes figuring out the nature(s) of problems that call for collective work precisely enough to join available expertise, develop it, and put it to use. The second challenge concerns how we work, how we make work communal and communicate, what kinds of routines we need to coordinate, what kinds of structures and infrastructures we need to support work of different kinds, and with what rhythms and tools to mesh these. The third challenge is motivating and justifying interdisciplinary work that escapes well-defined fields of expertise, while respecting existing drives and skills that inspire committed, well-informed work. These three aspects of interdisciplinary work, what it is about, how it is done, and why it is done, are interrelated and they are not fixed once and for all: 'whats', 'hows', and 'whys' all get negotiated and renegotiated, through collaborative, interdisciplinary work. We next see how.

2. Challenges in Action

2.1 *First Challenge: What is at Stake?*

Brought together to handle a pressing social issue, one of the first challenges collaborators face is understanding exactly what is at stake. How is a stated issue interpreted by each collaborator? One outcome of disciplinary training is that different disciplines tend to see the world differently. They specialize in studying different phenomena or different aspects of the same phenomenon.

235

One case of disagreement about what is at stake is the discussion of 'racial health disparities' in the United States. 'Racial health disparities' are differences measured in the average health outcomes of people from different 'race/ethnicity' groups in the US. For example, 'Black' adults are 40 per cent more likely to be diagnosed with diabetes than 'non-Hispanic White' adults, 71 per cent of people with HIV/AIDS reported in 2010 belonged to racial and ethnic minorities, tuberculosis was diagnosed 8.5 times more in 'Blacks' than in 'Whites' in 2007, and 'Black' infants are three times more likely to die of complications with low birth weight than 'non-Hispanic White' infants. Because of insurance and urban planning people identified with particular categories of 'race' and ethnicity have a harder time getting health care, and when they do get care, it is on average of poorer quality than health care given to 'non-Hispanic Whites'.

Money, effort, and concern are invested in addressing 'racial health disparities': one reason why the US instituted in 2010 a National Institute of Minority Health and Health Disparities (NIMHD). As the Director of the National Institutes of Health (NIH), Francis Collins, says:

> This change by Congress reflects the importance of studying the issue of health disparities with an even greater intensity. We need to learn much more about what causes disparities—including the role of society, the environment, and genes—and to find effective ways of overcoming or changing them.[1]

Director Collins sets out a problem and what matters for solving it. He says that researchers need to figure out the causes of these disparities and change them. Where should they look? Society, the environment, and genes. Like with other complex challenges, this one cuts across more than one field of expertise: social, environmental, and genetic expertise.

Health experts might agree on the challenge, broadly put: how can we get everyone to have good health, irrespective of their 'race' or ethnicity? Yet exactly what is at stake here is not so clear. Health scientists trained in the social sciences tend to see social and economic solutions to this problem, whereas scientists with training in genetics and molecular biology are pursuing pharmaceutical and pharmacogenetic solutions.

Experts in social sciences, including law, sociology, demography, gerontology, psychology, public health, and social epidemiology reason as follows: money and educational resources are distributed differently across 'race/ethnicity' categories; these in turn affect diet, mental health, access to, and quality of health care, which are directly responsible for the health outcomes recorded for 'non-White' groups. Thus to solve 'racial health disparities' we

---

[1] <http://www.nih.gov/news/health/sep2010/nimhd-27.htm>. Accessed Oct. 2013.

must tackle deeper structural inequalities in the social, economic, cultural, and educational opportunities among minority groups; we must eliminate the social causes for this phenomenon. At stake for these experts are matters of social inequality.

Experts in the life sciences and specifically in population genetics and genetic epidemiology think differently. They think that 'race' and ethnicity classifications can be biologically significant, independent of their history of racist use. Human population genetics examines the genetic similarities within groups of people ('populations') who have historically lived together but in isolation from other groups. Population geneticists argue that some inherited and heritable genetic features in people of different US 'race/ethnicity' groups can distinguish them on average from people of a different group. Further, there is some research on genetic markers that could help us figure out who will respond better to a drug and there is an argument that such markers vary regularly with 'race' and ethnicity. Some biomedical scientists thus think that 'race/ethnicity' categories can pick out, consistently, some differences of a biological sort and that these kinds of differences could be causing some health disparities.

If we follow this research programme, investigating factors on a genetic level that associate with how people of different 'race/ethnicity' respond to medications, then another possible way to tackle 'racial health disparities' emerges: look for better designed drugs that are 'personalized' to deal with the particular profiles of people depending on their 'race' or ethnicity. What is at stake for professionals working in the biosciences then is in part a biological, medically interesting, genetic phenomenon that census categories of 'race/ethnicity' help pick out.

All the while, disparities in the average health of different 'race/ethnicity' groups are politically important, irrespective of their medical significance. Economic, political, and educational resources are still unevenly available across these population groups in the US and also uneven across the private pharmaceutical industry and national health providers. There is a long history of racist science that abused people of colour and made claims about genetic differences between 'races'. It is thus challenging, especially for experts from social science backgrounds, to see bioscientists' projects as acceptable. Genetics experts think their research could provide equitable and effective solutions for drug development but social scientists see the mention of genetics as an evasion of the real source of health disparities: historical and continuing social, political, educational, and structural inequality across 'race/ethnicity' groups in the US. Thus the struggle for resources to understand and give solutions to 'racial health disparities' ends up being a struggle across disciplines, mirroring the complex struggles in the day-to-day lives of people identifying with different 'race' and ethnicity.

237

KEY: BE HUMBLE ABOUT WHAT YOUR DISCIPLINE CAN SEE/SHOW IS AT STAKE

Often our disciplinary training is targeted at recognizing and handling specific kinds of phenomena (e.g. biological phenomena, not societal ones). Specialization can make it so an expert sees only particular issues at stake. How should you deal with competing views on what is at stake? This is the kind of challenge that can weigh down a discussion or a research project from the outset, before there is even a chance to work on findings. While there is no formula for a universal solution there are some things to identify, acknowledge, and discuss explicitly as a group.

Negotiating conflicting ideas is not a challenge particular to interdisciplinary science; it also occurs in mono-disciplinary science and it can lead to new ideas. Take for example physics and the idea of 'length'. Classical physics thinks of length as fixed for all observers: measuring the length of a shoe in your room and the length of this shoe on a train does not change the measurement. But special relativity understands length (and time) as changing relative to the velocity of an observer and so the length of a shoe moving very fast relative to an observer would be shrunken relative to a stationary one. Correlatively time will move slower the faster you accelerate. So, concepts of length and time in physics vary depending on whether we do Newtonian or relativistic mechanics, i.e. moving at average velocities versus ones near the speed of light. The fact that we have developed more than one idea about length is a testimony to the progress of physics, even if relativistic ideas created tensions and competitions in science. And even if classical ideas can be defined as special cases of relativistic ones, we still use the old ideas to solve simpler problems in physics.

At issue in interdisciplinary domains is the lack of a common basis for deciding who is right about a question; methods and expertise that can help sort through competing explanations will be different across domains. Social scientists look for different things from their theories than geneticists do; though there may be internal debate about this, both have different criteria for calling their work 'good'. At the same time, the very fact of having come together to solve a problem suggests there should be some shared starting point for inquiry.

In STS we think of those common starting points as *boundary objects*: ideas or tools that straddle disciplinary work boundaries (Star and Griesemer 1989). These objects collect people and interests around them, and they help unify as well as distribute work on a topic. At the same time, seemingly common available ideas often need to get *founded* within different disciplinary domains to do proper scientific work. Different disciplines have different tools for proceeding to think precisely, and so can only use boundary objects meaningfully if they can articulate and found them within their particular scientific context.

In interdisciplinary work we are often in a bind between seeming to be talking about the same boundary thing but in effect having different founded ideas of it. In such cases it is worth tracing backwards through disciplinary logics and reasonings while considering at which points shared understandings may have diverged.

In the case of racial health disparities one seemingly shared organizing idea is '*race*'. Social science health professionals and bioscience experts all seem to be talking about 'race'. But are they?

'Race' is commonly used as a category for sorting people according to their: (a) physical features such as facial attributes, skin colour, hair texture, etc., (b) ancestry, examining one's parents and one's parents' parents, and (c) geographic origin, especially as relating to continental regions, such as Asia, Africa, America, or Europe. While the category of 'race' is controversial, it is used across disciplines to draw out questions on social justice and health. Some scientists use 'race' to study how (a) physical features, (b) ancestry, (c) geographic origin matter for socio-economic phenomena, such as education, financial or social achievement, legal rights and benefits, etc. On the other hand, bioscience experts embed notions of 'race' into their own research context by thinking about how (a) physical features, (b) ancestry, or (c) geographic origin relate to biomedical phenomena, such as disease-associated phenotype or genotype, evolutionary process, etc.

One way to keep track of multidisciplinary investigations on 'race' is to distinguish between how social science and life science disciplines respectively come to understand 'race', as '*sociorace*' and '*biorace*'. Renaming these ideas shows that they are discipline-specific ones and need not exhaust a phenomenon as complex as 'race'. It might turn out that racial health disparities have more to do with 'sociorace' than 'biorace' or it could be that 'biorace' differences really are much more significant than 'sociorace' disparities in how people respond to a drug. But in either case it is important not to minimize the effort and complexity of the problem(s) at stake by calling each others' categories empty.

This multiplicity of understandings is something to work from in interdisciplinary settings. We do not yet have familiar ways of thinking together about possible interactions across levels of life from the genetic to the environmental and societal. Most mainstream models of reasoning about disease and what causes it distinguish between genes and environment or between 'nature' and 'nurture', and focus on one or the other.

Interdisciplinary science need not negate context-specific understandings—this would get rid of a lot of the science we already know. The hope is that interdisciplinary viewpoints can synthesize new ways to understand complex challenges. Once grouped together in collaboration, scientists will often develop further special languages through day-to-day exchanges, as well as negotiations of discipline-specific terminologies, coming to form project-specific or other context-specific vocabularies. Developing new languages and new ideas in interdisciplinary settings demonstrates that simple explanations of a complex phenomenon will often not suffice for effective communication. We need extra work to get competing understandings of what is at stake sorted and negotiated. Figuring out what is at stake is a step towards that project.

2.2 Second Challenge: How do We Work Together?

A second area of challenges for interdisciplinarity is figuring out which methods and analyses are already available for each discipline to bring to the table, and when and how to use them. People with different ways of conducting research have to sort out which among their array of approaches should be applied to a task.

Work in different disciplines often happens in different geographical spaces, following different timelines and patterns of work activity. Coordinating work (or peripheral activities) and respecting each member's disciplinary habits may seem practically impossible within the same team. Further, divergences in methodology often couple with discipline-specific social worlds and negotiating work between disciplines often involves negotiating different work cultures (Strauss 1978). Often this is precisely the site where conflict among interdisciplinary participants is found.

Our case study here is an interdisciplinary group of scientists working to advise policy-makers on UK policy related to Population Ageing and Migration. The group we will call 'PAM' joined expertise from the same academic institution in three main fields: (a) Engineering and Computer Science, (b) Demography and Gerontology, and (c) Operational Research.

Our study of PAM was undertaken in the first eight months of the project by Efstathiou so we got to examine some initial stages in the collaboration. The social worlds of all three, computer scientists, social scientists, and management scientists, are different. We focus here on computer science and social science relations, as PAM members from these two disciplines had no prior history of collaboration. We examine how the groups go about learning about the issues they found to be at stake. We also consider the issue of infrastructure for temporal coordination among collaborators, and for that issue rely on research by Mirmalek among scientists and engineers conducting remote-robotic exploration of Mars, NASA's Mars Exploration Rovers mission.

KNOWING TOGETHER
Consider how PAM members study population ageing and migration. As mentioned, PAM includes social scientists from the fields of demography

and gerontology. Demography and gerontology study population change by measuring social characteristics, such as age, 'race', sex, marital status, educational achievement, and how these characteristics change—with gerontology focusing on changes related to ageing. Social science work in PAM is more akin to social statistics than sociology, emphasizing quantitative outcomes and models.

How do PAM social scientists produce knowledge about population ageing? What is their 'epistemic practice'? First consider how data is sourced. Social statistics relies substantially on actually or distally interrogating living (or data about deceased) individuals. Pursuing data, social scientists often design surveys. They carefully think out what questions to ask whom and in what order to get information about phenomena they think are important—and ones they hadn't considered as well. This information may possibly relate to historical data about a population, and it may be possible to analyse for recommendations on how to respond to foreseeable population changes as societies. Will we need more nursing homes? Should we give pensions to people later? Etc.

Typical concerns for PAM social scientists include choosing what groups to interrogate, what surveys to consult or conduct, what variables have been or should be recorded, and how to align and compare information from different data sources. Researchers seem to be at first seeking an accurate and comprehensive *description* of the social world, without a clear plan for intervention and modification of characteristics recorded. Social scientists want to get the right description now because they think this will increase the chances of effective social interventions in the future. Still, in the first instance it is description as opposed to intervention that is the aim of their epistemic practice.

The practice of computer scientists in the PAM group is interestingly different. These members come from the field of computer science called 'complexity science' that is especially tasked with studying complex systems, i.e. systems that cannot be studied by breaking them into simpler combinations of simpler parts. How do these complexity scientists work? To get knowledge the complexity scientists will often rely on *intervention* first, then description. Complexity scientists build simulations or models of a situation of interest, based on some background knowledge and educated guessing, and then play around with variables to establish interdependencies between components. Interventions are seen as of the essence for establishing how 'sensitive' the system is to different factors and so for making inferences regarding the causal processes involved in system behaviour. Modifying assumed characteristics of imagined agents to see how a model behaves is the bread and butter of building simulations. So it is common practice for PAM complexity scientists to intervene in virtual situations as opposed to carefully describing actual ones. At the same time complexity scientists do view their tools as helping derive descriptions: simulations can help describe mechanisms affecting the complex phenomenon in question. These two kinds of knowledge-gathering practice map onto what philosophers of science traditionally call inductive and deductive reasoning, building theory through respectively observation and testing hypotheses.

Notably, and related to the challenge of doctrine, what is at stake for complexity scientists need not be a social phenomenon. What complexity scientists study is first complex, then human or social. So, an 'agent' whose behaviour is modelled in a simulation can represent an individual human agent but also a population or a non-human structure, as long as the behaviour of the simulated agent displays characteristics of complexity, such as a non-linear evolution or the possibility of global system characteristics emerging (irreducibly) from interactions between individual parts.

BEING TOGETHER

Built and temporal structures are important for interdisciplinary work. Interdisciplinary group members necessarily have ways of working, communicating, and using technologies respective of their disciplinary backgrounds; thus explicit attention must be given to establishing shared meanings of technologies, processes, and goals.

Time, or temporality, is an essential component of any organizational structure, for any work environment (Zerubavel 1981). Clock time is a common technology used across disciplines and institutions that provides a shared language that supports communication among people and machines that may have an otherwise limited shared language. And yet it is so ubiquitous that it is often overlooked and underdeveloped in consideration of supporting the variety of temporal norms, habits, and practices that researchers employ.

Work is temporally differentiated even in a simple research project such as PAM (social science and complexity), but for a richer example consider the work of engineers, scientists, and ethnographers on NASA's Mars Exploration Rover (MER) mission 2003. This was an exploration of the planet Mars carried out by two solar-powered robots remotely operated by scientists and engineers on Earth. Mission members conducted their work while situated in Pasadena, California and organized their work schedules according to the time of day on Mars; i.e. people located in the Pacific Standard Time zone in California were working according to the time of day on Mars where a day is approximately 24 hours and 39.6 minutes long. To convert the time difference people on Earth had to set their clocks forward by 40 minutes every day (for ninety consecutive Mars days). In this collaborative science work, which brought together astrogeologists, atmospheric scientists, and mechanical engineers, to name a few, the mundane act of using clock time to coordinate work and communication (i.e. science analysis, meetings, breaks, meals, etc.) was novel and extra-terrestrial.

MER's interdisciplinary group came up with various technologies to help them tell time on Mars throughout their days and nights on Earth. Devices created to tell time on Mars included spreadsheets, a modified digital alarm clock, even modifying a traditional watch so that it ran slower. Despite different disciplinary relationships to temporality, mission members were inspired by and shared in the goals of producing Martian science via remotely operating robots on Mars, so much so that they cooperatively carried out additional work to support the very infrastructure provided by the organization to support them (Mirmalek 2008). This 'infrastructural maintenance work' appears in the forms of technology modifications and social processes necessary to maintain and support work, which for one reason or another are not included in the formal set of social arrangements and technologies provided for work. With disciplinary backgrounds and outlooks intact, mission members shared readiness to perform infrastructural maintenance work.

KEY: LIVE IN EACH OTHER'S WORLD
Working together relies on sharing some understanding and experience of each others' tools for producing knowledge. Sharing can be helped by combining approaches on specific problems and by obtaining broader understandings of each discipline's reasons for their ways of working.

In our study of the PAM group, social scientists seem to rely on the assumption that data collected today is relevant tomorrow. This assumes that significant social world features have a more or less stable structure. Complexity theorists reversely assume that interactions and unanticipated behaviours are definitive parts of complex systems; future behaviours can emerge from yet be distinct from current ones and in some cases it might just not be possible to offer any prediction of a system's behaviour, let alone predictions based on old data. This kind of divergence can cause friction. However it is generally good to shine a light on these issues because these are great candidate locations for developing new understandings and tools.

For example, a complexity scientist observed during a full team meeting that transition probabilities (probabilities of transitioning from one role or state to another, e.g. from being 'single' to being 'married') may vary with time. For example, how likely one is to get married may be on average different now than in five years. As a result, data collected today may be of little use tomorrow. The complexity scientist's challenge sparked a discussion between a demographer and the complexity scientist on whether simulating partners' behaviour during family formation could help predict variations in future transition probabilities. Could we model how behaviours might change?

The question seemed interesting but was not followed up in that instance. Another lead social scientist responded to the exchange by bringing the discussion back to a practical outcome: answering the grant proposal questions not bigger ones.

This kind of exchange is common in interdisciplinary settings. Some people in a team may be drawn to augment each other's thinking and relate to their perspectives, while others feel less easy with venturing to a question or realm outside the well-defined. Depending on the positions and responsibilities of team members, these tendencies influence team dynamics differently. But both tendencies are important in an interdisciplinary practice. The tendency to translate and share is productive for building a shared practice, but it can also lead to creations outside the mandated, expected, and more troublingly, the doable, so the attraction to what is known is important to respect and negotiate.

It can also be a matter of circumstance that allows joint ventures to move forward. In the PAM case, some interdisciplinary sharing was expedited by a change in roles. A senior demographer and a junior complexity scientist were invited to give a joint presentation; the junior complexity scientist got ill, so the presentation was given solely by the senior demographer, which motivated her to prepare by intensively reading up on complexity science, with direction from the junior scientist. This is an example of the growth in new understanding from crossing disciplinary boundaries and hierarchy. Indeed, the senior demographer described this sojourn into complexity science as an experience of sudden illumination, as a light bulb going off, once she realized one could build up different scenarios and see what the spread of possibilities could be, instead of relying on survey data.

This episode demonstrates the gains from interchanging roles and mutual learning. Openness to flexibility in roles among collaborators may enhance mutual understanding and appreciation of each other's work. It can help establish explicitly what some relevant questions are and to have a greater sense of responsibility for each other's work.

2.3 Third Challenge: Work with Divergent Ethos

So far we have discussed the challenges of figuring out exactly what is at stake for different disciplines and how to bring different practices together, what we broadly dubbed challenges of doctrine and discipline. The third challenge you face when doing interdisciplinary work is managing the different and at times conflicting values placed in this work by different stakeholders. As discussed, the ethos of a practice regards the kind of character it forms and promotes. In an interdisciplinary project aimed to tackle a socially relevant issue, experts, policy-makers, and publics with different ethos come together. Interdisciplinary work will need to figure out what is 'valuable', as well as 'valid' or 'accurate', in conversation with how experts or non-experts consider these points.

As someone working in that milieu, you need to consider at least: (a) what *society* values about your work, (b) what *scientists* not familiar with your expertise value about your work, and (c) what *you* yourself value about your work. Here are some examples of how things can get complicated when you try to combine all these.

First of all, a proper scientific method or result may not be acceptable once we consider the social context of its application. What you may value in one narrow, scientific context is the same thing to dismiss as useless or even harmful, once you think of the bigger picture.

For example, as discussed in Chapters 3 and 16, it is generally accepted that one of the best ways to know if a drug or treatment works is to do a 'randomized controlled trial' or RCT. In this scheme, a group of patients is divided randomly in two groups. The drug under test is given to one group and a placebo (a sugar pill) to the other and we then measure any differences in the health of one group versus the other. But is this always the best way to test a treatment?

In one case, doctors used an RCT to test if a new surgical procedure worked: the procedure called 'extra-corporeal membrane oxygenation' (ECMO), a system for pumping oxygen into the lungs of newborn babies who were at risk of suffocation. It seemed that newborns who got the procedure tended to survive, while without it many died. Still, it was deemed proper science to test the method using an RCT. Expectedly babies in the group not receiving surgery died. Running the RCT instead of trusting historical evidence that ECMO worked was valued by scientists who wanted to ensure that their procedure really worked. But it was arguably not valued by the parents of babies in the control arm who died. Though this was a case of 'proper' science, the test was arguably unethical: it allowed a foreseeable loss of human life (Worrall 2002).

The study is one example where doctors had to negotiate their ethos as medical researchers with the value (and responsibilities) that we place on human life. Ensuring interdisciplinary science is ethical relies on respecting human interests and values, alongside the values that different scientific methods have. As we see from Chapter 9, if you misrepresent or do not consider all the relevant facts, then the ethos of your research is questionable—and mistakes are exacerbated by the socially sensitive nature of this research. On the other hand, if you use unacceptable ways to come up with facts or technologies, or if these are possible to misuse in foreseeable ways that have not been controlled, then the ethos of the research is again often questioned.

KEY: BE REFLEXIVE; MAKE EXPLICIT AND DISCUSS YOUR AIMS AND MOTIVATIONS THROUGHOUT

It is important not to assume knowledge of each other's values and motivations, nor indeed of your own aims as these are under formation. Interdisciplinary motivations structure knowledge production and can revise individual and discipline-specific aims.

One way to address varying ethos among a group, as with conflicting worldviews or practices, is to figure out ways to make the differences visible. Acknowledging such challenges at the outset of collaborative work and allowing for the differences to be factors adds value in interdisciplinary knowledge production, and potentially prepares group members to better understand conflicts later in the process.

What you contribute to a collaborative project will depend on many factors, including the aspirations, prior experiences, and assumptions you bring to it. It is important to have ways for collaborating members to openly reflect on and express their motivations for doing interdisciplinary research. This can both aid awareness and help assess and modify the power of these work commitments in real time. Acknowledgements of this kind from the outset of collaborative work can be tricky, as people may have to admit they care about different things. However making differences explicit in an environment of curiosity and tolerance can help share and shape the collective ethos, allowing for motivations and values to form explicit factors that matter in knowledge production. Sharing a vision for the importance and ethos of an interdisciplinary collaboration is key for doing the maintenance work needed to support the infrastructures of work that are by default under formation.

3. Conclusion

To translate science results into solutions for complex, societal challenges we need to figure out how to best amalgamate already available but diverse knowledge. We must account for societal organizations, cultural values, and political processes, options for technology innovation, and their possible, unintended consequences. Further, for democratic governing we need researchers, entrepreneurs, policy-makers, and people with stakes in the decisions ('stakeholders') to agree on some approaches. And we need those productive interactions between social and natural scientists, ethics experts, and stakeholders early on in the process of policy and technology development as opposed to afterwards. Once we have started along a given direction it is hard to return to earlier stages of development, for example, to address impacts of an approach or technology (think of reactions to genetically modified food).

Social science, history, and philosophy as well as natural science are important here. Social sciences, history, and philosophy examine relationships between societies, technologies, and values. Research in STS shows that doing science research, even natural science research, is strongly influenced by the social and political context where the science happens—not only because societies decide to fund different projects differently (or not at all) but also because problems become apparent and possible to work on because of the very communities and social structures that scientific labour relies on. Conversely, the products of scientific and technological work change our everyday lives, give us new tools to raise new questions and solve older ones. They shape what we worry about and how we behave. This actual mutuality and interdependence of the development of social groups, material tools, and theoretical understandings is why we must think about the social, the human, and the scientific together to understand and reorient ourselves towards challenging situations.

In this chapter we have discussed three related challenges of being interdisciplinary investigated through particular examples:

- Finding a common basis for understanding *what* is at stake (doctrine)
- Deciding and coordinating *how* to deal with issues at stake (discipline)
- Justifying *why* we should pursue shared research on these matters (ethos)

And we offered some keys to help manage these challenges:

- Be *open* about what your discipline can see/show is at stake
- *Live* in each other's worlds
- Be *reflexive* and *discuss* your aims and motivations throughout

To develop guides for interdisciplinary collaboration we need more of all three: (1) work on central issues at stake, (2) creating and testing models for cooperation between science and socio-humanist scholars, and (3) jointly assessing guidelines for such collaborations. Doing and applying interdisciplinary science successfully is a case-by-case matter, but preparing for the kinds of challenges that may arise is a good start for learning to do interdisciplinary science well.

References

Alvargonzález, D. (2011). 'Multidisciplinarity, Interdisciplinarity, Transdisciplinarity, and the Sciences', *International Studies in the Philosophy of Science*, 25: 387–403.

Cunningham, A. (2002). 'The Pen and the Word: Recovering the Disciplinary Identity of Physiology and Anatomy before 1800 I: Old Physiology—the Pen', *Studies in History and Philosophy of Biological and Biomedical Sciences*, 33: 631–65.

Klein, J. (2010). 'A Taxonomy of Interdisciplinarity', in R. Frodeman, J. Klein, and C. Mitcham (eds), *The Oxford Handbook of Interdisciplinarity*. Oxford: Oxford University Press, 15–30.

Star, S., and Griesemer, J. (1989). 'Institutional Ecology, "Translations" and Boundary Objects: Amateurs and Professionals in Berkeley's Museum of Vertebrate Zoology, 1907–39', *Social Studies of Science*, 19: 387–420.

Strauss, A. (1978). 'A Social World Perspective', *Studies in Symbolic Interaction*, 1: 119–28.

Worrall, J. (2002). 'What Evidence in Evidence-Based Medicine?', *Philosophy of Science* (Proceedings), 3: S316–S330.

Zerubavel, E. (1981). *Hidden Rhythms*. Chicago: University of Chicago Press.

Further Readings

Bowker, G., and Star, S. (1999). *Sorting Things Out: Classification and its Consequences*. Cambridge, MA: MIT Press.

Jasanoff, S., Markle, G., Petersen, J., and Pinch, T., eds (1995). *Handbook of Science and Technology Studies*. New York: Sage.

Efstathiou, S. (2012). 'How Ordinary Race Concepts Get to be Usable in Biomedical Science: An Account of Founded Race Concepts', *Philosophy of Science*, 79: 701–13.

Mirmalek, Z. (2008). 'Working Time on Mars', *KronoScope*, 8(2): 159–78.

13

Social Epistemology in Practice

Miriam Solomon

1. Introduction

Sara G. is a 42-year-old woman who wants to take the best care that she can of her health. Should her preventative health care include a screening mammogram? This is a simple question, although it will get a complex answer in this chapter. The use of screening mammography in women aged 40–9 is controversial, and the standard tools of individual epistemology—logic, confirmation theory, and so forth—are not sufficient for understanding and evaluating the controversy. Epistemic concepts and tools from social epistemology will be introduced, in context, and first in **bold** text, to investigate the controversy over screening mammography. I use the case of Sara G. as an extended example throughout this chapter, although I will also mention other examples. After introducing a variety of social epistemic concepts, I will suggest that social epistemic analyses can be used for understanding and evaluating knowledge of all kinds.

First I will give a little background on the controversy over screening mammography. Recommendations for screening mammography have been controversial ever since the technology was developed in the late 1960s, more than forty years ago. Nine randomized controlled trials (two of these specifically for women aged 40–9) and extensive discussions in professional medical organizations have not settled the question of its routine use in women aged 40–9. (You will read about the special virtues randomized controlled trials are supposed to have in Chapters 3 and 16.)

In the US, the American Cancer Society, the National Cancer Institute, the Society for Breast Imaging, and the American College of Radiologists currently recommend annual screening starting at age 40, while the United States Preventative Services Task Force (USPSTF) and the American College

USPSTF & American College
of Physicians → No

of Physicians currently recommend against routine mammography for women aged 40–9. There is similar controversy in other developed countries. Positions have become polarized, with the American College of Radiology stating that the USPSTF recommendations are 'dangerous' and 'make unconscionable decisions about the value of human life',[1] and Michael Baum (an eminent breast surgeon from the UK) saying that the widespread acceptance of screening mammography as the standard of care is 'one of the greatest deceptions perpetuated on the women of the Western World' (quoted in Ehrenreich 2001). Such statements give the impression that the stakes are high, yet the uncertainty surrounding the recommendations continues.

2. From Traditional Individual Epistemology to Social Epistemology

Traditional individual epistemology approaches epistemic questions by asking about the strength of arguments and evidence. It is assumed that individuals produce the arguments and gather and evaluate the evidence. This approach has its roots in Descartes's strategy of beginning with firm foundations and carefully reasoning to logical conclusions. It is particularly suitable for mathematical claims, philosophical argumentation, and some everyday empirical knowledge, but it is less so for scientific knowledge. If Sara G. wants to know whether her bank statement is correct she can check the arithmetic herself. If Sara G. wants to know whether her sweater is on backwards she can gather the necessary evidence directly by looking in the mirror and then she can evaluate that evidence using her memory of what the sweater looked like the last time she wore it. However, if Sara G. wants to know the latest thinking on the origins of the solar system she is best off asking an astrophysicist or reading a book on cosmology; it would be impractical and pointless for her to generate or evaluate the evidence herself (unless she is an expert on astrophysics). Similarly, if Sara G. wants to know whether a screening mammogram offers a net benefit for her, she will not do her own experimentation. She will depend on the results of prior work done by medical researchers, perhaps asking her physician to interpret it for her. She needs to trust that this research is of sufficient quality.

Such **epistemic trust** between people (between individuals such as Sara G. and her physician and between them and the researchers who produced the evidence) involves both basic human trust and reliance on the **expertise**

[1] <http://www.acr.org/About-Us/Media-Center/Position-Statements/Position-Statements-Folder/Detailed-ACR-Statement-on-Ill-Advised-and-Dangerous-USPSTF-Mammography-Recommendations>. Accessed Oct. 2013.

of the researchers who are regarded as **authorities** (not as 'absolute' authorities who can never be wrong, but as having *some* authority) on the subject at hand. This in turn requires confidence in the system of **peer review** which decides which results should be published and thereby become part of the recognized evidence base.

Sara G. will typically also depend epistemically on others to come to a considered conclusion on the basis of the evidence. She might simply ask her doctor, 'What do you recommend?' relying on trust that her physician has her best interests at heart and also confidence in her physician's expertise. Or—perhaps aware of the controversy and aware that her physician is fallible—she may look at the evidence syntheses and clinical guidelines that are published on the topic of screening mammograms. Such syntheses and guidelines are typically produced by research groups and consensus panels, which I will discuss in the next section.

Epistemic trust, reliance on expertise, deference to epistemic authority, and confidence in the system of peer review are all social epistemic attitudes that need to be exercised with care. Some so-called experts are not as highly qualified as they seem to be, and the occasional poor study is not filtered out through peer review. On occasion, experts can deliberately deceive, although more commonly they produce unreliable results unintentionally, through bad luck, flawed study design, deficient experimental skills, or poor judgement.

You are probably familiar with the usual ways of verifying expertise, such as checking academic qualifications and questioning the experts about areas of uncertainty. You may also be aware of difficulties with the practice of peer review, such as non-concurrence of reviews by different experts and a tendency towards favouring established rather than innovative approaches. The social epistemological literature on trust and expertise looks more carefully at the judgements we make in these areas and attempts to improve them.

3. Expert Agreement and Consensus

If Sara G. does not simply take the recommendation of her physician, she may ask whether medical professional organizations have produced clinical guidelines on routine screening mammography for women aged 40–9. Clinical guidelines are typically produced in **expert consensus conferences**. Consensus conferences were invented at the USA's National Institutes of Health in the 1970s and are used by a wide range of professional medical organizations. They are social epistemic institutions designed to bring together a group of ten to twenty experts on a topic of clinical importance, with the goal of rationally discussing controversial aspects of the topic until agreement is reached. This process is usually given two to three days, and concludes with a consensus statement that is widely distributed to clinicians and to the public. In these days of evidence-based medicine (since the 1990s—you can read more about evidence-based policy in general in Chapter 3), consensus conferences are typically preceded by a systematic evidence review, produced by a group of experts on experimental methodology and statistics. So consensus conferences themselves often make use of a prior expert consensus. Consensus statements either include guidelines or are used to generate them.

In many cases in which clinical guidelines are consulted, there is either a single guideline or a few guidelines that agree with each other. For example, guidelines on screening for colorectal cancer—such those produced by the American College of Gastroenterology, the US Preventative Services Task Force, and the American College of Physicians—all concur that routine screening should begin at age 50. But guidelines on screening mammography for women aged 40–9 do not all concur, as was noted at the beginning of this chapter.

The epistemic authority of consensus conferences is due to the agreement of experts; when such conferences on the same topic agree with one another, epistemic authority is increased further. However, when individual experts or groups of experts disagree with one another, their authority is undermined. In general, controversy among authorities undermines their authority.

Scepticism and distrust are reasonable responses of laypersons to expert disagreement. If the experts do not agree, why should we believe any of them? Probably because of this response, the National Guidelines Clearinghouse (NGC) sometimes produces 'Guideline Syntheses' which describe the areas of dispute and then attempt to come to a more nuanced conclusion that acknowledges the rationales of the different guidelines, hopefully restoring their authority. The NGC considers only guidelines that are (a) produced by a recognized professional organization, (b) include an examination of relevant scientific evidence, and (c) have been produced within the past five years. This means that they exclude guidelines that are not of this quality, a reasonable general approach. In the case of screening mammography, however, the 'Guideline Synthesis' comes to an overall recommendation against annual mammographic screening for women aged 40–50 only by excluding two dissenting guidelines that do not clearly fail tests of quality. This does not help to resolve the controversy.

It is worth asking whether consensus statements *deserve* the authority that they have. Why *should* we take more seriously a statement on which the experts all agree? One answer is that the experts are assumed to check on one another's reasoning and correct for idiosyncratic error and individual biases.

In other words, a group of experts can produce a more reliable argument than an individual. Another answer is that the experts may come to the same answer for different reasons, so that their overall agreement signifies distinct lines of reasoning that arrive at the same conclusion, a kind of triangulation in which the experts' conclusions reinforce each other. However, it is also a possibility that consensus is the product of a social process such as 'group-think' in which individuals feel peer pressure, or pressure from leaders, to conform to a particular view. A classic example of groupthink is the Kennedy government's decision to accept the CIA plan to invade Cuba at the Bay of Pigs. When consensus is the product of groupthink it is unreliable. The only way to tell whether the consensus is the product of rational deliberation or the product of groupthink or some complex combination of each is to see how the *process* of coming to consensus takes place. There is considerable variation in the process.

Consensus conferences are not generally useful in science. When scientists disagree, they typically engage in further research; they do not call a consensus conference, sit around a table, and talk for three days. Consensus is not truth, it is merely agreement. In the past, scientists have agreed that the earth is the centre of the universe, that space is Euclidean, and that the continents are fixed; all turned out to be incorrect. Consensus conferences are important and appropriate when researchers want to speak authoritatively on a matter of public concern, such as health or the environment. Hence the consensus statements of the Intergovernmental Panel on Climate Change are important not because they settle a controversy among scientists (there is none) but because they provide a unified voice against the climate change deniers.

The case of screening mammography for women aged 40–9 differs from the case of climate change discussed in Chapter 2 because the active researchers are not in agreement. (For climate change, other interested parties, not the active researchers, are producing the controversy.) As a consequence, the case of screening mammography is a genuinely *scientific* controversy, while the case of climate change is better characterized as a clash between science and other enterprises.

Assessments of the arguments for and against screening mammography sometimes end here. It is common to find a recommendation that, since the experts are in disagreement, this is an area in which individual women can make a choice about what to do. Such a recommendation attempts to turn a difficult situation (expert disagreement) into an opportunity for 'patient-centred' medicine. This is a rhetorical achievement, but it is not really satisfactory. What is being said is that patients may exercise choice when the experts cannot decide on the best option, a paternalistic concession. At the same time, what is suggested is that patient choice in this case is not a reasoned choice, because reason cannot settle the issue. In other words, Sara G. will be told to exercise choice about whether or not to undergo a screening mammogram and told at the same time that the choice exists because the experts cannot find strong enough arguments for one side or the other, i.e. her choice does not really matter.

4. Hot Cognition

An important question to ask during a controversy is: what are the interests of the involved parties? It is well known by social psychologists that human reasoning, even with the best of intentions, can be biased by emotions such as desires to make money or gain power. Such bias is called '**hot cognition**' and distinguished from '**cold cognition**', or reasoning without emotionally caused bias (cold cognition may have other sources of bias, of course).

In the case of screening mammography, it is sometimes pointed out that radiologists have much at stake in the recommendations. Quanstrum and Hayward (2010), for example, discredit the recommendations of the Society for Breast Imaging and the American Society of Radiologists on the grounds that they are likely to be biased by self-interest.

If a process of hot cognition is sufficient to discredit the position that results, however, it is not clear that anyone will be left standing. There are possible or actual motives behind all the positions taken. Epidemiologists, who are usually allied with public health organizations, are often suspected of attempting to cut spending on healthcare, and their recommendations to end routine screening mammography for women aged 40–9 can thus be viewed with suspicion. The American Cancer Society, which is in the business of promoting optimism and personal empowerment about cancer treatment and screening, may wish to continue its messages about early detection quite independently of the actual success of mammography. Primary care practitioners may be invested in thinking that their recommendations for regular screening have helped their 40–9-year-old patients. Hot cognitive biases are pervasive, and it is not clear exactly how we should correct for them or take them into account. Nevertheless, we want to know about them in making our epistemic assessments.

5. Scientific Reasoning, Ideologies and Standpoint Critiques

Another approach to the mammography controversy is to consider scientific plausibility, given what we know about cancer. The reigning orthodoxy about cancer is that, if it is caught early enough, it can be excised and thereby cured. While this is true of some cancers, such as melanoma, cervical cancer, and colon cancer, it is not true of other cancers, such as gliomas and haematological malignancies. Breast cancer is in an intermediate position, with non-aggressive tumours curable if treated before metastasis, but aggressive cancers are not always curable when discovered early. This is because, even in early stages, breast cancer may be a systemic rather than (or in addition to) a local disease. Prognosis is affected by the type of cancer cell and by the host immune response to the cancer. In the case of breast cancer, it has been estimated that, even in the 50–70 age group (which benefits most from mammography), only 13 per cent of patients getting early diagnosis through mammographic screening have their life expectancy lengthened by that early diagnosis. Most of the time (87 per cent) mammographic detection and early treatment offers no benefit. This is not generally appreciated by breast cancer patients and their doctors, who frequently create and believe narratives about lives saved through early screening, detection, and treatment.

Michael Baum (2004) has extended the angiogenesis work of Judah Folkman. Angiogenesis is the formation of new blood vessels. Judah Folkman proposed that the growth of a cancer is limited by the richness of its blood supply, and that inhibiting such growth would be an effective cancer treatment. Baum suggested that mammography actually *causes* breast cancers, not only through exposure to radiation but also through the unforeseen effects of biopsy of suspicious lesions. Baum suggests that the injury caused by biopsy produces increased blood flow and stimulates angiogenesis in the area, and that this nourishes the cancer and enables it to spread. In the current state of knowledge about breast cancer and its mechanisms, this is a reasonable suggestion. In fact, one study, the Canadian National Breast Screening Study, found a higher death rate from breast cancer among women aged 40–9 who were screened than women who were not screened. (This result has usually been dismissed as a statistical fluke. But note that the data suggesting that screening is beneficial are not robust either.)

'Scientific plausibility' in the absence of supporting data does not count for much, because scientific predictions often fail. Sometimes the plausibility is the result of coherence with other (wider than 'scientific') beliefs, such as the widespread belief that our health is under our control and that if we act responsibly and go for regular check-ups we can avoid major health problems. Such a belief is more of an ideology than a scientific theory, and one that is particularly resonant with North American values. In contrast, Michael Baum's suggestion coheres with a belief that 'not meddling' is the best way to avoid health problems and a more British ethos of not going looking for trouble!

One of the tools of social epistemology is **standpoint theory**, which has its roots in Marxist and feminist thought and which you learn more about in Chapter 8. Standpoint theorists (such as Sandra Harding and Patricia Hill Collins) argue that there is often unacknowledged ideology underlying reasoning and that proper assessment of that reasoning also needs to recognize and critique the ideology. It is difficult to recognize one's own ideological presuppositions. Those in the best position to identify and critique ideology are those who are either disadvantaged by and/or outsiders to that ideology. So, for example, women who have occupied traditional homemaking roles are in a position to critique economic theories that do not value this labour. A standpoint is a social perspective that includes awareness of power relations. When there are ideologies underlying scientific claims, as is the case for the different theories about the early development of breast cancer, standpoint critique may be forthcoming from scientists who have developed critical awareness of these ideologies. This is the place to mention that, as someone who was raised in Britain but has spent most of her adult life in the USA, I have developed a critical distance from the ideologies favoured in both countries!

6. Goals and Values

Sara G.'s decision about whether or not to have a screening mammogram is not only a question about whether or not screening mammography prevents early deaths from breast cancer for women aged 40–9. The decision should take into account any other possible benefits as well as harms such as the pain and inconvenience of the screening itself, the anxiety while waiting for results, the anxiety and unnecessary invasive procedures (biopsies) resulting from false positives, and the damage caused by treatments such as surgery, radiation, and chemotherapy for tumours which might never become life-threatening. To save one life from breast cancer over about eleven years of screening in women aged 40–50, about 2,100 women would need to be screened regularly, about 690 would receive a false positive mammography at some point, about seventy-five would have an unnecessary breast biopsy, and five women will be diagnosed with DCIS or invasive cancer and be treated (unnecessarily) with surgery, radiation, and/or chemotherapy (CTFPHC 2011).

Some of the benefits and harms of mammography vary in magnitude for different people; for example, some women suffer more anxiety about breast cancer than others. The decision also needs to take into account available resources for preventative health care, both societal and individual. These are matters of negotiation and sensitive to values. If Sara G. is a US citizen with health insurance, her screening mammography is paid for; the reason for this is the late twentieth-century history of patient advocacy in breast cancer treatment, especially from the women's health movement. If Sara G. is a British citizen, her mammography will not be covered by the National Health Service (NHS) (unless she is judged to be at particularly high risk), and she will have to decide whether or not to use her own money to pay for it, or to pay for other potentially life-extending interventions, or to pay for something else entirely. In Britain, the NHS covers routine screening mammography only for women aged 50–70, and this is the product of a societal and governmental discussion and negotiation.

Social epistemologists acknowledge that **goals** and **values** vary across both individuals and communities and are relevant to practical decision-making, which as we see in Chapter 9 applies widely across areas of concern to both the natural and the social sciences. The results of inquiry depend in part upon the goals of inquiry, as Chapter 14 stresses as well.

7. Epistemic Diversity

People differ from one another in the ways in which they engage in inquiry. Some think boldly, others cautiously; some aim for simple unifying theories while others aim for more complex situational accounts; some are conservative and others flexible; some are particularly skilled at devising and carrying out experiments while others have creativity in devising theories. Standpoint is one kind of epistemic diversity, attained by some individuals for some questions.

Epistemic diversity, which is also discussed in Chapter 9, is generally beneficial in inquiry, for several reasons. First, it produces **division of cognitive labour**, i.e. it leads people to work on different aspects of a problem rather than simply attempt to replicate each other's work. Secondly, it increases the chances that a research group, composed of several different individuals, will include the necessary range of skills and knowledge, which are often far greater than can be accomplished by an individual. And third, it reduces the chances that an important idea or perspective will be overlooked.

How much epistemic diversity is desirable? This question can be asked generally, but also for particular epistemic issues such as the mammography debates. Sara G. could ask the question, 'Who are the people investigating mammographic screening and do they have enough epistemic diversity?' It is difficult to say exactly how much epistemic diversity is needed, but particular shortfalls on diversity are worth noting and addressing. For example, if the researchers were primarily senior clinicians, it would be worth asking,

'Would younger researchers come to less conservative conclusions?' If the researchers were all men, it would be worth asking, 'How does the matter look to a woman in her forties?' In the early years of mammography research (the 1970s), epistemic diversity was inadequate; it is probably much better now.

8. Testimonial Injustice

Even when epistemic diversity is adequate, the resulting scientific debate may be lacking because some perspectives are unjustly ignored, devalued, or rejected. For example, the Women's Health Movement of the 1960s and 1970s argued that patient perspectives have been dismissed because subjective patient experience is often regarded as unreliable and/or unscientific, even more so when it is the experience of women who are traditionally thought to be less reliable and less objective. Miranda Fricker (2007) has written extensively about testimonial injustice as both an ethical and an epistemic problem. Testimonial injustice can be systematic when it rests on prejudices such as stereotypes about women. When patient perspectives are ignored, patients are doubly harmed: once by not having their contributions to knowledge taken seriously and also by the fact that the knowledge produced, which concerns their health, will be less reliable. So they are harmed both as knowers and as patients.

Does Sara G. have to worry about testimonial injustice among mammography researchers? I expect that by now patient perspectives have been attended to, but there are other possible kinds of testimonial injustice that might be considered for this case. Is research from non-English speaking countries not taken as seriously as it should be? Do some kinds of medical specialists, e.g. radiologists, have too much say? Have some publications been overlooked because they have been published in non-prestigious journals? I am not aware of any particular testimonial injustices in the case of the research on screening mammography, but generally such questions are worth asking.

A good place to look for information about possible testimonial injustices related to screening mammography is patient advocacy organizations, such as Breast Cancer Action and the National Breast Cancer Coalition. These organizations have developed the standpoints (discussed in section 5) begun by the Women's Health Movement and other progressive communities to review the available evidence. The Women's Health Movement of the 1960s and 1970s was decidedly pro-mammogram, because that was a time when there was both optimism that screening mammography would greatly decrease the mortality from breast cancer and at the same time pressure to take women's health more seriously and devote more resources to it. Widespread insurance coverage for screening mammography for women of all ages is in part due to the advocacy of the Women's Health Movement. Breast Cancer Action and the National Breast Cancer Coalition were founded around 1990, and inherited the tradition of advocacy for women's health and healthy suspicion of the medical establishment and its supporting industries. By this time, the premise that mammography saves lives was being actively questioned. Breast Cancer Action and the National Breast Cancer Coalition did their own analyses of the evidence, and their current recommendations are that women should not begin routine mammographic screening until age 50.

Sara G. can be somewhat reassured that the evidence has been examined by advocacy organizations that would be quick to call out medical recommendations that were being made more on the basis of cost than on the basis of efficacy.

9. Agnatology

Jane Wells, a British public health physician, has written that 'The debate over the necessity for screening for breast cancer among women in their 40s has assumed an importance out of proportion to its potential impact on public health' (Wells 1998). There is a good deal of wisdom in this comment. If mammography offers a benefit to women in their forties, it is a very small benefit, and if mammography is an overall harm to women in their forties, it is a very small harm. If it were a larger benefit or harm, the data would be clearer. Arguably, more lives would be saved by directing the health care dollars devoted to screening mammography for women in their forties to other preventative health care interventions, such as vaccinations. Nevertheless, the debate persists and continues to consume more than its fair share of attention. For example, the Canadian Preventative Services Task Force, re-established in 2010, selected screening mammography as its first topic for discussion. The media are eager to cover the continuing debate and the public is eager to hear about it.

A new branch of social epistemology, called **agnatology**, looks critically at the ways in which cultures create and maintain ignorance about particular areas of inquiry. 'Agnatology' means the study of ignorance, and the field was named about ten years ago by historians of science Robert Proctor and Londa Schiebinger. An agnatologist would observe the excessive focus on the question of screening mammography for women in their forties and ask the question, 'What issues and questions are being ignored by this focus?' One answer that has been suggested is that the focus on screening distracts and diverts attention from the rising incidence of breast cancer and from questions about its environmental causation. Very little attention is paid to possible systemic environmental causes of breast cancer, such as air pollution and hormones and toxins in the food industry. Addressing these causes would be challenging and require a good deal of political courage. Focusing on what individual women can choose to do to detect breast cancer early is an effective distraction. Barbara Brenner, the former Executive Director of Breast Cancer Action, said this well in 1997:

> If there is any reason for outrage, it is this: as long as we are spending our time, energy and money on the mammogram debate, we are distracted from finding a nonradiation-based detection method that works, discovering effective treatments and offering primary prevention. Just as Nero fiddled while Rome burned, we are spending enormous resources on an aspect of breast cancer that ultimately does very little, if anything, to save lives.

Likewise, the oncologist and epidemiologist Steven Goodman writes:

> Even under the most optimistic assumptions, mammography still cannot prevent the vast majority of breast cancer deaths. Improving methods of risk prediction, communication, disease detection and treatment will probably yield more public health benefit than continued debate about mammography. (Goodman 2002: 364)

If Sara G. knows this, she can keep the significance of her clinical dilemma in proportion. It turns out that not much is at stake. If she wants to improve her own health, there are more effective practices to focus on. If she wants to engage in breast cancer advocacy, her time is best spent on issues such as aetiology, better diagnosis, and better therapies.

10. Special Circumstances

So far, Sara G. has been treated as though she has average risk of breast cancer, with no strong risk factors such as BRCA1 or BRCA2 genes or serious family history. This is implicit in the phrase 'routine screening mammography'. What happens if we know something about Sara G. that leads us to conclude that she is at greater risk of dying from breast cancer? For example, what if Sara G. is African-American? African-American women have greater breast cancer mortality than White Americans. At one time, it was thought that this was because of less screening of African-American women, but increased screening of African-American women has not closed the mortality gap. So knowing that Sara G. is African-American should not change the recommendations for routine screening. Another possibility is that Sara G. has a strong family history of the disease, with mother and sisters already diagnosed. Screening starting at an earlier age is likely to be beneficial in this case. I do not explore all the options for special circumstances here, because the main focus of this chapter is routine screening mammography.

11. General Normative Concerns

Some social epistemologists aim to give general accounts of how much epistemic diversity, forums for criticism, values discussions, and so forth is ideal. One of the most well-known such accounts is Helen Longino's (1990) 'critical contextual empiricism' which, as we see in Chapter 4, specifies four social standards for scientific knowledge: equality of intellectual authority (lack of testimonial injustice), shared standards for evaluation which include empirical success, public forums for criticism, and responsiveness to criticism. To the degree that scientific communities follow these norms, Longino argues, they produce objective science. Sara G. might benefit from a social normative account such as this one, which offers a checklist of the sorts of epistemic social phenomena to evaluate.

12. Conclusions

A traditional individual epistemological analysis of the mammography debate would only examine the logic of evidence and arguments and would end in simple uncertainty. A social epistemic analysis can go further, looking also at trust, expertise, authority, peer review, the results of consensus conferences, the likely presence of hot and cold cognitive bias, standpoint analysis, goals and values in inquiry, epistemic diversity, testimonial injustice, agnatology, and social norms. This leads to a deeper understanding of the debate and ultimately expands the options available to Sara G. I have used a variety of tools from social epistemology in answering the question, 'Should Sara G. have a routine mammogram?' The same tools can be used for many other questions, in medicine, technology, and other fields.

References

Baum, M. (2004). 'Commentary: False Premises, False Promises and False Positives— the Case Against Mammographic Screening for Breast Cancer', *International Journal of Epidemiology*, 33(1): 66–7; discussion 69–73.

Brenner, B. (1997). 'From the Executive Director: Fiddling While Rome Burns: The Latest Mammogram Controversy', *Breast Cancer Action Newsletter*, 41 (Apr.–May) <http://archive.bcaction.org/index.php?page=newsletter-41c>. Accessed Sept. 2013.

CTFPHC (Canadian Task Force on Preventive Health Care) (2011). *Guidelines for Screening for Breast Cancer*. <http://canadiantaskforce.ca/guidelines/2011-breast-cancer>. Accessed Oct. 2013.

Ehrenreich, B. (2001). 'Welcome to Cancerland', *Harper's Magazine*, Nov.: 43–53.

Fricker, M. (2007). *Epistemic Injustice: Power and the Ethics of Knowing*. Oxford: Oxford University Press.

Goodman, S. (2002). 'The Mammography Dilemma: A Crisis for Evidence Based Medicine?', *Annals of Internal Medicine*, 137(5): 363–4.

Longino, H. (1990). *Science as Social Knowledge: Values and Objectivity in Scientific Inquiry*. Princeton: Princeton University Press.

Quanstrum, K., and Hayward, R. (2010). 'Lessons from the Mammography Wars', *New England Journal of Medicine*, 363(11): 1076–9.

Wells, J. (1998). 'Mammography and the Politics of Randomised Controlled Trials', *British Medical Journal*, 317(7167): 1224–9.

Further Readings

Goldman, A. (1999). *Knowledge in a Social World*. Oxford: Clarendon Press.

Lackey, J. (2008). *Learning from Words: Testimony as a Source of Knowledge*. Oxford: Oxford University Press.

Solomon, M. (2001). *Social Empiricism*. Cambridge, MA: MIT Press.

Part VI
Research Methods

14

Measurement

Nancy Cartwright and Rosa Runhardt

1. Is Syria in Civil War?

At the time of writing this chapter, it is undecided whether we may classify the violent conflict in Syria that started in 2010 as a civil war. We know US President Barack Obama spoke of the 'grave dangers of all-out civil war' (Mason 2012) in the Arab state and that UN Secretary-General Ban Ki-Moon warned of civil war erupting (Black 2012). Who will decide whether it has and on what basis?

When classifications like this are made by social scientists, it is often called *coding*: assigning the conflict to a specific class (civil war/not civil war) or assigning it a specific number (say a level 5 rather than a level 4 civil war), using clear, articulated criteria. Coding is part of the process of measurement. Designing proper measures and carrying them out is one of the key jobs we expect science to accomplish. Properly defined and properly executed scientific measurements provide us with a precise picture of the things we study and give us the kind of information from which we can build scientific laws, models, and principles that can help us predict and change the world around us. This chapter is about how this is done in the social sciences. We begin by considering how civil wars are measured.

1.1 Intricacies of Categorizing a Conflict

Making measures may be one of the central jobs that the social sciences do, but we must from the very start be clear that how it is done can have implications well beyond the confines of the sciences, and scientific measures may for just that reason be hotly politically contested. Take the case of Syria. Both the Syrian government and the opposition activists have at the time of writing denied that the conflict is a civil war, because both are aware that, if the conflict is labelled a civil war, the international community may well respond to it in specific ways they don't want. Rather, they'd prefer the conflict to be called an act of terrorism (which would criticize the activists), or on the contrary, for it to be called a massacre (which would shed a positive light on the opposition). By calling the conflict a civil war we are stuck in the middle: the naming implies that there's an appreciable amount of force used on both sides, and neither of the two parties would be happy with that.

1.2 Civil War Studies

There are many intricacies when it comes to defining *civil war* and deciding if a conflict falls under the definition we settle on. Just think of the many cases of conflict that are called civil wars in common speech: both the nineteenth-century American War of Secession and the current conflicts in Colombia fall under this label. What connects them?

In the social science civil-war literature, the most common definition focuses on four aspects. A civil war is a war that involves fighting internal to the metropole, the national government participates actively, both sides employ an appreciable amount of force (the 'effective resistance criterion', which may require, for example, that the opposition is responsible for at least 5 per cent of deaths, or at least a hundred government deaths), and a certain number of deaths result from the conflict (the 'death threshold') (Sambanis 2004).

All this can seem ad hoc and especially the choice of threshold levels and percentages. There is nothing in nature that tells us what a civil war is; it's not a category in the same way that atoms or elm trees are. Rather, war scholars use case studies and statistical analysis to find out what kinds of categories help them understand conflicts and accomplish other goals they have in view—like monitoring what is happening, making comparisons across countries, regions, or times, preventing harm or predicting the future, and doing so in either the long or the short run and either globally or locally. On that basis, they've judged definitions requiring these four elements helpful. Importantly, it turns out that internal conflicts that have these characteristics in common have other characteristics in common as well. As a stunning example, scholars have found some evidence that states with a secondary school enrolment of ten percentage points higher than the average have a reduced risk of about three percentage points to break out in civil war—at least as civil war is characterized by this kind of definition (Collier and Hoeffler 2004).

Even if scholars agree on a definition, that is not the end of the story. Before the definition can be applied, civil war scholars must 'operationalize' the definition—i.e. specify just what procedures need to be carried out to decide if the definition is satisfied. This can involve entire new layers of definition. For instance, what exactly is to count as a war death? Deaths of combatants? 'Collateral deaths' of 'civilians' directly due to conflict? Deaths that arise indirectly due to damages to health care and delivery systems, water supplies, food resources, etc.? And then, who counts as a combatant and who counts as a civilian? Must one be armed at the point of death to count as a combatant? More on-the-ground problems arise when it comes to collecting the actual data needed to check whether a state is in civil war. Counting deaths in a conflict is tricky, especially when both sides of the conflict try to hide the number of casualties they have taken and that they have caused to the other party.

2. Three Requirements for Measurement

Coding for civil war—categorizing a violent conflict as a civil war on clear, articulated criteria—is, as we noted, an example of measurement in social science. You may most immediately associate measurement with assigning a number to a specific unit (think, for instance, of measuring someone's height). But deciding to put an individual unit in a specific category is as much a measurement as assigning to them a number or value for some quantity like height or income. If we want to be formal about it, we can think of categories as quantities with two values: individual units (which can be persons, countries, regions, institutions, etc.) take the value 'yes' or 1 for this quantity if they fall within the category and 'no' or zero otherwise.

Measurement, though, isn't just assigning values or numbers or putting things into categories; it is doing so in a systematic and grounded way. This involves three different kinds of activities: *characterization*—laying out clearly and explicitly what the quantity or category is, including any features of it that we intend to make use of in assigning a number or category to a unit; *representation*—providing a way to represent the quantity or category in our scientific work; and *procedures*—describing just what must be done to carry out the measurement successfully. It is important that the three activities mesh. They should not only be consistent but also mutually supporting, as we shall illustrate.

2.1 *Characterization*

Before we can measure a quantity or specify procedures for deciding if an individual unit fits into a category, we need to be clear what that quantity or category is. We shall illustrate with 'yes–no' quantities for now, pursuing our original example. Categorizing an individual requires a couple of things that have been illustrated by the case of civil war. First, a category must be formulated, a category that is *useful for purpose*—for the specific purposes to be served in measuring the category. For instance, if we are interested in finding ways to lower the probability of armed conflict between government and some opposition groups espousing opposed ideals, we may delineate the category *civil war* one way. On the other hand, if we are more interested in preventing the spread of HIV/AIDS as result of violent conflicts (which may occur by infected members of one side of the conflict purposely raping civilians), the category we have delineated under the label *civil war* for the first purpose may be not so useful. So, delineation depends on the aim of the social science research.

Why not, you may ask, just keep working on the problem till we manage to formulate the 'correct' delineation of civil war? That's the tricky thing about *civil war* as a category, and similarly with a great many of our other concepts in social science. Civil war is not something 'just there' in nature, like a hydrogen atom or a birch tree or the planet Jupiter. It is not what is called a 'natural kind'. Rather, it is a concept that is socially constructed. It is socially constructed in two senses. First, civil war is an activity that depends on human actions to occur; and second, this concept is only formulated because we care about, and thus wish to focus on, particular kinds of conflicts, like those currently going on in Somalia, Sudan, and Colombia.

Second, *civil war* is not something that has definite boundaries nor, it seems, is there some one set of characteristics that all things we label as civil wars have in common, by contrast for instance with electrons, which are all negatively charged, or with the number of people whose births are recorded in the local church registry for 1847. Rather, the different violent conflicts that get called civil wars all differ from one another. This reminds us of the way members of a family look alike. They might look like Smiths and each one may look in some significant way like some of the others, but there is probably no set of visible characteristics that all or even most members of the Smith family have in common. The Smith family look alike to us not because they share one common feature, but because there's sufficient overlap among them with respect to the visible features that we take note of. Civil wars seem to be like that. But to make matters more complicated, some civil wars have more elements in common with non-civil wars than they do with other civil wars.

In order to describe this fuzziness we find in concepts like *civil war*, we call them *Ballung* concepts: concepts that are characterized by family resemblance between individuals rather than by a definite property. *Ballung* is a German word for a concentrated cluster; the term *Ballungsgebiet* (*Ballung* region) is used to describe sprawling congested urban complexes like the area from New York to Washington on the East Coast of the US. We take the term from left-wing leader of the Vienna Circle between the Great Wars, Otto Neurath. Neurath worried about the role that Ballung concepts can play in 'proper science' since it seems there can be no strict universal relations of the kind typical in physics (and perhaps other natural sciences) between concepts that have neither strict boundaries nor whose instances share any essential features in common (Neurath 1936). When we are trying to find an apt categorization to suit the aims of the social science research we are doing, we must find some way to deal with both the Ballung fuzziness of many social concepts as well as the fact that many are socially constructed.

A third problem for characterization is that, even if we construct a category or quantity that we are interested in, there is no guarantee that we will be able to do fruitful research using this category or quantity. If we have a category that consists of individuals that have little in common except the fact that they're grouped in this category, we can't do much with our categorization. If instead it turns out that they also have other properties in common—perhaps all the states we say are in civil war are also very poor, or perhaps they all have a high unemployment rate for young men—then we can begin to formulate some useful claims using these concepts.

One of the important features that social scientists look for in delineating a quantity or category is that there be some shared set of causes or some shared effects from being in the category or possessing specific values of the quantity, though the sets of causes and effects may, like the concepts themselves, have only rough boundaries and no strict criteria of inclusion.

One of the ways in which categorization can go wrong is when we use a category that is so general that all causes become invisible. We can use civil war again as an example. Suppose we take for granted that we have a decent database of all violent conflicts in states since 1945 (such as the Correlates of War (COW) project database founded by political scientist J. David Singer and hosted at Pennsylvania State University since 2003) and that we can do good statistical research on these conflicts. Using the characterization of *civil war* in section 1.2 but considering various different values for the threshold of deaths and the effective resistance criterion, social scientists have looked for a correlation between whether a country is in civil war and how much ethnic diversity it has. For some values of the threshold and criterion they find a small correlation; for others, none. This suggests that ethnic diversity is not a real cause of the kinds of conflicts we are trying to focus on using the concept *civil war* (Sambanis 2004).

But this is surprising because our intuitions, as well as a large body of literature in international relations and a number of case studies in different countries, paint a different picture. In these other kinds of studies, it seems as if countries that are ethnically diverse are likely to develop conflicts. Why then does it not show up in the statistical research? The reason that some social scientists adduce is that as a category *civil war* as characterized in section 1.2 is too general. By averaging across all conflicts that satisfy that characterization, we lose the information about ethnic diversity. To resolve this problem, a more narrow category of *ethnic civil war* has been devised. For instance, Nicholas Sambanis defines *ethnic civil war* as 'war among communities (ethnicities) that are in conflict over the power relationship that exists between those communities and the state'. Statistical research with this category provides evidence, or at least so it is claimed, that ethnic diversity in a country does indeed increase the probability of ethnic civil war there (Sambanis 2001).

Another familiar way that characterization can go wrong is when different scholars seem to be talking about the same thing but report very different results for it. They seem to be talking about the same thing because they call it by the same name, like 'civil war', or 'degree of poverty', or 'level of inflation'. But often in actuality they are not disagreeing. Instead, they are measuring different concepts, different because they have characterized them in different ways. Some authors might say, for instance, that Somalia is at civil war in a certain year, while others might disagree because they have adopted different thresholds for the number of deaths.

EXAMPLE: CPI
Moreover, the way we characterize a concept for policy can have different consequences for different groups of people. Consider for example the US Consumer Price Index (CPI), which is meant to be a measure of inflation in the price of consumer goods. To measure the rate of inflation from one year to another, the average price of a basket of goods is compared between the two years. To do that, the CPI procedures specify that a sample be made of the prices of these goods from various kinds of stores across the country. So to provide a detailed characterization of this concept that will be relatively easy to proceduralize, a great many questions need to be answered, amongst which is: at what kinds of stores do individuals do their shopping?

One of the issues in more recent years is that people have started shopping at discount stores rather than through traditional distribution channels such as grocers. The Boskin commission, a panel of experts appointed by the US Senate Finance Committee to study the accuracy of the CPI, observed this gain in market share of discount stores and decided to adjust the CPI accordingly. This made a difference to the CPI value and correlatively to the welfare of a great many people whose income—like social security and veterans' benefits—is pegged to the CPI. However, groups differ in crucial respects when it comes to the stores they go to. There are large groups of people in the US, like the elderly and poor veterans dependent on their benefits, who are unable to go to discount stores, which are often located far away from town centres. The elderly and poor veterans are therefore disadvantaged by the new categorization of inflation compared to the people who do shop at discount stores.

Note that this example also shows that the consequences of using a specific measure rather than another can require a very specific form of expertise. Not only do those appraising the consequences of using one CPI rather than another need to be experts in economics, they also need knowledge of the shopping patterns of, for example, the elderly.

2.2 Representation

Once social scientists have come to a specific characterization of a social science concept, they need to devise a method of representing the concept in their scientific work—in their claims, their calculations, and their studies. It is important that the representations adopted do justice to the characterization. This is true for all kinds of social science concepts. Think, for instance, of *poverty*. We can characterize poverty in various ways that make it a yes–no matter: either you're poor, or you're not. For instance, do you earn less than $2 a day, or less than two-thirds of the median income in your country? In this case poverty should be represented as a two-valued variable. Alternatively the concept of interest may be not *poverty* but *degree of poverty*. This might be characterized in terms of which quartile of the population your income falls in, in which case it would be represented by a variable that takes four values. Alternatively one could simply characterize *degree of poverty* as how much income one earns. Then it would be represented as a continuous variable. Or we may have a more nuanced concept characterized in terms of various aspects of being poor that concern us. For instance we may define a concept where not only income matters but also amount of access to clean water, electricity, education, and housing. In this case the concept should be represented by a table of different indicators, where the indicators themselves may be yes–no variables or multivalued.

Similarly, there are several ways in which we can represent *civil war*. First, we may represent civil war with a two-valued variable. In that case we judge that either there is no civil war in a state, and we assign a 0 to that state, or there is, and we assign a 1 to it. This is done by many social scientists interested in civil war, particularly by those who wish to undertake purely quantitative, statistical research. Recently, however, this two-valued representation has come into question. For one, some commentators feel it is wrong to suggest that civil war is the same no matter where it takes place. The civil war in Sudan is different from the one in Colombia. But the two-valued representation can make it seem as if all civil wars are the same by lumping the countries in which they occur together under the label '1—engaged in civil war'. This means that the two-valued representation does not do justice to the characterizations of *civil war* that these commentators have in view (even if they have not provided a characterization explicitly).

If we look at other characterizations of civil war, like some of those we will describe in this chapter, it is more reasonable to argue against the two-valued indicator. This kind of back-and-forth process of mutual adjustment is typical in devising measures in both the natural and the social sciences. Characterization and representation must get changed in tandem. They must also change in step with the procedures for measurement (which we turn to in section 2.3) and vice versa. A change or improvement in any one of the three typically produces the need for change in the other two.

It is useful to note here Stanley Smith Stevens's distinctions to summarize some familiar types of representation that social scientists make use of. Stevens (1951) describes four ways of representing a concept. We have already seen the first type. We may represent a concept using a *numeral* scale by assigning different numbers or letters or names to the different units that fall under the concept. This is the kind of representation we employ when we use a two-valued variable, as in the case of *civil war* where countries are divided into two groups, conventionally labelled '1' and '0'. But the numbers are just labels—we don't treat them as numbers.

Stevens's second type of representation is the *ordinal* scale. Using an ordinal scale means *ranking* the units that fall under the concept. Here the numbers do mean something. The higher the number assigned an individual unit, the more of the quantity it possesses. So we might rank *degree of poverty* on a scale from 1 to 10. With a merely ordinal scale the size of the differences between any two numbers doesn't mean anything. There is no implication with an ordinal scale that, for instance, the difference in the degree of poverty between individuals assigned '4'and those assigned '6' is the same as that between those assigned '8' and those assigned '10', nor that there is twice the difference in the degree of poverty for individuals falling in either of these groups as the differences between individuals assigned '1' versus '2' or '7' versus '8'. This contrasts with Stevens's third type of scale, the *interval* scale, which both orders individual units and has equal intervals between points with equal numerical separation. (You see a similar distinction to that between interval and ordinal scales discussed in Chapter 10 between cardinal and ordinal scales.)

Fourth, social scientists may rank the units under study on a *ratio* scale—an interval scale with a natural zero point. We would for instance be using a ratio scale if we assigned the label *degree of civil war* according to the number of deaths, e.g. this civil war claimed 5,000 deaths, whilst that one claimed 23,000.

A different way of representing civil war is with a probability distribution. In line with the idea that a different representation generally presupposes a different concept—a different characterization—the representation in this case is not of *civil war* as characterized in section 1.2, but of 'probability of civil war onset in a state'. Nicholas Sambanis, for instance, uses this representation in order to explore and represent how strongly various different social and economic factors are conducive to civil war. He wishes to know what other aspects of a state influence the chances of civil war breaking out. He then uses the conditional probability for civil war onset, conditional on these other aspects, as an indicator that these aspects influence the onset of civil war. We have already seen an example of this research in the case of the conditional probability of civil war onset given a specific unemployment rate and/or school enrolment rate for young men. Another conditional probability we encountered was the probability of civil war breaking out given a certain amount of ethnic diversity.

In general, this probability research goes as follows. Faced with a certain state, say Angola, the civil war scholar tries to find the value of a set of parameters that are meant to represent properties of that country. These parameters might include the school enrolment rate and amount of ethnic diversity already mentioned, but also how poor the country is (represented perhaps by the GDP, Gross Domestic Product), the percentage of the country that has a mountainous area (which is of interest because it is thought that rebels might hide there and thus be able to put up more effective resistance against the government), how many valuable goods (like diamonds or oil) are exported, how weak the government is, etc. Then, the scholar also looks at whether there is civil war in the country. Data on these parameters are collected across as many countries and as many different kinds of countries as possible. The data are then subjected to various kinds of statistical analysis to see if any significant correlations can be found. Of course, as Chapter 16 in this book stresses, this is not a proof of genuine influence since 'correlation ≠ causation'. But it can be helpful in suggesting causal hypotheses to subject to further tests.

Yet another way to represent social science concepts is with a table of indicators. This is generally a good representation for Ballung-type concepts where a number of features matter to the concept but no one or two can be singled out as essential and where it is not clear which combinations of features are better or worse than which others. The table simply lists what values the individual to be measured takes for each of the features that matter.

For instance, the European Union has adopted a common set of social indicators in order to represent social exclusion in a three-layer table. The first layer contains seven lead indicators that are supposed to be important aspects of social inclusion/exclusion throughout the European Union, such as the proportion of 18 to 24 year olds who have only lower secondary education and are not in education or training leading to such a qualification, or the proportion of people living in households that lack specified housing amenities or have specified housing faults. The second layer contains additional indicators taken to be important to the concept but less central, such as the proportion of the population aged 18 to 64 with only lower secondary education, and an indicator for the proportion of people living in overcrowded housing. The third layer contains factors that matter only more locally and that member states decide for themselves to include, so these can differ from country to country. Member states should amongst others include non-monetary indicators of deprivation that are particular to their context. Italy for instance measures the percentage of elderly persons living alone without living siblings or children; Belgium measures the relation between education of parents and children; and Finland measures the number of people on the waiting list for their State Housing Board rental accommodation.

As with all representations there are advantages and disadvantages to tables of indicators. Two related advantages stand out. First, often this kind of representation is the only appropriate one for the concept we have in mind. When the concept we care about is a Ballung-type concept made of many aspects and with fuzzy edges, simpler measures end up omitting aspects and drawing boundaries that can leave individuals on the wrong side. Second, a table of indicators provides a far more detailed picture that allows us to survey the range of plusses and minuses that contribute to assigning individuals into or out of the category. We can, for instance, measure the poverty or welfare of a country on a ratio scale via GDP per capita. But the fact that many low GDP countries have had higher life expectancy at various times than would be predicted from such a measure—like Sri Lanka, Costa Rica, the Indian state of Kerala, China, some of the Soviet socialist states, or Jamaica—suggests that the individuals in these countries are not as 'poor' as this measure would make them out to be. One standard account is that the societies provide things that individuals cannot buy for themselves, like an educational system, clean water, and health care facilities, and many individuals in the country have access to them. This is one of the reasons we might think of, say, lack of access to clean water for its citizens as part of what we mean by categorizing a society as poor.

The chief disadvantage of a table of indicators is that it does not allow for comparisons, either across time or across different units falling under the concept, except for rare cases where one unit performs better on every indicator in the table than does another. Yet we do want to compare, both to see how things are changing in time and to see which social systems work better for reducing or enhancing the characteristics of societies that we care about. So it is not unusual to turn a table of indicators into an index number by weighting the different aspects in some way to come up with a single number. The *HDI—Human Development Index*—is a good example. The HDI, a number between 0 and 1, is the geometric mean of normalized measures of life expectancy, education level, and national income. Norway and Australia, for instance, have HDIs above .920, and Niger and the Democratic Republic of Congo below .300.

As usual there is a trade-off. For Ballung-type concepts there is generally no appropriate way to weigh the various items from a table that makes good sense across all applications. The weightings are, in that sense, arbitrary. This matters because different ways of weighing will give rise to different rankings, both for the same units across time—are they improving or getting worse—and in comparing units to each other.

This provides yet another illustration of the fact that different methods of representation generally mean that it is really different concepts—different characterizations—being represented. For instance, one of the aspects of civil wars that some scholars believe are not currently well represented in civil war studies is the variation in the conflict in a state over time. By giving only a 0 for a year in which a state is not in civil war and a 1 for a year in which it is, we ignore a large amount of information about the development of the conflict over time. A 1 in one of the first years of conflict may hide a very different kind of situation than a 1 in one of the last years of conflict. Similarly, by focusing on a 0 or 1 for an entire state rather than for a location in the country, the social scientist ignores information on local armed conflicts.

Which of these representation/characterization pairs is best? As we have stressed, for the most part there is no correct answer. It depends on purposes. If we want a very accurate account of just what the poverty (or lack of it) of the inhabitants is like in a country, a Ballung-type concept with its associated table of indicators would generally be best. If we must have rankings for some reason, we will need an index. And again, which is the best index, weighting which factors in which way, depends on purpose.

This may suggest that to serve all our different purposes we should construct more and more different measures surrounding the same basic idea like *civil war* or *poverty* or *human development*. This will naturally make for more accuracy. On the other hand this has its disadvantages.

First, too many measures are confusing, not only for the general public but for social scientists themselves. Having a great many measures available also makes it easier for those who want to bend the results to fit their own ends to cherry-pick the measures, choosing to use or report just those that make them look good. Generally it will take a real expert in the various measures and what they really mean to spot that this is going on. A second important disadvantage is that it is difficult to accumulate knowledge when social science studies use different measures and thus turn out to be studying different things. Third, it becomes difficult to make genuine comparisons since different measures can give different verdicts. What's better on one measure is worse on another. But it may be important to be able to make comparisons. Consider the HDI indicators for example. It seems important to identify the developing countries that have performed better than others in terms of these indicators so that we can study the relation of this progress to the nature of these economies and to public policies pursued. In civil war studies it is also common to compare different states to see what causes some of them to break out in civil war (say, Burundi) whilst others (say, Kenya) do not. Finally, we know that data collection is very difficult and expensive and we simply are unable to collect the right kind of data for each measure when measures multiply.

All this drives us to try to devise *common metrics* for central social science concepts—one way of characterizing, representing, and proceduralizing that is widely used, researched, and reported. But, as we noted, that can distort what we mean, fail to be fit for purpose, and lack nuance, detail, and accuracy. Finding a good balance among all these different aims and needs is one of the central problems that social scientists continuously confront in their efforts to measure society.

2.3 *Procedures*

In this section, we will discuss what on-the-ground procedures entail, and some problems we face in devising them for measurement of social science concepts. To that end, we will give several examples: *civil war, human well-being,* and the *disability-adjusted life year (DALY)*. These examples show that often coming to correct procedures means we have to get back to earlier stages in the process of developing measurements (characterization and representation) in order fully to do the concepts justice. Social science measurement is thus a process that involves continuous feedback and refinement, even at the procedures stage.

Let us start by giving a brief account of what we mean by *on-the-ground procedures*. Assume for this purpose that we have found a satisfactory characterization and representation of a concept, e.g. *poverty*. Let's say we have characterized poverty as living on less than $2 a day and represent it as a two-valued variable (i.e. you're poor, or you're not). Now we wish to measure, say for every person over 18 in Cameroon, who is poor and who is not. The methods we use to find out who is poor are called the *procedures*. We may, in this example, look at civil service records already in place; we may conduct a census; or we may gather a representative sample of the population and extrapolate from the data we collect from them. Which procedure is right for any given characterization depends on which one—if any—is most accurate: in this case, which is most accurate in grouping the adults in Cameroon in the poor and the not-poor categories according to the criterion of 'living on less than \$2 a day'. However, generally there are also other considerations we must take into account. Some procedures may be more costly or time-consuming to undertake, and some procedures may be unfair or unethical. So it is not just the degree of accuracy that helps us choose a procedure. It is very much a matter of prioritizing (e.g. we ask: is the extra accuracy worth the extra time and money?), just as we have seen with choosing characterizations and representations.

This mock example is an easy case, one in which we do not encounter many further difficulties with the concept itself when settling on and carrying out the procedure for conducting our measurement. Unfortunately, social scientists are rarely so lucky. Often, scholars do not measure the parameters they need for their study independently of other scholars' work. Data collection is expensive and difficult. So most social scientists need to depend on shared databases for their figures. In the civil war case there are several databases they can use, such as that collected by the COW or the Uppsala Conflict Data Programme (UCDP) at Uppsala University in Sweden. Each of these databases uses different measures to come to, for instance, the number of fatalities. For instance, the COW database started out by using a death count that refers to military deaths only. In later years this has been changed for civil wars to include civilian deaths, although the matter is still at time of writing under discussion in the COW community. Thus, although social scientists may use the figures in these databases for their own purposes, they have to rely on the procedures someone else has devised and these may not fit well with the concept they need for the purposes of their own study. It is a constant challenge to social scientists, on the one hand, to devise procedures for data collection that can allow for wide usage and, on the other hand, to try to figure out information needed about their specific concepts from data that measures something different.

Even given that a set of specific procedures has been settled on, there can still be problems on the ground in interpreting them. Measuring fatalities on the ground is difficult. Not only do both sides of the conflict tend to give a skewed image of the number of deaths to favour their own side, there are also difficulties in classifying a death. Say we find a young adult male in civilian clothing who has been fatally shot. We then tend to classify him as a civilian death. What, however, if he was carrying a weapon that he threw on the ground just before he was shot? Is this still a civilian death, or is it a battle death? Social scientists need to be both sure of how their procedures dictate the death should be classified in this situation and sure of what the database collectors they are relying on have done. These two need to match up, but whether they do requires both further specification on the part of the social scientists and clear communication on the part of database collectors.

So far, we've seen that coming to correct procedures involves setting priorities (e.g. accuracy versus costliness) and questioning whether the data we use from others were collected with our aims in mind. Further difficulties in settling on the right procedures come from issues involving specification and de-abstraction. Imagine, for example, that our characterization of *civil war* calls for over 1,000 deaths each year, and we correlatively represent civil war as a two-valued variable. Now someone asks, 'Is Syria at civil war or not?' We then realize that, though they use the same characterization and representation, some scholars classify Syria as being at civil war, while we do not. We look for the differences in the procedures of these social scientists and find to our great surprise that we are only measuring deaths of combatants whereas the other scholars are also measuring deaths of civilians. This then indicates to us that we need to find a more detailed characterization of civil war that specifies which deaths to take into account. Problems with our procedures force us to refine our characterization.

We have already stressed one reason that this problem may come up for social science concepts much more than it does for natural science concepts, like *electrons* and *oranges*: there is no right or wrong characterization of these Ballung, socially constructed concepts. We have a different concept of *civil war* if we count different kinds of deaths, but this is neither a right nor a wrong concept. By contrast, although some thinkers disagree, it is widely maintained that if we characterized electrons or oranges differently we would simply get the concept wrong.

Of course, there is an upside to the civil war example. Though measuring the number of deaths in a population requires sophisticated procedures, in the end we know that either someone is dead or they're not. Proceduralizing is generally more problematic than this in social science. In the remainder of this section, we will consider two examples that require more sophisticated specification.

CAPABILITIES

Suppose we want to measure well-being, perhaps to see if the well-being of the inhabitants of a country or an ethnic group is improving, or to study how on average well-being might be affected by wealth, education, employment, health, etc., or to compare the well-being of different groups. We can see from Chapter 1 how complex and controversial the concept *human well-being* is. Here we introduce it to illustrate some of the problems raised by abstract concepts and some of the problems solved by using them.

The Human Development Index, which we have already described, is used by the United Nations as a measure of well-being. The HDI represents well-being as the geometric mean of three features, which we can take to be the core of the characterization of this particular concept: education, life expectancy, and income. Let us not for now worry about the geometric mean but concentrate instead on these three factors. Do these constitute *well-being*? Is that really what we mean by this concept? Probably not. Still they may be relevant to measuring well-being. For instance they might be tools that are relatively necessary to secure well-being, or alternatively they might be features that fairly regularly accompany well-being. In either of these cases they might serve as reasonably good indicators of the degree of well-being in a country. Both these, however, depend on having some other concept of well-being which these features are good indictors of or good tools for securing. Whatever that concept is, it needs a proper characterization if it is to play a serious role in social science. What can it be?

Consider the proposal from Amartya Sen (1999), already discussed in Chapter 1. For Sen, human well-being consists in having a good amount of *substantive freedom*. *Freedom* for Sen involves having choice; *substantive* freedom, having choice among things we have reason to value. *Substantive freedom* for Sen consists then in having the choice of many *lives worth living*. We can only live one of them, but we have many that we can freely choose among.

Sen represents these ideas using notions of *functioning* and *capability*. A *functioning* is anything you can do or be, like being well or poorly nourished, a doctor, a runner, trapped in an unhappy marriage, or a loving parent. Because of our abilities and the constraints of our positions only certain functionings are available to us and only certain combinations can be taken up in one life. We cannot simultaneously be an Artic explorer and also work daily in our local homeless shelter. Your *capability set* is the set of all the consistent sets of functionings available to you. As with an ordinal scale, this representation provides an ordering of substantive freedoms; but unlike ordinal scales, it is only a *partial order* (which is also the case with tables of indicators). If your capability set contains all the lives worth living that mine does and then some more, you have more substantive freedom than I do. If the sets are just different, no order is decreed. Judgements can be made from case to case but they come from independent sources not from the notion of *substantive freedom* characterized and represented as we have just described.

This characterization is very abstract, using concepts like *substantive freedom* and *lives worth living*. This gives it certain advantages. Although it may be a controversial proposal, in part by virtue of its abstractness it can get far closer to what one might actually intend with a concept of *human well-being* than a more concrete concept like *life expectancy* or *income* can. It also puts us more squarely in the realm of moral discourse, which, as you see in Chapter 9 and we will discuss briefly in the next section, many would argue cannot be avoided with central social science concepts. As Chapter 1 explains, this is especially true with *human well-being*: surely what constitutes human well-being depends on what we think constitutes a good for humans and a good way of life.

These two advantages are the flip side of its two central disadvantages. First, moral debate cannot in the end be avoided. Definitions cannot be agreed on just by conducting 'proper science'. To apply Sen's concept of *well-being*, decisions must be made about which combinations of functionings make for *lives we have reason to value* and that is not a purely scientific matter. Second, this kind of characterization and its correlative representation is extremely difficult to operationalize. Just what procedures shall we follow to decide which and how many lives worth living are available to individuals? The problem is not just that it is difficult to come up with procedures or that the procedures might be difficult to carry out. It is that the characterization does not contain enough information to help. For any procedures we settle on, the fit between the concept and the procedure carried out to measure it will be extremely loose. This can result in dramatically different verdicts being given by different procedures for what is supposed to be the same concept. By contrast a far more concrete concept like HDI will have a far closer fit with the procedures used to carry out measurements of it on the ground.

This is yet another problem that social science must continuously deal with, and without any specified prescriptions for how to do so. There is no easy way to balance the advantages and disadvantages of adopting more abstract versus more concrete concepts or of using concepts that engage moral issues directly versus ones that appear to duck them but may therefore be less true to our intended meanings.

DISABILITY-ADJUSTED LIFE YEAR

As a second briefer example, consider the disability-adjusted life year (DALY). This measure for health liability combines the years of life lost with the years lived with disability in one single measure. In order to formulate a specific procedure for measuring DALYs, social scientists have to specify the concept further. For instance, to find a DALY figure for the death of a 25 year old versus that of a 70 year old, a 'social weighting' is specified in order to compare the value of life depending on age. The life of a 70 year old may be discounted at a specific rate so that it is worth less than that of a 25 year old. As we have stressed in discussing other concepts, these specifications should be sensitive to the aims and values the social science project has in measuring the DALY. Discounting the lives of the elderly could, for instance, indicate that the project values the potential for further productivity of an individual.

As a second example, to come to a procedure for measuring DALYs we must also specify a trade-off between keeping people alive and enhancing their standard of living. Are five years lived in full health worth the same as ten years lived with a serious disability? So, as with *human well-being,* we see that the DALY too is a case where a very abstract, value-laden characterization needs to be further specified and de-abstracted in order to formulate reasonable procedures for measurement.

3. Values in Social Science Measurement

In the last section, we will give an analysis of how values influence social science measurement. We will not here argue in favour or against the use of values in different kinds of scientific practice, but we will highlight several areas of social science work where the interaction between values and social science measurement is more complex than it may seem at first. We will start by briefly touching on the existing general literature of values in both natural and social science, before applying this literature to the social science measurement case.

3.1 *General Issues of Values in Science*

As you see in Chapter 9, there is wide agreement within philosophy as well as in both the natural and social sciences that several areas of a scientist's job are influenced by values. First, when scientists decide to study a particular topic rather than another, most agree that they do this for reasons that may not have anything to do with science. It is also widely agreed that this may well have no negative impact on science's search for truth. For example, if a scientist decides to study the global distribution of a particular kind of blue algae because her favourite professor did his doctoral work on this topic, that does not suggest that her results will be biased. Or, if a scholar wants to study the violent conflict in Rwanda rather than Colombia because she is more familiar with African internal politics than with that of South America, this is not judged as an illicit intrusion of personal interest or values into her scientific work.

Further, once we've measured a concept in a certain way, e.g. once we've measured that 24 per cent of Cameroon's population lives under the $2 per day poverty line, then what we subsequently do with that information depends on value judgements. For instance, we may decide to recommend that our government should increase the amount of development aid we send to Cameroon, or we may decide that this situation is not bad enough to deserve this recommendation. Similarly, once we've discovered nuclear fission, applying that research to build nuclear weapons is based on a value judgement. We may disagree with building weapons because we do not share these values, but that is not grounds to argue that the application is not going to work, i.e. that the bombs are not going to go off.

There are also aspects of science that may be negatively impacted if value judgements or personal interests play a crucial role. For instance, the traditional view in philosophy of science is that values ought not to play a role in gathering evidence and in choosing what hypothesis or theory to accept. This normative standpoint that scientists may not make value judgements in carrying out these practices is, as we see in Chapter 9, called the *value-free ideal*. For instance, when we are gathering evidence, or when we are categorizing data into groups, or when we are checking if certain evidence supports a hypothesis, the value-free ideal dictates that the scientist not let values supplant the evidence. This means that we do not want scientists to say the evidence supports a hypothesis simply because they agree with the hypothesis or on a whim or for personal or political reasons. Nor do we want scientists to consider only evidence that supports their initial beliefs; nor to claim that one theory is more likely to be true than another because they are paid to get that outcome or because having that theory adopted advantages some group they support.

But Amartya Sen points out a closely related social science practice that, he argues, is necessarily value-laden: the action of giving a certain account (Sen 1983). Say a social scientist has done a statistical study into the causes of ethnic civil war and finds that it could be prevented by isolating different ethnic minorities in a country from one another by mass displacement. The question is: would the action of publishing this result be right? Sen maintains that this is a kind of question the social scientist cannot avoid (nor, in fact, can any other type of scientist). Publishing is an action one performs and one's actions can always be subject to moral scrutiny, whether one does them wearing the hat of a social scientist or as an ordinary citizen or as a parent, a teacher, a grocer, etc. Whether it is or isn't ethically wrong is not our topic. What we want is to alert you to Sen's claim that *the question needs to be asked by the social scientist*—that giving an account, publishing a statement, choosing a research topic, and all else that social scientists do, these are all actions; and as actions, they are subject to moral scrutiny. So their evaluation cannot avoid value judgements.

One may argue against Sen's view, thinking: doesn't truth (and therefore also publishing an account if true) trump all other considerations in science? Is it not the task of the scientist to uncover truth at all costs, i.e. regardless of the consequences that outing the truth will have? Perhaps this is universally correct. Or perhaps it is correct over some questions and not others—like carrying out research on biological warfare or on the Manhattan project to build the atom bomb, both of which have a number of arguments pro and con. Perhaps it depends on how immediate and easy to predict the consequences are. Perhaps not. The insight we get from Sen's arguments is that the answers to these questions themselves require value judgements, including judgements about what the aims of science should be.

3.2 Values in Social Science Measurement

With this backdrop in mind, we can revisit the case of social science measurement. What we find is that most of the issues that arise there may be interpreted as issues of values influencing science, but in a unique social science way that does not always match up with the general problems of values in science just described.

First, however, let's look at the overlap. Just as happens in science in general, the motivation behind choosing a certain field to study may be personal. A scholar might decide to measure ethnic diversity rather than poverty because she is part of an ethnic minority. Similarly, applying theory in a certain way is a value judgement. Using a statistical study's result to try to influence NGO policy rather than governmental policy is our own choice. There are, however, many more areas of social science measurement where values necessarily play a role.

We've already come across one aspect of social science measurement that is value-laden in section 2.1, where we saw that, in the characterization stage of measurement, social scientists work with an uneasy tension between two aims. First, there is the aim of studying those concepts that they and the society they work in are concerned about. The father of sociology, Max Weber, argued that this is essential to social science (Weber 1949). It is the job of social science to study the things that our societies care about—which in large part depends on what we value and disvalue. Second, there is the aim of finding concepts that aid in explanation, prediction, and control. As we've noted, it is not always easy to bring these aims into accordance. Sometimes the concepts we're interested in (like *civil war* or *poverty* or *well-being*) cannot be brought into the kinds of systematic relations with other concepts that allow prediction and control. There might, for instance, be no specific features that can help us to predict or explain those conflicts we want to label as civil wars, nor any interventions that would have a good chance of preventing even a reasonable percentage of conflicts we want to label that way. Similarly there may not be any significant systematic effects we can expect from conflicts falling into this category. Pushed by the second aim, we may be forced to abandon the concepts we care about and to study others that are not really the same. We may refine our concept of civil war, for instance, by looking at ethnic civil wars, even though we were interested in the more general concept of civil war in the first instance.

A special case of this is the refinement of Ballung concepts. As we have seen, a Ballung concept is characterized by family resemblance and can be usefully represented by a table of indicators. This makes a reasonable level of prediction, explanation, and control unlikely since some features in the table may have one set of causes, other features very different causes, and some may themselves not be the kinds of features that have stable systematic relations with others. For predicting and control we generally need more narrow concepts and especially ones chosen because they do have definable causes and effects. This leads us to refine our Ballung concepts, substituting for them other concepts that do not have the same meaning but are better for prediction and explanation. The way in which we refine a Ballung concept is, however, not uniquely determined. There are many ways of doing it and what concepts we end up with will, therefore, depend on value judgements. As we see from Chapter 9 and in the discussion of *human well-being* here and in Chapter 1, one reason that social science measures are often value-laden is that social science concepts often do what Weber says they should: they refer to things we care about, things we value and disvalue.

A second reason that social science measures are value-laden, more so probably than measures of natural science concepts like *neutrino stars, finches,* or *natrium chloride,* is one we have mentioned repeatedly, that many social science concepts are not already there in nature for us to find out about. They are socially constructed concepts. This makes them susceptible to value judgement, because there is in principle no right or wrong characterization over and above the demand they help us achieve the aims of our social science projects. This situation then is similar to the initial choice of the social scientist to study ethnic diversity rather than poverty; her characterization of ethnic diversity will be inherently value-laden as well. There is no unique right way of doing it.

By this point, it will be clear that a similar situation to the one for concept characterization holds for representation and procedures; there, also, there is no unique right way of doing things. Thus, social science measurement is value-laden through and through. In general, we can say that *the aims we have with social science measurement decisively influence the results we will find.* If we aim to find a causal mechanism that tells us what properties of a country cause ethnic civil war, we will characterize, represent, and proceduralize the concept *civil war* differently than when we aim to give an explanation for the development of the conflict in Syria between 2010 and 2012, and different again if we aim to count how many civil wars there are in the decade 2000–2010 as opposed to 1950–60 using some broad Ballung-type concept of *civil war* that captures something that we care about far better than any of the more refined concepts. These aims are value-laden. Thus, social science measurement is value-laden.

Suppose though that characterization, representation, and procedures have been settled on for some purposes. What of the scientific work that comes after this, the categorization of individuals? We may want to insist that, once the characterization and procedures have been specified, the decision of what individuals fit the concept should be based on facts alone, and not on values. Consider, for example, the measurement of which individuals have Asperger syndrome. This measurement is important for social policy as it may determine whether or not an individual qualifies for benefits or special arrangements in the workplace. Now assume that a characterization, representation, and procedure for measuring whether a person has Asperger's have been settled on. The procedures might, for instance, require individuals to score a certain number on the autism spectrum disorder severity scale. Then we may want to ensure that the classification of an individual as having or not having Asperger's should not be influenced by values, for instance by the judgement that this particular individual is especially deserving of help.

This is one reason we see such attention to the details of procedures and the recent drive to 'mechanize' classification as far as possible. There is a concern that, when judgements enter, values may play a role they should not, whether consciously or unconsciously. On the other hand, it is difficult in a fuzzy world to design systems that cover all cases and our best efforts can end up making absurd rulings in many real applications. Also, as we have seen, there is often equally good reason to choose different measures and sometimes we feel we are confronted with a case that should fit the label, and does under a different measure than the one that has been chosen, perhaps chosen arbitrarily. How should we weigh up the dangers of overmechanization versus the dangers of conscious and unconscious bias? Here is yet another area where good decisions require delicate case-by-case balancing.

4. Conclusion

This chapter has discussed measurement in the social sciences. In it we have seen that both assigning a number to an individual unit (e.g. GDP to a country) and assigning the unit to a specific category (e.g. calling the Syrian conflict a civil war) are instances of measurement. Measurement involves three mutually interlinked stages: characterization, representation, and on-the-ground procedures. We have seen that how social science should fill these in depends on the aims of the research. So, a social science project that aims to prevent the mass displacement of civilians due to internal armed conflict may choose different ways of characterizing and representing and different on-the-ground procedures than one that aims to find a causal mechanism linking some economic variables of a country with civil war duration. We have also seen how designing good measures requires trade-offs and balancing among a great variety of different demands and aims.

Asking whether Syria is at civil war is not sensible unless we say to what end we would like to classify Syria as at civil war or not. If we want to know whether the conflict will have certain effects, so that we can act to prevent these, then we will most likely give a different answer than if we wanted to explain the development of the conflict since 2010. Neither of these two answers will be simply right or wrong; they will only be right for a certain purpose.

References

Black, I. (2012). 'Syria: Ban Ki-Moon Warns of Catastrophic Civil War', *Guardian*, 31 May <http://www.guardian.co.uk/world/2012/may/31/syria-ban-ki-moon-civil-war>. Accessed Sept. 2013.

Collier, P., and Hoeffler, A. (2004). 'Greed and Grievance in Civil War', *Oxford Economic Papers*, 56(4): 563–95. Figure on 581.

Mason, J. (2012). 'Obama Says China, Russia "Not Signed on" for Assad's Removal', *Reuters*, 19 July <http://www.reuters.com/article/2012/06/20/us-g20-syria-obama-idUSBRE85J01620120620>. Accessed Sept. 2013.

Neurath, O. (1936). 'Physikalismus und Erkenntnisforschung', *Theoria*, 2: 97–105 and 234–7. Tr. as 'Physicalism and Investigation of Knowledge', in R. Cohen and M. Neurath (eds), *Philosophical Papers 1913–1946*. Dordrecht: Reidel, 1983, 159–67.

Sambanis, N. (2001). 'Do Ethnic and Nonethnic Civil Wars Have the Same Causes? A Theoretical and Empirical Enquiry (Part 1)', *Journal of Conflict Resolution*, 45(3): 259–82.

Sambanis, N. (2004). 'What is Civil War?', *Journal of Conflict Resolution*, 48(6): 814–58.

Sen, A. (1983). 'Accounts, Actions and Values: Objectivity in Social Science', in C. Lloyd (ed.), *Social Theory and Political Practice: Wolfson College Lectures 1981*. Oxford: Clarendon Press, 87–107.

Sen, A. (1999). *Development as Freedom*. Oxford: Oxford University Press.

Stevens, S. (1951). 'Mathematics, Measurement, and Psychophysics', in S. Stevens (ed.), *Handbook of Experimental Psychology*. New York: Wiley, 1–49.

Weber, M. (1949). *The Methodology of the Social Sciences*. Glencoe, IL: Free Press.

Further Readings

Cartwright, N., and Bradburn, N. (2011). 'A Theory of Measurement', in R. M. Li (ed.), *The Importance of Common Metrics for Advancing Social Science Theory and Research: A Workshop Summary*. Washington, DC: National Academies Press, 53–70.

Cartwright, N., and Chang, H. (2008). 'Measurement', in S. Psillos, and M. Curd (eds), *The Routledge Companion to Philosophy of Science*. New York: Routledge, 360–75.

Reiss, J. (2008). *Error in Economics: Towards a More Evidence-Based Methodology*. London: Routledge, chapters 2–4.

Reiss, J. (2013). *The Philosophy of Economics: A Contemporary Introduction*. New York: Routledge, chapter 8, 'Measurement'.

Sarkees, M. (2000). 'The Correlates of War Data on War: An Update to 1997', *Conflict Management and Peace Science*, 18(1): 123–44.

15

Case Studies

Mary S. Morgan

1. 'Case Studies' in the Social Sciences: Epistemic Genres and Definitional Issues

Many different 'styles' or modes of scientific reasoning can be found amongst the social sciences, including statistical, experimental, taxonomic, even mathematical modelling, but what is particularly symptomatic of social science research is a strong tradition of case study work. Case studies are used in the social sciences to varying degrees and with various status levels. They appear regularly in sociology, political science, and in those management fields based on sociology, anthropology, and psychology. In contrast, in economics, case studies do not command the high status of research work using either mathematical models or statistics. But lest one think that case studies are limited to the social science domains, it is worth a reminder that they are also found in medical sciences such as neurology, and may be understood to have cousins in the field studies of ecology, the model organisms of biology, and the exemplary narratives of the humanities.

The authority of science—and the legitimacy of scientific knowledge when it travels beyond the immediate base of its production—rests not narrowly on methods, or means of investigation, but more broadly upon ways of reasoning that work in conjunction with those means of investigation. The historian Alistair Crombie (1994), in writing his monumental account of the history of science in the Western traditions, wrote of these as 'styles of thinking', defining them in the order that they were developed from ancient times:

- mathematical postulation and proof
- experiment
- analogical or hypothetical modelling

- taxonomy and the classification of natural kinds
- statistical thinking
- historical-genetic thinking.

The philosopher of science Ian Hacking argued that these were practical and active modes of investigation and reasoning, i.e. broad practical ways of *doing* science not just *thinking* (Hacking 1992). For example, experiment is not a narrowly defined 'method', but one legitimate way of doing science according to established codes of control and intervention developed and epitomized in laboratory science but applicable in various ways outside the laboratory. Statistical thinking as a way to scientific knowledge relies not primarily on knowing how to calculate a correlation coefficient or how to take a random sample; it is rather about using the combination of probability laws, along with statistical concepts and methods, to construct ways of designing investigations, gathering data, and analysing the results in ways that hold validity within that mode of reasoning. In other words, there are different ways of doing science that are to be understood not just as techniques or methods, but rather as legitimate generic recipes for finding out about the world which can be referred to as 'epistemic genres'.

Case studies as an epistemic genre did not appear in this well-known list of such genres given by Crombie and discussed by Hacking, but was added by a seminal paper of John Forrester (1996): 'If p, Then What? Thinking in Cases'. His paper did not make any marked distinction between 'a case', one of a series of objects or events that might be compared or be similar enough to be studied together, and 'a case study', an in-depth study of one single whole. The difference may appear clear, yet as objects of scientific reasoning, it is not so easy to draw lines between the 'case studies' of social sciences, the 'case histories' of medicine or the 'case notes' of psychoanalysis, and the 'cases' of forensic science and law.

Historically, cases and case studies have several roots. Forrester, thinking about psychiatry in the early twentieth century, points to the long centuries of medical tradition that created case notes and case histories of individuals, records of observations both given by patients and made by doctors. The idea of 'a case' here implies a single patient, or, as in law, the account of a single event and its development: in both, the boundaries of the case are relatively clear. Yet, for sociology and certain parts of management, case study subjects are much less closely bounded, and the approach is closer to that of field science. This points to an alternative historical root, akin to that taken by anthropologists to their subject matter, even while the latter do not use the term case studies for their work. Thus Henrika Kuklick points to the tradition of field work that involved intense personal experience as an instrument for observing specific peoples in specific places and of recording those observations, a field work ethos that was shared by anthropologists with glaciologists, oceanographers, geologists, geographers, and naturalists in the late nineteenth and early twentieth centuries (Kuklick 2011). Thus, in sociology, by the mid-twentieth century, one could find—as equally valid research approaches—the taking of life histories of individuals alongside ethnography-based community studies. Another root lies in history itself. The in-depth studies of particular past events in political science and international relations, as of specific firms or industries in industrial economics and management, owe much to the importance of historical examples in developing evidence-based concepts and in theory development in these fields. Noting these roots of cases and case studies as a way of doing social science offers myriad possibilities for how to think about what they are and what they do.

The first problem for characterizing case studies as a separate epistemic genre lies in providing a good definition of 'the case study' as genre of research in social scientific fields. This is difficult for a number of reasons: definitions have changed over time; case studies as a mode of research have gone in and out of fashion (even while they continue to be used); and both the terminologies and what gets labelled a case study vary between disciplines. In addition, various social scientists will single out different elements in their accounts of case study work. Some will say it means qualitative (vs. quantitative) study; some that it is a study of a single object rather than multiple ones; some that it involves a narrative mode of arguing; some that it is an event study (one process/object that evolves over time); some that it involves ethnography; and others that the research mode is open-ended. Sometimes case studies are defined by stating an opposition in terms of methods, i.e. a case study is not a statistical study, nor a modelling exercise; and sometimes they are defined only by that opposition: life histories versus surveys, qualitative vs. quantitative. Such definitions are particularly misleading, for case studies in general are not characterized or defined by any one particular research technique; rather the opposite, case studies often involve a variety of specific methods of research, for example, they can involve statistical and ethnographic methods, or counterfactual reasoning along with historical description. Such is the lack of standardized terminology that case study 'definitions' are regularly contested by other practitioners.

Despite these varieties of expressed opinion from within the social scientific communities, I suggest a definition of case studies which works across the social sciences. This definition derives from taking note of the characteristics of things referred to as case studies in the social sciences rather than by following social scientists' given definitions. A case study is defined by the following characteristics:

1. *A case study investigates a bounded whole (not single) object of analysis.* The unit of analysis points to the fact that it is wholeness not singleness that matters in the material (i.e., not a single, but a whole industry, firm, town, street corner community, military engagement, or ritual); within that whole there may be many single elements (i.e. many firms in an industry, people in the town etc.).
2. *Case study research maintains a considerable degree of open-endedness; and the boundary between subject of analysis and context is not clear at the start of the research and may remain fluid during the study.* The topic or problematic of the research question is chosen in broad terms, but the extent of the work undertaken, what studied, and the divide into content and environment or context, emerge only during the process of research.
3. *A case study involves researching directly a 'real-life' whole, which creates a considerable depth of engagement with the subject and dense evidential materials across a range of aspects of the topic.* This contrasts with the relatively thinner (but internally comparable) materials produced by the statistical genre, or the more artificial materials produced from the isolated and controlled world of the laboratory experiment or from modelling of various kinds.
4. *Many potential research methods may be used within the case study.* A case study in the social sciences may involve many different techniques: survey work, statistical work, ethnographic work, historical work, etc.
5. *The outcome is a complex, often narrated, account that typically contains some of the raw evidence as well as its analysis, and that ties together the many different bits of evidence in the study.*

Notably this definition makes no mention of the place of 'theory'—not because theories are absent in the work of doing case studies. On the contrary, relevant sets of theories are usually called upon in case studies, but researchers are not necessarily willing or able to commit themselves in advance to focus on concise accounts of causal relationships within a case study, largely because of the complexity of case work. Analysis is almost everywhere within a case study, for conceptual and theorizing work is integrated into the account of the evidence, so though the outcome may appear 'descriptive' this appearance is usually deceptive.

The second problem (after defining case study work) lies in figuring out how research within such an epistemic genre—using this definition of case studies—can be used to develop scientific knowledge. While Forrester's paper raised an important question, exactly what 'reasoning in', or perhaps 'with', cases consists of remains difficult to characterize. How are case studies argued with and to what end? How are case studies to be defended as a way of doing social science? While there are few analyses from philosophers of science, practitioners in the social sciences have provided a considerable, and methodologically sophisticated, literature analysing case studies as a mode of reasoning in their fields. This literature—both critical and positive, defensive and supportive—is written in a language, and offered in forms, which are grist to the mill of philosophy of science.

2. The Critique and Defence of Case Studies as an Epistemic Genre

Both the conventional critiques and the defences social scientists offer for case studies are conducted by comparing them with, and understanding them as a version of, two other epistemic genres, namely laboratory experiments and statistics. It is worth examining these arguments in some detail as both practising social scientists and philosophical studies of the topic of case studies come up against these critiques and defences, and because these arguments do illuminate some of the characteristics of the knowledge-making claims of case studies.

The critiques of case studies are taken first. In the comparison with statistical studies, case studies are usually derided for offering only a case of $N = 1$ observation whereas statistics relies for its epistemic power on $N = $ many observations. Statistics relies on being able to draw accurate measurements and evidenced conclusions for a hypothesis under study from many individual observations using probability laws. In contrast a case study provides evidence from one whole event, or community, or life, and—so the argument goes—one case can never say anything useful with respect to some general claim or even about other similar events, communities, or lives. After all, 'it is only one case' and who can tell what will happen in the rest of them? In the comparison with laboratory experiments, $N = 1$ in both genres. In the laboratory, a result is obtained from a controlled experiment conducted under very carefully controlled conditions. That is, not only is the environment completely controlled so nothing interferes with the experiment, but the experiment itself is done with clean apparatus, with carefully measured elements of attested qualities, and with an exact process designed to isolate one particular interaction or event. In contrast, the case study scientist investigates an event taking place within a changing and not fully known environment, with many different factors influencing the event, and in which there are many different characteristics of the events to be studied concurrently. Whereas the many kinds of controls invoked for the experiment may well enable the experimenter to draw conclusive results about the event, the critique argues that the very lack of such controls in the case study makes inferring results about the case deeply problematic. And moreover, the evidence of case studies often comes from kinds of participant-observation methods seen as insufficiently 'objective' compared to the means of collecting statistical evidence or the witnessing of results in laboratory experiments.

Given this extensive critique, scientists in fields such as sociology and social psychology have recently developed a research form they call the 'quasi-experiment'. This is actually a hybrid between the epistemic genres of experiment and statistical reasoning developed for use outside the laboratory. Quasi-experiments rely on carefully designed methods of grouping, selecting, and even randomizing across the elements in the field to be studied, so that statistical analysis on the data collected will be valid. These quasi-experiments are similar to the randomized controlled trials developed for agricultural field science in the 1920s and 1930s, and recently taken to be 'the gold standard' for assessment of medical treatments and for evidence-based social policy, as we see in Chapter 3. For those conducting case studies incorporating such quasi-experiments, this is seen as a positive move which enables valid inferences to be made by using a small number of carefully selected cases, or by partitioning material within the case study. For detractors, such case studies still remain invalid—for hypotheses testing purposes—on both the experimental and statistical grounds at the same time, for the problems of insufficient numbers of observations and lack of real control remain in the quasi-experiment.

On the defensive side, social scientists argue that case studies can be understood as a version of either experiment or of statistical work. In the former argument, case studies are sometimes presented *as a form of* experiment—not a controlled laboratory experiment, but an experiment in the world which has the features of a controlled experiment. Rarely is this defence constructed in terms of a 'natural experiment' (an event that occurs outside the laboratory within its own natural/social sphere which can be reinterpreted as an experiment). Some case studies clearly could fall into this class. For example, the sociologist Robert Merton (1946) introduces his case study of a radio fund-raiser for 'war bonds' during the Second World War in just such terms, though without using the label of 'natural experiment'. In this event, the radio star Kate Smith 'sold' $39 million of war bonds—loans from individuals to the US government to fund the war effort—in one day in September 1943. Over an eighteen-hour period, she spoke sixty-eight times, with different stories, anecdotes, messages, and elements, each making an appeal to the public to buy war bonds. Previous, but more limited, radio fund-raisers had raised only $1 million or $2 million so this was a very unusual event. Nevertheless, it was an event in which Merton claimed the cultural and political context was rather stable (a reasonable claim given that the 'experiment' took place over only eighteen hours), and so the stimulus-response of the real-life event in the social realm could be investigated as if it were a some kind of natural experiment.

More usually, researching the complex whole does not lend itself to the label of natural experiment, but it can be presented as an uncontrolled experiment in the world. The associated alternative defence rests on the argument that,

because the study goes into such detail of the *whole* event (point 1 in the definition), all the relevant factors that affect the event can be taken into account.
They are not removed, or shielded, or held *ceteris paribus* (as in the controlled laboratory experiment), but remain present; and because their variations become
known during the case study, the critical variables can be parsed out and their
influence can be assessed. For example, Robert Burgelman's (1994) study of
Intel, a computer-chip-making company and its decision to alter its product
range, can be interpreted in this light. The study took place over an extended
time period and the research team investigated a range of causal factors in different sections of the firm to show how the product switch emerged not from a
top-management strategic decision that reached downwards into the firm but
from a series of individual moves by middle managers and particular decisions
by groups, both reacting to the industrial (competitive) context of their day.
In this 'case study as an uncontrolled experiment' defence, $N = 1$: there is only
one whole event, and so one thing observed, but it is a multiply-dimensioned
observation on the complex whole over time, not a single-dimensioned observation on a single element within that whole. It is notable that, despite these
very different kinds of defence of case studies as a form of experiment, both
Merton's and Burgelman's research teams used a range of methods to gather
evidence (such as ethnographic, formal interviews, surveys, statistical data)
and related kinds of analyses within their case study work.

On the latter defence with respect to statistical work, case studies are presented by social scientists *not as a form of* statistical study, but as having *some
of the equivalent features*. Most especially, $N = $ many, but instead of many comparable, numerically expressed, observations on a rather small number of
aspects of the object as in most statistical work (e.g. on the size of firms,
turnover, and profit of 100 firms, so $N = 100$), there are multiple observations in many different forms on very many different elements and aspects
of the whole object/event that is the focus of the case study. (Thus, in the
Burgelman case, the researchers gathered all the information they could in
any form on that one firm and one major strategic change of direction for that
firm.) The variety and multi-dimensioned nature of the observations creates a
difficulty: there is no route to statistical validation of the case study because
the pieces of information are complementary rather than comparable. But
Donald Campbell (1975), a statistician and previously a fierce critic of case
studies on just these grounds, found a way to turn this evidential richness
to advantage in the context of justification. He was converted by examining
a work in psycho-analytic anthropology of the Yurok Indians of Northern
California by Erik Erikson in the 1940s. Erikson had failed to find evidence of
a 'Freudian anal syndrome' as he expected, and tried 'innumerable alternative' hypotheses, making use of both 'multiple implications' of these theories
and 'multiple observations' from the site to arrive at a very different account

of their behaviour patterns. From studying Erikson's work, Campbell argued that case studies had considerable power to 'infirm' (weaken) as opposed to 'confirm' (strengthen) degrees of acceptance for a theory under consideration. This power to infirm came from the multiple implications of the theory in such a case study, each of which could be infirmed by one bit of evidence.

Campbell portrayed his new understanding of case studies in terms of the concept of 'degrees of freedom', an important notion in statistical reasoning. Namely, the more information or data points relative to the parameters of the theory, the more degrees of freedom there are in fitting a hypothesized relationship to the many data points. (The term has a technical definition, but for informal illustration: if a researcher has only two data points, fitting a linear relationship involves two parameters and so involves no degrees of freedom to fit any but one line; having many data points offers many possible lines—there are more degrees of freedom.) The more degrees of freedom, the more possible relationships can be fitted, and so when one statistical relationship coalesces, a certain confidence is gained in that relation. Carrying the idea over—case study research produces observations on many different things and creates the possibility of multiple interpretations, but few of those interpretations (or 'theories') will likely be consistent with *all* the details of evidence. Most accounts would be 'infirmed' by some of the evidence. But, if all the bits of information were to be found consistent with one interpretation, more confidence would adhere to that account.

And, an additional point often made by those invoking such a defence, case studies in the social sciences are often carried out by a team of several different researchers, so it is not only a question of multiple observations on different elements that need to fit together but the use of multiple observers who must triangulate their different bits of evidence to ensure all the bits are admissible and consistent in the case study account.

In summary, the two critiques of case studies as a way of doing science are that it provides only one uncontrolled experiment or one statistical observation. The social scientists' defence of the virtues and validity of case studies rests on the evidential density (point 3 in the definition) on a whole unit (point 1) to enable a full analysis of all the influencing factors and to use the multiplicity of different observations to justify the case account.

3. The Context of Justification: Validity and Transportability of Case Study Knowledge

Two general points arise from this analysis of these practitioner defences of case studies. The first point to raise is: why should the judgement of the worth of case studies be made by comparison with experiments, or statistics, or any other epistemic genre? The second point to make is to suggest that, if such comparisons are made, they should be made on broader criteria by asking: how does the validity and transportability of case study results compare with work in those other genres?

Answers to the first point here seem to have much to do with the fact that statistical and experimental work have accepted status amongst philosophers of science, a status which is reflected in the social scientists' own focus for their defensive arguments. Yet Ian Hacking's writings about epistemic genres argued that there is no appeal from within any of these genres to any higher, broader, philosophical argument which validates all the different ways of doing science as versions of one general method of science. Rather, each one in the list of epistemic genres can be used to justify the knowledge obtained using them, but they do so only within the context of their own genre. There are ways of doing experiments (with control and limited intervention) that deliver experimental knowledge of objects' behaviour. There are ways of doing mathematics that ensure knowledge through deductive or inductive means. There is no more general philosophical argument that gives either genre their justification. There is no absolute source of legitimation.

It seems almost forgotten now, but what Hacking did was to mark out a path between the logical positivist philosophers' desire to establish (or at least to arbitrate) the 'truth claims' of scientific knowledge and the sociologists' social constructivist critique of science as 'true' knowledge. The importance of Crombie's work was to show that it was a historical process for each epistemic genre to become acceptable as a way of doing science (e.g. experiments in the seventeenth century and statistics in the nineteenth century). It was a matter of history that each epistemic genre developed its own generic way of finding and validating knowledge, so that work within that genre came to be judged as a valid route to knowledge within that epistemic genre and by its community of practitioners, not according to the rules, or in the terms, of any other genre. The importance of Hacking's commentaries was to show how the scientific authority of each genre rested upon its own mode of investigation and reasoning to support its claims to knowledge. So each of these genres have to be separately characterized both historically and philosophically.

The easiest way to communicate what all this means is to say—as Hacking did—that once an epistemic genre is accepted in a field as the (or a valid) way to do science, it becomes what it means 'to reason rightly' in that field. Any scientist's ability to reason in a chosen style is thus dependent on the contingent history of that discipline and whether that method is accepted within it. Yet, once more or less adopted within a discipline, that style, as Hacking says, becomes a timeless canon of objectivity, a standard or model of what it is to be reasonable about this or that type of subject matter. We do not check to see whether mathematical proof or laboratory investigation or statistical 'studies' are the right way to reason: they have become (after fierce struggles) what it is to reason rightly, to be reasonable in this or that domain. (1992: 10)

Once accepted by a group of scientists, a style of reasoning comes to seem natural to them; they neither question its historical origins, nor the objectivity of the knowledge gained from using the method, nor do they appeal to any outside or higher level for its justification. Once accepted as a legitimate mode of doing science, knowledge acquired with that mode—provided the mode is carried through properly—carries the badge of science, just as postage stamps, passports, and monies traditionally carry a badge of the state that proves their legitimacy and authorizes the passage of the letters, persons, and values, carried under those badges.

The legitimacy of scientific knowledge obtained within a genre depends upon it meeting the requirements of that genre as a way of doing science. But this is not a radical relativism for each mode can be, individually, justified as an epistemic genre, a way to knowledge. So, it no more makes sense to judge, in any definitive way, the epistemic genre of taxonomy and classification according to the characteristics of the experimental mode nor—equally—the genre of case studies according to the character of either statistics or laboratory experiment. Nevertheless, reciprocal or systematic comparisons between the genres along various dimensions are valid and may be insightful.

The main thrust of the arguments outlined earlier, and so of the comparisons made, are concerned with the project of 'justification', namely of testing specific theories or causal hypotheses within case studies and of providing valid justification for such findings. These concerns are important because if this 'internal validity' of the analysis and results cannot be judged, then any validity of the findings beyond the case will not even come under consideration. Yet, as philosophers of science well know, scientists using other epistemic genres—such as experiments or statistics or modelling—also have difficulties, both in establishing or justifying the internal validity of their results and then in grounding the transportability of those findings beyond the specific example. Here comparisons reveal as much about the genres of experiment and statistics as they do about the epistemic genre of case studies.

Statistics fares rather well in these particular comparisons. As a genre of research, it relies on lots of independent observations of a comparable kind on a limited number of characteristics on an object of interest; and statisticians have worked out rules for combining that sample of observations in a way that depends on statistical theory to ground the analysis and obtain valid results. Inferences beyond the sample to a wider population likewise rest on well-established and highly developed statistical and probability theory. In contrast, case studies rely on lots of different observations of different kinds on the object of interest and on combining them to obtain an internally valid account of the case. Unfortunately, there are no systematic rules governing the way that such combination is made. Nor are there rules for inferring—or transporting—findings beyond the single case study (or even beyond two or three such case studies that suggest the same results) to the wider group of cases as there are in statistical work.

On the other side of the comparison—with experiments—case studies fare rather better. There are no systematic rules for establishing internal validity in the individual case study just as one might argue that there are no systematic rules for ensuring internal validity within the single experiment where the validity of experimental results usually rests on a claim about the replicability or reproducibility of any single experiment to validate the initial results. But such validation is still only *internal*, i.e. within the artificial domain of the experimental set-up, not *external*—it does not extend to the same kind of events in the uncontrolled world and environment. Case studies are conducted, and results generated, in a 'natural' (i.e. social) setting. They cannot (usually) be repeated, and so internal validity has to be created by multiple evidential coherence (when no one piece of evidence infirms the account). Case studies in social sciences are generally thought to be unique. Their uniqueness stems not just from the difficulty of repeating any piece of case study work in the same place and time, but also from the uniqueness of events/situations and their context: nothing in the uncontrolled social world is ever exactly the same. So internal validity is a characteristic which may be established for each particular case study but may not be moveable to any other—thus *general* validity is problematic.

It is clear then that this lack of transportability of scientific knowledge beyond its immediate site of production is a problem that occurs in other epistemic genres, though in somewhat different forms. While the experimental method suffers from the problem of establishing 'external validity' for its findings outside the lab in the natural environment, and 'parallelism' is the equivalent problem for how far findings from the small world of a mathematical model parallel the events in the real world, the problem for case studies is how to establish the 'general validity' of the case findings for other similar social (natural) cases and other social (natural) environments. This issue is discussed further in Chapter 3 on evidence-based policy.

But this context of justification (which prompts questions of internal validity and the associated issues of transportability: external or general validity) is not the only space within which social scientists argue for the usefulness of case studies, nor should it be for a philosopher of science. This leads to a more positive analysis of case studies as an epistemic genre.

4. Case Studies: Vehicles of Discovery?

Social scientists, at various times and in various fields, have argued that case studies are not primarily vehicles for theory testing, i.e. they are not concerned with this problem of 'justification'—of proving a theory useful or not. Rather, so it is claimed, case studies are research in *the context and service of discovery, not justification*. 'Discovery' is much more difficult territory for philosophers of science, perhaps because discovering things is less open to philosophical analysis than to other kinds of analyses. It may also be because the philosophical picture we have of discovery is too simplistic: most work of discovery—however difficult the practical scientific process may be—is not about finding a new star, or discovering a hidden property of a chemical. 'Discovery' in practice is more prosaic and more pragmatic, and it covers a range of elements that have been associated with case study work. Case studies have been found useful for the formation of evidence-based concepts, for the development of measurement structures, the place where types are defined and kinds isolated, where partial accounts are spliced together to create full accounts, and where phenomena are revealed and theories about them developed.

Because of the difficulty of dealing with these various elements of 'discovery' in abstract philosophical terms, I will use examples from the social science literature to put more flesh on these claims of the important role of case studies in the domain of discovery. Again I draw on the characteristics of case studies given in the definition earlier, in particular with points (1) the importance of the whole object of study, (3) that it is a real-life case (not an abstract mathematical model nor a laboratory controlled world), and (5) that the explanatory account integrates a variety of evidence.

The first example begins with a case study of a large American firm by Rosabeth Moss Kanter (1977) which proved instrumental in exposing the internal power structures of the modern American corporation. It was particularly revealing about the ways these structures affected the behaviour of those who worked there, and especially about the position of women in such an organization. It quickly became regarded as a classic case study (in both sociology and management fields) just because it showed how the structures of the firm and the behaviour of its people interacted. During the 1980s, research across a number of firms was used to pin down the barriers that created the 'glass ceiling' that prevented women getting promotions in such corporations. American social scientists from different disciplines, in both academic and public positions, and using a variety of different methods, were then able to characterize in detail a number of the other barriers that accounted for the 'glass ceiling' phenomenon: not just the glass ceilings that prevented promotions at the top level, but the 'glass walls' that prevented the sideways promotions that provided women with the experience needed to break the glass ceilings, and the 'sticky floors' that prevented low-skilled women (and male ethnic minorities) from making even the first career progressions within institutions. Although these individual elements became quite well understood from statistical studies, survey work, and formal interviews, it was case studies (as a genre) that proved able to integrate these elements together to show how all the different barriers worked together. One exemplary case study that did such integration was Leonie Still's (1997) commissioned study of the Australian finance industry, one of the largest industries in which women are employed in Australia. As Morgan (forthcoming) shows, at several critical points in this research track on glass ceilings, at the beginning and near the end, case studies proved critical in revealing and labelling the conceptual elements of the glass ceiling phenomenon and in creating and developing a fuller and integrated account of the phenomenon.

The second example is about the problem for social scientists of developing constructs which will work well at both conceptual and evidential levels. 'Class', for example, is one of these concepts (like 'civil war', discussed in Chapter 14) which is slippery to operationalize; it has been done so in many ways, usually relying on statistical and survey work. But case studies are not without merit in such circumstances. For example, while the standard assumption of early American sociology had been that a society either had a class structure (as in Great Britain) or a caste structure (as in India), it was believed these would never occur together. *Deep South*, a 1930s study of a small town and associated rural area in the USA (Natchez, Mississippi), showed not only that class and caste divisions existed together, but developed the analytical constructs to show how these social groups labelled each other and to formalize diagrammatically the interaction between them as well as developing an account of 'cliques', a third level of social group within that same class- and caste-ridden society. This ethnographic account, by a team consisting of two white and two black anthropologists (Davis et al. 1941) was certainly not an abstract account, for members of the society could each be slotted into their different class, caste, and clique membership groups. This was one of a series of community studies in mid-century that revealed American society to itself. Of course neither class nor caste were new concepts; rather the case study developed a way of showing not just that they did exist together, but how they interrelated, a classic piece of anthropology.

These two examples show how important case studies can be in developing the evidence base for concepts and in defining the nature of a phenomenon, activities that fit within a broad notion of discovery. But case studies have also proved an important research genre for a somewhat narrower definition of discovery—namely in their capacity to reveal phenomena. One of the oft-quoted practitioner texts by Robert Yin (various editions from 1994 to 2009), argues that one of the true benefits of the case study method is that objects are studied in their context (point 2 in the definition). This can be seen as an important virtue in comparison with other genres in which the objects of case study research are divorced from context (as in the abstract modelling of economics), or have their context heavily controlled (as in the laboratory experiments of psychology and sociology). Yin goes on to suggest that it is often difficult for the researcher to draw lines between the object of interest and its context because of the open-endedness of the research question and because the object emerges as fully distinguished from its context only during the course of the research. This difficulty illuminates how and why case studies can play an important role in the context of discovery. For any scientist, locating a phenomenon involves being able to distinguish that object from its background and to filter out the context in order to study the object more clearly, which is exactly what happens in doing case studies. It is not likely that a social phenomenon will emerge as a distinct self-contained object from its environment like an egg from a chicken. Rather, distinguishing a phenomenon from its context involves identifying an element in the social field that is of particular interest, defining the important aspects of it, describing its characteristics and suggesting its function or importance in the social field. Discovering new phenomena in the social field will involve identification, description, conceptualization, and explanation as found in our next two examples.

Our first example is the case study that defined the characteristics of 'street corner society', and coined the label for that phenomenon. This—both as a conceptual notion for a potentially widespread phenomenon and as a specific example—was 'discovered' in the book of that name, by William Foote Whyte (1943). There was no one moment in the study when one could say that the phenomenon of street corner society had been identified, rather it emerged as the outcome of a case study of a group of young men living in an urban US (North Boston) community. The detailed case work of this (largely) ethnographic study was originally undertaken to study the interactions of individuals within a small group. But the open-endedness of the case study enabled Whyte to branch out into new areas from that initial base, i.e. from interactions within the one group (on the corner, in the café, in the bowling alley, or in street gambling), into relationships with other groups (such as the 'college boys'), and between such groups and with the wider society in the form of the police and the political machine. The lack of boundary between subject of interest and context freed Whyte to develop an account of a slum community as an organized society that failed 'to mesh with the structure of the society around it' (Whyte 1943: 273). Against a theoretical background in sociology of the day in which slum communities were understood not to be communities at all but rather to be a disorganized set of inhabitants lacking social organization, the study revealed something very different.

Another 'discovery' example, from the field of industrial economics or management, is found in Charles Baden-Fuller's (1989) case study on the steel castings industry in the UK. Here, initially, context seemed all important: it was an industry in terminal decline, a context which might seem to swamp any other considerations, and the focus of the study was the performance of a government scheme to help save the industry. This too was a study undertaken against the backdrop of a strong theoretical assumption, namely, the economists' absolute belief that firms left an industry in the order of their profitability, with the least profitable exiting first (that exit was 'efficient'), though there were few empirical studies of the matter. Although this assumption was not the focus of the research, when the case study found the order of exit was contrary to that assumption, it documented a phenomenon of potentially much wider relevance. Despite the general decline of the industry, from which one might have expected all firms to close, some stayed open much longer than seemed reasonable given their profitability. The order of exit was found to depend on the size and diversity of the firm as well as its resources (it costs money to close), and its ownership structure (single units with owner-managers tended to be less willing to close their foundries than large diversified, non-owner-managed, companies). Here we find a mix of methods—statistical, mathematical modelling, and ethnographic—and the development of middle-level theories to explore the various reasons why this unexpected phenomenon occurred.

The scientific communities' response to both these examples—'street corner society' and 'inefficient industry exit'—was similar. For them, the case studies revealed phenomena that were unexpected against the standard assumptions and beliefs of the time and produced evidence of the phenomena that could not be explained within those original terms but could be explained in other terms. And in both cases, those phenomena were not even the original focus of interest. So these cases were not understood as examples of something already known and established. Nor were they seen as hypotheses-testing case studies, though both studies developed explanations of the social structures or causal elements in the process of exploring their phenomena. Rather, the scientific community's response was to understand the phenomena revealed as potentially generic, i.e. likely to be found beyond the individual case studies. These two case studies proved a starting point for research activities each in their own social scientific communities: searching for other similar cases of the phenomena, exploring the nature of the phenomena they revealed, and testing out the accounts they gave of the phenomena across a range of other cases and with other methods.

5. Case Studies and Criteria for Internal Validity

Just what makes these discovery domain case accounts valid to the community of social scientists? That is, what are the positive criteria that operate as the flip side for the notion of infirming? I suggest that case study accounts rely on the same kind of criteria in producing their explanations as MacCormick argues establish the validity of narrative accounts made in legal cases in the courtroom. That is, the accounts exhibit: (i) consistency with all the evidence found, (ii) coherence within the account (the bits of evidence fit together), and (iii) credibility of the explanation. For MacCormick, this last criterion means that the explanation has to provide a satisfactory 'causal or motivational account of the whole complex of events' (MacCormick 2005). For social sciences, this does not necessarily mean that the explanation has to start from the individuals in their situations (as in law)—it means rather that the explanation has to be formulated in social science conceptual terms that are understood as having a grip within the social science concerned. So, regardless of the level of explanation (individual, holistic, or functional), these three criteria from law can be used to assess the internal validity of the explanation in relation to the materials of the case study at hand.[1] And while such explanations and criteria do not allow for any direct inference to events, times, and places beyond the case study, the conceptual materials, the measurement constructs, the phenomena discovered, and any other elements of discovery from the case studies, may well travel beyond the individual case study as we have indicated with both the firm exit case and the street corner society account.

These criteria need to be unpacked. Different disciplines, using different methods in their case studies (point 4 in the definition), seek this internal consistency and create their accounts in different ways to attain coherence and social scientific credibility. Whyte (like other social-anthropology ethnographers) created an internally valid account of *Street Corner Society* in a way which relied on dense reporting of detailed evidence in a narrative process that drew the reader into direct engagement with the evidence, and then stood back a little to draw threads of the evidence together and to analyse the materials to provide an account and explanation of the phenomenon of that society. Other fields seek more complementarity between the case study account and their experiments, models, or theories. So Baden-Fuller's account of firm exit from an industry iterated in quite formal ways, between the data that he

---

[1] As explained in Ch. 10, social science explanations that begin with the individual are often termed those based on 'methodological individualism' (as in most of economics) in comparison with ones that begin from society or communities and their structures (some kind of holistic explanation as often in sociology), or are based on some other kind of conceptualized social characteristics that may have functional power (such as the rituals of anthropology).

gathered on firms and his different technical methods of analysis to provide the separate elements of the account. These were then knitted together to provide an overall explanation of the pattern of firm exit and the reasons for that pattern. Both these accounts—and regardless of the particular methods used—showed how the phenomena were revealed and how the various bits of different evidence that supported the account were joined up and integrated into an account that explained that particular case and revealed how those explanations relied on conceptual and theoretical materials.

This process of creating internally valid accounts—consistent, coherent, and credible—within the case study points to characteristic features of the way case study evidence is combined. Perhaps all this seems obvious, but it is in marked contrast with how internal validity is established in statistical accounts. Recall that statistics defends itself with the argument that it works with lots of comparable, but independent, observations on a small number of characteristics (relative to case study evidence) on the object of interest. These are treated, cumulated, and analysed in order to establish a pattern which has a much smaller dimension of elements compared to the number of observations collected. These data processes are subject to rules laid down in statistical theory, which also provide the criteria for assessing the validity of the account given.

The coherence and credibility of case studies is built upon something else— not upon *independence* of *comparable* and *similar* kinds of observations, but on the *interdependence* of *different* kinds and bits of evidence and upon the fact that these different elements must be *connected* bits of evidence. Here is where wholeness (point 1 of the definition) matters—for the case study assumption is that social life is inherently multi-dimensional and multi-connected, and that is why the case account or explanation has to integrate the evidence into an account of the whole, and not just concentrate on some bits of evidence that fit together and ignore outlier observations (as might happen in statistical work). Case study work and accounts concentrate on fitting together a jigsaw of pieces to reveal a picture of one particular social world in its natural (i.e. social) environment rather than in a controlled environment (as in laboratory experiment) or in searching for patterns that hold in similar elements across different environments (as in statistical work). Case study findings rely on connecting the different bits and pieces of evidence together to create a coherent picture in the account (point 5 in the definition), one that must be credible to the social scientific community.

Once this is understood, we can also begin to see how these processes of integrating elements of the evidence together can also be found in case studies used in the domain of justification: those that seek to account for a particular example of an already known phenomenon and are concerned with building justified accounts of that phenomenon. Thus, the 'analytical narratives' of social science history construct accounts of a set of known examples of social science phenomena in an iterative process between evidence and theories; they may end up throwing out some of the explanatory structure as a result but not the bits of evidence. For example, Robert Bates (1998) gives an account of the International Coffee Organization, a cartel of buyers/consumers set up to control the price of coffee and balance the power of the largest producer, Brazil. His account moves in sequence from a general historical narrative of the events to economic analysis using game theory, to a narrative about the elements that lay unexplained in the first analysis, thence to a political science analysis of those elements, and so forth as more different models and theories are used to give a valid account (consistent and coherent with all the evidence) of the elements of the history.

A similar problem of explanation for already recognized phenomena is found in 'process tracing', the generic term used in political science for the development of an internally valid account of the historical record of some specific political events. Such process tracing looks to trace the 'causes of effects': particular causes that created particular effects in specific events in the political and international affairs arena (in contrast to statistical studies which seek the average 'effects of causes'). Crasnow (2012) explores how this happens in the case of the 'democratic peace' hypothesis of the international relations field, the thesis that democracies tend not to go to war with each other compared to democracy/non-democracy or non/non-democracy engagements in the international relations sphere. This has been 'tested' by the counting of cases, to establish that the thesis holds water. But in examining why this should be so, political sciences have relied on a series of case studies—e.g. of the Fashoda incident between Britain and France in conflict over the division of Africa in the late twentieth century—looking in detail at these democracy–democracy engagements to trace the causal processes or mechanisms by which democracies avoid war. Process tracing within such a case study necessarily includes historical work tracing the process by which such an event was caused and explaining its development; it may also involve counterfactual reasoning or even the use of some comparable cases. These are primarily justificatory exercises: theory or hypotheses generate the research within the case study to explain some already known events, and the modes of testing can be translated into standard kinds of testing regimes for causal accounts. Consistency is a strong criteria in these justificatory exercises, consistency to create a coherent account, an account that is not infirmed by any piece of the evidence.

However, the integration of bits of evidence with explanations in ways that colligate the processes of observation, analysis, and inference typically found in phenomena-revealing social science case studies seems to call for something more than an account that relates failure to infirm to justification, or that merely points to the criteria for internal validity in a case study explanation. What kind of explanation do the joint criteria of consistency, coherence, and credibility produce in the context of discovery?

The answer may be phrased in terms of the philosopher of science C. G. Hempel's discussion of 'why-questions', a discussion he thought as relevant for the social as the natural sciences. He distinguished between 'reason-seeking, or epistemic why-questions' and 'explanation-seeking why-questions' (1965: 333–5). The former ask for grounds (epistemic reasons) for believing something is true, the latter takes something to be true and asks for the explanation (substantive reasons) why it is so. Case study research and their reports attack both questions together. Is it true that firms in the steel castings industry exited in an inefficient order, and if so, what were the reasons why this was so? Is it true that small corner gangs have a well-ordered social system, and if so, what are the features of that system that make it so? In both cases, despite standard theory, an unexpected phenomenon was observed to be true—according to social scientific research that looked to epistemic criteria of (i) consistency and (ii) coherence between the evidence and the account to answer 'the epistemic why question'. But in each case, the phenomenon was explained in ways that took care to offer (ii) coherent and (iii) credible explanations to their own social scientific community, i.e. to answer the 'explanation-seeking' why-question. These involved criteria relating to the details of explanation but also to broader criteria of subject matter coherence and credibility. Such phenomena-revealing case studies answer the epistemic why-question as to the existence of the phenomena, at the same time as giving substantive explanations of those phenomena without separating out the two kinds of questions. Such a feature of answering both kinds of why-questions together may well be a feature of other epistemic genres when they operate in the domain of discovery, but perhaps the answers do not appear in quite such an integrated form as in the epistemic genre of case study research in the social sciences, not least because, compared to other genres of research, the mode of reporting case studies invites the integration we have seen here.

References

Baden-Fuller, C. (1989). 'Exit from Declining Industries and the Case of Steel Castings', *Economic Journal*, 99: 949–61.

Bates, R. (1998). 'The International Coffee Organization: An International Institution', in R. Bates et al. (eds), *Analytical Narratives*. Princeton: Princeton University Press. 194–230.

Burgelman, R. (1994). 'Fading Memories: A Process Theory of Strategic Business Exit in Dynamic Environments', *Administrative Science Quarterly*, 39(1): 24–56.

Campbell, D. (1975). ' "Degrees of Freedom" and the Case Study', *Comparative Political Studies*, 8(2): 178–93.

Crasnow, S. (2012). 'The Role of Case Studies in Political Science Research', *Philosophy of Science*, 79(5): 655–66.

Crombie, A. (1994). *Styles of Scientific Thinking in the European Traditions*, I–III. London: Duckworth.

Davis, A., Gardner, B., and Gardner, M. (1941). *Deep South: A Social Anthropology of Caste and Class*. Chicago: University of Chicago Press.

Forrester, J. (1996). 'If *p*, Then What? Thinking in Cases', *History of the Human Sciences*, 9(3): 1–25.

Hacking, I. (1992). ' "Style" for Historians and Philosophers', *Studies in the History and Philosophy of Science Part A*, 23(1): 1–20.

Hempel, C. G. (1965). *Aspects of Scientific Explanation*. New York: Free Press.

Kanter, R. M. (1977). *Men and Women of the Corporation*. New York: Basic Books.

Kuklick, H. (2011). 'Personal Equations: Reflections on the History of Fieldwork, with Special Reference to Sociocultural Anthropology', *Isis*, 102: 1–33.

MacCormick, N. (2005). *Rhetoric and the Rule of Law: A Theory of Legal Reasoning*. Oxford: Oxford University Press.

Merton, R. (1946). *Mass Persuasion: The Social Psychology of a War Bond Drive*. New York: Harper & Brothers.

Morgan, M. S. (forthcoming). 'Recognising Glass Ceilings and Sticky Floors', in E. Fox-Keller and K. Chemla (eds), *Culture without Culturalism*.

Still, L. (1997). *Glass Ceilings and Sticky Floors: Barriers to the Careers of Women in the Australian Finance Industry*. A report prepared for the Human Rights and Equal Opportunity Commission and Westpac. Canberra: Commonwealth of Australia.

Whyte, W. F. (1943). *Street Corner Society: The Social Structure of an Italian Slum*. Chicago: University of Chicago Press.

Yin, R. (2009). *Case Study Research: Design and Methods*. London: Sage.

Further Readings

Byrne, D., and Ragin, C. (2009). *The Sage Handbook of Case-Based Methods*. London: Sage.

Gerring, J. (2001). *Social Science Methodology: A Criterial Framework*. Cambridge: Cambridge University Press.

Morgan, M. S. (2013). 'Nature's Experiments and Natural Experiments in the Social Sciences', *Philosophy of the Social Sciences*, 43: 341–57.

16

Causal Inference

Nancy Cartwright

1. Problems for Causation

Causation has long been a vexed notion across the sciences, so much so that there have been repeated cries that it must be banished forever from both the natural and the social sciences. Yet, whatever is the case with the natural sciences, causation remains at the heart of the social sciences. For example, the London School of Economics and Political Science (LSE), which is one of the foremost social science institutions in the world, has as its motto, *Rerum cognoscere causas*: 'To know the causes of things'.

Why is causality so central? Because, it is widely believed, it is knowledge of the causes of things that allows us to understand the world, to predict the future, to build better social systems, to change the world we live in. Why, then, try to banish causation? Because the notion faces serious problems and there is no widespread agreement how, or even that, the problems can be solved. The problems can be grouped under three headings: meaning, method, and metaphysics.

1.1 *Meaning*

The eighteenth-century Scottish philosopher David Hume argued that our notion of causation is not what we think it is (see e.g. Garrett 2009). He claimed that all of our concepts (he called them 'ideas') come from experience. They are copies of the impressions that make up our experiences. Where, then, in our experience of happenings in the world is the impression of causation? Nowhere, he argued. Look as hard as you will. You only really see shapes, and colours, and motions, never a 'making something happen'. So where does the concept come from?

What we call causes are regularly followed by what we label as their effects, said Hume. Human beings, he believed, are deeply prone to forming habits. So, having observed a regular association between two kinds of events, we come to expect the second when we see the first. Looking inwards at ourselves, we notice this feeling of expectation; we get an impression of it. Our concept of causation, Hume claimed, is a copy of that impression of expectation. All that is happening in the external world that contributes to our coming to have this concept is a regular association of events. The concept itself derives from an impression of our own internal state.

Although no one nowadays subscribes to Hume's theory of concept formation, his conclusion still has a powerful grip, and it is not uncommon to find contemporary thinkers who hold what is called a *regularity theory* of causality, that all there is to causality is association, though many now would allow that the association may be merely probabilistic, not one that holds with full regularity.

Independent of the influence of thinking like Hume's, there is good reason to care about just what the concept of causation is if we are to employ it in social science. For it is one of the central norms of science, whether it be natural science or social science, that its claims be clear and unambiguous and that the concepts employed in them be well defined and well understood. When we talk in science, we are supposed to be clear exactly what we are saying. So philosophers and social scientists alike have invested a great deal of effort trying to get straight the meaning of 'cause'. We shall review some of the central recent attempts in section 2.

1.2 Method

Just as good science demands clarity about the meaning of the concepts it employs, it also demands that there be clear, explicit methods for determining just when a concept applies to something in the world and when it does not. Without such methods, claims involving the concept will be untestable. There will be no way to judge whether they are true of the world or not. It will also be difficult to use the concepts to make predictions or to provide instructions for how to bring about change in the world. So much effort is also put into devising sound methods for establishing when relations hold and when they do not. We will look at some of these in section 2.

As Chapter 14 of this book stresses, the two endeavours of characterizing or defining concepts, on the one hand, and of devising methods for determining when they obtain, on the other, must go hand-in-hand. The methods must be geared to showing whether the very concept that has been defined holds, so that we can be sure that our methods are teaching us about what we think we are learning about. You will not be surprised then that some of the characterizations of causation you will see are almost read directly off from some of our favoured methods for establishing causal relations, and vice versa.

1.3 *Metaphysics*

The problems under this heading concern the nature of the causal relations themselves. Social science studies causal relations at two levels. The first is the *singular*: what are the causes and effects of specific single events? Using an example from Chapter 14, what caused the civil war in Angola in 1975? The second is the *general*: what kind of features are generally connected as cause and effect? For instance, 'Ethnic diversity is among the causes of ethnic civil war', or 'Skill loss during periods of unemployment causes persistence of high levels of unemployment.' Claims in social sciences about general causal relations are often called *causal principles*.

Probably the most central metaphysical problems facing singular causal relations arise from questions about how they behave in time. Are they instantaneous or extended in time? Is the cause temporally contiguous with the effect or is there a gap between them? Bertrand Russell (1912–13) argued that there cannot be a gap. Otherwise what would make the effect pop into existence when the cause was no longer there to produce it? This implies, he argued, that neither the cause nor the effect can be extended in time because the earlier parts of the cause, if they were to matter, would have to have an influence across a time gap; and so too with later parts of the effect. So causes must be instantaneous and contiguous with their effects. But that is impossible because time is continuous. Between any two instants there are infinitely many more, no matter how close together those two instants are. So, said Russell, the notion of one thing causing another does not make sense. We can sensibly talk of what values quantities have at each instant through continuous time, as when we use a line to represent the changing locations or changing velocity of the centre of mass of an object; but not of causality. That's part of why the concept should be banned from both natural and social science.

Social scientists have not worried much about Russell's problems. But they do worry about similar ones. There is a general consensus that in the single case there should be some continuous causal process connecting cause and effect. But the causes represented in social science studies are often aggregates, like GDP; they are often characteristics of institutions, like the managerial structure of Enron; and they are often norms or practices, like tax evasion. For causes like these, it can be hard to identify a causal process connecting cause and effect. What, for instance, might connect the high ethnic diversity in Angola in the period before 1975 with the ethnic civil war there in 1975 that it is supposed to have helped cause? Or suppose we want to argue that the GDP in a country in one quarter caused the rise in consumer spending there next quarter. What temporally continuous causal process connects these aggregate quantities? How even should we think about GDP itself with respect to time? Suppose all the production processes in a country are stopped for a day to mourn a dead leader. Does GDP go to zero then? Although these are live questions from social science, there has not been much headway on them recently and we shall not discuss them further here.

The dominant questions at the general level have to do with, first, the relation between the singular and the general. Must every singular causing fall under a general principle? We may say that the event reported in paragraph three of the lead story in today's *New York Times* caused the event reported in the first paragraph on page five. Surely we do not think there is a general principle that 'Events reported in paragraph three of the lead story of the *New York Times* cause events reported in the first paragraph of page five.' But must there be some feature of the event reported in the lead story—say, that it involves a high level of ethnic diversity—and some feature of the event reported in page five—say that it is an ethnic civil war—which are connected by a general principle? This is an important question for how we approach the understanding of singular events in the social sciences, which is the meat of what is done in anthropology and in policy evaluation (did the policy really produce the improved outcomes we observe?). Philosophers over the last two and a half decades have tended to answer 'yes' to this question. Although there was a lively debate about the question involving both philosophers and social scientists in the 1960s (see e.g. Roberts 1995) concerning historical explanation, social scientists have not had much to say about it lately. The exception is the recent literature on evidence-based policy, to which we will turn.

The second dominant question at the general level is one that confronts all principles in science whether they are causal principles or some other kind of law and whether they are in natural or in social science. What makes a general truth a law? Don't some facts just happen to be true generally? They hold by accident and we would not want to include them as principles in our scientific theories. For instance it is true that Venetian sea levels rise and so do bread prices. But this general association does not seem to be a law. Though this can be an important question, it is widely—and well—addressed in texts on philosophy of science in general, so we shall not pursue it here.

In what follows we shall discuss first general causation and then singular and, because of the close connection between the two, we shall discus meaning and method together.

2. Meaning and Method

What does it mean to say, at the general level, 'Ethnic diversity causes (or is among the causes of) ethnic civil war'? Or 'Rising inflation causes decreases in unemployment'? Or, as Chapter 1 discusses, that wives slimmer than their husbands make for happy marriages? Most recent attempts to answer this question are not *reductive*. They do not attempt to define causation in totally non-causal terms. They suppose, to the contrary, that causation is a basic fact of nature that cannot be properly characterized in totally non-causal terms any more than central physics concepts, such as *electron*, can be characterized without using other concepts from physics theory, like *proton* and *electromagnetic field*. The view that causation cannot be characterized in entirely non-causal language and correlatively that the validity of our methods to test causal claims will always rest on some specific causal assumptions gets summed up in the slogan, 'No causes in, no causes out.' Nevertheless, even if a reductive characterization is not possible, if the concept is to play a role in social science, it is still essential that it have clear unambiguous meaning and that our methods for testing for it be appropriate to the concept as thus understood. Four main ideas are used in recent attempts to characterize causation, which we address in turn: probabilistic association; manipulation or intervention; mechanism; powers.

How do these four different approaches to causation relate? Are they all different theories about the very same thing, perhaps a special kind of relation that holds between events or a special kind of general truth or a special kind of law of nature? If so which, if any, is correct; and might they all, or at least more than one, be correct, perhaps by focusing on different aspects of this one thing? If they are not about the same thing, are each of them—or at least some of them—correct about something? Perhaps they focus on somewhat different kinds of relations in the social world, though are similar enough to go under the same loose title 'causal'? These are important questions requiring both philosophical and empirical input. We will not discuss these here but leave them as topics in a more advanced course since they cannot be tackled till after we have a good idea what the different approaches are, which we do aim to provide here.

We shall also not discuss the relation between causation and explanation, on which there is a large philosophical literature (see e.g. Reiss 2013: chs 5–7).

2.1 *Probabilistic Association*

When a cause is present there should be more of the effect than if it were absent. That is the root idea of the probabilistic theory of causation. If C-type events occurring at some arbitrary time t cause E type of events at a time t' later, then we should expect $\text{Prob}(E_{t'} \mid C_t) > \text{Prob}(E_{t'} \mid \neg C_t)$. But that's similar to saying $E_{t'}$ and C_t are correlated—they tend to occur together; and it is a well-known mantra that correlation is not causation. High candy consumption in one month is correlated with low divorce rate the next. But eating candy does not prevent divorce. The correlation is due to the fact that candy eating is correlated with being young and young people have generally not been married long enough to get divorced. So, something more needs to be said.

Suppose you were able to control for all the other factors causing or preventing $E_{t'}$.[1] Imagine you could look in a population where all of these took some fixed value. So everyone is the same age, the same religion, is undergoing the same stress at work, has the same number of children, etc. In this population it seems reasonable to expect that if candy consumption does cause low divorce rate, it will increase the probability; and the probability will increase only if it does so since in this population there's no other way to account for an increase in probability. Somewhat more formally, let K_i represent a population where all the causes of E_t other than C_t take some fixed value, where i ranges over all the sets of values these causes can take. Then C_t causes $E_{t'}$ in K_i if and only if $\text{Prob}(E_{t'} \mid C_t + K_i) > \text{Prob}(E_{t'} \mid \neg C_t + K_i)$.

This is the gist of the probabilistic theory of causation, though more details need to be ironed out. For instance, note that this characterization is relative to the population satisfying K_i. What then about a larger population that contains K_i? That is one of the points of dispute. Some philosophers and social scientists insist on keeping the relativization to the K_i. Others allow that C_t causes $E_{t'}$ in any population that contains K_i, though this can lead to it being true both that C_t causes $E_{t'}$ in a population and also prevents $E_{t'}$ there in cases where in one subpopulation C_t increases the probability of $E_{t'}$ and in another it decreases it. Under any circumstances this kind of characterization will always be relativized to a population since different populations will have different probabilities over the same variables and also they may well have other general causal relations holding, hence different factors for determining the K_is. Chapter 3 worries about taking studies that show that a policy worked—i.e. caused the targeted outcomes—in one situation as evidence that it will have the same effects elsewhere. It is just this kind of relativity of causal claims to other causal factors (those that pick out the K_is) that creates this worry: whether C_t causes $E_{t'}$ or prevents it or does nothing to $E_{t'}$ at all in a given situation can depend very much on what other causal factors are there in the situation along with C_t.

---

[1] Except those on the causal pathway between C_t and $E_{t'}$ if it exists.

Note also that seen as a characterization of general level causality—as a way of providing clear unambiguous sense for the concept—the probabilistic theory of causation is not reductive since we need to refer to general causal relations in specifying what K_i is and thus we refer to other general causal relations in explaining what is required for any given general causal relation to hold. It is, however, very constraining. Each of the factors in K_i must satisfy a similar formula with respect to C_t and the remaining factors in K_i since each of these is itself meant to be a cause of $E_{t'}$. Although this may not narrow the choice of causes for $E_{t'}$ to a single choice, it will rule out a huge number of alternatives. And adding some information about a few factors, that they are indeed a cause of $E_{t'}$ or that they are not, can sometimes fix the set entirely given the probabilities.

This way of characterizing causality has the advantage that it connects immediately with standard statistical methods used in the social sciences to test for causal relations. These methods are used in what are called 'observational studies', which means that the data come from populations in their natural settings and not from specially selected populations enrolled in experiments. In the populations under study, social scientists measure *correlations* or *regressions* between factors to begin to test whether there is a causal connection between them in that population. These are weaker notions than conditional probabilities, like $\text{Prob}(E_{t'} \mid C_t)$ and $\text{Prob}(E_{t'} \mid \neg C_t)$, but are closely related. In a better test, they measure *partial correlations* or *partial regressions*, holding fixed other variables that they hope represent the other causes. This is akin to the partial conditional probabilities $\text{Prob}(E_{t'} \mid C_t + K_i)$ and $\text{Prob}(E_{t'} \mid \neg C_t + K_i)$. Similar kinds of ideas are used in econometrics, in estimating the coefficients that appear in economic equations that will hopefully represent causal relations.

The two assumptions of the probabilistic theory—that an effect is always probabilistically dependent on its cause and that this kind of dependency disappears when other causes are held fixed—are also at the core of what are called 'Bayes nets methods' for causal inference, for which computer programmes can generate all sets of causal relations among a given set of variables that are possible, given information about probabilistic dependencies among the variables, supposing the fundamental assumptions linking causes and probabilities are satisfied.

These two assumptions are also at the core of the reasoning behind randomized controlled trials (RCTs), which are highly touted as the gold standard for causal testing in medicine and, as we see in Chapter 3, in evidence-based policy, and are being pushed throughout the social sciences now, especially in development economics. The neat thing about RCTs is that they help with one of the central problems that the statistical methods discussed so far face: that we generally don't know what the other causal factors are and so don't know what to hold fixed.

In an RCT, the individuals in a population enrolled in the experiment—which could be individuals, schools, countries, etc.—are randomly assigned either to the treatment group, which will be subject to the cause (C_t), or to the control group, which will not have the cause ($\neg C_t$), but may perhaps receive a placebo. There should be as much masking as possible: the individuals in the experiment should not know which group they are in, nor should anyone involved in further monitoring or treatment, or in reading out the results to see if $E_{t'}$ obtains or not, or in carrying out the statistical analysis. This is to guard against conscious or unconscious bias that may influence the results that are finally recorded. The aim is to ensure that both groups have the same distribution for all the other causal factors influencing the outcome, so that every arrangement of them—every K_i—has the same frequency in both groups. This aim can very rarely be achieved and moreover, we won't know when it has been: statistics can tell us how often in the long run random assignment will produce any particular imbalance but we do not have even that kind of assessment when it comes to how well the masking has succeeded. So, as always in scientific work, we must not place too much confidence in the results of a single study, even one that has been very well conducted.

In order to see the logic of the causal inference, let us suppose, though, that the other causal factors have the same frequency in the treatment and control groups. The Prob($E_{t'}$) in the treatment group will then be an average across the probability of $E_{t'}$ given C_t in each of the subpopulations in it—i.e. each of the K_i. So it will be an average over Prob($E_{t'} \mid C_t + K_i$). Similarly, the Prob($E_{t'}$) in the control is the average of the probability of $E_{t'}$ given $\neg C_t$ in each of the subpopulations represented there—each of the K_i. So it is an average over Prob($E_{t'} \mid \neg C_t + K_i$). By our hypothesis that the other causal factors have the same distribution in the two groups, the frequency of each K_i subpopulation is the same in both. So if the probability of $E_{t'}$ is greater in the treatment group than in the control group, that implies that for one of the K_i subpopulations, Prob($E_{t'} \mid C_t + K_i$) > Prob($E_{t'} \mid \neg C_t + K_i$). It follows that there is at least one subpopulation—one K_i—of the experimental population in which 'C_t causes $E_{t'}$ in K_i' is true, or at least is true under the probabilistic theory's way of characterizing causality.

Can we conclude from the experiment 'C_t causes $E_{t'}$ in the experimental population'? That depends on the decision referred to earlier about what to say about 'C_t causes $E_{t'}$' in a population given that C_t causes $E_{t'}$ in one of its subpopulations. What matters is that, however this decision is made, those using the claim should understand it and not read more out of it than the study supports. In particular, the higher probability in the treatment over the control group shows only that C_t causes $E_{t'}$ in some subpopulation of the population enrolled in the experiment. It may hold in specific other populations or even across most. But C_t may have exactly the opposite effect on $E_{t'}$ in some subpopulations than it does in others. Finding out whether that is true requires a great deal more social science work.

2.2 *Intervention and Manipulation*

The manipulation view of causation revolves around the idea that causes give us effective strategies for producing effects we want, or preventing those we do not; by manipulating the cause we can manipulate the effect in a predictable way. So manipulation theories characterize general-level causation roughly this way, where again there is a dispute about the exact details of the formulation: for any two times t and t', 'C_t causes $E_{t'}$ in situations of type S' just in case manipulating C at t—making it bigger or smaller, or bringing it in or taking it away—is regularly followed by appropriate changes in E at t' '. For this to be true, we must be careful how these manipulations are carried out. 'Reducing class sizes causes improved reading scores' is true in many populations. But not if you lower teacher quality at the same time as reducing class size. Alternatively the manipulation of one factor may be followed by improvement in another without any causal connection. For instance new programmes for teaching reading may be followed by better reading scores not because the programmes cause better scores but because the teachers adopting them are regularly the better teachers or they become more enthusiastic when trying out new programmes.

This is where the concept of *intervention* comes in. 'Intervention' has been given a variety of formal definitions, but the basic idea is that an intervention is a manipulation that is done in the 'right way' to make the causal relation, or lack of it, apparent. The right way will be one in which neither other causes nor other preventatives of the effect change, an idea we are familiar with from the probabilistic theory. Nor can any causal relations involving the effect change during the intervention. That's because it is not a fair test of a causal relation if suddenly there are a lot of new causal relations produced between the effect and other factors that were not causes before. This includes changes in the very relation under test. One familiar way in which the requirement that causal relations involving the effect not change during intervention is violated is when the manipulation of the cause is so ham-fisted that it busts up the causal relation we are trying to test. One familiar example is when we wind up the toy soldier to see if that will make it march, but we wind too tightly and break the mechanism that makes it work.

Nobel-prize-winning Chicago School economist Robert Lucas claims this is frequently true with attempts to manipulate economic variables to bring about desired change. For instance, inflation, when it occurs naturally, can in the short run cause reductions in unemployment. That's because, so the story goes, entrepreneurs mistakenly see the universal rise in prices as a real rise in prices in their sector and so hire more workers to produce more goods to meet increased demand. If, though, the government manipulates inflation to improve unemployment, entrepreneurs will recognize the rise in prices for what it is—just inflation—and will not open new jobs. The government's very attempt to use the causal relation between inflation and unemployment will break it. Or at least so says Lucas's model.

As with probabilistic theory, the characterization of general causation using the concept of manipulation is not reductive since the definition of an intervention, however the details are worked out, will have to refer to other general causal relations.

Also, as with the probabilistic theory, the characterization of causality in terms of manipulation is closely linked with familiar methods for testing, in this case with real non-statistical experiments where other causes are held fixed and only the cause under test is varied. Here too we are often stymied by our lack of knowledge of what these other causes are. This is the problem that plagues standard *before-and-after studies*. In before-and-after studies the cause is administered and we look to see if the effect changes. But, are we sure that nothing else changed at the same time as the cause? One of the tricks of social science is to find situations where we can have reasonable confidence that nothing else that could influence the effect has changed even if we do not have a catalogue of what all the other influences might be to check on them. This is the strategy that is used in what are called 'instrumental variables' models in economics. For instance Joshua Angrist in a classic paper uses the Vietnam era draft lottery to measure the effect of veteran status on earnings (Angrist 1990). Since whether an individual was drafted was determined on the basis of a randomly assigned number, we can be fairly confident that factors that affect earnings, like education, were equally distributed between the group of individuals who were drafted and the group of individuals who were not, as in an RCT. And so we can be fairly confident that the comparison between the average earnings in one group and the average earnings in the other tells us something about the effect of veteran status on earnings.

The manipulation theory of general-level causation is closely akin to the *counterfactual theory* of singular causation, which is based on the idea that one specific event, c, is a cause of a later event, e, just in case e would not have occurred unless c had. You can see immediately that this kind of claim will be hard to test since c and e are specific events that either occur or do not; so we can never observe what would have happened had things been different. There are also huge problems of formulation. There is a vast literature available in philosophy on counterfactuals and causes in which you can read more about these (see e.g. Paul 2009 and references therein).

Similar counterfactuals have come to the fore in social science lately because of the rise of the evaluation industry for social policy. As Chapter 3 explains, there is a great demand to know whether the policies we have implemented have 'worked': Has the policy genuinely produced the change intended? To answer that, it helps to know what would have happened otherwise. RCTs are often employed to this end. But of course they cannot tell us of a specific case whether the policy brought about the effect there, since they only look at groups. If an RCT shows more positive results in the treatment group, the group in which the policy was implemented, than in the group where it was not, we can conclude that in some of the cases in the treatment group the policy produced the effect. But we do not know which; we have no way to sort cases where the policy brought about the effect from those where something else was responsible. So for reliable evaluation of the single case, some different way of reasoning is required. This often involves process tracing which we shall discuss in the next section.

Not only do we not know from the RCT for which individuals the policy worked. We do not know what sets of characteristics matter. We know that there is at least one arrangement of characteristics that individuals might have—one K_i—for which the policy promotes the desired outcome. We call these 'support factors'. But we do not know which it is. This matters when it comes to putting the claims established in RCTs to use in predicting what will happen if the policy were to be implemented elsewhere. If the population elsewhere has no individuals with just the right arrangement of support factors (no individuals described by the successful K_is), or not enough to make it pay, the policy will not produce the desired outcomes in the new setting. Given good reason to think that the new setting does have enough individuals with the right arrangements, we have good reason to suppose the policy will work for some individuals there. But without good reason to suppose this, the RCT results will not be much use in predicting results in the new setting.

Consider for instance Oportunidades, a Mexican programme for poverty reduction. Because Oportunidades was itself designed as an RCT, there is very good evidence that it did contribute to reducing poverty where it was implemented. Does the success of Oportunidades provide evidence supporting predictions regarding what would happen were a similar programme implemented in some other population? Only if enough individuals in this target population have the right arrangement of support factors. And one cannot assume without evidence that this will be so. This point is illustrated by the case of Opportunity NYC, a poverty reduction programme modelled—and named—after Oportunidades which was implemented in New York City in 2007 but discontinued in 2010 because it failed to produce the expected effects. The success of Oportunidades in Mexico did not, by itself, provide sufficient evidence to support the prediction that Opportunity NYC would produce similar results, and the mistaken assumption that it did led to a poor policy decision.

2.3 *Mechanisms*

There are three senses of the term 'mechanism' in play currently in work on causation in philosophy and in the social and in the biomedical sciences. These include notions of *causal process, invariance*, and *underlying structure*.

CAUSAL PROCESSES

For singular causation it is widely held that a cause must be connected with its effect by some spatio-temporally continuous process between them. So tracing the causal process between them can be a good way to tell whether two events are related as cause and effect, a good way IF we know how to tell a causal process when we see one. So what distinguishes a continuous sequence of events that constitutes a causal process from one that does not? One popular philosophical account answers that in causal processes energy is transferred at each step in between. But this is not of much help in social science (see e.g. Dowe 2009).

A standard procedure in social science and in policy evaluation is to break the sequence into small steps where it is easier to determine for each step whether it is a genuine cause of the next. For instance, the Global Environment Facility evaluated the effectiveness of one of its programmes, the end-goal of which was to 'establish a long-term conservation finance mechanism to support biodiversity conservation' in the Bwindi national park (Uganda), by determining whether this programme had an effect on four intermediate outcomes (e.g. the establishment of a Bwindi Trust) which in turn were supposed to contribute to achieving the end-goal of the program (GEF 2007: 6).

Process tracing necessarily focuses on singular causation. But it can be a tool for general causation as well. If in situations of kind S, an event of kind C at t is regularly followed by an event of kind E at t' and it regularly happens that the same kind of causal process connects the individual events, then we can conclude at the general level that 'In S-type situations, C_t causes $E_{t'}$'. This kind of reasoning has played a significant role in the biomedical sciences. For instance, tracing the process by which the chemicals in cigarette smoke lead to lung cancer provided a central piece of the evidence that showed that smoking causes lung cancer.

INVARIANCE

Suppose we observe that in a particular kind of situation S one kind of feature F2 regularly changes after another, F1, changes. That is mere correlation and we know that correlation does not equal causation. But suppose that F1 changes by intervention. If F1 causes F2 we expect that F2 will change following the intervention in the way that it always has; but not, if F1 does not. Changing levels of candy consumption may be regularly followed by changing probabilities of divorce. But this relationship is not invariant under intervention. If we intervene to change candy consumption—'intervene', so the only change is in the amount of candy consumed—the divorce rate will not change in tandem. This observation has given rise to the invariance account of causality now in fashion in philosophy of science. The basic idea is that, supposing C_t and $E_{t'}$ are regularly associated in S, then 'C_t causes $E_{t'}$ in S' just in case the association between C_t and $E_{t'}$ is invariant under interventions on C_t.

This account is clearly closely connected with the manipulation account, and it shares one major drawback with that account that we have not yet discussed. The manipulation account is grounded in the idea that causes provide strategies for changing the world. Suppose we do characterize causation as invariance under intervention. Then changing C_t will be a good way to change $E_{t'}$—but that follows only if C_t is changed by intervention. But interventions are hard to come by. We are in a far more powerful position to predict what will happen and to engineer what we want if we know about a regular association that is invariant under the method of implementation that we will in fact employ. This gives rise to another, different characterization of general-level causation, one that we can find in contemporary economics (see e.g. Hoover 2001: ch. 2). Roughly, if C_t and $E_{t'}$ are regularly associated in S, then C_t causes $E_{t'}$ in S relative to ϕ just in case the association between C_t and $E_{t'}$ is invariant when C_t is changed by ϕ, where ϕ can then represent the method by which we will in fact change C_t. Knowing that C_t causes $E_{t'}$ under this characterization of causation immediately provides an effective strategy for changing E at t'.

Notice that these different versions of the invariance account can give different verdicts about whether C_t causes $E_{t'}$ in any given situation. This underlines the importance of being clear exactly what we mean when we make causal claims in social science.

UNDERLYING STRUCTURES

Different causal relations hold in different social, cultural, and economic settings. What is a required politeness in one culture can cause insult in another. Why? What causal relations hold in a social setting depends on the underlying system, the underlying social, economic, and cultural structure. It is now standard in philosophy of biology to call the structures that underlie causal relations there 'mechanisms', and sometimes this usage is adopted in the social sciences as well. Though there is no widely used mechanistic characterization of causation, there is widespread sense that, if we are to follow the injunction of the LSE motto, to know the causes of things, we should come to understand the underlying mechanism that make the particular causal principles that hold for a given population possible.

This is clearly of central importance in social planning and policy. Consider recent problems in child welfare in the UK, where attention tended to focus on causal processes. When a tragic child death occurs, 'The standard response is to hold an inquiry... trying to get a picture of the causal sequence of events that ended in the child's death... We are tracing a chain of events back in time to understand how it happened.' So says Eileen Munro (2005: 377), author of Chapter 3 and of the 2012 UK government report on child protection. Munro recommends instead a 'systems' approach. That means focusing on the underlying mechanism or social structure that makes these kinds of processes possible, or even probable. As a US National Academy of Science report on building safer health systems explains, 'The focus must shift from blaming individuals for past errors to a focus on preventing future errors by designing safety into the system' (Kohn et al. 2000: 5).

So it is clear that it is important to study social mechanisms in social science. What is not clear is what kinds of concepts should be used to describe these mechanisms and their operation, nor what tool kit of methods will help us to understand them. This is one of the central tasks right now on which philosophy and social science intersect.

2.4 Powers

John Stuart Mill argued that women have the same powers of leadership and imagination as men, and we have these powers even should they be seldom displayed. Give women the same education, upbringing, situation, and opportunities as men and they will display these qualities equally with men. And he used this claim to argue for dramatic changes in the social policies and practices in play at the time regarding the role of women in society.

As with all concepts, if the concept *power* is to play an important role like this in social science or in social policy deliberation, we should be clear what is meant by it. This is a big topic in metaphysics nowadays and, to a lesser extent, in philosophy of science (see e.g. Mumford 2009). It is usual to make at least four assumptions about powers. First, a system—an object, a person, an institution—can have a power without displaying it. Second, the power will be displayed if the conditions are right. Third, what actually happens when a power is displayed depends on the setting. So what happens when a woman displays her imagination will depend on whether she is at a laboratory work bench or addressing Parliament or tending her children. Fourth, when a power operates in a situation, what happens there will depend in some intelligible way on the display of the power (as when a heavy metal object does not fall to the ground because the power of a magnet is displayed).

The most typical characterizations of powers 'back' define them from their displays. Roughly, A has the power to α just in case when properly enabled and failing something stopping it doing so (which we sometimes express as 'nothing interferes with the display'), A does α. This characterization is dramatically non-reductive because of the concepts of *enablement* and *interference*. Contrast this with an alternative: 'A has the power to α just in case there are some circumstances Cα such that it is a law of nature that in Cα, A does α', where Cα is to be filled in by some possibly very long list of features that can be characterized without any power-related notions, like 'is schooled at Eton', 'learns Latin', 'does not play with dolls', etc. Many powers advocates do not adopt this alternative because, they argue, there is never a list that does the job. In each actual situation there is a fact of the matter about whether the circumstances that obtain there constitute an interference and whether they are enabling, but there is nothing these facts share in common that we could fill in for Cα other than that they are enabling or they interfere. This is taken by many to be particularly problematic since philosophers have not succeeded in having much enlightening to say about interferences and enablers at the general level.

Why then take powers seriously? Philosophers offer a panoply of metaphysical arguments. But for social science the answer seems to lie in the usefulness of the concept, as with Mill, who argued for the centrality of the related notion of *tendency* in political economy. Another word used for much the same idea is 'capacity'. In order to link it with our contemporary discourse, I shall use the word 'power' throughout for all these related notions. Mill's model for powers comes from Newtonian mechanics. The sun has the power to attract the planets. Nothing ever interferes with it so the sun constantly displays this power (called 'gravity'). What happens when it displays it? The planets move around it in elliptical orbits. By contrast, when the earth displays its power to attract a cannonball shot at an enemy ship, the cannonball moves along a parabola. What actually happens when the power of gravitational attraction is displayed (i.e. when the sun or earth attract other objects) depends on the setting. To make a link with our immediately previous discussion, we may think of the earth–cannonball pair as a mechanism, in the sense of an underlying structure, giving rise to the causal principle, 'The earth displaying its power of gravitational attraction causes cannonballs to move along parabolas'; and the planetary system as a mechanism giving rise to the causal principle 'The sun displaying its power of gravitational attraction causes the planets to move along ellipses around it'.

How do we know what happens when a power is displayed in a given setting? That's easy, at least in principle, in Newtonian mechanics. All that's relevant to how a power affects motions is what other powers are displayed in the situation. The display of the power is represented by what we call a force, represented by a vector. When several forces are displayed at once, we add these vectors, call the result 'the total force, F_T', and calculate the acceleration of any object in the situation by the familiar formula $F_T = ma$, where m is the mass of the object. That is what we do, for instance, when we want to know how a pin will behave when a magnet attracts it upward and the earth attracts it downward, or how an electron in an atom behaves when it is attracted by both the mass of the nucleus and the charge on the protons there.

That's all physics. Life is not so easy in social science, which may have some knowledge of powers but little knowledge of methods for calculating just what happens in different situations when the powers are displayed. Consider an economics example already mentioned, the one involving skill loss during unemployment. Earlier I suggested that economics entertains a causal principle that skill loss perpetuates high levels of unemployment. That is probably a mistaken way to look at it. It is seldom the case that skill loss is the only thing going on that affects unemployment. There are, for instance, sometimes vigorous successful government efforts to combat unemployment. In these cases skill loss may be followed by improving levels of employment, contrary to what is suggested by this causal principle. A better way to put it might be 'Skill loss has the power to cause continuing high unemployment'. This will not lead us to expect that skill loss actually produces unemployment whenever it occurs, but only that, to understand the levels of employment that actually occur, we shall have to take the downward push of skill loss into account.

So, we return to the question, 'How do we take it into account?' How do we predict what happens when a socio-economic power is displayed? There is no systematic answer. This is one of the problems social scientists constantly confront in trying to put their isolated parcels of hard-won knowledge—like the knowledge of specific powers such as the power of skill loss to perpetuate unemployment—to use.

3. Putting Causal Knowledge to Use

Chapter 14 in this book teaches us that the meaning we assign a scientific concept must be closely paired with our methods for finding out whether it obtains. We should have good arguments to show that the methods we employ provide a good way to find out about just what we claim we are finding out about. That message has been echoed throughout this chapter with respect to the concept of causation when it is used in the social sciences. It is not just meaning and method that must match, however. So too must use. The use to which we put our social scientific claims—the inferences we draw from them and the practices we adopt on the basis of them—should be supported by what those claims actually say; and what they say that supports our inference should in turn be supported by our methods for deciding that what they say is true. It is no good making a very broad claim whose first half is well supported by the evidence but then draw our inferences from the second half, which is unsupported.

We have looked at a number of accounts of what causal claims say. The claims say different things because they employ different concepts of causation. These concepts may all go under the same title, 'general causal relation', but they require different conditions to be met in order to obtain. So different methods must be used to find out about them and different uses made of them. So, of what use is knowledge of the causes of things? Knowing causes helps us to understand how things work. But it is also supposed to be of practical value. Knowing the causes of things should help us to change the world.

Here we must be cautious though. There is a tendency to too much haste, to try to read off directly from our causal claims just what we must do to bring about the change we desire. That will work with some kinds of causal knowledge but not most. Consider the manipulation concept of causation found in economics that I mentioned in discussing invariance: C_t causes $E_{t'}$ relative to ϕ just in case manipulating C_t by ϕ is followed by $E_{t'}$, where ϕ is one of the methods available to us to change C at t. Suppose we know that. Then we are in a powerful position to change E at t'.

But suppose we have established instead a different causal claim, say a manipulationist claim of the kind favoured in philosophy—C_t causes $E_{t'}$ just in case if C_t changes by intervention $E_{t'}$ changes—or in invariance-type claim—C_t causes $E_{t'}$ just in case the association between them is invariant when C_t changes by intervention. That too can be of immediate use—if we have an intervention to hand, which we usually do not. We have seen the same kind of problem with knowledge of powers. Knowing about what powers a system has will not by itself tell us what to expect to happen in particular circumstances nor how to build circumstances to get what we want. Nor does knowing the causal relations, on the probabilistic theory, that hold in one population, perhaps the population enrolled in an RCT, give us immediate guidance about how to bring about change in a different population.

This does not, however, in any way make causal knowledge in social science useless. It just puts it more on a par with similar knowledge in the natural sciences, where strategies are built by splinting together a very great many different pieces of knowledge and often undertaking designated new researches and developing new theory to fill in gaps. The great nineteenth-century physicist Lord Kelvin laid the first Atlantic cable in 1866. His knowledge of causes in physics was essential to his success but it definitely did not tell him just what to do. Similarly, the large team of physicists, engineers, mathematicians, and technicians who developed the US Second World War radar took many months to do so, despite the vast repository of causal knowledge the team members brought to the project. The conclusion I propose is that the causal knowledge we work so hard to gain in the social sciences can be of immense use. But there is no reason to think it should be easier to put our social science knowledge to use than it is to use our knowledge in the natural sciences.

References

Angrist, J. (1990). 'Lifetime Earnings and the Vietnam Era Draft Lottery: Evidence from Social Security Administrative Records', *American Economic Review*, 80(3): 313–36.

Dowe, P. (2009). 'Causal Process Theories' in H. Beebee et al. (eds), *Oxford Handbook of Causation*. Oxford: Oxford University Press, 213–33.

Garrett, D. (2009). 'Hume', in H. Beebee et al. (eds), *Oxford Handbook of Causation*. Oxford: Oxford University Press, 73–91.

GEF (2007). *Case Study: Bwindi Impenetrable National Park and Mgahinga Gorilla National Park Conservation Project*. Impact Evaluation Information Document, 7. Washington, DC: Global Environment Facility, Evaluation Office.

Hoover, K. (2001). *Causality in Macroeconomics*. Cambridge: Cambridge University Press.

Kohn, L., Corrigan, J., and Donaldson, M., eds (2000). *To Err is Human: Building a Safer Health System*. Washington, DC: Committee on Quality of Health Care in America, Institute of Medicine.

Mumford, S. (2009). 'Causal Powers and Capacities', in H. Beebee et al. (eds), *Oxford Handbook of Causation*. Oxford: Oxford University Press, 265–78.

Munro, E. (2005). 'Improving Practice: Child Protection as a Systems Problem', *Child and Youth Services Review*, 27: 375–91.

Paul, L. A. (2009). 'Counterfactual Theories', in H. Beebee et al. (eds), *Oxford Handbook of Causation*. Oxford: Oxford University Press, 158–84.

Reiss, J. (2013). *Philosophy of Economics: A Contemporary Introduction*. London: Routledge.

Roberts, C. (1995). *The Logic of Historical Explanation*. University Park, PA: Pennsylvania State University Press.

Russell, B. (1912–13). 'On the Notion of Cause', *Proceedings of the Aristotelian Society*, 13: 1–26.

Further Readings

Beebee, H., Hitchcock, C., and Menzies, P., eds. (2009). *Oxford Handbook of Causation*. Oxford: Oxford University Press.

Campaner, R., and Galavotti, M. C. (2007). 'Plurality in Causality', in P. Machamer and G. Wolters (eds), *Thinking about Causes: From Greek Philosophy to Modern Physics*. Pittsburgh: University of Pittsburgh Press. 178–99.

Cartwright, N. (2007). *Hunting Causes and Using Them*. Cambridge: Cambridge University Press.

McKim, V., and Turner, S., eds (1997). *Causality in Crisis: Statistical Methods and the Search for Causal Knowledge in the Social Sciences*. South Bend, IN: University of Notre Dame Press.

Russo, F. (2009). *Causality and Causal Modelling in the Social Sciences*. New York: Springer.

Index

Lightning Source UK Ltd.
Milton Keynes UK
UKHW010136080121
376652UK00001B/1